BRITISH RAILWAYS

LOCOMOTIVES & COACHING STOCK

2005

The Complete Guide to all Locomotives & Coaching Stock which operate on National Rail & Eurotunnel

Robert Pritchard, Peter Fox & Peter Hall

ISBN 1 902336 44 5

© 2005. Platform 5 Publishing Ltd., 3 Wyvern House, Sark Road, Sheffield, S2 4HG, England.

CONTENTS

SECTION 5 – NON-PASSENGER COACHING STOCK

SECTION 6 – SERVICE STOCK

SECTION 7 – CODES

COVER PHOTOGRAPHS

Front Cover: As this book closed for press the repaint programme for the First Great Western HST fleet was completed. On 24 July 2004 a full set in First Group livery is seen leaving Newton Abbot, with power cars 43021 and 43189 "RAILWAY HERITAGE TRUST" forming the 11.33 London Paddington–Paignton.
Jason Rogers

Rear Cover: The Siemens-built Class 444s entered service for South West Trains in 2004, mainly working services on the London to Portsmouth corridor. On 21 June 2004 444 021 and 444 020 are seen near Bedhampton with the 10.17 Portsmouth Harbour–Waterloo.
Chris Wilson

PROVISION OF INFORMATION

This book has been compiled with care to be as accurate as possible, but in some cases official information is not available and the publisher cannot be held responsible for any errors or omissions. We would like to thank the companies and individuals which have been co-operative in supplying information to us. The authors of this book will be pleased to receive notification of any inaccuracies readers may find in the series, and also any additional information to supplement our records and thus enhance future editions. Please send comments to:

Locomotives, DMUs & EMUs: Robert Pritchard, Platform 5 Publishing Ltd., 3 Wyvern House, Sark Road, Sheffield, S2 4HG, England.
Tel: 0114 255 2625 **Fax:** 0114 255 2471
e-mail: robert@platform5.com

Coaching Stock: Peter Hall, 4 Ladies Spring Court, Ladies Spring Grove, Dore, Sheffield, S17 3LR. (Tel: 0114 262 0693; e-mail: peter@hall59.freeserve.co.uk)

Both the author and the staff of Platform 5 regret they are unable to answer specific queries regarding locomotives and rolling stock.

This book is updated to 1 January 2005.

ACKNOWLEDGEMENTS

The author would like to thank all Train Operating Companies, Freight Companies and Leasing Companies that have helped with the compilation of this book.

Thanks are also due to the following individuals for their reports of changes observed during 2004 (for the **entrain** "Stock Changes" column) and for corrections given to the "pocket book" series:

Brian Loughlin, Tony Russell, Keith Foster, Shaun Bamford, Nick Lawford, John Patston, Jason Rogers, John Hall, Chris Wilson, Ian Lothian, RC Hardiment, John Cundy, Allan Staite, Martin Haywood, Michel Crisp, Peter Hintz, Andrew Mcfarlane, Steve Hutton, N. Tooth, Iain Mansell, Andy Harkness, Brian Ovington, Joe Patrick, Mike Taplin, Richard Oakley, Andrew Marsh, Matt Forbes, Adrian Jackson, Jon Barlow, Phil Wright, John Henley, BJ Brotherton, Steve Taylor, Martyn Osbourne, Nigel Farebroker, Edward Tucker, Roger Templeman, Donald J. Bishop, Alan Costello, Mark Beal, David Haydock, Mike Stone, Mark Allatt, J. Bogucki, Allan Staite, Brian Garvin, Nick Chadha, Ian Hardy, Keith Cox, Garry Sparks, Ben Williams, Kevin Lee, Alan Spencer, Barry Monk, David Denton and many others – keep the observations coming!

BRITAIN'S RAILWAY SYSTEM

INFRASTRUCTURE & OPERATION

Britain's national railway infrastructure is now owned by a "not for dividend" company, Network Rail. Many stations and maintenance depots are leased to and operated by Train Operating Companies (TOCs), but some larger stations remain under Network Rail control. The only exception is the infrastructure on the Isle of Wight, which is nationally owned and is leased to the Island Line franchisee.

Trains are operated by TOCs over Network Rail, regulated by access agreements between the parties involved. In general, TOCs are responsible for the provision and maintenance of the locomotives, rolling stock and staff necessary for the direct operation of services, whilst Network Rail is responsible for the provision and maintenance of the infrastructure and also for staff needed to regulate the operation of services.

DOMESTIC PASSENGER TRAIN OPERATORS

The large majority of passenger trains are operated by the TOCs on fixed term franchises. Franchise expiry dates are shown in parentheses in the list of franchisees below:

Franchise	Franchisee	Trading Name
Central Trains[1]	National Express Group plc (until 1 April 2006)	Central Trains
Chiltern Railways	M40 Trains Ltd. (until December 2021)	Chiltern Railways
Cross-Country[2]	Virgin Rail Group Ltd. (until further notice)	Virgin Trains
Gatwick Express[3]	National Express Group plc (until 27 April 2011)	Gatwick Express
Great Western Trains[4]	First Group plc (until 31 March 2006)	First Great Western
Greater Anglia[5]	National Express Group plc (until 31 March 2014)	"One"
InterCity East Coast[6]	GNER Holdings Ltd. (until 4 April 2005)	Great North Eastern Railway
InterCity West Coast	Virgin Rail Group Ltd. (until 8 March 2012)	Virgin Trains
Island Line	Stagecoach Holdings plc (until February 2007)	Island Line
LTS Rail	National Express Group plc (until 25 May 2011)	c2c
Merseyrail Electrics[7]	Serco/NedRail (until 20 July 2028)	Merseyrail Electrics

Midland Main Line	National Express Group plc (until 27 April 2008)	Midland Mainline
North London Railways	National Express Group plc (until 17 October 2006)	Silverlink Train Services
Northern Rail[8]	Serco/NedRail (until 11 September 2013)	Northern
ScotRail	First Group plc (until 16 October 2011)	First ScotRail
South Central	GoVia Ltd. (Go-Ahead/Keolis). (until May 2010)	Southern
South Eastern[9]		South Eastern Trains
South West	Stagecoach Holdings plc (until 3 February 2007)	South West Trains
Thames[4]	First Group plc (until 31 March 2006)	First Great Western Link
Thameslink	GoVia Ltd. (until 1 April 2006)	Thameslink Rail
Trans-Pennine Express	First Group/Keolis (until 31 January 2012)	First Trans-Pennine Express
Wales & Borders	Arriva Trains Ltd (until 6 December 2018)	Arriva Trains Wales
Wessex Trains[4]	National Express Group plc (until 31 March 2006)	Wessex Trains
Great Northern[10]	National Express Group plc (until 4 April 2006)	WAGN

Notes:

[1] Due to be abolished on expiry. Services expected to be split between Chiltern, Midland Mainline, Northern, "One", Silverlink, Trans-Pennine Express and Cross-Country.

[2] At the time of going to press the future of this franchise was in doubt following its renegotiation, as the Strategic Rail Authority (SRA) then announced that Virgin's best and final offer for a single-tender deal running until 2012 did not represent value for money. The SRA has therefore told Virgin that it reserves the right to terminate the franchise.

[3] Gatwick Express has been proposed for possible absorption by Southern as part of the SRA's Brighton Main Line Route Utilisation Strategy. This could take place before the expiry of the current Gatwick Express franchise.

[4] Due to transfer to the new Greater Western franchise on 1 April 2006.

[5] Incorporates the former Anglia and Great Eastern franchises and the West Anglia half of West Anglia Great Northern. Awarded for seven years with a likely extension for a further three.

[6] The preferred bidder for the new East Coast franchise is due to be announced in March 2005, slightly later than originally planned. Because of this the current franchise is likely to be extended for a short period beyond 4 April.

[7] Now under control of Merseyrail PTE instead of the SRA. Franchise due to be reviewed after seven years and then every five years to fit in with Merseyside

Local Transport Plan.

[8] Urban and rural services previously run by Arriva Trains Northern and First North Western were transferred to the new Northern franchise on 12 December 2004. Trans-Pennine services formerly run by these operators were taken over by the new Trans-Pennine Express franchise on 1 February 2004. The Northern franchise runs for up to 8¾ years.

[9] New interim management company known as South Eastern Trains (SET) formed on 9 November 2003, pending award of new Integrated Kent franchise expected in the latter part of 2005. SET is a subsidiary of the SRA.

[10] The West Anglia half of WAGN transferred to new Greater Anglia franchise. The Great Northern half remains separate until its absorption by the new Thameslink franchise in 2006. Despite this, Great Northern continues to use the brand name WAGN and has said it now wishes to be referred to as "W-A-G-N", not as WAGN.

A major reorganisation of franchises is under way. See **entrain** for developments.

The following operators run non-franchised services only:

Operator	Trading Name	Route
British Airports Authority	Heathrow Express	London Paddington–Heathrow Airport
Hull Trains§	Hull Trains	London King's Cross–Hull
West Coast Railway Co.	West Coast Railway	Birmingham Snow Hill–Stratford-on-Avon
		Fort William–Mallaig*
		York–Scarborough*

* Special summer-dated services only.
§ Now owned by First Group.

INTERNATIONAL PASSENGER OPERATIONS

Eurostar (UK) operates international passenger-only services between the United Kingdom and continental Europe, jointly with French National Railways (SNCF) and Belgian National Railways (SNCB/NMBS). Eurostar (UK) is a subsidiary of London & Continental Railways, which is jointly owned by National Express Group plc and British Airways.

In addition, a service for the conveyance of accompanied road vehicles through the Channel Tunnel is provided by the tunnel operating company, Eurotunnel.

FREIGHT TRAIN OPERATIONS

The following operators operate freight train services under "Open Access" arrangements:

English Welsh & Scottish Railway Ltd (EWS).
Freightliner Ltd.
GB Railfreight Ltd. (now owned by First Group)
Direct Rail Services Ltd.

1. LOCOMOTIVES

INTRODUCTION

SCOPE

This section contains details of all locomotives which can run on Britain's national railway network, plus those of Eurotunnel. Locomotives which are owned by EWS and Freightliner which have been withdrawn from service and awaiting disposal are now listed in the main list, as are those owned by companies such as FM Rail, Harry Needle and DRS which are awaiting possible restoration to service. Only preserved locomotives which are currently used or are likely to be used on the national network in the foreseeable future are included. Others, which may be Network Rail registered but not at present certified for use, are not included, but will be found in the Platform 5 book, "Preserved locomotives and Multiple Units".

LOCO CLASSES

Loco classes are listed in numerical order of class. Principal details and dimensions are quoted for each class in metric and/or imperial units as considered appropriate bearing in mind common UK usage.

Builders: These are shown in class headings. Abbreviations used are found in section 7.8.

All dimensions and weights are quoted for locomotives in an "as new" condition with all necessary supplies (e.g. oil, water and sand) on board. Dimensions are quoted in the order length x width. Lengths quoted are over buffers or couplers as appropriate. All widths quoted are maxima. Where two different wheel diameter dimensions are shown, the first refers to powered wheels and the second refers to non-powered wheels.

NUMERICAL LISTINGS

Locomotives are listed in numerical order. Where numbers actually carried are different from those officially allocated, these are noted in class headings where appropriate. Where locomotives have been recently renumbered, the most immediate previous number is shown in parentheses. Each locomotive entry is laid out as in one of the following examples:

RSL No. Detail Livery Owner Pool Allocn. Name

67010 r **E** A WABK TO Unicorn

In some cases where few members of a class are named, names are appended as a separate list at the end of the class listings to save space.

Detail Differences. Only detail differences which currently affect the areas and types of train which locomotives may work are shown. All other detail differences are specifically excluded. Where such differences occur within a class or part class, they are shown in the "Detail" column alongside the individual locomotive number.

Standard abbreviations used are:

a	Train air brake equipment only.
b	Drophead buckeye couplers.
c	Scharfenberg couplers.
d	Fitted with retractable Dellner couplers (for coupling to Pendolinos).
k	Fitted with Swinghead Automatic "buckeye" combination couplers.
p	Train air, vacuum and electro-pneumatic brakes.
r	RETB fitted
s	Slow Speed Control equipment.
v	Train vacuum brake only.
x	Train air and vacuum brakes ("Dual brakes").
+	Additional fuel tank capacity.
§	Sandite laying equipment.

In all cases use of the above abbreviations indicates the equipment indicated is normally operable. Meaning of non-standard abbreviations and symbols is detailed in individual class headings.

Codes. Codes are used to denote the livery, owner, pool and depot of each locomotive. Details of these will be found in section 7 of this book.

Names. Only names carried with official sanction are listed. As far as possible names are shown in UPPER/lower case characters as actually shown on the name carried on the locomotive.

GENERAL INFORMATION

CLASSIFICATION AND NUMBERING

All locomotives are classified and allocated numbers by the Rolling Stock Library under the TOPS numbering system, introduced in 1972. This comprises a two-digit class number followed by a three-digit serial number. Where the actual number carried by a locomotive differs from the allocated number, or where an additional number is carried to the allocated number, this is shown by a note in the class heading.

For diesel locomotives, class numbers offer an indication of engine horsepower as shown in the table below.

Class No. Range	Engine h.p.
01–14	0–799
15–20	800–1000
21–31	1001–1499
32–39	1500–1999
40–54, 57	2000–2999
55–56, 58–69	3000+

For electric locomotives class numbers are allocated in ascending numerical order under the following scheme:

Class 70–80	direct current and DC/diesel dual system locomotives.
Class 81 onwards	alternating current and AC/DC dual system locos.

Numbers in the 89xxx series (except 89001) are allocated by the Rolling Stock Library to locomotives which have been de-registered but subsequently re-registered for use on the Netwrk Rail network and whose original number has already been re-used. 89xxx numbers are normally only carried inside locomotive cabs and are not carried externally in normal circumstances.

WHEEL ARRANGEMENT

For main line locomotives the number of driven axles on a bogie or frame is denoted by a letter (A = 1, B = 2, C = 3 etc.) and the number of non-powered axles is denoted by a number. The use of the letter 'o' after a letter indicates each axle is individually powered, whilst the '+' symbol indicates bogies are inter-coupled.

For shunting locomotives, the Whyte notation is used. In this notation the number of leading wheels are given, followed by the number of driving wheels and then the trailing wheels.

HAULAGE CAPABILITY OF DIESEL LOCOMOTIVES

The haulage capability of a diesel locomotive depends upon three basic factors:

1. Adhesive weight. The greater the weight on the driving wheels, the greater the adhesion and more tractive power can be applied before wheelslip occurs.

2. The characteristics of its transmission. To start a train the locomotive has to exert a pull at standstill. A direct drive diesel engine cannot do this, hence the need for transmission. This may be mechanical, hydraulic or electric. The present British Standard for locomotives is electric transmission. Here the diesel engine drives a generator or alternator and the current produced is fed to the traction motors. The force produced by each driven wheel depends on the current in its traction motor. In other words, the larger the current, the harder it pulls. As the locomotive speed increases, the current in the traction motor falls, hence the *Maximum Tractive Effort* is the maximum force at its wheels the locomotive can exert at a standstill. The electrical equipment cannot take such high currents for long without overheating. Hence the *Continuous Tractive Effort* is quoted which represents the current which the equipment can take continuously.

3. The power of its engine. Not all power reaches the rail, as electrical machines are approximately 90% efficient. As the electrical energy passes through two such machines (the generator or alternator and the traction motors), the *Power at Rail* is approximately 81% (90% of 90%) of the engine power, less a further amount used for auxiliary equipment such as radiator fans, traction motor blowers, air compressors, battery charging, cab heating, Electric Train Supply (ETS) etc. The power of the locomotive is proportional to the tractive effort times the speed. Hence when on full power there is a speed corresponding to the continuous tractive effort.

HAULAGE CAPABILITY OF ELECTRIC LOCOMOTIVES

Unlike a diesel locomotive, an electric locomotive does not develop its power on board and its performance is determined only by two factors, namely its weight and the characteristics of its electrical equipment. Whereas a diesel locomotive tends to be a constant power machine, the power of an electric locomotive varies considerably. Up to a certain speed it can produce virtually a constant tractive effort. Hence power rises with speed according to the formula given in section three above, until a maximum speed is reached at which tractive effort falls, such that the power also falls. Hence the power at the speed corresponding to the maximum tractive effort is lower than the maximum speed.

BRAKE FORCE

The brake force is a measure of the braking power of a locomotive. This is shown on the locomotive data panels so operating staff can ensure sufficient brake power is available on freight trains.

ELECTRIC TRAIN SUPPLY (ETS)

A number of locomotives are equipped to provide a supply of electricity to the train being hauled to power auxiliaries such as heating, cooling fans, air conditioning and kitchen equipment. ETS is provided from the locomotive by means of a separate alternator (except Class 33 locos, which have a DC generator). The ETS index of a locomotive is a measure of the electrical power available for train supply.

Similarly, most loco-hauled coaches also have an ETS index, which in this case is a measure of the power required to operate equipment mounted in the coach. The sum of the ETS indices of all the hauled vehicles in a train must not exceed the ETS index of the locomotive.

ETS is commonly (but incorrectly) known as ETH (Electric Train Heating), which is a throwback to the days before loco-hauled coaches were equipped with electrically powered auxiliary equipment other than for train heating.

ROUTE AVAILABILITY (RA)

This is a measure of a railway vehicle's axle load. The higher the axle load of a vehicle, the higher the RA number on a scale from 1 to 10. Each Network Rail route has a RA number and in general no vehicle with a higher RA number may travel on that route without special clearance.

MULTIPLE & PUSH-PULL WORKING

Multiple working between vehicles (i.e. two or more powered vehicles being driven from one cab) is facilitated by jumper cables connecting the vehicles. However, not all types are compatible with each other, and a number of different systems are in use, each system being incompatible with any other.

Association of American Railroads (AAR) System: Classes 59, 66, and 67.
Blue Star Coupling Code: Classes 20, 25, 31, 33, & 37.
Green Circle Coupling Code: Class 47 (not all equipped).
Orange Square Coupling Code: Class 50.
Red Diamond Coupling Code: Classes 56 and 58.
SR System: Classes 33/1, 73 and various electric multiple units.
Within Own Class only: Classes 43 and 60.

Many locomotives use a time-division multiplex (TDM) system for push-pull and multiple working which utilises the existing RCH jumper cables fitted to coaching stock vehicles. Previously these cables had only been used to control train lighting and public address systems.

Class 47 locos 47701–47717 were equipped with a older non-standard TDM system.

1.1. DIESEL LOCOMOTIVES

Note: The 01/5 series has been allocated for shunting locomotives of various types which may operate on the Network Rail system. Only those actually registered on TOPS, or ex-BR locos are included here.

SERIES 01/5   H-B/CATERPILLAR   0-6-0

Built: 1971 by The Hunslet Engine Company at Leeds (Works No. 7018), for the National Coal Board, Western Area (No. 8D). Subsequently sold to Hunslet-Barclay, Kilmarnock and rebuilt prior to sale to The Felixstowe Dock and Railway Company in 1999. Registered for use on the Railtrack network in 1999. Normally used at Felixstowe South Container Terminal.
Engine: Caterpillar 3412C DITA of 475 kW (640 h.p.) at ? r.p.m.
Transmission: Hydraulic. Twin Disc 13800 series torque converter coupled to a Hunslet final drive.
Maximum Tractive Effort: 180 kN (40365 lbf).
Train Brakes: Air.

Brake Force: 48 t.	
Weight: 64.3 t.	**Dimensions:** 3.95 x 2.51 m.
Design Speed: 15 m.p.h.	**Wheel Diameter:** 1143 mm.
Fuel Capacity: 930 litres.	**Maximum Speed:** 15 m.p.h.
Train Supply: Not equipped.	**RA:** 7.
	Multiple Working: Not equipped.

Non standard numbering: Also carries number H4323.

01531	**FX**	FX	MBDL	FX	COLONEL TOMLINE

SERIES 01/5   ENGLISH ELECTRIC/RR   0-4-0

Built: 1966 by English Electric at Vulcan Foundry, Newton le Willows (Works No. D1122), for the Central Electricity Generating Board at Croydon 'B' Power Station (No. 2). Subsequently acquired by RFS(E), Doncaster (now Wabtec).
Engine: ? of 235 kW (315 h.p.) at ? r.p.m.
Transmission: Hydraulic.
Maximum Tractive Effort:
Train Brakes: Air.

Brake Force: 10 t.	**Dimensions:** 7.32 x ? m.
Weight: 24.0 t.	**Wheel Diameter:**
Design Speed: 10 m.p.h.	**Maximum Speed:** 10 m.p.h.
Fuel Capacity: 1365 litres.	**RA:** 0.
Train Supply: Not equipped.	**Multiple Working:** Not equipped.

Non standard livery: RFS(E) livery of blue, lined out in silver.

01551	**0**	WA	MBDL	ZB	

SERIES 01/5   HNRC/ROLLS-ROYCE   0-6-0

Built: 1966 by Thomas Hill at Vanguard Works, Kilnhurst (Works No. 167V), for ICI Billingham (No. D3). Subsequently sold to Harry Needle Railroad Company in 1995 and rebuilt 2000. Registered for use on the Railtrack network in 2000, and hired to Creative Logistics, for use at Salford International Railfreight Terminal.

Engine: Rolls Royce 8-cylinder of 275 kW (370 h.p.) at ? r.p.m.
Transmission: Hydraulic. Twin Disc 11800 torque converter coupled to a RF final drive unit.
Maximum Tractive Effort:
Train Brakes: Air.
Brake Force: 19 t.
Weight: 49.0 t.
Design Speed: 10 m.p.h.
Fuel Capacity: 1360 litres.
Train Supply: Not equipped.
Dimensions: 9.14 x ? m.
Wheel Diameter:
Maximum Speed: 10 m.p.h.
RA: 5.
Multiple Working: Not equipped.
Non standard livery: Creative Logistics livery of blue and green.

01552   **0**   HN   MBDL   BH

SERIES 01/5   BR/ENGLISH ELECTRIC   0-6-0

Built: 1950 by BR at Derby Locomotive Works to LMS design as BR Class 11 No. 12082. Withdrawn from service in 1971 and sold to Shellstar (UK), Ince (later UK Fertilisers) in 1972. Purchased by Harry Needle in 19??, and registered for use on the Railtrack network in 2000. Part of the Harry Needle hire fleet.
Engine: English Electric 6KT of 260 kW (350 h.p.) at 600 r.p.m.
Main Generator: English Electric 801.
Traction Motors: Two English Electric 506.
Maximum Tractive Effort: 156 kN (35000 lbf).
Continuous Tractive Effort: ? at 8.5 m.p.h.
Power at Rail:
Brake Force: 19 t.
Weight: 48.60 t.
Design Speed: 20 m.p.h.
Fuel Capacity: 3000 litres.
Train Supply: Not equipped.
Train Brakes: Air.
Dimensions: 8.88 x 2.59 m.
Wheel Diameter: 1232 mm.
Maximum Speed: 20 m.p.h.
RA: 5.
Multiple Working: Not equipped.
Non-standard numbering: Also carries original number 12082.

01553 (12082)   **HN**   HN   HNRL   BH

CLASS 03   BR/GARDNER   0-6-0

Built: 1962 by BR at Swindon Works.
Engine: Gardner 8L3 of 152 kW (204 h.p.) at 1200 r.p.m.
Transmission: Mechanical. Fluidrive type 23 hydraulic coupling to Wilson-Drewry CA5R7 gearbox with SCG type RF11 final drive.
Maximum Tractive Effort: 68 kN (15300 lbf).
Continuous Tractive Effort: 68 kN (15300 lbf) at 3.75 m.p.h.
Train Brakes: Air & vacuum.
Brake Force: 13 t.
Weight: 31.3 t.
Design Speed: 28.5 m.p.h.
Fuel Capacity: 1364 litres.
Train Supply: Not equipped.
Dimensions: 7.93 x 2.59 m.
Wheel Diameter: 1092 mm.
Maximum Speed: 28.5 m.p.h.
RA: 1.
Multiple Working: Not equipped.

Originally numbered D 2179.

03179   **WN**   WN   HQXX   HE   CLIVE

CLASS 07 RUSTON & HORNSBY/PAXMAN 0-6-0

Built: 1962 by Ruston & Hornsby, Lincoln, as BR D2985 for shunting duties in Southampton Docks. Withdrawn from service in 1977 and sold to Tilsley & Lovatt, Stoke-on-Trent in 1978. Resold to Staveley Lime Company (later Peakstone Ltd.), Peak Dale, in 1978. Purchased by Harry Needle in 1989 and registered for use on the national network in 2000. Part of the Harry Needle Railroad Company hire fleet.
Engine: Paxman 6RPHL Mk. 3 of 204 kW (275 h.p.) at 1360 r.p.m.
Main Generator: AEI RTB 6652.
Traction Motors: AEI RTA 6652.
Maximum Tractive Effort: 126 kN (28240 lbf).
Continuous Tractive Effort: ? at 4.4 m.p.h.

Power at Rail:	**Train Brakes:** Air.
Brake Force: 21 t.	**Dimensions:** 8.13 x 2.57 m.
Weight: 42.25 t.	**Wheel Diameter:** 1067 mm.
Design Speed: 20 m.p.h.	**Maximum Speed:** 20 m.p.h.
Fuel Capacity:	**RA:** 6.
Train Supply: Not equipped.	**Multiple Working:** Not equipped.

Originally numbered D 2985.

07001   **HN**   HN   HNRL   BH

CLASS 08   BR/ENGLISH ELECTRIC   0-6-0

Built: 1955–1962 by BR at Crewe, Darlington, Derby Locomotive, Doncaster or Horwich Works.
Engine: English Electric 6KT of 298 kW (400 h.p.) at 680 r.p.m.
Main Generator: English Electric 801.
Traction Motors: Two English Electric 506.
Maximum Tractive Effort: 156 kN (35000 lbf).
Continuous Tractive Effort: 49 kN (11100 lbf) at 8.8 m.p.h.

Power At Rail: 194 kW (260 h.p.).	**Train Brakes:** Air & vacuum.
Brake Force: 19 t.	**Dimensions:** 8.92 x 2.59 m.
Weight: 49.6–50.4 t.	**Wheel Diameter:** 1372 mm.
Design Speed: 20 m.p.h.	**Maximum Speed:** 15 m.p.h.
Fuel Capacity: 3037 litres.	**RA:** 5.
Train Supply: Not equipped.	**Multiple Working:** Not equipped.

Notes: † – Equipped with remote control (Hima Sella system) for working at Celsa (formerly Allied Steel & Wire), Cardiff.
§ – Equipped with remote control (Cattron system) for evaluation purposes.

Non-standard liveries/numbering:

08414 As **DG**, but with BR & Railfreight Distribution logos and large bodyside numbers. Carries number D3529.
08442 Dark grey lower bodyside with light grey upper bodyside.
08460 Light grey with black underframe, cab doors, window surrounds and roof. Carries number D3575.

08527 White with a black roof, blue bodyside stripe and "Ilford Level 5" branding.
08568 and 08730 Special Alstom (Springburn) livery. Dark grey lower bodyside with a light grey upper bodyside. Red solebar stripe.
08601 London Midland & Scottish Railway style black.
08613 Blue with a white bodyside stripe and BOMBARDIER TRANSPORTATION branding.
08616 Carries number 3783.
08629 Red with italic numbers.
08642 London & South Western Railway style black. Carries number D3809.
08648 Yellow with black cabsides and roof.
08649 Grey with blue, white and red stripes and Alstom logo. Carries number D3816.
08678 Glaxochem grey and blue.
08682 Dark blue with a grey roof.
08715 "Day-glo" orange.
08721 As **B**, but with a black roof and "Express parcels" branding with red and yellow stripe.
08805 London Midland & Scottish Railway style maroon. Carries number 3973.
08834 RFS(E) livery of blue with silver lining.
08883 Caledonian Railway style blue.
08928 As **F0** with large bodyside numbers and light blue solebar.

Originally numbered in series D3000–D4192.

Class 08/0. Standard Design.

08077		**FL**	P	DFLS	FD	08483	a	**GL**	FG	HJXX	PM
08308	a	**CS**	RT	MOLO	IS	08484	a	**DG**	AM	ARZN	ZN
08331		**GN**	WA	RFSH	EC	08485	a	**B**	E	WZTS	CU
08350		**G**	LW	MBDL	CP	08489	a	**E**	E	WZTS	MH
08375	a	**RT**	RT	MOLO	ZG	08492	a	**B**	E	WSYX	ML
08389	a	**E**	E	WSWM	BS	08493	a	**B**	RT	MOLO	ZF
08393	a	**E**	E	WSEM	TO	08495		**E**	E	WSNE	TE
08397	a	**E**	E	WZTS	AN	08499	a	**E**	E	WSXX	CF
08401	a	**DG**	E	WZTS	IM	08500		**E**	E	WSSC	ML
08402	a	**E**	E	WNXX	ML	08506	a	**B**	E	WNXX	OC
08405	a	**E**	E	WSLN	TD	08507	a	**HN**	HN	HNRL	CZ
08410	a	**GL**	FG	HJXX	PZ	08509	a	**F**	E	WNYX	IM
08411	a	**B**	E	WNYX	AN	08510	a	**B**	E	WZTS	EH
08414	a	**0**	E	WNYX	TO	08511	a	**E**	E	WNYX	AY
08417	a	**SB**	SO	CDJD	ZA	08512	a	**E**	E	WSEM	TO
08418	a	**E**	E	WZTS	BS	08514	a	**E**	E	WSNE	TE
08428	a	**B**	E	WSEM	TO	08516	a	**E**	E	WSXX	BK
08441	a	**E**	E	WNYX	ML	08523		**ML**	RT	MOLS	CP
08442	a	**0**	E	WNXX	EH	08525		**MA**	MA	HISL	NL
08451		**GB**	VW	ATLO	WN	08526		**E**	E	WSWR	OC
08454		**SL**	VW	ATXX	WN	08527		**0**	BT	KCSI	ZI (S)
08460	a	**0**	E	WZTS	WA	08528		**DG**	E	WRWM	BS
08466	a†	**E**	E	WSEM	TO	08529		**B**	E	WNXX	DR
08472	a	**BR**	WA	RFSH	ZB	08530		**FL**	P	DFLS	FD
08480	a	**E**	E	WZTS	TO	08531	a	**DG**	P	DFLS	FD
08481		**B**	E	WNXX	SP	08534		**DG**	E	WNXX	ML
08482	a	**E**	E	WNTR	OC	08535		**DG**	RT	MOLS	CP

08536		**B**	MA	HISE	DY (S)	08663 a	**GL**	FG	HJSL	PM
08538		**DG**	E	WRWM	BS	08664		**E**	E	WSLS	OC
08540		**E**	E	WNYX	TO	08665		**E**	E	WNYX	HM
08541		**DG**	E	WNYX	OC	08669 a		**WA**	WA	RFSH	BN
08542		**F**	E	WNYX	BS	08670 a		**E**	E	WNYX	ML
08543		**DG**	E	WNYX	BS	08675		**F**	E	WNXX	ML
08561		**B**	E	WSWR	OC	08676		**E**	E	WSWR	OC
08567		**E**	E	WNYX	WA	08678		**0**	WC	MBDL	CS
08568 a		**0**	AM	ARZH	ZH	08682		**0**	BT	KDSD	ZF
08569		**E**	E	WNTR	TO	08683		**E**	E	WNXX	TO
08571 a		**WA**	WA	HBSH	PC	08685		**E**	E	WNTR	AY
08573		**K**	RT	MOLO	RG	08689 a		**E**	E	WSSC	ML
08575		**FL**	P	DFLS	FD	08690		**MA**	MA	HISE	DY (S)
08577		**E**	E	WNTR	BS	08691		**FL**	WA	DFLS	FD
08578		**E**	E	WSWM	BS	08694 a		**E**	E	WNXX	OC
08580		**E**	E	WSWM	BS	08695 a		**E**	E	WNYX	AY
08582 a		**DG**	E	WNXX	DR	08696 a		**G**	VW	ATLO	MA
08585		**FL**	P	DFLS	FD	08697		**B**	MA	HISE	DY (S)
08587		**E**	E	WREM	TO	08698 a		**E**	E	WNTS	DR
08588		**BR**	MA	HISL	ZB (S)	08701 a		**RX**	E	WSXX	CE
08593		**E**	E	WSWM	BS	08703 a		**E**	E	WSEM	TO
08596 a†		**WA**	WA	RFSH	ZB	08706		**E**	E	WSWM	BS
08597		**E**	E	WNTR	DR	08709		**E**	E	WSWM	BS
08599		**E**	E	WNTR	IM	08711 k		**RX**	E	WSEM	TO
08601		**0**	HN	HNRS	SP	08714		**E**	E	WRGW	MG
08605		**E**	E	WSSC	ML	08715 v		**0**	E	WNXX	CU
08611		**V**	VW	ATLO	MA	08720 a		**E**	E	WNYX	ML
08613		**0**	RT	KCSI	ZI	08721		**0**	VW	ATLO	LL
08615		**WA**	WA	RFSH	EC	08724		**WA**	WA	HBSH	EC
08616		**GW**	MA	HGSS	TS	08730		**0**	AM	ARZH	ZH
08617		**VP**	VW	ATLO	WN	08735		**E**	E	WSEM	TO
08623		**E**	E	WZTS	AN	08737 a		**FE**	E	WZTS	AN
08624		**FL**	P	DFLS	FD	08738		**E**	E	WSSC	ML
08628		**B**	E	WNYX	SY	08739		**B**	E	WNYX	AN
08629		**0**	AM	ARZN	ZN	08740		**F**	E	WNXX	FB
08630		**E**	E	WSGW	MG	08742		**RX**	E	WSWM	BS
08631		**N**	FM	SDFR	DF	08743		**EN**	EN	MBDL	BG
08632		**E**	E	WSWM	BS	08745		**FE**	P	DFLS	FD
08633		**E**	E	WSEM	TO	08750 a		**K**	RT	MOLO	QU
08635		**B**	E	WNYX	TO	08752 †		**E**	E	WNXX	DR
08641		**GL**	FG	HJSL	LA	08754		**FL**	RT	MOLO	ZB
08642		**0**	P	DFLS	LD (S)	08756		**DG**	RT	MOLO	ZB
08644		**GL**	FG	HJSL	LA	08757		**RG**	E	WRWR	OC
08645		**GL**	FG	HJSL	LA	08762		**K**	RT	MOLO	NW
08646		**F**	E	WNXX	TD	08765		**E**	E	WSLS	OC
08648		**0**	RT	MOLO	NW	08768		**B**	E	WNXX	ML
08649		**0**	AM	ARZG	ZG	08770 a		**DG**	E	WZTS	MG
08651 a		**DG**	E	WNYX	CF	08775		**E**	E	WNTR	WB
08653		**E**	E	WRWM	BS	08776 a		**DG**	E	WNTS	CE
08655		**B**	E	WNYX	TE	08782 a		**CU**	E	WRWM	BS
08662		**E**	E	WSGW	MG	08783		**E**	E	WNTR	WB

08784		**E**	E	WSNE	TE	08883		**0**	E	WNYX	ML
08785	a	**FL**	P	DFLS	FD	08884		**B**	E	WZTS	BS
08786	a	**DG**	E	WNTR	EH	08886	§	**E**	E	WRSC	ML
08788		**RT**	RT	MOLO	IS	08887	a	**VP**	VW	ATLO	MA
08790		**B**	VW	ATLO	MA	08888		**E**	E	WZTS	IM
08792		**F**	E	WNXX	CF	08890		**DG**	E	WSXX	EH
08795		**GL**	FG	HJSE	LE	08891		**FL**	P	DFLS	FD
08798		**E**	E	WSLN	TD	08892		**GN**	WA	RFSH	ZB
08799	a	**E**	E	WSNE	TE	08893		**DG**	E	WSYX	FB
08802		**RX**	E	WNTS	AN	08894		**B**	E	WNYX	AN
08804		**E**	E	WSWR	OC	08896		**E**	E	WNXX	TO
08805		**0**	MA	HGSS	SI	08897		**E**	E	WSWM	BS
08806	a	**F**	E	WNXX	TE	08899		**MM**	MA	HISE	ZB
08807		**BR**	E	WZTS	ML	08900		**DG**	E	WSAW	MG
08809		**AR**	CD	CREL	NC	08901		**B**	E	WSYX	FB
08810	a	**AR**	LW	MBDL	CP	08902		**B**	E	WNYX	AN
08813	a	**DG**	E	WSYX	TE	08903		**EN**	EN	MBDL	BG
08815		**B**	E	WSYX	SP	08904		**E**	E	WSLN	TD
08817		**BR**	HN	HNRS	SP	08905		**E**	E	WNTS	BS
08818		**HN**	HN	HNRL	MY	08906		**B**	E	WNXX	ML
08819		**DG**	RT	MOLO	ZB	08907		**E**	E	WRLS	OC
08822		**GL**	FG	HJSE	PM	08908		**MM**	MA	HISL	NL
08823	a	**B**	BT	KDSD	ZF	08909		**ML**	E	WZTS	DM
08824	ak	**F**	E	WSEM	TO	08910		**B**	E	WNYX	TO
08825	a	**B**	E	WSYX	SP	08911		**DG**	NM	MBDL	YK
08827	a	**B**	E	WSYX	ML	08912		**B**	E	WNYX	TO
08828	a	**E**	E	WNYX	BS	08913		**E**	E	WZTS	DC
08830		**LW**	LW	MBDL	CP	08914		**B**	E	WSYX	FB
08834		**0**	WA	HBSH	DV	08915		**F**	E	WNXX	TO
08836		**GL**	FG	HJXX	PM	08918		**DG**	E	WSLN	TD
08837		**DG**	E	WNYX	AN	08919		**RX**	E	WNYX	OC
08842		**E**	E	WSLN	TD	08920		**F**	E	WNXX	BS
08844		**E**	E	WNTR	WB	08921	†	**E**	E	WNTS	TD
08847		**CD**	CD	CREL	NC	08922		**DG**	E	WSWM	BS
08853	a	**B**	WA	RFSH	BN	08924		**E**	E	WSSC	ML
08854	†	**E**	E	WNXX	TD	08925		**B**	E	WNXX	DR
08856		**B**	E	WNXX	DC	08926		**B**	E	WNYX	AN
08865		**E**	E	WSWR	OC	08927		**B**	E	WRSC	ML
08866		**E**	E	WSSC	ML	08928		**0**	HN	HNRS	BH
08867		**K**	E	WNXX	FB	08932		**B**	E	WNXX	CD
08868		**B**	HN	HNRL	FX	08933		**E**	E	WRSC	ML
08869		**G**	HN	HNRS	BH	08934	a	**VP**	VW	ATLO	WN
08870		**RL**	RL	MBDL	KE	08936		**HN**	HN	HNRL	MY
08871		**CD**	CD	CREL	DV	08939		**E**	E	WZTS	BS
08872		**E**	E	WZTS	TD	08941		**E**	E	WRGW	MG
08873		**RX**	RT	MOLO	CP	08942		**B**	E	WNYX	TO
08874		**SL**	RT	MOLO	BY	08946		**FE**	E	WNYX	AN
08877		**DG**	E	WSXX	SP	08947		**B**	E	WNXX	WY
08879		**E**	E	WSLS	OC	08948	c	**EP**	EU	GPSS	BH
08880		**B**	E	WNYX	AN	08950		**MA**	MA	HISL	NL
08881		**DG**	E	WZTS	ML	08951	†	**E**	E	WNTS	AN

| 08953 | a | **DG** | E | WSEM | TO | 08955 | **F** | E | WNXX | CF |
| 08954 | | **F** | E | WNXX | WA | 08956 | **SB** | SO | CDJD | ZA |

Names:

08389	NOEL KIRTON OBE
08483	DUSTY Driver David Miller
08568	St. Rollox
08585	Vicky
08616	COOKIE
08631	EAGLE
08649	G.H. Stratton
08664	DON GATES 1952–2000
08682	Lionheart
08691	Terri
08694	PAT BARR
08701	The Sorter
08714	Cambridge
08730	The Caley
08743	Brian Turner
08782	CASTLETON WORKS
08790	M.A. SMITH
08799	ANDY BOWER
08804	RICHARD J.WENHAM EASTLEIGH DEPOT DECEMBER 1989–JULY 1999
08805	CONCORDE
08818	MOLLY
08844	CHRIS WREN 1955–2002
08872	TONY LONG STRATFORD DEPOT 1971–2002
08874	Catherine
08903	John W Antill
08919	Steep Holm
08951	FRED

Class 08/9. Reduced height cab. Converted 1985–1987 by BR at Landore T&RSMD.

08993		**E**	E	WNTR	BZ	ASHBURNHAM
08994	a	**E**	E	WNTR	CF	
08995	a	**E**	E	WNTR	MG	

CLASS 09   BR/ENGLISH ELECTRIC   0-6-0

Built: 1959–1962 by BR at Darlington or Horwich Works.
Engine: English Electric 6KT of 298 kW (400 h.p.) at 680 r.p.m.
Main Generator: English Electric 801.
Traction Motors: English Electric 506.
Maximum Tractive Effort: 111 kN (25000 lbf).
Continuous Tractive Effort: 39 kN (8800 lbf) at 11.6 m.p.h.
Power At Rail: 201 kW (269 h.p.).   **Train Brakes:** Air & vacuum.

Brake Force: 19 t.
Weight: 50 t.
Design Speed: 27 m.p.h.
Fuel Capacity: 3037 litres.
Train Supply: Not equipped.

Dimensions: 8.92 x 2.59 m.
Wheel Diameter: 1372 mm.
Maximum Speed: 27 m.p.h.
RA: 5.
Multiple Working: Not equipped. Class 09/0 were originally numbered D3665–D3671, D3719–3721, D4099–D4114.

Class 09/0. Built as Class 09.

09001	**E**	E	WSAW	MG	
09003	**E**	E	WSWR	OC	
09005 k	**E**	E	WRLS	OC	
09006	**E**	E	WSLS	OC	
09007	**ML**	E	WSEM	TO	
09008	**E**	E	WNTR	CF	
09009	**E**	E	WNXX	SL	Three Bridges C.E.D.
09010	**DG**	E	WNTR	HG	
09011	**DG**	E	WSGW	MG	
09012	**DG**	E	WNXX	HG	Dick Hardy
09013	**DG**	E	WSWR	OC	
09014	**DG**	E	WSNE	TE	
09015	**E**	E	WSGW	MG	
09016	**E**	E	WNXX	BZ	
09017	**E**	E	WRGW	MG	
09018	**E**	E	WNXX	HG	
09019	**ML**	E	WSWR	OC	
09020	**E**	E	WNTR	TE	
09021	**E**	E	WNXX	DR	
09022 a	**E**	E	WSWM	BS	
09023 a	**E**	E	WSEM	TO	
09024	**ML**	E	WSLS	OC	
09025	**CX**	SN	HWSU	SU	
09026	**G**	SN	HWSU	BI	Cedric Wares

Class 09/1. Converted from Class 08/0. 110 V electrical equipment.

Converted: 1992–1993 by RFS Industries, Kilnhurst.

09101 (08833)	**DG**	E	WSGW	MG	
09102 (08832)	**DG**	E	WSGW	MG	
09103 (08766)	**DG**	E	WSSC	ML	
09104 (08749)	**DG**	E	WNXX	AN	
09105 (08835)	**DG**	E	WSGW	MG	
09106 (08759)	**DG**	E	WNTR	DR	
09107 (08845)	**DG**	E	WNTR	DR	

Class 09/2. Converted from Class 08. 90 V electrical equipment.

Converted: 1992 by RFS Industries, Kilnhurst.

09201 (08421) ak	**DG**	E	WSNE	TE	
09202 (08732)	**DG**	E	WSNE	TE	
09203 (08781)	**DG**	E	WSGW	MG	
09204 (08717)	**DG**	E	WNXX	TY	
09205 (08620)	**DG**	E	WSNE	TE	

CLASS 20   ENGLISH ELECTRIC   Bo-Bo

Built: 1957–1968 by English Electric Company at Vulcan Foundry, Newton le Willows or by Robert Stephenson & Hawthorn at Darlington.
Engine: English Electric 8SVT Mk. II of 746 kW (1000 h.p.) at 850 r.p.m.
Main Generator: English Electric 819/3C.
Traction Motors: English Electric 526/5D or 526/8D.
Maximum Tractive Effort: 187 kN (42000 lbf).
Continuous Tractive Effort: 111 kN (25000 lbf) at 11 m.p.h.
Power At Rail: 574 kW (770 h.p.).   **Train Brakes:** Air & vacuum.
Brake Force: 35 t.   **Dimensions:** 14.25 x 2.67 m.
Weight: 73.4–73.5 t.   **Wheel Diameter:** 1092 mm.
Design Speed: 75 m.p.h.   **Maximum Speed:** 75 m.p.h.
Fuel Capacity: 1727 litres.   **RA:** 5.
Train Supply: Not equipped.   **Multiple Working:** Blue Star.

Non-standard liveries:

20088, 20105, and 20145 are in RFS grey.
20092 is in Central Services grey & red livery.
20132, 20138 and 20215 are as **F0** but with a red solebar stripe.

Originally numbered in series D8007–D8190, D8315–D8325.

Class 20/0. Standard Design.

20016	**B**	HN	HNRS	LT
20032	**B**	HN	HNRS	LT
20056	**G**	HN	HNRL	BH
20057	**B**	HN	HNRS	LT
20066	**B**	HN	HNRS	BH
20072	**B**	HN	HNRS	LT
20073	**B**	HN	HNRS	LT
20081	**B**	HN	HNRS	LT
20088	**0**	HN	HNRS	LT
20092	**0**	HN	HNRS	LT
20105	**0**	HN	HNRS	BF
20121	**B**	HN	HNRS	BH
20132	**0**	HN	HNRS	BH
20138	**0**	HN	HNRS	LT
20145	**0**	HN	HNRS	LT
20168	**LA**	HN	HNRL	EA	SIR GEORGE EARLE
20215	**0**	HN	HNRS	LT

Class 20/3. Direct Rail Services refurbished locos. Details as Class 20/0 except:

Refurbished: 1995–1996 by Brush Traction at Loughborough (20301–20305) or 1997–1998 by RFS(E) at Doncaster (20306–20315). Disc indicators or headcode panels removed.
Train Brakes: Air.   **Maximum Speed:** 75 m.p.h.
Brake Force: 31 t.   **Fuel Capacity:** 2900 (+ 4909) litres.
Multiple Working: Blue Star (20301–20305 at nose end only).

20301	(20047)	+	**DR**	DR XHMW	ZH	Max Joule 1958–1999
20302	(20084)		**DR**	DR XHSD	KM	
20303	(20127)	+	**DR**	DR XHMW	LB	
20304	(20120)		**DR**	DR XHSD	KM	
20305	(20095)		**DR**	DR XHMW	ZH	
20306	(20131)	+	**DR**	DR XHSD	KM	
20307	(20128)	+	**DR**	DR XHMW	LB	
20308	(20187)	+	**DR**	DR XHSD	KM	
20309	(20075)	+	**DR**	DR XHSD	KM	
20310	(20190)	+	**DR**	DR XHMW	LB	
20311	(20102)	+	**DR**	DR XHSD	KM	
20312	(20042)	+	**DR**	DR XHSD	KM	
20313	(20194)	+	**DR**	DR XHSD	KM	
20314	(20117)	+	**DR**	DR XHSD	KM	
20315	(20104)	+	**DR**	DR XHSD	KM	

Class 20/9. Harry Needle Railroad Company (former Hunslet-Barclay and DRS) locos.
Details as Class 20/0 except:

Refurbished: 1989 by Hunslet-Barclay at Kilmarnock.
Train Brakes: Air.   **Fuel Capacity:** 1727 (+ 4727) litres.

20901	(20101)		**DR**	HN HNRS	KM
20902	(20060)	+	**DR**	HN HNRS	BH
20903	(20083)	+	**DR**	HN HNRS	KM
20904	(20041)		**DR**	HN HNRS	KM
20905	(20225)	+	**DR**	HN HNRS	KM
20906	(20219)		**DR**	HN HNRS	CP

CLASS 31 BRUSH/ENGLISH ELECTRIC A1A-A1A

Built: 1958–1962 by Brush Traction at Loughborough.
Engine: English Electric 12SVT of 1100 kW (1470 h.p.) at 850 r.p.m.
Main Generator: Brush TG160-48.   **Traction Motors:** Brush TM73-68.
Maximum Tractive Effort: 160 kN (35900 lbf).
Continuous Tractive Effort: 83 kN (18700 lbf) at 23.5 m.p.h.
Power At Rail: 872 kW (1170 h.p.).   **Train Brakes:** Air & vacuum.
Brake Force: 49 t.   **Dimensions:** 17.30 x 2.67 m.
Weight: 106.7–111 t.   **Wheel Diameter:** 1092/1003 mm.
Design Speed: 90 m.p.h.   **Maximum Speed:** 90 m.p.h.
Fuel Capacity: 2409 (+ 4820) litres.   **RA:** 5 or 6.
Train Supply: Not equipped.   **Multiple Working:** Blue Star.

Originally numbered D5520–D5699, D5800–D5862 (not in order).

Non-standard livery/numbering:

31110 Carries number D5528.
31301 As **F0** but with a red solebar stripe.

Class 31/1. Standard Design. RA: 5.

31102	**CE**	NR QADD	TH (S)
31105	**Y**	NR QADD	DF

31106	**FR**	HJ	SDPP	DF	SPALDING TOWN
31107	**CE**	NR	QADD	DF (S)	
31110 a	**G**	E	WMOC	BH (S)	TRACTION magazine
31128	**FR**	FM	SDPP	DF	CHARYBDIS
31154	**CE**	FM	SDXL	DY	
31190	**RK**	FM	SDFR	DF	GRYPHON
31200	**F**	NR	QADD	TH (S)	
31206	**CE**	CD	CROL	LB	
31233 a	**Y**	NR	QADD	DF	
31275	**F**	HN	HNRS	CS	
31285	**Y**	NR	QADD	DF	
31301	**0**	FM	SDXL	MQ	
31306	**CE**	HN	HNRS	OC	
31308	**CE**	HN	HNRS	OC	
31319	**F**	NR	QADD	TH (S)	

Class 31/4. Electric Train Supply equipment. RA: 6.
Class 31/5. Train Heating Equipment isolated. RA: 6.

31407	**ML**	FM	SDXL	BH	
31411	**DG**	FM	SDXL	BH	
31412	**CE**	FM	SDXL	BH	
31415	**B**	FM	SDXL	MQ	
31417	**DG**	FM	SDXL	BH	
31420	**IM**	E	WNXX	OC	
31422	**IM**	FM	SDXL	TM	
31423	**IM**	FM	SDXL	MQ	
31426	**CE**	FM	SDXL	MQ	
31427	**B**	E	WNXX	OC	
31433	**CE**	FM	SDXL	BH	
31437	**CE**	FM	SDXL	MQ	
31439	**RR**	FM	SDXL	MQ	
31449	**CE**	FM	SDXL	TM	
31452	**FR**	FM	SDPP	DF	MINOTAUR
31454	**IC**	FM	SDPP	DF	THE HEART OF WESSEX
31458	**CE**	FM	SDXL	TM	
31459	**FR**	FM	SDPP	DF	CERBERUS
31460	**B**	FM	SDXL	BH	
31461 +	**DG**	FM	SDXL	DF	
31462	**DG**	FM	SDXL	TM	
31465	**RR**	HN	HNRS	OC	
31466 a	**E**	E	WNXX	OC	
31468	**FR**	FM	SDPP	DF	HYDRA
31514	**CE**	HN	HNRS	OC	
31524	**CE**	FM	SDXL	BH	

Class 31/6. ETS through wiring and controls. RA: 5.

31601	(31186)	**WX**	FM	SDPP	DF	THE MAYOR OF CASTERBRIDGE
31602	(31191)	**FR**	FM	SDPP	DF	CHIMAERA

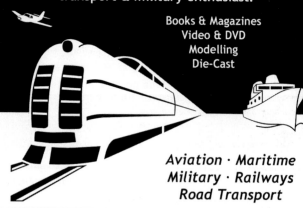

CLASS 33   BRCW/SULZER   Bo-Bo

Built: 1960–1962 by the Birmingham Railway Carriage & Wagon Company at Smethwick.
Engine: Sulzer 8LDA28 of 1160 kW (1550 h.p.) at 750 r.p.m.
Main Generator: Crompton Parkinson CG391B1.
Traction Motors: Crompton Parkinson C171C2.
Maximum Tractive Effort: 200 kN (45000 lbf).
Continuous Tractive Effort: 116 kN (26000 lbf) at 17.5 m.p.h.
Power At Rail: 906 kW (1215 h.p.). **Train Brakes:** Air & vacuum.
Brake Force: 35 t.   **Dimensions:** 15.47 x 2.82 (2.64 m. 33/2).
Weight: 77.7 t.   **Wheel Diameter:** 1092 mm.
Design Speed: 85 m.p.h.   **Maximum Speed:** 85 m.p.h.
Fuel Capacity: 3410 litres.   **RA:** 6.
Train Supply: Electric, index 48 (750 V DC only).
Multiple Working: Blue Star.

Originally numbered in series D6500–D6597 but not in order.

Non-standard liveries/numbering:

33046 All over mid-blue. Carries no number.
33109 Carries number D6525.
33116 Carries number D6535.
33208 Carries number D6593.

Class 33/0. Standard Design.

33008	**G**	HN	HNRS	LT	
33019	**CE**	FM	SDXL	BF	
33021	**FR**	WF	SDFR	DF	Eastleigh
33025	**DR**	DR	XHSD	KM	
33029	**B**	DR	XHSS	DF	
33030	**DR**	DR	XHSD	KM	
33046	**O**	FM	SDXL	DF	
33053	**F**	HN	HNRS	LT	
33057	**CE**	HN	HNRS	LT	

Class 33/1. Fitted with Buckeye Couplings & SR Multiple Working Equipment for use with SR EMUs, TC stock & Class 73. Also fitted with flashing light adaptor for use on Weymouth Quay line.

33103	b	**FR**	CM	SDFR	DF	SWORDFISH
33108	b	**FR**	11	SDFR	DF	VAMPIRE
33109	b	**B**	71	MBDL	CP	
33116	b	**B**	E	WNZX	OC	

Class 33/2. Built to Former Loading Gauge of Tonbridge–Battle Line.
All equipped with slow speed control.

33202	**FR**	FM	SDFR	DF	METEOR
33203	**F**	HN	HNRS	LT	
33207	**DR**	DR	XHSD	KM	
33208	**G**	71	MBDL	RL	

CLASS 37   ENGLISH ELECTRIC   Co-Co

Built: 1960–1965 by English Electric Company at Vulcan Foundry, Newton le Willows or by Robert Stephenson & Hawthorn at Darlington.
Engine: English Electric 12CSVT of 1300 kW (1750 h.p.) at 850 r.p.m.
Main Generator: English Electric 822/10G.
Traction Motors: English Electric 538/A.
Maximum Tractive Effort: 245 kN (55500 lbf).
Continuous Tractive Effort: 156 kN (35000 lbf) at 13.6 m.p.h.
Power At Rail: 932 kW (1250 h.p.).   **Train Brakes:** Air & vacuum.
Brake Force: 50 t.   **Dimensions:** 18.75 x 2.74 m.
Weight: 102.8–108.4 t.   **Wheel Diameter:** 1092 mm.
Design Speed: 90 m.p.h.   **Maximum Speed:** 80 m.p.h.
Fuel Capacity: 4046 (+ 7678) litres.   **RA:** 5 (§ 6).
Train Supply: Not equipped.   **Multiple Working:** Blue Star.

Originally numbered D6600–D6608, D6700–D6999 (not in order).

Non-standard liveries/numbering:

37137 Has been used for paint trials.
37351 Carries number 37002 on one side only.
37402 Light grey lower bodyside & dark grey upper bodyside.
37403 Carries number D6607.

Class 37/0. Standard Design. Details as above.

37010	a	**CE**	E	WNZX	SP
37013		**ML**	DR	XHSS	LB
37023		**ML**	E	WNXX	OC
37029	§	**DR**	DR	XHCK	KM	Stratford TMD
37038		**DR**	DR	XHMW	LB
37040		**E**	E	WNZX	SP
37042	+	**E**	E	WNTR	DR
37046	a	**CE**	E	WZKF	TY
37047	+	**ML**	E	WNTA	HG
37051		**E**	E	WNTR	TD
37055	+	**ML**	E	WNXX	TE
37057	+	**E**	E	WNTA	CE	Viking
37058	a+	**CE**	E	WZKF	TY
37059	a+	**DR**	DR	XHCK	KM
37065	+	**ML**	E	WNTR	TT
37068		**F**	HN	HNRS	LB
37069	a+	**DR**	DR	XHSD	KM
37071	a+	**CE**	E	WNZX	SP
37074	a+	**ML**	E	WNZX	SP
37077	a	**ML**	E	WZKF	BK
37087	a	**HN**	DR	XHCK	KM
37095		**CE**	HN	HNRS	CS
37100	a	**F**	E	WNXX	TY
37109		**E**	E	WNTA	HG
37114	r+	**E**	E	WNTA	BS	City of Worcester

37116	+	**B**	E	WNYX	EH
37131	+	**F**	E	WNZX	SP
37137		**0**	E	WNSO	TT
37141		**CE**	HN	HNRS	CS
37146	a	**CE**	E	WNXX	TY
37152		**IC**	E	WNYX	ML
37162	+	**DG**	E	WNZX	SP
37165	a+	**CE**	X	HNRS	CS
37170	a	**CE**	E	WNZX	SP
37174	a	**E**	E	WNTS	BS
37175	a	**CE**	E	WMOC	OC (S)
37178	+	**F**	E	WNYX	EH
37185	+	**CE**	E	WNZX	SP
37188		**CE**	X	WNSO	CS
37194		**DR**	DR	XHCK	KM
37196	a	**CE**	E	WZKF	TY
37197		**IR**	WC	MBDL	CS
37203		**ML**	E	WNTR	BS
37216	+	**ML**	E	WNTR	ML
37217	+	**B**	X	WNSO	AY
37218		**DR**	DR	XHSD	KM
37219		**ML**	E	WNXX	EH
37220	+	**E**	E	WNXX	TT
37221	a	**F**	E	WZKF	TY
37222		**F**	HN	HNRS	CS
37229	§	**DR**	DR	XHCK	KM
37230	+	**CE**	E	WNYX	TT
37235		**F**	WC	MBDL	BQ (S)
37238	a+	**F**	E	WZKF	TY
37248	+	**ML**	E	WNTR	MG
37250	a+	**F**	E	WZKF	TY
37259		**DR**	DR	XHSD	KM
37261	a+	**G**	WC	MBDL	CS
37293	a+	**ML**	E	WZKF	TY
37294	a+	**CE**	E	WNXX	CD
37298	a+	**E**	E	WNZX	SP
37308	+	**B**	E	WNTR	TO

Class 37/3. Re-geared (CP7) bogies. Details as Class 37/0 except:

Maximum Tractive Effort: 250 kN (56180 lbf).
Continuous Tractive Effort: 184 kN (41250 lbf) at 11.4 m.p.h.
Design Speed: 80 m.p.h.

37334		**F**	HN	HNRS	LB
37344		**F**	HN	HNRS	LB
37351	+	**CE**	E	WNXX	CD
37358	+	**F**	X	WNSO	IM
37359		**F**	HN	HNRS	CS
37370	a	**E**	E	WNZX	SP
37372		**ML**	E	WNTA	ML
37375	a+	**ML**	E	WNTS	TT

37376	a+	**F**	E	WNZX	SP	
37377	+	**U**	E	WZKF	BK	
37379	a	**ML**	E	WNXX	BK	Ipswich WRD Quality Approved
37383	+	**ML**	RV	RTLS	CP	
37384		**CE**	DR	XHSS	LB	

Class 37/4. Refurbished with electric train supply equipment. Main generator replaced by alternator. Re-geared (CP7) bogies. Details as Class 37/0 except:
Main Alternator: Brush BA1005A.   **Power At Rail:** 935 kW (1254 h.p.).
Maximum Tractive Effort: 256 kN (57440 lbf).
Continuous Tractive Effort: 184 kN (41250 lbf) at 11.4 m.p.h.
Weight: 107 t.
Design Speed: 80 m.p.h.
Fuel Capacity: 7678 litres.
Train Supply: Electric, index 38.

37401	r	**GS**	E	WKBM	ML	The Royal Scotsman
37402		**0**	E	WNTR	BS	Bont Y Bermo
37403	a	**G**	E	WNYX	MG	
37405		**E**	E	WKCK	MG	
37406	r	**E**	E	WKBM	ML	The Saltire Society
37407		**F**	E	WNXX	SP	
37408		**E**	E	WKCK	MG	Loch Rannoch
37409		**F**	E	WNXX	ML	
37410		**E**	E	WNTA	TO	
37411		**E**	E	WKCK	MG	The Scottish Railway Preservation Society
37412		**F**	E	WNXX	MG	Driver John Elliott
37413		**E**	E	WNXX	MG	
37414		**RR**	E	WNYX	SP	
37415		**E**	E	WNXX	MG	
37416	r	**GS**	E	WKBM	ML	
37417	ra	**E**	E	WKBM	ML	Richard Trevithick
37418	r	**E**	E	WKSN	ML	East Lancashire Railway
37419		**E**	E	WNTA	MG	
37420		**RR**	E	WNXX	CD	The Scottish Hosteller
37421	r	**E**	E	WKSN	ML	
37422		**E**	E	WNTS	TO	Cardiff Canton
37423		**F**	WC	MBDL	CS (S)	
37424		**F**	E	WNYX	ML	
37425		**E**	E	WKCK	MG	
37426		**E**	E	WNXX	CD	
37427	r	**E**	E	WKAD	TO	
37428		**GS**	E	WNXX	MG	
37429		**RR**	E	WNXX	TT	
37430	a	**F**	E	WNYX	ML	

Class 37/5. Refurbished without train supply equipment. Main generator replaced by alternator. Re-geared (CP7) bogies.
Details as Class 37/4 except:
Maximum Tractive Effort: 248 kN (55590 lbf).
Weight: 106.1–110.0) t.

37503	r§ **E**	E	WNTA	DR	
37505	a§ **F**	E	WZKF	AY	British Steel Workington
37509	a§ **F**	E	WNXX	CF	
37510	a **IC**	HN	HNRS	BH	
37513	as§ **LH**	E	WNXX	OC	
37515	as **HN**	DR	XHCK	KM	
37516	s§ **LH**	E	WNTA	DR	
37517	as§ **LH**	E	WNTA	TO	
37518	a§ **F**	E	WZKF	AY	
37519	**F**	E	WZKF	EH	
37520	r§ **E**	E	WNXX	CD	
37521	r§ **E**	E	WNTA	DR	English China Clays

Class 37/6. Originally refurbished for Nightstar services. Main generator replaced by alternator, re-geared bogies and UIC jumpers. Details as Class 37/5 except:

Maximum Speed: 90 m.p.h.   **Train Brake:** Air.
Train Supply: Not equipped, but electric through wired.
Multiple Working: TDM († plus Blue Star).

37601	**EP**	EU	GPSV	OC	
37602 †	**DR**	DR	XHCK	KM	
37603	**EP**	EU	GPSV	OC	
37604	**EP**	EU	GPSV	OC	
37605 †	**DR**	DR	XHCK	KM	
37606 †	**DR**	DR	XHCK	KM	
37607 †	**DR**	DR	XHCK	KM	
37608 †	**DR**	DR	XHMW	LB	
37609 †	**DR**	DR	XHCK	KM	
37610 †	**DR**	DR	XHMW	LB	The MALCOLM Group
37611 †	**DR**	DR	XHCK	KM	
37612 †	**DR**	DR	XHCK	KM	

Class 37/5 continued.

37667	rs§ **E**	E	WNTR	BS	Meldon Quarry Centenary
37668	s§ **E**	E	WNTA	WA	
37669	r§ **E**	E	WKAD	TO	
37670	r§ **E**	E	WNTR	TD	St. Blazey T&RS Depot
37671	a **F**	E	WZKF	TY	
37672	as **F**	E	WNXX	TE	
37673	§ **F**	E	WNXX	TE	
37674	§ **F**	E	WNTA	ML	Saint Blaise Church 1445–1995
37675	as§ **F**	E	WNTA	BK	Margam TMD
37676	a§ **F**	E	WNTA	TO	
37677	a§ **F**	E	WNXX	IM	
37678	a§ **F**	E	WNXX	BS	

37679	a§ **F**	E	WZKF	AY	
37680	a§ **F**	E	WNXX	TE	
37682	r§ **E**	E	WNTA	CE	Hartlepool Pipe Mill
37683	a **F**	E	WNXX	TE	
37684	ar§ **E**	E	WNTA	MG	Peak National Park
37685	a§ **IC**	E	WNTA	TO	
37686	a **F**	E	WNZX	SP	
37688	§ **E**	E	WNTR	HM	
37689	a§ **F**	E	WNTA	WA	
37692	s§ **F**	E	WNTA	MG	Didcot Depot
37693	as **F**	E	WZKF	TY	
37694	§ **E**	E	WNTR	TD	
37695	s§ **E**	E	WNTR	HM	
37696	as **F**	E	WZKF	BK	
37697	**E**	E	WNZX	SP	
37698	a§ **LH**	E	WNTA	MG	

Class 37/7. Refurbished locos. Main generator replaced by alternator. Re-geared (CP7) bogies. Ballast weights added. Details as Class 37/5 except:
Main Alternator: GEC G564AZ (37796–803) Brush BA1005A (others).
Maximum Tractive Effort: 276 kN (62000 lbf).
Weight: 120 t.   **RA:** 7.

37701	as **F**	E	WZKF	OC	
37702	s **GIF**	E	WZKS	ES	
37703	**GIF**	E	WZKS	ES	
37704	s **E**	E	WNYX	MG	
37705	**F**	E	WZKF	ML	
37706	**E**	E	WNTA	TO	
37707	**E**	E	WNTA	BS	
37708	a **F**	E	WNXX	HM	
37709	**F**	E	WNTA	MH	
37710	**LH**	E	WNTA	WA	
37711	**F**	E	WNZX	SP	
37712	a **E**	E	WNTA	WA	
37713	**LH**	HN	HNRS	CD	
37714	a **GIF**	E	WZKS	ES	
37715	**F**	E	WNZX	SP	
37716	**GIF**	E	WZKS	ES	
37717	**E**	E	WNTA	TO	Berwick Middle School Railsafe Trophy Winners 1998
37718	**GIF**	E	WZKS	ES	
37719	a **F**	E	WZKF	OC	
37796	as **F**	E	WZKF	TY	
37797	s **E**	E	WNTR	TT	
37798	**ML**	E	WNTA	MG	
37799	as **GIF**	E	WZKS	ES	
37800	a **GIF**	E	WZKS	ES	
37801	s **GIF**	E	WZKS	ES	
37803	a **ML**	E	WNXX	TY	
37883	**GIF**	E	WZKS	ES	
37884	**GIF**	E	WZKS	ES	

37886	E	E	WNTA	MH	Sir Dyfed/County of Dyfed
37887 s	F	E	WZKF	IM	
37888	GIF	E	WZKS	ES	
37889	F	HN	HNRS	CD	
37890 a	F	E	WNTA	MG	
37891 a	F	E	WZKF	TY	
37892	F	E	WZKF	OC	Ripple Lane
37893	F	E	WNTA	BS	
37894 as	F	E	WZKF	TY	
37895 s	E	E	WNTA	BS	
37896 s	F	E	WNTA	MG	
37897 s	F	E	WNXX	BS	
37898 s	F	HN	HNRS	MG	

Class 37/9. Refurbished locos. New power unit. Main generator replaced by alternator.
Ballast weights added. Details as Class 37/4 except:

Engine: Mirrlees MB275T of 1340 kW (1800 h.p.) at 1000 r.p.m. (§ Ruston RK270T of 1340 kW (1800 h.p.) at 900 r.p.m.).
Train supply: Not equipped.
Main Alternator: Brush BA1005A (ç GEC G564AZ).
Maximum Tractive Effort: 279 kN (62680 lbf).
Continuous Tractive Effort: 184 kN (41250 lbf) at 11.4 m.p.h.
Weight: 120 t.   **RA:** 7.

37902	F	DR	XHSS	KM	
37903	F	HN	HNRS	CD	
37905 s	F	E	WNYX	IM	
37906 s	F0	E	WMOC	KR	

CLASS 40   ENGLISH ELECTRIC   1Co-Co1

Built: 1958–1962 by the English Electric Co. at Vulcan Foundry, Newton le Willows.
Engine: English Electric 16SVT Mk2 of 1490 kW (2000 h.p.) at 850 r.p.m.
Main Generator: English Electric 822.
Traction Motors: English Electric 526/5D.
Maximum Tractive Effort: 231 kN (52000 lbf).
Continuous Tractive Effort: 137 kN (30900 lbf) at 18.8 m.p.h.

Power At Rail: 1160 kW (1550 h.p.).	**Train Brakes:** Air & vacuum.
Brake Force: 51 t.	**Dimensions:** 21.18 x 2.78 m.
Weight: 132 t.	**Wheel Diameter:** 914/1143 mm.
Design Speed: 90 m.p.h.	**Maximum Speed:** 90 m.p.h.
Fuel Capacity: 3250 litres.	**RA:** 6.
Train Supply: Steam.	**Multiple Working:** Not equipped.

| 40145 | B | 40 | MBDL | BQ |

CLASS 43   BREL/PAXMAN   Bo-Bo

Built: 1976–1982 by BREL at Crewe Works.
Engine: Paxman Valenta 12RP200L of 1680 kW (2250 h.p.) at 1500 r.p.m.
(* Paxman 12VP185 of 1680 kW (2250 h.p.) at 1500 r.p.m.).
(§ MTU 16V4000 of 1680kW (2280 h.p.) at 1500 r.p.m.). Experimentally fitted by
Angel Trains to two power cars.
Main Alternator: Brush BA1001B.
Traction Motors: Brush TMH68–46 or GEC G417AZ, frame mounted.
Maximum Tractive Effort: 80 kN (17980 lbf).
Continuous Tractive Effort: 46 kN (10340 lbf) at 64.5 m.p.h.
Power At Rail: 1320 kW (1770 h.p.).   **Train Brakes:** Air.
Brake Force: 35 t.   **Dimensions:** 17.79 x 2.71 m.
Weight: 70.25 t.   **Wheel Diameter:** 1020 mm.
Design Speed: 125 m.p.h.   **Maximum Speed:** 125 m.p.h.
Fuel Capacity: 4500 litres.   **RA:** 5.
Train Supply: Three-phase electric.
Multiple Working: Within class, jumpers at non-driving end only.

Notes:

† Buffer fitted.

43013, 43014 and 43062 are fitted with measuring apparatus and front-end
cameras.

Non-standard livery:

43101 All over black with a red cab.

43002	FG	A	IWRP	PM	TECHNIQUEST
43003	FG	A	IWRP	PM	
43004 §	FP	A	SCXL	LB	
43005	FG	A	IWRP	LA	
43006	GN	A	IECP	EC	Kingdom of Fife
43007	MN	A	IMLP	NL	
43008	GN	A	IECP	EC	City of Aberdeen
43009 §	FP	A	SCXL	LB	
43010	FG	A	IWRP	PM	
43012	FG	A	IWRP	PM	
43013 †	Y	P	QCAR	EC	
43014 †	Y	P	QCAR	EC	
43015	FG	A	IWRP	PM	
43016	FG	A	IWRP	PM	Peninsula Medical School
43017	FG	A	IWRP	PM	
43018	FG	A	IWRP	PM	The Red Cross
43019	FG	A	SCXL	ZC	City of Swansea/Dinas Abertawe
43020	FG	A	IWRP	LA	John Grooms
43021	FG	A	IWRP	LA	
43022	FG	A	IWRP	PM	
43023	FG	A	IWRP	PM	County of Cornwall
43024	FG	A	IWRP	PM	
43025	FG	A	IWRP	PM	Exeter

43026		FG	A	IWRP	PM	City of Westminster
43027		FG	A	IWRP	PM	Glorious Devon
43028		FG	A	IWRP	PM	
43029		FG	A	IWRP	PM	
43030		FG	A	IWRP	PM	Christian Lewis Trust
43031		FG	A	IWRP	PM	
43032		FG	A	IWRP	PM	The Royal Regiment of Wales
43033		FG	A	IWRP	PM	Driver Brian Cooper
						15 June 1947–5 October 1999
43034		FG	A	IWRP	PM	The Black Horse
43035		FG	A	IWRP	PM	
43036		FG	A	IWRP	PM	
43037		FG	A	IWRP	PM	PENYDARREN
43038		GN	A	IECP	EC	City of Dundee
43039		GN	A	IECP	EC	The Royal Dragoon Guards
43040		FG	A	IWRP	PM	Bristol St. Philips Marsh
43041		FG	A	IWRP	PM	City of Discovery
43042		FG	A	IWRP	PM	
43043	*	MM	P	IMLP	NL	LEICESTERSHIRE COUNTY
						CRICKET CLUB
43044	*	MN	P	IMLP	NL	
43045	*	MN	P	IMLP	NL	
43046		MM	P	IMLP	NL	Royal Philharmonic
43047	*	MM	P	IMLP	NL	
43048	*	MN	P	IMLP	NL	Neville Hill
43049	*	MM	P	IMLP	NL	
43050	*	MN	P	IMLP	NL	
43051		MN	P	IMLP	NL	
43052	*	MN	P	IMLP	NL	
43053		MN	P	IMLP	NL	
43054		MM	P	IMLP	NL	
43055	*	MM	P	IMLP	NL	Sheffield Star
43056		MN	P	IMLP	NL	
43057		MN	P	IMLP	NL	
43058		MN	P	IMLP	NL	
43059	*	MN	P	IMLP	NL	COUNTY OF LEICESTERSHIRE
43060	*	MM	P	IMLP	NL	
43061	*	MN	P	IMLP	NL	
43062		Y	P	QCAR	EC	
43063		FG	P	IWRP	LA	
43064		MM	P	IMLP	NL	
43065	†	V	P	SBXL	BR	
43066		MM	P	IMLP	NL	Nottingham Playhouse
43067	†	GN	P	IECP	EC	
43068	†	V	FG	FGXP	BR	
43069		MN	P	SBXL	YK	Rio Enterprise
43070		MN	P	SBXL	YK	Rio Pathfinder
43071		FG	P	IWRP	LA	
43072	*	MM	P	IMLP	NL	Derby Etches Park
43073	*	MM	P	IMLP	NL	
43074	*	MN	P	IMLP	NL	

43075	*	MM	P	IMLP	NL	
43076	*	MM	P	IMLP	NL	THE MASTER CUTLER 1947–1997
43077		MM	P	IMLP	NL	
43078		GN	P	IECP	EC	
43079		FG	P	IWRP	LA	
43080	†	GN	P	IECP	EC	
43081		MM	P	IMLP	NL	
43082	*	MN	P	IMLP	NL	
43083		MM	P	IMLP	NL	
43084	†	V	FG	FGXP	BR	
43085		MN	P	IMLP	NL	
43086		MN	P	SBXL	BR	Rio Talisman
43087		MN	P	SBXL	ZC	Rio Invader
43088		FG	P	IWRP	LA	
43089		MN	P	IMLP	NL	Rio Thunderer
43090		V	P	SBXL	BR	
43091		FG	P	IWRP	LA	
43092		V	FG	FGXP	BR	
43093		V	FG	FGXP	WS	
43094		V	FG	FGXP	PM	
43095		GN	A	IECP	EC	Perth
43096		GN	A	IECP	EC	Stirling Castle
43097		V	FG	FGXP	BR	
43098		V	FG	FGXP	BR	
43099		GN	P	IECP	EC	
43100		V	P	SBXL	BR	
43101		0	P	SBXL	LB	
43102		GN	P	IECP	EC	
43103		V	P	SBXL	BR	
43104		MN	A	IMLP	NL	
43105		GN	A	IECP	EC	City of Inverness
43106		GN	A	IECP	EC	Fountains Abbey
43107		GN	A	IECP	EC	Tayside
43108		GN	A	IECP	EC	Old Course St. Andrews
43109		GN	A	IECP	EC	
43110		GN	A	IECP	EC	Stirlingshire
43111		GN	A	IECP	EC	Scone Palace
43112		GN	A	IECP	EC	Doncaster
43113		GN	A	IECP	EC	The Highlands
43114		GN	A	IECP	EC	East Riding of Yorkshire
43115		GN	A	IECP	EC	Aberdeenshire
43116		GN	A	IECP	EC	
43117		GN	A	IECP	EC	Bonnie Prince Charlie
43118		GN	A	IECP	EC	City of Kingston upon Hull
43119		GN	A	IECP	EC	Harrogate Spa
43120		GN	A	IECP	EC	
43121		V	P	SBXL	BR	
43122		V	FG	FGXP	BR	South Yorkshire Metropolitan County
43123	†	V	FG	FGXP	WS	
43124		FG	A	IWRP	LE	
43125		FG	A	IWRP	LE	Merchant Venturer

43126	FG	A	IWRP	LE	City of Bristol
43127	FG	A	IWRP	LE	Sir Peter Parker 1924–2002
					Cotswold Line 150
43128	FG	A	IWRP	LE	
43129	FG	A	IWRP	LE	
43130	FG	A	IWRP	LE	Sulis Minerva
43131	FG	A	IWRP	LE	Sir Felix Pole
43132	FG	A	IWRP	LE	
43133	FG	A	IWRP	LE	
43134	FG	A	IWRP	LE	County of Somerset
43135	FG	A	IWRP	LE	
43136	FG	A	IWRP	LE	
43137	FG	A	IWRP	LE	Newton Abbot 150
43138	FG	A	IWRP	LE	
43139	FG	A	IWRP	LE	
43140	FG	A	IWRP	LE	
43141	FG	A	IWRP	LE	
43142	FG	A	IWRP	LE	
43143	FG	A	IWRP	LE	Stroud 700
43144	FG	A	IWRP	LE	
43145	FG	A	IWRP	LE	
43146	FG	A	IWRP	LE	
43147	FG	A	IWRP	LE	
43148	FG	A	IWRP	LE	
43149	FG	A	IWRP	LE	B.B.C. Wales Today
43150	FG	A	IWRP	LE	Bristol Evening Post
43151	FG	A	IWRP	LE	
43152	FG	A	IWRP	LE	
43153	V	FG	FGXP	BR	
43154	Y	P	QCAR	EC	
43155	V	FG	FGXP	WS	
43156	FG	P	IWRP	LA	
43157	V	P	IMLP	NL	
43158	V	P	SBXL	BR	
43159	MN	P	SBXL	BR	Rio Warrior
43160	V	P	SBXL	LB	
43161	FG	P	IWRP	LA	
43162	FG	P	IWRP	LA	
43163	FG	A	IWRP	LA	
43164	FG	A	IWRP	LA	
43165 *	FG	A	IWRP	LA	
43166	MN	A	IMLP	NL	
43167	GN	A	IECP	EC	
43168 *	FG	A	IWRP	LA	
43169 *	FG	A	IWRP	LA	The National Trust
43170 *	FG	A	IWRP	LA	Edward Paxman
43171	FG	A	IWRP	LA	
43172	FG	A	IWRP	LA	
43174	FG	A	IWRP	LA	Bristol–Bordeaux
43175	FG	A	IWRP	LA	
43176	FG	A	IWRP	LA	

43177	*	FG	A	IWRP	LA	University of Exeter
43178		MN	A	IMLP	NL	
43179	*	FG	A	IWRP	LA	Pride of Laira
43180		FG	P	IWRP	LA	
43181		FG	A	IWRP	LA	Devonport Royal Dockyard 1693–1993
43182		FG	A	IWRP	LA	
43183		FG	A	IWRP	LA	
43184		MN	A	IMLP	NL	
43185		FG	A	IWRP	LA	Great Western
43186		FG	A	IWRP	LA	Sir Francis Drake
43187		FG	A	IWRP	LA	
43188		FG	A	IWRP	LA	City of Plymouth
43189		FG	A	IWRP	LA	RAILWAY HERITAGE TRUST
43190		FG	A	IWRP	LA	
43191	*	FG	A	IWRP	LA	Seahawk
43192		FG	A	IWRP	LA	City of Truro
43193		MN	P	IMLP	NL	Rio Triumph
43194		V	P	SBXL	BR	
43195		FG	P	IWRP	LA	
43196		MN	P	SBXL	ZC	Rio Prince
43197		GN	P	IECP	EC	
43198		MN	FG	FGXP	PM	Rio Victorious

CLASS 45   BR/SULZER   1Co-Co1

Built: 1963 by BR at Derby Locomotive Works.
Engine: Sulzer 12LDA28B of 1860 kW (2500 h.p.) at 750 r.p.m.
Main Generator: Crompton-Parkinson CG426 A1.
Traction Motors: Crompton-Parkinson C172 A1.
Maximum Tractive Effort: 245 kN (55000 lbf).
Continuous Tractive Effort: 134 kN (31600 lbf) at 22.3 m.p.h.
Power At Rail: 1490 kW (2000 h.p.).   **Train Brakes:** Air & vacuum.
Brake Force: 63 t.   **Dimensions:** 20.70 x 2.78 m.
Weight: 140 t.   **Wheel Diameter:** 914/1143 mm.
Design Speed: 90 m.p.h.   **Maximum Speed:** 90 m.p.h.
Fuel Capacity: 3591 litres.   **RA:** 7.
Train Supply: Electric.   **Multiple Working:** Not equipped.

Originally numbered D61.

45112	B	FM	SDMS	DF	THE ROYAL ARMY ORDNANCE CORPS

CLASS 46   BR/SULZER   1Co-Co1

Built: 1963 by BR at Derby Locomotive Works.
Engine: Sulzer 12LDA28B of 1860 kW (2500 h.p.) at 750 r.p.m.
Main Generator: Brush TG160-60.   **Traction Motors:** Brush TM73-68 Mk3.
Maximum Tractive Effort: 245 kN (55000 lbf).
Continuous Tractive Effort: 141 kN (31600 lbf) at 22.3 m.p.h.
Power At Rail: 1460 kW (1960 h.p.).   **Train Brakes:** Air & vacuum.

Brake Force: 63 t.
Weight: 140 t.
Design Speed: 90 m.p.h.
Fuel Capacity: 3591 litres.
Train Supply: Not equipped.

Dimensions: 20.70 x 2.78 m.
Wheel Diameter: 914/1143 mm.
Maximum Speed: 75 m.p.h.
RA: 7.
Multiple Working: Not equipped.

46035	**B**	WH	MBDL	CQ

CLASS 47   BR/BRUSH/SULZER   Co-Co

Built: 1963–1967 by Brush Traction, at Loughborough or by BR at Crewe Works.
Engine: Sulzer 12LDA28C of 1920 kW (2580 h.p.) at 750 r.p.m.
Main Generator: Brush TG160-60 Mk4 or TM172-50 Mk1.
Traction Motors: Brush TM64-68 Mk1 or Mk1A.
Maximum Tractive Effort: 267 kN (60000 lbf).
Continuous Tractive Effort: 133 kN (30000 lbf) at 26 m.p.h.
Power At Rail: 1550 kW (2080 h.p.).   **Train Brakes:** Air.
Brake Force: 61 t.   **Dimensions:** 19.38 x 2.79 m.
Weight: 111.5–120.6 t.   **Wheel Diameter:** 1143 mm.
Design Speed: 95 m.p.h.   **Maximum Speed:** 95 m.p.h. (*75
m.p.h.).
Fuel Capacity: 3273 (+ 5550).
Train Supply: Not equipped.
Multiple Working: Green Circle (n – not equipped).

Originally numbered in series D1100–D1111, D1500–D1999 but not in order.

Note: The DFFT locos have "Dock Mode" slow speed traction control system for working trains from Felixstowe North Container Terminal.

Non-standard liveries/numbering:
47004 Carries number D1524.
47145 Dark blue with Railfreight Distribution logos.
47515 Livery IM on one side and all-over white on the other side.
47519 Carries number D1102.
47803 BR experimental Infrastructure livery. Yellow & white with a red stripe.
47829 "Police" livery of white with a broad red band outlined in yellow.
47851 Carries number D1648.
47853 "XP64 blue" with red cabside panels. Carries number D1733.
47972 BR Central Services livery of red & grey.

Class 47/0 (Dual-braked locos) or Class 47/2 (Air-braked locos). Standard Design. Details as above.

47004	xn	**GG**	E	WMOC	OC (S)	
47033		**CD**	CD	CRUR	ZB	
47053	+	**FE**	FM	SDXL	BH	
47095	+	**FE**	HN	HNRS	CS	
47145	+	**0**	FM	SDFL	DF	MYRDDIN EMRYS
47146	+	**FE**	E	WNZX	SP	
47150	*+	**FL**	FL	DFLH	FD	
47156	F		HN	HNRS	ZH	
47186	+	**FE**	FM	SDXL	KT	

47188 +	**FE**	X	CROL	CD	
47194	**F**	FM	SDXL	CS	
47197 n*	**FF**	P	DFLH	FD	
47200 +	**CD**	CD	CRRH	MM	The Fosse Way
47201 +	**FE**	FM	SDXL	KT	
47213 +	**F**	X	CROL	CD	
47217 +	**FE**	E	WNZX	SP	
47219 +	**FE**	FM	SDXL	KT	
47223	**F**	HN	HNRS	ZH	
47224 xn*	**F**	P	DHLT	CP	
47226 +	**F**	FM	SDXL	KT	
47228 +	**FE**	FM	SDXL	KT	
47229 +	**F**	FM	SDXL	BH	
47236 +	**FE**	FM	SDXL	CS	
47237 +	**DR**	DR	XHMW	LB	
47241 +	**FE**	E	WNYX	SP	
47245 +	**FE**	WC	MBDL	CS	
47270 *n	**FL**	P	DHLT	CP	Cory Brothers 1842–1992
47279 *+	**FL**	P	DHLT	BA	
47280 +	**F**	FM	SDXL	KT	
47289 *+	**FF**	P	DHLT	CP	
47292 *+	**FL**	P	DHLT	BA	
47293 +	**FE**	FM	SDXL	KT	
47298 +	**DR**	DR	XHSD	KM	

Class 47/3 (Dual-braked locos) or Class 47/2 (Air-braked locos).
Details as Class 47/0 except:
Weight: 113.7 t.

47302 +	**FF**	FL	DHLT	BA	
47303 *+	**FF**	P	DFLM	FD	Freightliner Cleveland
47306 +	**FE**	E	WMOC	BZ (S)	The Sapper
47307 +	**FE**	FM	SDXL	KT	
47309 *+	**FF**	FL	DFFT	FD	European Rail Operator of The Year
47313 +	**F**	FM	SDXL	KT	
47314 +	**F**	FM	SDXL	KT	
47316 +	**CD**	CD	CRRH	MM	Cam Peak
47326 +	**FE**	CD	CROL	ZB	
47328 +	**F**	E	WNZX	SP	
47331 xns	**CE**	HN	HNRS	SP	
47335 +	**F**	FM	SDXL	KT	
47338 +	**FE**	CD	CRUR	ZB	
47345 n	**FF**	P	SBXL	LB	
47348 +	**FE**	FM	SDXL	MQ	
47355	**FB**	FM	SDFL	DF	AVOCET
47358 *+	**FF**	P	DFLM	FD	
47360 +	**FE**	FM	SDXL	KT	
47363	**F**	FM	SDXL	CS	
47365 +	**FE**	CD	CRUR	CO	
47368 xn	**F**	FM	SDXL	CS	
47370 *+	**FF**	P	DHLT	IP	Andrew A Hodgkinson
47375 +	**FB**	FM	SDFL	DF (S)	

Class 47/4. Electric Train Supply equipment.
Details as Class 47/0 except:

Weight: 120.4–125.1 t.	**Fuel Capacity:** 3273 (+ 5887) litres.
Train Supply: Electric. ETH 66.	**RA:** 7.
Multiple Working: Not equipped (m – Green Circle).	

47474	x	**RG**	E	WNZX	SP
47475	x	**RX**	CD	CROL	HM
47478	x	**B**	HN	HNRS	SP
47484	x	**GW**	DR	XHSS	ZH
47488	x	**GG**	FM	SDFR	BH (S)
47489	x	**RG**	FM	SDXL	CS
47492	x	**RX**	GD	MBDL	CS (S)
47501	x	**DR**	DR	XHSD	KM
47515	x	**0**	HN	HNRS	CY
47519	x+	**GG**	E	WNZX	SP
47525	x	**FE**	FM	SDXL	CS
47526	x	**BL**	FM	SDXL	CS
47528	x	**IM**	CD	CRUR	ZB
47536	x	**RX**	E	WNZX	SP
47550	x	**IM**	FM	SDXL	IR
47566	x	**RX**	E	WNZX	SP
47575	x	**RG**	RV	RTLS	BH
47576	x	**RX**	E	WNZX	SP
47624	x	**RX**	E	WNZX	SP
47628	x	**RX**	FM	SDXL	BH
47635	x	**BL**	E	WNTR	OC	The Lass O' Ballochmyle

Class 47/7. Fitted with an older form of TDM.

Details as Class 47/4 except:
Weight: 118.7 t. **Fuel Capacity:** 5887 litres.
Maximum Speed: 100 m.p.h.

47701	x	**FR**	WF	SDFR	LU (S)	Waverley
47703	x	**FR**	FM	SDFR	DF	HERMES
47704	x	**RX**	FM	SDXL	TH	
47707	x	**RX**	FM	SDXL	BH	
47709	x	**FR**	FM	SDFR	DF	DIONYSOS
47710	x	**FR**	FM	SDFR	DF (S)	
47712	x	**FR**	FM	SDFR	DF	ARTEMIS
47714	x	**AR**	CD	IANA	NC	
47715	x	**FR**	FM	SDXL	YK	POSEIDON
47717	x	**RG**	FM	SDXL	BH	

Class 47/7. Former Railnet dedicated locos. All have twin fuel tanks and are fitted with RCH jumper cables for operation with Propelling Control Vehicles (PCVs).

47721	**RX**	E	WNXX	TT	Saint Bede
47722	**V**	E	WNXX	TT	
47725	**RX**	E	WNZX	SP	
47726	**RX**	E	WNXX	TT	Manchester Airport Progress

47727	**E**	E	WNTR	WN	Castell Caerffili/Caerphilly Castle
47732 x	**RX**	E	WNTR	HM	
47733	**RX**	E	WNTR	HM	
47734	**RX**	E	WNTR	HM	
47736	**RX**	E	WNXX	CD	Cambridge Traction & Rolling Stock Depot
47737	**RX**	E	WNSS	HM	
47739	**RX**	E	WNSS	ML	Resourceful
47741	**V**	E	WNXX	TT	Resilient
47742	**RX**	E	WNXX	TT	The Enterprising Scot
47744	**E**	FM	SDXL	CD	Royal Mail Cheltenham
47746	**RX**	E	WNTR	CD	The Bobby
47747	**E**	E	WNTR	MH	Florence Nightingale
47749	**RX**	E	WNXX	CE	Atlantic College
47750	**V**	E	WNXX	HM	
47756	**RX**	E	WNXX	OC	Royal Mail Tyneside
47757	**E**	E	WNXX	CL	
47758 x	**E**	E	WNXX	TT	
47759	**RX**	E	WNXX	CD	
47760	**E**	E	WNTR	CE	
47761	**RX**	E	WNTR	MG	
47762	**RX**	E	WNZX	SP	
47764	**RX**	E	WNZX	SP	
47765 x	**RX**	E	WNZX	SP	
47767	**E**	FM	SDXL	TT	
47768 x	**RX**	E	WNZX	SP	
47769	**V**	RV	RTLO	BQ	
47770	**RX**	E	WNXX	BS	Reserved
47772 x	**RX**	E	WNTR	MG	
47773	**E**	E	WNXX	HM	
47774 x	**RX**	HN	HNRS	CD	Poste Restante
47775 x	**RX**	HN	HNRS	CD	
47776 x	**RX**	E	WNXX	HM	
47778	**E**	E	WNXX	SP	
47779	**RX**	E	WNZX	SP	
47780	**RX**	FM	SDXL	BH	
47781	**RX**	E	WNXX	TT	Isle of Iona
47782	**RX**	E	WNXX	OC	
47783	**RX**	E	WNXX	CD	Saint Peter
47784	**RX**	E	WNXX	CD	Condover Hall
47785	**E**	E	WNTR	ML	
47786	**E**	E	WNXX	HM	
47787	**E**	E	WNXX	HM	
47789	**RX**	E	WNSS	TT	
47790	**E**	E	WNTR	HM	
47791	**RX**	E	WNXX	SY	
47792	**E**	E	WNTR	HM	
47793	**E**	E	WNTR	HM	

Class 47/4 continued. RA6.

47798	**RP**	NM	MBDL	YK	Prince William
47799	**RP**	E	WNXX	FB	Prince Henry

47802	+	**DR**	DR	XHSD	KM
47803		**0**	FM	SDXL	AS
47805	+	**V**	RV	RTLO	CP
47810	+	**V**	P	ATSP	WN	PORTERBROOK
47811	+	**GL**	P	DFLH	FD
47812	+	**V**	RV	RTLO	CP
47813	+	**GL**	CD	CREL	NC
47815	+	**GG**	RV	RTLO	CP
47816	+	**GL**	P	DFLH	FD
47818	+	**1**	CD	IANA	NC
47826	+	**IC**	P	ATSP	WN	Springburn
47828	+	**CD**	CD	CREL	NC
47829	+	**0**	RV	RTLO	CP
47830	+	**GL**	P	ATSP	WN
47832	+	**GL**	FM	SDFR	DF
47839	+	**RV**	RV	RTLO	CP
47840	+	**B**	P	ATSP	WN	NORTH STAR
47841	+	**V**	P	DFLH	FD
47843	+	**V**	RV	RTLO	CP	VULCAN
47847	+	**BL**	RV	RTLO	CP	Railway World Magazine/Brian Morrison
47848	+	**V**	RV	RTLO	CP	Newton Abbot Festival of Transport
47851	+	**GG**	P	ATSP	WN	Traction Magazine
47853	+	**0**	RV	RTLO	CP	RAIL EXPRESS
47854	+	**WC**	WC	MBDL	CS
47972		**0**	FM	SDXL	CS

CLASS 50   ENGLISH ELECTRIC   Co-Co

Built: 1967–1968 by English Electric at Vulcan Foundry, Newton-le-Willows.
Engine: English Electric 16CVST of 2010 kW (2700 h.p.) at 850 r.p.m.
Main Generator: English Electric 840/4B.
Traction Motors: English Electric 538/5A.
Maximum Tractive Effort: 216 kN (48500 lbf).
Continuous Tractive Effort: 147 kN (33000 lbf) at 23.5 m.p.h.

Power At Rail: 1540 kW (2070 h.p.).	**Train Brakes:** Air & vacuum.
Brake Force: 59 t.	**Dimensions:** 20.88 x 2.78 m.
Weight: 116.9 t.	**Wheel Diameter:** 1092 mm.
Design Speed: 105 m.p.h.	**Maximum Speed:** 90 (* 100) m.p.h.
Fuel Capacity: 4796 litres.	**RA:** 6.
Train Supply: Electric, index 66.	**Multiple Working:** Orange Square.

Originally numbered D417–D449, D400.

Non-standard livery/numbering:

50017 "LMS Coronation Scot" style maroon with four gold bands.
50044 Carries number D444.

50017	*	**0**	JK	MBDL	TM (S)
50031		**BL**	50	MBDL	KR	Hood
50044		**GG**	50	MBDL	OC
50049		**BL**	50	MBDL	KR	Defiance
50050		**BL**	HS	MBDL	YJ (S)	Fearless

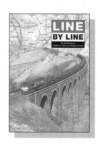

CLASS 52   WESTERN   C-C

Built: 1961–1964.
Engine: Two Maybach MD655 of 1007 kW (1350 h.p) at 1500 r.p.m.
Transmission: Hydraulic. Voith L630rV.
Maximum Tractive Effort: 297 kN (66700 lbf).
Continuous Tractive Effort: 201 kN (45200 lbf) at 14.5 m.p.h.

Power At Rail: 1490 kW (2000 h.p.).	**Train Brakes:** Air & vacuum.
Brake Force: 65 t.	**Dimensions:** 20.7 m x 2.78 m.
Weight: 111 t.	**Wheel Diameter:** 1092 mm.
Design Speed: 90 m.p.h.	**Maximum Speed:** 90 m.p.h.
Fuel Capacity: 3900 litres.	**RA:** 7.
Train Supply: Steam.	**Multiple Working:** Not equipped.

Non-standard livery: Golden ochre.

Never allocated a number in the 1972 number series.

D1015	**0**	DT	MBDL	OC	SIR MISHA BLACK

CLASS 55   ENGLISH ELECTRIC   Co-Co

Built: 1961 by English Electric at Vulcan Foundry, Newton-le-Willows.
Engine: Two Napier-Deltic D18-25 of 1230 kW (1650 h.p.) each at 1500 r.p.m.
Main Generators: Two English Electric 829.
Traction Motors: English Electric 538/A.
Maximum Tractive Effort: 222 kN (50000 lbf).
Continuous Tractive Effort: 136 kN (30500 lbf) at 32.5 m.p.h.

Power At Rail: 1969 kW (2640 h.p.).	**Train Brakes:** Air & vacuum.
Brake Force: 51 t.	**Dimensions:** 21.18 x 2.68 m.
Weight: 104.7 t.	**Wheel Diameter:** 1092 mm.
Design Speed: 105 m.p.h.	**Maximum Speed:** 100 m.p.h.
Fuel Capacity: 3755 litres.	**RA:** 5.
Train Supply: Electric, index 66.	**Multiple Working:** Not equipped.

Originally numbered D9009–D9019, D9000.

Non-standard numbering:

55009 Carries number D9009.
55016 Carries number 9016.
55022 Carries number D9000.

55009	**GG**	DP	MBDL	BH (S)	ALYCIDON
55016	**GG**	PO	MBDL	TM (S)	GORDON HIGHLANDER
55019	**B**	DP	MBDL	BH (S)	ROYAL HIGHLAND FUSILIER
55022	**GG**	MW	MBDL	BH (S)	ROYAL SCOTS GREY

CLASS 56   BRUSH/BR/PAXMAN   Co-Co

Built: 1976–1984 by Electroputere at Craiova, Romania (as sub contractors for Brush) or BREL at Doncaster or Crewe Works.
Engine: Ruston Paxman 16RK3CT of 2460 kW (3250 h.p.) at 900 r.p.m.
Main Alternator: Brush BA1101A.
Traction Motors: Brush TM73-62.
Maximum Tractive Effort: 275 kN (61800 lbf).
Continuous Tractive Effort: 240 kN (53950 lbf) at 16.8 m.p.h.
Power At Rail: 1790 kW (2400 h.p.).   **Train Brakes:** Air.
Brake Force: 60 t.   **Dimensions:** 19.36 x 2.79 m.
Weight: 125.2 t.   **Wheel Diameter:** 1143 mm.
Design Speed: 80 m.p.h.   **Maximum Speed:** 80 m.p.h.
Fuel Capacity: 5228 litres.   **RA:** 7.
Train Supply: Not equipped.   **Multiple Working:** Red Diamond.

Notes: All equipped with Slow Speed Control.
56110 Carries its name on one side only.

Non-standard liveries:

56063 As **F**, but with the light grey replaced by a darker grey.
56027 and 56109 Are **LH** but with the Loadhaul branding on one side only.

56004	**B**	E	WNZX	SP	
56006	**B**	E	WNSS	BH	
56007	**F**	E	WZGF	OC	
56011	**E**	E	WNXX	IM	
56018	**E**	E	WNSS	IM	
56021	**LH**	E	WNXX	IM	
56022	**F**	FM	SDXL	IR	
56025	**F**	E	WNXX	IM	
56027	**LH**	E	WNXX	IM	
56029	**F**	E	WNZX	SP	
56031	**CE**	E	WZGF	OC	
56032	**E**	E	WNSS	IM	
56033	**F**	E	WNXX	IM	Shotton Paper Mill
56034	**LH**	E	WNZX	SP	
56036	**CE**	E	WNZX	SP	
56037	**E**	E	WNXX	IM	
56038	**FER**	E	WZGF	FN	
56040	**F**	E	WNXX	IM	
56041	**E**	E	WNXX	IM	
56043	**F**	E	WNXX	IM	
56044	**F**	E	WNYX	IM	
56046	**CE**	E	WNXX	TO	
56048	**CE**	E	WNXX	IM	
56049	**CE**	E	WZGF	BK	
56051	**E**	E	WZGF	BK	
56052	**F**	E	WNXX	IM	
56053	**F**	E	WNXX	HM	
56054	**F**	E	WNXX	FB	

56055	**LH**	E	WNXX	HM	
56056	**F**	E	WNTR	HM	
56058	**E**	E	WZGF	BS	
56059	**FER**	E	WZGF	FN	
56060	**FER**	E	WZGF	FN	
56061	**F**	FM	SDXL	TT	
56062	**E**	E	WNSS	MG	
56063	**0**	E	WNXX	IM	
56064	**F**	E	WNXX	IM	
56065	**E**	E	WZGF	BK	
56066	**F**	FM	SDXL	SP	
56067	**E**	E	WNXX	FB	
56068	**E**	E	WNXX	IM	
56069	**FER**	E	WZGF	FN	
56070	**F**	E	WNTR	HM	
56071	**E**	E	WNTR	HM	
56072	**F**	E	WNSS	HM	
56073	**F**	E	WNXX	TO	
56074	**LH**	E	WZGF	OC	
56076	**F**	E	WNXX	IM	
56077	**LH**	E	WNXX	CD	
56078	**FER**	E	WZGF	FN	
56079	**F**	E	WNXX	IM	
56081	**E**	E	WZGF	EH	
56082	**F**	E	WNXX	IM	
56083	**LH**	E	WNXX	FB	
56084	**LH**	E	WNXX	IM	
56085	**LH**	E	WNXX	TE	
56086	**F**	E	WNXX	IM	
56087	**FER**	E	WZGF	FN	
56088	**E**	E	WNSS	TE	
56089	**E**	E	WNXX	IM	
56090	**FER**	E	WZGF	FN	
56091	**E**	E	WNTR	HM	
56093	**F**	E	WNXX	HM	
56094	**E**	E	WNTR	HM	
56095	**E**	E	WNTR	HM	
56096	**E**	E	WZGF	TO	
56098	**F**	E	WNXX	IM	
56099	**F**	E	WZGF	TO	
56100	**LH**	E	WNXX	MG	
56101	**F**	E	WNXX	IM	
56102	**LH**	E	WNXX	TE	
56103	**E**	E	WNSS	IM	STORA
56104	**F**	E	WNTR	IM	
56105	**E**	E	WZGF	TO	
56106	**LH**	E	WZGF	TO	
56107	**LH**	E	WNTR	FB	
56108	**F**	E	WNXX	TE	
56109	**LH**	E	WNXX	FB	
56110	**LH**	E	WNXX	IM	Croft

56111	**LH**	E	WNXX	TE	
56112	**LH**	E	WNXX	IM	
56113	**E**	E	WNTR	HM	Stainless Pioneer
56114	**E**	E	WNTR	IM	
56115	**E**	E	WNTR	HM	
56116	**LH**	E	WNXX	IM	
56117	**FER**	E	WZGF	FN	
56118	**FER**	E	WZGF	FN	
56119	**E**	E	WNTR	HM	
56120	**E**	E	WNXX	FB	
56121	**F**	E	WNZX	SP	
56124	**F**	HN	HNRS	KY	
56125	**F**	FM	SDXL	DF	
56127	**F**	E	WNXX	TE	
56128	**F**	E	WNXX	TO	
56129	**F**	E	WNXX	TE	
56131	**F**	E	WNXX	IM	
56132	**F**	E	WNZX	SP	
56133	**F**	E	WNTR	HM	
56134	**F**	E	WNXX	IM	Blyth Power

CLASS 57   BRUSH/GM   Co-Co

Built: 1964–1965 by Brush Traction at Loughborough or BR at Crewe Works as Class 47. Rebuilt 1997–2004 by Brush Traction at Loughborough.
Engine: General Motors 645-12E3 of 1860 kW (2500 h.p.) at 900 r.p.m.
Main Alternator: Brush BA1101A.
Traction Motors: Brush TM68-46.
Maximum Tractive Effort: 244.5 kN (55000 lbf).
Continuous Tractive Effort: 140 kN (31500 lbf) at ?? m.p.h.
Power at Rail: 1507 kW (2025 h.p.).   **Train Brakes:** Air.
Brake Force: 80 t.   **Dimensions:** 19.38 x 2.79 m.
Weight: 120.6 t.   **Wheel Diameter:** 1143 mm.
Design Speed: 75 m.p.h.   **Maximum Speed:** 75 m.p.h.
Fuel Capacity: 5550 litres.   **RA:** 6
Train Supply: Not equipped.   **Multiple Working:** Not equipped.

Class 57/0. No Train Supply Equipment.

57001	(47356)	**FL**	P	DFTZ	FD	Freightliner Pioneer
57002	(47322)	**FL**	P	DFTZ	FD	Freightliner Phoenix
57003	(47317)	**FL**	P	DFTZ	FD	Freightliner Evolution
57004	(47347)	**FL**	P	DFTZ	FD	Freightliner Quality
57005	(47350)	**FL**	P	DFTZ	FD	Freightliner Excellence
57006	(47187)	**FL**	P	DFTZ	FD	Freightliner Reliance
57007	(47332)	**FL**	P	DFTZ	FD	Freightliner Bond
57008	(47060)	**FL**	P	DFTZ	FD	Freightliner Explorer
57009	(47079)	**FL**	P	DFTZ	FD	Freightliner Venturer
57010	(47231)	**FL**	P	DFTZ	FD	Freightliner Crusader
57011	(47329)	**FL**	P	DFTZ	FD	Freightliner Challenger
57012	(47204)	**FL**	P	DFTZ	FD	Freightliner Envoy

Class 57/3. Electric Train Supply Equipment. Virgin Trains locos. Details as Class 57/0 except:

Engine: General Motors 645-F3B-12 Cylinder of 2050 kW (2750 h.p.).
Fuel Capacity: 5887 litres.   **Train Supply:** Electric, index 100.
Design Speed: 95 m.p.h.   **Maximum Speed:** 95 m.p.h.
Brake Force: 60 t.   **Weight:** 117 t.

57301	(47845)	d	**VT**	P	ATTB	WN	SCOTT TRACY
57302	(47827)	d	**VT**	P	ATTB	WN	VIRGIL TRACY
57303	(47705)	d	**VT**	P	ATTB	WN	ALAN TRACY
57304	(47807)	d	**VT**	P	ATTB	WN	GORDON TRACY
57305	(47822)	d	**VT**	P	ATTB	WN	JOHN TRACY
57306	(47814)	d	**VT**	P	ATTB	WN	JEFF TRACY
57307	(47225)	d	**VT**	P	ATTB	WN	LADY PENELOPE
57308	(47846)	d	**VT**	P	ATTB	WN	TIN TIN
57309	(47806)	d	**VT**	P	ATTB	WN	BRAINS
57310	(47831)	d	**VT**	P	ATTB	WN	KYRANO
57311	(47817)	d	**VT**	P	ATTB	WN	PARKER
57312	(47330)	d	**VT**	P	ATTB	WN	THE HOOD
57313	(47371)	d	**VT**	P	ATTB	WN	TRACY ISLAND
57314	(47372)	d	**VT**	P	ATTB	WN	FIREFLY
57315	(47234)	d	**VT**	P	ATTB	WN	THE MOLE
57316	(47290)	d	**VT**	P	ATTB	WN	FAB 1

Class 57/6. Electric Train Supply Equipment. Prototype loco (rebuilt 2001).

Fuel Capacity: 5887 litres.   **Train Supply:** Electric, index 100.
Design Speed: 95 m.p.h.   **Maximum Speed:** 95 m.p.h.

57601	(47825)	**WC**	WC MBDL	CS	

Class 57/6. Electric Train Supply Equipment. First Great Western locos. Details as Class 57/3.

57602	(47337)	**GL**	P	IWLA	LA	Restormel Castle
57603	(47349)	**GL**	P	IWLA	LA	Tintagel Castle
57604	(47209)	**GL**	P	IWLA	LA	Pendennis Castle
57605	(47206)	**GL**	P	IWLA	LA	Totnes Castle

CLASS 58   BREL/PAXMAN   Co-Co

Built: 1983–1987 by BREL at Doncaster Works.
Engine: Ruston Paxman 12RK3ACT of 2460 kW (3300 h.p.) at 1000 r.p.m.
Main Alternator: Brush BA1101B.   **Traction Motors:** Brush TM73-62.
Maximum Tractive Effort: 275 kN (61800 lbf).
Continuous Tractive Effort: 240 kN (53950 lbf) at 17.4 m.p.h.
Power At Rail: 1780 kW (2387 h.p.).   **Train Brakes:** Air.
Brake Force: 62 t.   **Dimensions:** 19.13 x 2.72 m.
Weight: 130 t.   **Wheel Diameter:** 1120 mm.
Design Speed: 80 m.p.h.   **Maximum Speed:** 80 m.p.h.
Fuel Capacity: 4214 litres.   **RA:** 7.
Train Supply: Not equipped.   **Multiple Working:** Red Diamond.

Notes: All equipped with Slow Speed Control.

Non-standard livery:

58001 As **FO** but with a red solebar stripe.

58001	**O**	E	WNXX	BH	
58002	**ML**	E	WNXX	EH	Daw Mill Colliery
58003	**F**	E	WNXX	TT	Markham Colliery
58004	**FER**	E	WZFF	FN	
58005	**ML**	E	WZFF	LR	
58006	**F**	E	WZFF	EH	
58007	**SCO**	E	WZFF	FN	
58008	**ML**	E	WNXX	TT	
58009	**SCO**	E	WZFF	FN	
58010	**F**	E	WZFF	EH	
58011	**F**	E	WZFF	EH	
58012	**F**	E	WNXX	TT	
58013	**ML**	E	WZFF	EH	
58014	**ML**	E	WNXX	TT	
58015	**FER**	E	WZFF	FN	
58016	**E**	E	WZFF	EH	
58017	**F**	E	WZFF	EH	
58018	**F**	E	WZFF	EH	
58019	**F**	E	WNXX	TO	Shirebrook Colliery
58020	**GIF**	E	WZFS	ES	
58021	**ML**	E	WZFF	EH	Hither Green Depot
58022	**F**	E	WNXX	CD	
58023	**ML**	E	WNXX	TT	
58024	**GIF**	E	WZFS	ES	
58025	**GIF**	E	WZFS	ES	
58026	**F**	E	WZFF	EH	
58027	**SCO**	E	WZFF	FN	
58028	**F**	E	WNXX	TT	
58029	**GIF**	E	WZFS	ES	
58030	**GIF**	E	WZFS	ES	
58031	**GIF**	E	WZFS	ES	
58032	**FER**	E	WZFF	FN	
58033	**TSO**	E	WZFF	FN	
58034	**FER**	E	WZFF	FN	
58035	**FER**	E	WZFF	FN	
58036	**ML**	E	WZFH	TT	
58037	**E**	E	WNXX	EH	
58038	**ML**	E	WZFH	TO	
58039	**ACT**	E	WZFH	TB	
58040	**SCO**	E	WZFF	FN	
58041	**GIF**	E	WZFS	ES	
58042	**ML**	E	WNXX	EH	
58043	**GIF**	E	WZFS	ES	
58044	**ACT**	E	WZFH	TB	
58045	**F**	E	WNXX	OC	
58046	**FER**	E	WZFF	FN	

58047	**TSO**	E	WZFF	FN
58048	**E**	E	WNXX	TT
58049	**TSO**	E	WZFF	FN
58050	**TSO**	E	WZFF	FN

CLASS 59 GENERAL MOTORS Co-Co

Built: 1985 (59001/59002/59004) or 1989 (59005) by General Motors, La Grange, Illinois, USA or 1990 (59101–59104), 1994 (59201) and 1995 (59202–59206) by General Motors, London, Ontario, Canada.
Engine: General Motors 645E3C two stroke of 2460 kW (3300 h.p.) at 900 r.p.m.
Main Alternator: General Motors AR11 MLD-D14A.
Traction Motors: General Motors D77B.
Maximum Tractive Effort: 506 kN (113 550 lbf).
Continuous Tractive Effort: 291 kN (65 300 lbf) at 14.3 m.p.h.

Power At Rail: 1889 kW (2533 h.p.).	**Train Brakes:** Air.
Brake Force: 69 t.	**Dimensions:** 21.35 x 2.65 m.
Weight: 121 t.	**Wheel Diameter:** 1067 mm.
Design Speed: 60 (* 75) m.p.h.	**Maximum Speed:** 60 (* 75) m.p.h.
Fuel Capacity: 4546 litres.	**RA:** 7.
Train Supply: Not equipped.	**Multiple Working:** AAR System.

Class 59/0. Owned by Foster-Yeoman.

59001	**FY**	FY	XYPO	MD	YEOMAN ENDEAVOUR
59002	**MR**	FY	XYPO	MD	ALAN J DAY
59004	**FY**	FY	XYPO	MD	PAUL A HAMMOND
59005	**FY**	FY	XYPO	MD	KENNETH J PAINTER

Class 59/1. Owned by Hanson Quarry Products.

59101	**HA**	HA	XYPA	MD	Village of Whatley
59102	**HA**	HA	XYPA	MD	Village of Chantry
59103	**HA**	HA	XYPA	MD	Village of Mells
59104	**HA**	HA	XYPA	MD	Village of Great Elm

Class 59/2. Owned by EWS.

59201	*	**E**	E	WDAG	TD	Vale of York
59202	*	**E**	E	WDAG	TD	Vale of White Horse
59203	*	**E**	E	WDAG	TD	Vale of Pickering
59204	*	**E**	E	WDAG	TD	Vale of Glamorgan
59205	b*	**E**	E	WDAG	TD	L. Keith McNair
59206	b*	**E**	E	WDAG	TD	Pride of Ferrybridge

CLASS 60   BRUSH/MIRRLEES   Co-Co

Built: 1989–1993 by Brush Traction at Loughborough.
Engine: Mirrlees 8MB275T of 2310 kW (3100 h.p.) at 1000 r.p.m.
Main Alternator: Brush BA1000.   **Traction Motors:** Brush TM216.
Maximum Tractive Effort: 500 kN (106500 lbf).
Continuous Tractive Effort: 336 kN (71570 lbf) at 17.4 m.p.h.
Power At Rail: 1800 kW (2415 h.p.)   **Train Brakes:** Air.
Brake Force: 74 (+ 62) t.   **Dimensions:** 21.34 x 2.64 m.
Weight: 129 (+ 131) t.   **Wheel Diameter:** 1118 mm.
Design Speed: 62 m.p.h.   **Maximum Speed:** 60 m.p.h.
Fuel Capacity: 4546 (+ 5225) litres.   **RA:** 7.
Train Supply: Not equipped.   **Multiple Working:** Within class.

Notes: All equipped with Slow Speed Control.
60034, 60038, 60061, 60064, 60066, 60072, 60073, 60077, 60079, 60082, 60084 and 60088 carry their names on one side only.

60001	E	E	WCAN	IM	The Railway Observer
60002 +	E	E	WCBN	IM	High Peak
60003 +	E	E	WCBN	IM	FREIGHT TRANSPORT ASSOCIATION
60004 +	E	E	WCBN	IM	
60005 +	E	E	WCBN	IM	BP Gas Avonmouth
60006	CU	E	WNTS	TO	Scunthorpe Ironmaster
60007 +	LH	E	WNTR	IM	
60008	LH	E	WCAN	IM	GYPSUM QUEEN II
60009 +	E	E	WCBN	IM	
60010 +	E	E	WCBN	IM	
60011	ML	E	WCAN	IM	
60012 +	E	E	WCBN	IM	
60013	F	E	WCAN	IM	Robert Boyle
60014	F	E	WCAN	IM	Alexander Fleming
60015 +	F	E	WCBN	IM	Bow Fell
60017 +	E	E	WCAN	IM	Shotton Works Centenary Year 1996
60018	E	E	WCAN	IM	
60019	E	E	WNTR	IM	PATHFINDER TOURS
					30 YEARS OF RAILTOURING 1973–2003
60020 +	E	E	WCBN	IM	
60021 +	E	E	WCBN	IM	Star of the East
60022 +	E	E	WCBN	IM	
60023 +	E	E	WCBN	IM	
60024	E	E	WCAN	IM	
60025 +	E	E	WCBN	IM	Caledonian Paper
60026 +	E	E	WCBN	IM	
60027 +	E	E	WCBN	IM	
60028 +	F	E	WCBN	IM	John Flamsteed
60029	E	E	WNTR	IM	Clitheroe Castle
60030 +	E	E	WCBN	IM	
60031	E	E	WCAN	IM	ABP Connect
60032	F	E	WCAN	IM	William Booth
60033 +	CU	E	WCBN	IM	Tees Steel Express

60034	F	E	WCAN	IM	Carnedd Llewelyn
60035	E	E	WCAN	IM	
60036	E	E	WCAN	IM	GEFCO
60037 +	E	E	WCBN	IM	Aberddawan/Aberthaw
60038 +	E	E	WCBN	IM	AvestaPolarit
60039	E	E	WCAN	IM	
60040	E	E	WCAN	IM	
60041 +	E	E	WCBN	IM	
60042	E	E	WCAN	IM	The Hundred of Hoo
60043	E	E	WNTR	IM	
60044	ML	E	WCAN	IM	
60045	E	E	WCAN	IM	The Permanent Way Institution
60046 +	F	E	WCBN	IM	William Wilberforce
60047	E	E	WCAN	IM	
60048	E	E	WCAN	IM	EASTERN
60049	E	E	WCAN	IM	
60050	E	E	WCAN	IM	
60051 +	E	E	WCBN	IM	
60052 +	E	E	WCBN	IM	Glofa Twr – The last deep mine in Wales – Tower Colliery
60053	E	E	WCAN	IM	NORDIC TERMINAL
60054 +	F	E	WCBN	IM	Charles Babbage
60055 +	F	E	WNTR	IM	Thomas Barnardo
60056 +	F	E	WNTR	TE	William Beveridge
60057	F	E	WNTR	TE	Adam Smith
60058 +	E	E	WCBN	IM	
60059 +	LH	E	WCBN	IM	Swinden Dalesman
60060	F	E	WCAN	IM	James Watt
60061	F	E	WCAN	IM	Alexander Graham Bell
60062	E	E	WCAN	IM	
60063	F	E	WCAN	IM	James Murray
60064 +	F	E	WCBN	IM	Back Tor
60065	E	E	WCAN	IM	Spirit of JAGUAR
60066	F	E	WCAN	IM	John Logie Baird
60067	F	E	WCAN	IM	James Clerk-Maxwell
60068	F	E	WCAN	IM	Charles Darwin
60069	E	E	WCAN	IM	Slioch
60070 +	F	E	WNTR	IM	John Loudon McAdam
60071 +	E	E	WCBN	IM	Ribblehead Viaduct
60072	F	E	WCAN	IM	Cairn Toul
60073	F	E	WCAN	IM	Cairn Gorm
60074	F	E	WCAN	IM	
60075	E	E	WNTR	IM	
60076	F	E	WCAN	IM	
60077 +	F	E	WCBN	IM	Canisp
60078	ML	E	WCAN	IM	
60079	F	E	WNTR	IM	Foinaven
60080 +	E	E	WCBN	IM	Stanley Common C of E Primary School Ilkeston EWS Rail Safety Competition Winners 2003
60081 +	GW	E	WCBN	IM	ISAMBARD KINGDOM BRUNEL

60082	F	E	WCAN	IM	Mam Tor
60083	E	E	WCAN	IM	Mountsorrel
60084	F	E	WCAN	IM	Cross Fell
60085	E	E	WCAN	IM	MINI Pride of Oxford
60086	F	E	WCAN	IM	Schiehallion
60087	E	E	WCAN	IM	Barry Needham
60088	F	E	WCAN	IM	Buachaille Etive Mor
60089 +	E	E	WNTR	IM	THE RAILWAY HORSE
60090 +	F	E	WNTR	IM	Quinag
60091 +	F	E	WCBN	IM	An Teallach
60092 +	F	E	WNTR	TO	Reginald Munns
60093	E	E	WCAN	IM	Adrian Harrington 1955–2003
					Royal Navy/Burges Salmon
60094	E	E	WCAN	IM	Rugby Flyer
60095	F	E	WNTR	TO	
60096 +	E	E	WCBN	IM	
60097 +	E	E	WNTS	TO	ABP Port of Grimsby & Immingham
60098 +	E	E	WNTR	IM	Charles Francis Brush
60099	F	E	WCAN	IM	Ben More Assynt
60100	E	E	WCAN	IM	Pride of Acton
60500	E	E	WCAN	IM	RAIL Magazine (ex 60016)

CLASS 66   GENERAL MOTORS   Co-Co

Built: 1998–20 by General Motors, London, Ontario, Canada (Model JT42CWR).
Engine: General Motors 12N-710G3B-EC two stroke of 2385 kW (3200 h.p.)
at 900 r.p.m.
Main Alternator: General Motors AR8/C86.
Traction Motors: General Motors D43TR.
Maximum Tractive Effort: 409 kN (92000 lbf).
Continuous Tractive Effort: 260 kN (58390 lbf) at 15.9 m.p.h.
Power At Rail: 1850 kW (2480 h.p.).   **Train Brakes:** Air.
Brake Force: 68 t.   **Dimensions:** 21.35 x 2.64 m.
Weight: 126 t.   **Wheel Diameter:** 1120 mm.
Design Speed: 87.5 m.p.h.   **Maximum Speed:** 75 m.p.h.
Fuel Capacity: 6550 litres.   **RA:** 7.
Train Supply: Not equipped.   **Multiple Working:** AAR System.

Note: All equipped with Slow Speed Control.

Class 66/0. EWS-operated locomotives.

66001		E	A	WBAN	TO	66012	k	E	A	WBAN	TO
66002		E	A	WBAN	TO	66013	k	E	A	WBAN	TO
66003	k	E	A	WBAN	TO	66014	k	E	A	WBAN	TO
66004	k	E	A	WBAN	TO	66015	k	E	A	WBAN	TO
66005	k	E	A	WBAN	TO	66016	k	E	A	WBAN	TO
66006	k	E	A	WBAN	TO	66017	k	E	A	WBAN	TO
66007	k	E	A	WBAN	TO	66018	k	E	A	WBAN	TO
66008	k	E	A	WBAN	TO	66019	k	E	A	WBAN	TO
66009	k	E	A	WBAN	TO	66020	k	E	A	WBAN	TO
66010	k	E	A	WBAN	TO	66021	k	E	A	WBAN	TO
66011	k	E	A	WBAN	TO	66022	k	E	A	WBAN	TO

66023	k	E	A	WBAN	TO	66074	k	E	A	WBAN	TO
66024	k	E	A	WBAN	TO	66075	k	E	A	WBAN	TO
66025	k	E	A	WBAN	TO	66076	k	E	A	WBAN	TO
66026	k	E	A	WBAN	TO	66077	k	E	A	WBAN	TO
66027	k	E	A	WBAN	TO	66078	k	E	A	WBAN	TO
66028	k	E	A	WBAN	TO	66079	k	E	A	WBAN	TO
66029	k	E	A	WBAN	TO	66080	k	E	A	WBAN	TO
66030	k	E	A	WBAN	TO	66081	k	E	A	WBAN	TO
66031	k	E	A	WBAN	TO	66082	k	E	A	WBAN	TO
66032	k	E	A	WBAN	TO	66083	k	E	A	WBAN	TO
66033	k	E	A	WBAN	TO	66084	k	E	A	WBAN	TO
66034	k	E	A	WBAN	TO	66085	k	E	A	WBAN	TO
66035	k	E	A	WBAN	TO	66086	k	E	A	WBAN	TO
66036	k	E	A	WBAN	TO	66087	k	E	A	WBAN	TO
66037	k	E	A	WBAN	TO	66088	k	E	A	WBAN	TO
66038	k	E	A	WBAN	TO	66089	k	E	A	WBAN	TO
66039	k	E	A	WBAN	TO	66090	k	E	A	WBAN	TO
66040	k	E	A	WBAN	TO	66091	k	E	A	WBAN	TO
66041	k	E	A	WBAN	TO	66092	k	E	A	WBAN	TO
66042	k	E	A	WBAN	TO	66093	k	E	A	WBAN	TO
66043	k	E	A	WBAN	TO	66094	k	E	A	WBAN	TO
66044	k	E	A	WBAN	TO	66095	k	E	A	WBAN	TO
66045	k	E	A	WBAN	TO	66096	k	E	A	WBAN	TO
66046	k	E	A	WBAN	TO	66097	k	E	A	WBAN	TO
66047	k	E	A	WBAN	TO	66098	k	E	A	WBAN	TO
66048	k	E	A	WBAN	TO	66099	kr	E	A	WBBM	TO
66049	k	E	A	WBAN	TO	66100	kr	E	A	WBBM	TO
66050	k	E	A	WBAN	TO	66101	kr	E	A	WBBM	TO
66051	k	E	A	WBAN	TO	66102	kr	E	A	WBBM	TO
66052	k	E	A	WBAN	TO	66103	kr	E	A	WBBM	TO
66053	k	E	A	WBAN	TO	66104	kr	E	A	WBBM	TO
66054	k	E	A	WBAN	TO	66105	kr	E	A	WBBM	TO
66055	k	E	A	WBLN	TO	66106	kr	E	A	WBBM	TO
66056	k	E	A	WBLN	TO	66107	kr	E	A	WBBM	TO
66057	k	E	A	WBLN	TO	66108	kr	E	A	WBBM	TO
66058	k	E	A	WBLN	TO	66109	k	E	A	WBAN	TO
66059	k	E	A	WBLN	TO	66110	kr	E	A	WBBM	TO
66060	k	E	A	WBAN	TO	66111	kr	E	A	WBBM	TO
66061	k	E	A	WBAN	TO	66112	kr	E	A	WBBM	TO
66062	k	E	A	WBAN	TO	66113	kr	E	A	WBBM	TO
66063	k	E	A	WBAN	TO	66114	kr	E	A	WBBM	TO
66064	k	E	A	WBAN	TO	66115	k	E	A	WBAN	TO
66065	k	E	A	WBAN	TO	66116	k	E	A	WBAN	TO
66066	k	E	A	WBAN	TO	66117	k	E	A	WBAN	TO
66067	k	E	A	WBAN	TO	66118	k	E	A	WBAN	TO
66068	k	E	A	WBAN	TO	66119	k	E	A	WBAN	TO
66069	k	E	A	WBAN	TO	66120	k	E	A	WBAN	TO
66070	k	E	A	WBAN	TO	66121	k	E	A	WBAN	TO
66071	k	E	A	WBAN	TO	66122	k	E	A	WBAN	TO
66072	k	E	A	WBAN	TO	66123	k	E	A	WBAN	TO
66073	k	E	A	WBAN	TO	66124	k	E	A	WBAN	TO

66125	k	E	A	WBAN	TO	66176	k	E	A	WBAN	TO
66126	k	E	A	WBAN	TO	66177	k	E	A	WBAN	TO
66127	k	E	A	WBAN	TO	66178	k	E	A	WBAN	TO
66128	k	E	A	WBAN	TO	66179	k	E	A	WBAN	TO
66129	k	E	A	WBAN	TO	66180	k	E	A	WBAN	TO
66130	k	E	A	WBAN	TO	66181	k	E	A	WBAN	TO
66131	k	E	A	WBAN	TO	66182	k	E	A	WBAN	TO
66132	k	E	A	WBAN	TO	66183	k	E	A	WBAN	TO
66133	k	E	A	WBAN	TO	66184	k	E	A	WBAN	TO
66134	k	E	A	WBAN	TO	66185	k	E	A	WBAN	TO
66135	k	E	A	WBAN	TO	66186	k	E	A	WBAN	TO
66136	k	E	A	WBAN	TO	66187	k	E	A	WBAN	TO
66137	k	E	A	WBAN	TO	66188	k	E	A	WBAN	TO
66138	k	E	A	WBAN	TO	66189	k	E	A	WBAN	TO
66139	k	E	A	WBAN	TO	66190	k	E	A	WBAN	TO
66140	k	E	A	WBAN	TO	66191	k	E	A	WBAN	TO
66141	k	E	A	WBAN	TO	66192	k	E	A	WBAN	TO
66142	k	E	A	WBAN	TO	66193	k	E	A	WBAN	TO
66143	k	E	A	WBAN	TO	66194	k	E	A	WBAN	TO
66144	k	E	A	WBAN	TO	66195	k	E	A	WBAN	TO
66145	k	E	A	WBAN	TO	66196	k	E	A	WBAN	TO
66146	k	E	A	WBAN	TO	66197	k	E	A	WBAN	TO
66147	k	E	A	WBAN	TO	66198	k	E	A	WBAN	TO
66148	k	E	A	WBAN	TO	66199	k	E	A	WBAN	TO
66149	k	E	A	WBAN	TO	66200	k	E	A	WBAN	TO
66150	k	E	A	WBAN	TO	66201	k	E	A	WBAN	TO
66151	k	E	A	WBAN	TO	66202	k	E	A	WBAN	TO
66152	k	E	A	WBAN	TO	66203	k	E	A	WBAN	TO
66153	k	E	A	WBAN	TO	66204	k	E	A	WBAN	TO
66154	k	E	A	WBAN	TO	66205	k	E	A	WBAN	TO
66155	k	E	A	WBAN	TO	66206	k	E	A	WBAN	TO
66156	k	E	A	WBAN	TO	66207	k	E	A	WBAN	TO
66157	k	E	A	WBAN	TO	66208	k	E	A	WBAN	TO
66158	k	E	A	WBAN	TO	66209	k	E	A	WBAN	TO
66159	k	E	A	WBAN	TO	66210	k	E	A	WBAN	TO
66160	k	E	A	WBAN	TO	66211	k	E	A	WBAN	TO
66161	k	E	A	WBAN	TO	66212	k	E	A	WBAN	TO
66162	k	E	A	WBAN	TO	66213	k	E	A	WBAN	TO
66163	k	E	A	WBAN	TO	66214	k	E	A	WBAN	TO
66164	k	E	A	WBAN	TO	66215	k	E	A	WBAN	TO
66165	k	E	A	WBAN	TO	66216	k	E	A	WBAN	TO
66166	k	E	A	WBAN	TO	66217	k	E	A	WBAN	TO
66167	k	E	A	WBAN	TO	66218	k	E	A	WBAN	TO
66168	k	E	A	WBAN	TO	66219	k	E	A	WBAN	TO
66169	k	E	A	WBAN	TO	66220	k	E	A	WBAN	TO
66170	k	E	A	WBAN	TO	66221	k	E	A	WBAN	TO
66171	k	E	A	WBAN	TO	66222	k	E	A	WBAN	TO
66172	k	E	A	WBAN	TO	66223	k	E	A	WBAN	TO
66173	k	E	A	WBAN	TO	66224	k	E	A	WBAN	TO
66174	k	E	A	WBAN	TO	66225	k	E	A	WBAN	TO
66175	k	E	A	WBAN	TO	66226	k	E	A	WBAN	TO

66227	k	**E**	A	WBAN	TO	66239	k	**E**	A	WBAN	TO
66228	k	**E**	A	WBAN	TO	66240	k	**E**	A	WBAN	TO
66229	k	**E**	A	WBAN	TO	66241	k	**E**	A	WBAN	TO
66230	k	**E**	A	WBAN	TO	66242	k	**E**	A	WBAN	TO
66231	k	**E**	A	WBAN	TO	66243	k	**E**	A	WBAN	TO
66232	k	**E**	A	WBAN	TO	66244	k	**E**	A	WBAN	TO
66233	k	**E**	A	WBAN	TO	66245	k	**E**	A	WBAN	TO
66234	k	**E**	A	WBAN	TO	66246	k	**E**	A	WBAN	TO
66235	k	**E**	A	WBAN	TO	66247	k	**E**	A	WBAN	TO
66236	k	**E**	A	WBAN	TO	66248	k	**E**	A	WBAN	TO
66237	k	**E**	A	WBAN	TO	66249	k	**E**	A	WBAN	TO
66238	k	**E**	A	WBAN	TO	66250	k	**E**	A	WBAN	TO

Names:

66002 Lafarge Quorn
66022 Lafarge Charnwood
66042 Lafarge Buddon Wood
66077 Benjamin Gimbert G.C.
66079 James Nightall G.C.
66200 RAILWAY HERITAGE COMMITTEE

Class 66/4. Direct Rail Services-operated locomotives. Details as Class 66/0.

Advertising Livery: 66405 WH Malcolm (DRS Blue with WH Malcolm logos).

66401	**DS**	P	XHCK	KM
66402	**DS**	P	XHCK	KM
66403	**DS**	P	XHCK	KM
66404	**DS**	P	XHCK	KM
66405	**AL**	P	XHCK	KM
66406	**DS**	P	XHCK	KM
66407	**DS**	P	XHCK	KM
66408	**DS**	P	XHCK	KM
66409	**DS**	P	XHCK	KM
66410	**DS**	P	XHCK	KM

Class 66/5. Freightliner-operated locomotives. Details as Class 66/0.

Advertising Livery: 66522 Shanks Waste (one half of loco Freightliner green and one half Shanks' Waste light green).

66501	**FL**	P	DFGM	FD	Japan 2001
66502	**FL**	P	DFGM	FD	Basford Hall Centenary 2001
66503	**FL**	P	DFGM	FD	The RAILWAY MAGAZINE
66504	**FL**	P	DFGM	FD	
66505	**FL**	P	DFGM	FD	
66506	**FL**	H	DFRT	FD	Crewe Regeneration
66507	**FL**	H	DFRT	FD	
66508	**FL**	H	DFRT	FD	
66509	**FL**	H	DFRT	FD	
66510	**FL**	H	DFRT	FD	
66511	**FL**	H	DFRT	FD	
66512	**FL**	H	DFRT	FD	
66513	**FL**	H	DFRT	FD	

66514	**FL**	H	DFRT	FD	
66515	**FL**	H	DFRT	FD	
66516	**FL**	H	DFRT	FD	
66517	**FL**	H	DFRT	FD	
66518	**FL**	H	DFRT	FD	
66519	**FL**	H	DFRT	FD	
66520	**FL**	H	DFRT	FD	
66521	**FL**	H	SAXL	LD	
66522	**AL**	H	DFHH	LD	
66523	**FL**	H	DFHH	FD	
66524	**FL**	H	DFHH	LD	
66525	**FL**	H	DFHH	FD	
66526	**FL**	P	DFHH	LD	Driver Steve Dunn (George)
66527	**FL**	P	DFHH	LD	Don Raider
66528	**FL**	P	DFHH	FD	
66529	**FL**	P	DFHH	FD	
66530	**FL**	P	DFHH	LD	
66531	**FL**	P	DFHH	FD	
66532	**FL**	P	DFGM	FD	P&O Nedlloyd Atlas
66533	**FL**	P	DFGM	FD	Hanjin Express/Senator Express
66534	**FL**	P	DFGM	FD	OOCL Express
66535	**FL**	P	DFGM	FD	
66536	**FL**	P	DFGM	FD	
66537	**FL**	P	DFGM	FD	
66538	**FL**	H	DFGM	FD	
66539	**FL**	H	DFGM	FD	
66540	**FL**	H	DFGM	FD	
66541	**FL**	H	DFGM	FD	
66542	**FL**	H	DFGM	FD	
66543	**FL**	H	DFGM	FD	
66544	**FL**	P	DFHH	LD	
66545	**FL**	P	DFHH	FD	
66546	**FL**	P	DFHH	FD	
66547	**FL**	P	DFHH	LD	
66548	**FL**	P	DFHH	LD	
66549	**FL**	P	DFHH	LD	
66550	**FL**	P	DFHH	LD	
66551	**FL**	P	DFHH	LD	
66552	**FL**	P	DFHH	LD	Maltby Raider
66553	**FL**	P	DFHH	LD	
66554	**FL**	H	DFHH	LD	
66555	**FL**	H	DFHH	LD	
66556	**FL**	H	DFHH	LD	
66557	**FL**	H	DFHH	FD	
66558	**FL**	H	DFHH	FD	
66559	**FL**	H	DFHH	LD	
66560	**FL**	H	DFHH	FD	
66561	**FL**	H	DFHH	FD	
66562	**FL**	H	DFHH	LD	
66563	**FL**	H	DFHH	FD	
66564	**FL**	H	DFHH	LD	

66565	**FL**	H	DFHH	LD	
66566	**FL**	H	DFHH	LD	
66567	**FL**	H	DFGM	FD	
66568	**FL**	H	DFGM	FD	
66569	**FL**	H	DFGM	FD	
66570	**FL**	H	DFGM	FD	
66571	**FL**	H	DFGM	FD	
66572	**FL**	H	DFGM	FD	
66573	**FL**	H	DFGM	FD	
66574	**FL**	H	DFGM	FD	
66575	**FL**	H	DFGM	FD	
66576	**FL**	H	DFGM	FD	Hamburg Sud Advantage
66577	**FL**	H	DFGM	FD	
66578	**FL**	H			
66579	**FL**	H			
66580	**FL**	H			
66581	**FL**	H			

Class 66/6. Freightliner-operated locomotives with modified gear ratios. Details as Class 66/0 except:

Maximum Tractive Effort: 467 kN (105080 lbf).
Continuous Tractive Effort: 296 kN (66630 lbf) at 14.0 m.p.h.
Design Speed: 65 m.p.h.   **Maximum Speed:** 65 m.p.h.

66601	**FL**	P	DFHH	FD	The Hope Valley
66602	**FL**	P	DFRT	FD	
66603	**FL**	P	DFRT	FD	
66604	**FL**	P	DFRT	FD	
66605	**FL**	P	DFRT	FD	
66606	**FL**	P	DFRT	FD	
66607	**FL**	P	DFHH	FD	
66608	**FL**	P	DFHH	FD	
66609	**FL**	P	DFHH	FD	
66610	**FL**	P	DFHH	FD	
66611	**FL**	P	DFHH	FD	
66612	**FL**	P	DFHH	FD	Forth Raider
66613	**FL**	H	DFHH	FD	
66614	**FL**	H	DFHH	FD	
66615	**FL**	H	DFHH	FD	
66616	**FL**	H	DFHH	FD	
66617	**FL**	H	DFHH	FD	
66618	**FL**	H	DFHH	FD	Railways Illustrated Annual Photographic Awards Ian Lothian
66619	**FL**	H			
66620	**FL**	H			
66621	**FL**	H			
66622	**FL**	H			

Class 66/7. GB Railfreight-operated locomotives.

Details as Class 66/0.

Non Standard/Advertising liveries:

66705 **GB** livery but with the addition of "Union Jack" bodyside vinyls.
66709 Black and Orange with MEDITE branding.

66701	**GB**	H	GBRT	WN	Whitemoor
66702	**GB**	H	GBRT	WN	Blue Lightning
66703	**GB**	H	GBRT	WN	Doncaster PSB 1981–2002
66704	**GB**	H	GBRT	WN	Colchester Power Signalbox
66705	**GB**	H	GBCM	WN	Golden Jubilee
66706	**GB**	H	GBCM	WN	Nene Valley
66707	**GB**	H	GBRT	WN	Sir Sam Fay GREAT CENTRAL RAILWAY
66708	**GB**	H	GBRT	WN	
66709	**AL**	H	GBRT	WN	Joseph Arnold Davies
66710	**GB**	H	GBCM	WN	
66711	**GB**	H	GBCM	WN	
66712	**GB**	H	GBCM	WN	
66713	**GB**	H	GBCM	WN	Forest City
66714	**GB**	H	GBCM	WN	Cromer Lifeboat
66715	**GB**	H	GBCM	WN	VALOUR – IN MEMORY OF ALL RAILWAY EMPLOYEES WHO GAVE THEIR LIVES FOR THEIR COUNTRY
66716	**GB**	H	GBCM	WN	Willesden Traincare Centre
66717	**GB**	H	GBCM	WN	

66718–66722. New "low emission" engines. On order and due for delivery September 2005.

66718	H
66719	H
66720	H
66721	H
66722	H

Class 66/9. Freightliner locos. New "low emission" engines. Full details awaited. Not yet Network Rail approved. Currently based at Dagenham for use on CTRL 2 trains.
Fuel Capacity: 5150 litres.

66951	**FL**	H	DFHC	FD
66952	**FL**	H	DFHC	FD

CLASS 67 ALSTOM/GENERAL MOTORS EMD Bo-Bo

Built: 1999–2000 by Alstom at Valencia, Spain, as sub-contractors for General Motors (General Motors model JT42 HW-HS).
Engine: General Motors 12N-710G3B-EC two stroke of 2385 kW (3200 h.p.) at 900 r.p.m.
Main Alternator: General Motors AR9/HE3/CA6B.
Traction Motors: General Motors D43FM.
Maximum Tractive Effort: 141 kN (31750 lbf).
Continuous Tractive Effort: 90 kN (20200 lbf) at ?? m.p.h.
Power At Rail: 1860 kW.   **Train Brakes:** Air.
Brake Force: 78 t.   **Dimensions:** 19.74 x 2.72 m.
Weight: 90 t.   **Wheel Diameter:** 965 mm.
Design Speed: 125 m.p.h.   **Maximum Speed:** 125 m.p.h.
Fuel Capacity: 4927 litres.   **RA:** 8.
Train Supply: Electric, index 66.   **Multiple Working:** AAR System.

Notes: All equipped with Slow Speed Control and Swinghead Automatic "Buckeye" Combination Couplers.

Non Standard livery: 67029 All over silver with EWS logos (EWS "Special Train").

67001	E	A	WNTR	TO	
67002	E	A	WAAK	TO	Special Delivery
67003	E	A	WAAK	TO	
67004 r	E	A	WABK	TO	Post Haste
67005	RZ	A	WAAK	TO	Queen's Messenger
67006	RZ	A	WAAK	TO	
67007 r	E	A	WABK	TO	
67008 r	E	A	WABK	TO	
67009 r	E	A	WABK	TO	
67010 r	E	A	WABK	TO	Unicorn
67011	E	A	WAAK	TO	
67012	E	A	WAAK	TO	
67013	E	A	WAAK	TO	
67014	E	A	WAAK	TO	
67015	E	A	WAAK	TO	
67016	E	A	WAAK	TO	
67017	E	A	WAAK	TO	Arrow
67018	E	A	WNTR	DR	Rapid
67019	E	A	WAAK	TO	
67020	E	A	WAAK	TO	
67021	E	A	WAAK	TO	
67022	E	A	WAAK	TO	
67023	E	A	WAAK	TO	
67024	E	A	WAAK	TO	
67025	E	A	WAAK	TO	Western Star
67026	E	A	WNTR	ML	
67027	E	A	WAAK	TO	Rising Star
67028	E	A	WAAK	TO	
67029	0	A	WAAK	TO	
67030	E	A	WNTR	TO	

▲ First Great Western green-liveried 08641 is seen at Plymouth station on 08/07/04. **Robert Pritchard**

▼ EWS-liveried 09006 is seen shunting at Hoo Junction on 09/09/04.
Anthony Kay

▲ DRS-liveried 20314 and 20308 approach Whitchester Tunnel on the Tyne Valley line with 6M60 12.53 Seaton-on-Tees–Carlisle on 27/05/04. **Dave McAlone**

▼ Wessex Trains-liveried 31601 "BLETCHLEY PARK 'STATION X'" runs through Avoncliff at the head of the 08.28 Bristol–Weymouth on 22/06/04. **John Chalcraft**

33202 "METEOR" and 33021 "Eastleigh", both in Fragonset livery, are seen near Chertsey with the 09.45 Hoo Junction–Eastleigh on 09/12/03. The locos were on hire to EWS for driver training.   **Rodney Lissenden**

▲ 37416 nears Strathcarron with a Kyle–Carrbridge leg of the Royal Scotsman on 08/07/04. This loco is in the special Royal Scotsman livery.　**John Chalcraft**

▼ 37612 and 37611 head 6K73 15.35 Sellafield–Crewe nuclear flask train through Kirkby-in-Furness on 09/07/03.　**George Allsop**

Several First Great Western power cars remain in the old Great Western green livery. One of these is 43005. On 05/07/04 it leads 43028 (out of sight) at Horse Cove with the 12.35 Paddington–Plymouth.

Robert Pritchard

▲ A GNER-liveried HST with power cars 43105 "City of Inverness" and 43112 "Doncaster" is seen at Bardrill Road near Blackford, Gleneagles with the 07.55 Inverness–King's Cross on 29/10/03.   **Ian Lothian**

▼ Fragonset-operated Class 45 "Peak" 45112 "THE ROYAL ARMY ORDNANCE CORPS" storms through Warrington Bank Quay on 07/07/04 with the 14.06 Carlisle–Crewe Network Rail Inspection train.   **Robert Pritchard**

▲ Fragonset freight-liveried 47355 "AVOCET" leads non-standard-liveried 47145 "MYRDDIN EMRYS" at Wilmorton, Derby with 6Z57 Shirebrook–Derby on 22/04/04. **Paul Robertson**

▼ Riviera Trains-liveried 47839 passes Rowton, Cheshire with 1G11 14.00 Holyhead– Birmingham on 02/08/03. **Doug Birmingham**

▲ Several EWS Class 56s have been repainted into Fertis grey livery, prior to being used for a contract in France. On 19/10/04 56118 and 56087 lead two line ups of locos at St. Hilaire stabling point, France. **David Haydock**

▼ Freightliner-liveried 57008 "Freightliner Explorer" passes the aggregates terminal at Banbury with a Lawley Street–Southampton Freightliner on 07/06/04. **Kim Fullbrook**

▲ First Great Western green-liveried 57602 "Pendennis Castle" is seen at Penzance on 05/10/04 after arrival with the 23.50 Paddington–Penzance Sleeper service. All four FGW 57/6s are now in service and named after famous castles in the West Country. **Darren Ford**

▼ 58046, ex-works in Fertis livery, at Toton depot on 07/09/04. **EWS**

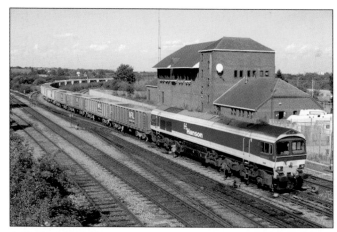

▲ Hanson-liveried 59101 "Village of Whatley" is seen at Westbury with 7C76 14.21 Acton–Westbury empty stone train on 23/07/04.   **Shaun Bamford**

▼ Two of a kind at Hindlow in the Peak District on 18/10/03. 60010 and 60022, both in EWS livery, wait to depart with loaded stone trains.   **Les Nixon**

EWS were the first company to order General Motors Class 66 locos, Freightliner, GBRf and DRS followed. On 17/04/04 66121 is seen at Penmaenmawr prior to departure with 6Z52 10.47 loaded stone train to Acton. **Paul Shannon**

▲ 66564 leads a well loaded 4M26 14.41 Dagenham Dock–Crewe car/van train past Castle thorpe, north of Milton Keynes, on 29/03/04.　　**Anthony Kay**

▼ In the revised DRS Class 66 livery 66406 passes Cowperthwaite near Grayrigg, Cumbria with 4M44 06.20 Coatbridge–Daventry DRS Intermodal on 05/12/03.
Dave McAlone

Revised Royal Train-liveried 67005 "Queen's Messenger" passes Bristol Barton Hill with Virgin Cross-Country's 1M89 08.43 Paignton–Preston on 14/08/04.

Jason Rogers

▲ 73205, in GBRf livery, stands in Tonbridge yard on 12/05/04. **Rodney Lissenden**

▼ Freightliner Green-liveried 86620 "Philip G Walton" and 86612 pass Bradley, north of Wigan, with 4M27 05.00 Coatbridge–Crewe Freightliner on 07/08/04.
Paul Senior

▲ 87031 "Hal o' the Wynd"" heads a diverted Euston–Manchester Virgin service past Bathpool, Kidsgrove on 03/05/04. **Cliff Beeton**

▼ "One"-liveried 90004 leads a One Anglia Mark 3 set at Brantham near Manningtree with the 09.40 Norwich–Liverpool Street on 18/05/04. **Anthony Kay**

▲ GNER-liveried 91104 "Grantham" approaches Colton Junction with a King's Cross–Newcastle setvice on 05/06/04. **Les Nixon**

▼ EPS-liveried 92037 "Sullivan" passes Slindon, Staffordshire with 6S75 11.30 Wembley–Mossend Enterprise on 14/06/04. **Hugh Ballantyne**

1.2. ELECTRO-DIESEL & ELECTRIC LOCOMOTIVES

CLASS 73   BR/ENGLISH ELECTRIC   Bo-Bo

Electro-diesel locomotives which can operate either from a DC supply or using power from a diesel engine.

Built: 1965–1967 by English Electric Co. at Vulcan Foundry, Newton le Willows.
Main Generator: English Electric 824/5D.
Traction Motors: English Electric 546/1B.
Maximum Tractive Effort (Electric): 179 kN (40000 lbf).
Maximum Tractive Effort (Diesel): 160 kN (36000 lbf).
Continuous Rating (Electric): 1060 kW (1420 h.p.) giving a tractive effort of 35 kN (7800 lbf) at 68 m.p.h.
Continuous Tractive Effort (Diesel): 60 kN (13600 lbf) at 11.5 m.p.h.
Maximum Rail Power (Electric): 2350 kW (3150 h.p.) at 42 m.p.h.
Train Brakes: Air, vacuum & electro-pneumatic († Air & electro-pneumatic).
Brake Force: 31 t.   **Dimensions:** 16.36 x 2.64 m.
Weight: 77 t.   **Wheel Diameter:** 1016 mm.
Design Speed: 90 m.p.h.   **Maximum Speed:** 90 m.p.h.
Fuel Capacity: 1409 litres.
Train Supply: Electric, index 66 (on electric power only).
Multiple Working: SR System.

Formerly numbered E6001–E6020/E6022–E6026/E6028–E6049 (not in order).

Notes: Locomotives numbered in the 732xx series are classed as 73/2 and were originally dedicated to Gatwick Express services.

73103	**IM**	FM	SDXL	MQ	
73107	**FB**	FM	SDED	DF	SPITFIRE
73109	**ST**	SW	HYSB	BM	Battle of Britain 50th Anniversary
73117	**IM**	FM	SDXL	MQ	
73118 †c	**EP**	EU	GPSN	OC	
73130 †c	**EP**	EU	GPSN	OC	
73132	**IM**	NR	QADD	DF (S)	
73141	**IM**	NR	QAED	LU (S)	
73201 †	**GX**	P	IVGA	SL	
73202 †	**GX**	P	IVGA	SL	
73203 †	**GX**	GB	GBZZ	PB	
73204 †	**GB**	GB	GBED	DF	Janice
73205 †	**GB**	GB	GBED	DF	Jeanette
73206 †	**GB**	GB	GBED	DF	Lisa
73207 †	**GX**	GB	GBZZ	PB	
73208 †	**GX**	P	IVGA	SL	
73209 †	**GB**	GB	GBED	DF	Alison
73210 †	**GX**	P	SBXL	ZG	
73211 †	**GX**	P	SBXL	ZG	

73212	†	**RK**	NR	QAED	DF
73213	†	**RK**	NR	QAED	DF
73235	†	**SD**	SW	HYSB	BM

CLASS 86   BR/ENGLISH   ELECTRIC   Bo-Bo

Built: 1965–1966 by English Electric Co. at Vulcan Foundry, Newton le Willows or by BR at Doncaster Works.
Electric Supply System: 25 kV AC 50 Hz overhead.
Train Brakes: Air.   **Brake Force:** 40 t.
Dimensions: 17.83 x 2.65 m.   **Weight:** 83–86.8 t.
RA: 6.   **Multiple Working:** TDM system.
Train Supply: Electric, index 74.

Formerly numbered E3101–E3200 (not in order).

Non standard Liveries:

86227 **AR** but with the addition of "Union Jack" bodyside vinyls.
86233 BR "Electric Blue" livery.

Class 86/1. Class 87-type bogies & motors.
Details as above except:
Maximum Tractive Effort: 258 kN (58000 lbf).
Traction Motors: GEC 412AZ frame mounted.
Continuous Rating: 3730 kW (5000 h.p.) giving a tractive effort of 95 kN (21300 lbf) at 87 m.p.h.
Maximum Rail Power: 5860 kW (7860 h.p.) at 50.8 m.p.h.
Weight: 86.8 t.   **Wheel Diameter:** 1150 mm.
Design Speed: 110 m.p.h.   **Maximum Speed:** 110 m.p.h.

| 86101 | **IC** | H | SAXL | LT | |
| 86102 | **IC** | H | SAXL | LT | Robert A Riddles |

Class 86/2. Standard Design rebuilt with resilient wheels and Flexicoil suspension.

Traction Motors: AEI 282BZ axle hung.
Maximum Tractive Effort: 207 kN (46500 lbf).
Continuous Rating: 3010 kW (4040 h.p.) giving a tractive effort of 85 kN (19200 lbf) at 77.5 m.p.h.
Maximum Rail Power: 4550 kW (6100 h.p.) at 49.5 m.p.h.
Wheel Diameter: 1156 mm.   **Weight:** 85–86.2 t.
Design Speed: 125 m.p.h.   **Maximum Speed:** 100 m.p.h.

86205	**V**	H	SAXL	IR	
86207	**IC**	H	SAXL	LT	City of Lichfield
86209	**AR**	H	SAXL	PY	
86212	**V**	H	SAXL	OY	
86213	**IC**	H	SAXL	BH	Lancashire Witch
86214	**IC**	H	SAXL	LT	Sans Pareil
86215	**AR**	H	SAXL	PY	
86217	**AR**	H	SAXL	OY	
86218	**AR**	H	IANA	NC	NHS 50

86223	**AR**	H	SAXL	OY	Norwich Union
86224	**IC**	H	SAXL	LT	
86225	**V**	H	SAXL	LT	Hardwicke
86226	**V**	H	SAXL	IR	
86227	**AR**	H	SAXL	PY	
86228	**IC**	H	SAXL	ZH	Vulcan Heritage
86229	**V**	H	SAXL	OY	
86230	**AR**	H	SAXL	PY	
86231	**V**	H	SAXL	OY	
86232	**AR**	H	IANA	NC	Norfolk and Norwich Festival
86233	**O**	H	SAXL	OY	
86234	**AR**	H	IANA	NC	Suffolk Relax.Refresh.Return
86235	**AR**	H	IANA	NC	Crown Point
86238	**AR**	H	SAXL	PY	
86240	**V**	H	SAXL	PY	
86242	**AR**	H	SAXL	PY	
86245	**V**	H	SAXL	IR	
86246	**AR**	H	IANA	NC	Royal Anglian Regiment
86247	**V**	H	SAXL	IR	
86248	**V**	H	SAXL	ZH	Sir Clwyd/County of Clwyd
86249	**IC**	H	SAXL	PC	County of Merseyside
86250	**AR**	H	SAXL	OY	
86251	**V**	H	SAXL	OY	
86256	**V**	H	SAXL	LT	Pebble Mill
86258	**V**	H	SAXL	ZH	
86259	**V**	H	SAXL	IR	
86260	**AR**	H	IANA	NC	

Class 86/4. EWS/Network Rail-owned locomotives.

Traction Motors: AEI 282AZ axle hung.
Maximum Tractive Effort: 258 kN (58000 lbf).
Continuous Rating: 2680 kW (3600 h.p.) giving a tractive effort of 89 kN (20000 lbf) at 67 m.p.h.
Maximum Rail Power: 4400 kW (5900 h.p.) at 38 m.p.h.
Wheel Diameter: 1156 mm. **Weight:** 83–83.9 t.
Design Speed: 100 m.p.h. **Maximum Speed:** 100 m.p.h.

86424		**RX**	NR	SDXL	AS
86426	x	**FL**	E	WNXX	CE
86430	x	**FL**	E	WNXX	CE

Class 86/5. Regeared locomotive operated by Freightliner.
Details as Class 86/4 except:

Continuous Rating: 2680 kW (3600 h.p.) giving a tractive effort of 117 kN (26300 lbf) at 67 m.p.h.
Maximum Speed: 75 m.p.h. **Train Supply:** Electric, isolated.

| 86501 | (86608) | **FL** | FL | DFGC | FE |

Class 86/6. Freightliner-operated locomotives.

Details as Class 86/4 except:
Maximum Speed: 75 m.p.h.   **Train Supply:** Electric, isolated.

86602	**FL**	FL	DFHC	FE	
86603	**FE**	X	DHLT	SP	
86604	**FL**	FL	DHLT	CP	
86605	**FL**	FL	DFNC	FE	
86606	**FF**	FL	DHLT	CE	
86607	**FL**	FL	DFNC	FE	
86609	**FL**	FL	DFNC	FE	
86610	**FL**	FL	DFNC	FE	
86612	**FL**	P	DFNC	FE	
86613	**FL**	P	DFNC	FE	
86614	**FF**	P	DFNC	FE	
86615	**FL**	P	DFNC	FE	Rotary International
86620	**FL**	P	DFNC	FE	Philip G Walton
86621	**FL**	P	DFNC	FE	
86622	**FF**	P	DFNC	FE	
86623	**FF**	P	DHLT	BA	
86627	**FL**	P	DFNC	FE	
86628	**FL**	P	DFNC	FE	
86632	**FL**	P	DFNC	FE	
86633	**FF**	P	DHLT	BA	Wulfruna
86635	**FL**	P	DHLT	BA	
86637	**FF**	P	DFNC	FE	
86638	**FL**	P	DFNC	FE	
86639	**FL**	P	DFNC	FE	

Class 86/9. Network Rail-owned locomotives. Rebuilt for use as Mobile Load Bank test locos to test Overhead Line Equipment, initially on the WCML. No. 1 end Traction Motors isolated. Can still move under own power.

Maximum Speed: 60 m.p.h.

86901	(86253)	**Y**	NR	QACL	RU	
86902	(86210)	**Y**	NR	QACL	RU	RAIL VEHICLE ENGINEERING

CLASS 87   BREL/GEC   Bo-Bo

Built: 1973–1975 by BREL at Crewe Works.
Electric Supply System: 25 kV AC 50 Hz overhead.
Traction Motors: GEC G412AZ frame mounted.
Maximum Tractive Effort: 258 kN (58000 lbf).
Continuous Rating: 3730 kW (5000 h.p.) giving a tractive effort of 95 kN (21300 lbf) at 87 m.p.h.
Maximum Rail Power: 5860 kW (7860 h.p.) at 50.8 m.p.h.
Train Brakes: Air.   **Brake Force:** 40 t.
Dimensions: 17.83 x 2.65 m.   **Weight:** 83.3 t.
Wheel Diameter: 1150 mm.   **Design Speed:** 110 m.p.h.
Maximum Speed: 110 m.p.h.   **Train Supply:** Electric, index 95.
RA: 6.   **Multiple Working:** TDM system.

87001	B	P	IWCA	WN	STEPHENSON
87002	P	P	IWCA	WN	
87003	V	P	IWCA	WN	Patriot
87004	V	P	IWCA	WN	Britannia
87005	V	P	SBXL	WN	
87006	DR	P	XHAC	WN	
87007	V	P	SBXL	WN	
87008	V	P	SBXL	WN	
87009	V	P	SBXL	BR	
87010	V	P	IWCA	WN	King Arthur
87011	V	P	SBXL	BR	
87012	V	P	IWCA	WN	Coeur de Lion
87013	V	P	GBAC	WN	
87014	V	P	GBAC	WN	
87015	V	P	SBXL	WN	Howard of Effingham
87017	V	P	SBXL	BR	
87018	V	P	SBXL	BR	
87019	V	P	IWCA	WN	Sir Winston Churchill
87020	V	P	SBXL	BR	
87021	V	P	SBXL	WN	Robert The Bruce
87022	DR	P	XHAC	WN	
87023	V	P	SBXL	WN	
87024	V	P	SBXL	WN	Lord of the Isles
87025	V	P	SBXL	WN	
87026	V	P	SBXL	WN	Sir Richard Arkwright
87027	V	P	SBXL	NC	
87028	DR	P	XHAC	WN	
87029	V	P	SBXL	WN	
87030	V	P	IWCA	WN	Black Douglas
87031	V	P	SBXL	WN	
87032	V	P	XHAC	WN	
87033	V	P	IWCA	WN	Thane of Fife
87034	V	P	SBXL	BR	
87035	V	P	SBXL	WN	

CLASS 89   BRUSH   Co-Co

Built: 1986 by BREL at Crewe Works (as sub-contractors for Brush).
Electric Supply System: 25 kV AC 50 Hz overhead.
Traction Motors: Brush. Frame mounted.
Maximum Tractive Effort: 205 kN (46000 lbf).
Continuous Rating: 4350 kW (5850 h.p.) giving a tractive effort of 105 kN (23600 lbf) at 92 m.p.h.

Maximum Rail Power:	**Train Brakes:** Air.
Brake Force: 50 t.	**Dimensions:** 19.80 x 2.74 m.
Weight: 104 t.	**Wheel Diameter:** 1150 mm.
Design Speed: 125 m.p.h.	**Maximum Speed:** 125 m.p.h.
Train Supply: Electric, index 95.	**RA:** 6.
Multiple Working: TDM system.	

| 89001 | GN | SA | IECB | BH (S) |

CLASS 90   GEC   Bo-Bo

Built: 1987–1990 by BREL at Crewe Works (as sub contractors for GEC).
Electric Supply System: 25 kV AC 50 Hz overhead.
Traction Motors: GEC G412CY frame mounted.
Maximum Tractive Effort: 258 kN (58000 lbf).
Continuous Rating: 3730 kW (5000 h.p.) giving a tractive effort of 95 kN (21300 lbf) at 87 m.p.h.
Maximum Rail Power: 5860 kW (7860 h.p.) at 68.3 m.p.h.
Train Brakes: Air.
Brake Force: 40 t.
Weight: 84.5 t.
Design Speed: 110 m.p.h.
Train Supply: Electric, index 95.
Multiple Working: TDM system.

Dimensions: 18.80 x 2.74 m.
Wheel Diameter: 1156 mm.
Maximum Speed: 110 m.p.h.
RA: 7.

Non-standard liveries:

90036 As **FE**, but has a yellow roof.

90001	b	1	P	IANA	NC
90002	b	1	P	IANA	NC
90003	b	1	P	IANA	NC	Raedwald of East Anglia
90004	b	1	P	IANA	NC
90005	b	V	P	IANA	NC
90006	b	1	P	IANA	NC	Modern Railways Magazine/ Roger Ford
90007	b	V	P	IANA	NC
90008	b	V	P	IANA	NC
90009	b	V	P	IANA	NC
90010	b	1	P	IANA	NC
90011	b	V	P	IANA	NC
90012	b	V	P	IANA	NC
90013	b	1	P	IANA	NC
90014	b	V	P	IANA	NC
90015	b	1	P	IANA	NC
90016	b	RX	E	DFLC	FE
90017	b	E	E	WEFE	CE
90018	b	E	E	WEFE	CE
90019	b	RX	E	WNTR	CE	Penny Black
90020	b	E	E	WEFE	CE	Sir Michael Heron
90021		FE	E	WEFE	CE
90022		FE	E	WEFE	CE	Freightconnection
90023		E	E	WEFE	CE
90024		GN	E	WEFE	CE
90025		F	E	WNTR	CE
90026		E	E	WEFE	CE
90027		F	E	WEFE	CE	Allerton T&RS Depot
90028		F	E	WEFE	CE	Hertfordshire Rail Tours
90029		E	E	WEFE	CE	The Institution of Civil Engineers
90030		E	E	WEFE	CE	Crewe Locomotive Works

90031	E	E	WEFE	CE	The Railway Children Partnership Working For Street Children Worldwide
90032	E	E	WNTR	CE	
90033	FE	E	WEFE	CE	
90034	E	E	WEFE	CE	
90035	E	E	WEFE	CE	
90036	0	E	WEFE	CE	
90037	E	E	WEFE	CE	Spirit of Dagenham
90038	FE	E	WNTR	CE	
90039	E	E	WEFE	CE	
90040	E	E	WNTR	CE	The Railway Mission
90041	FL	P	DFLC	FE	
90042	FF	P	DFLC	FE	
90043	FF	P	DFLC	FE	Freightliner Coatbridge
90044	FF	P	DFLC	FE	
90045	FF	P	DFLC	FE	
90046	FF	P	DFLC	FE	
90047	FF	P	DFLC	FE	
90048	FF	P	DFLC	FE	
90049	FF	P	DFLC	FE	
90050	FF	P	WNTS	CE	

CLASS 91   GEC   Bo-Bo

Built: 1988–1991 by BREL at Crewe Works (as sub contractors for GEC).
Electric Supply System: 25 kV AC 50 Hz overhead.
Traction Motors: GEC G426AZ.   **Maximum Tractive Effort:**
Continuous Rating: 4540 kW (6090 h.p.) giving a tractive effort of ?? kN at ?? m.p.h.
Maximum Rail Power: 4700 kW (6300 h.p.) at ?? m.p.h.
Train Brakes: Air.
Brake Force: 45 t.   **Dimensions:** 19.41 x 2.74 m.
Weight: 84 t.   **Wheel Diameter:** 1000 mm.
Design Speed: 140 m.p.h.   **Maximum Speed:** 125 m.p.h.
Train Supply: Electric, index 95.   **RA:** 7.
Multiple Working: TDM system.

Note: Locos originally numbered in the 910xx series, but renumbered upon completion of overhauls at Bombardier, Doncaster by the addition of 100 to their original number. The exception to this rule was 91023 which was renumbered 91132.

91101	GN	H	IECA	BN	City of London
91102	GN	H	IECA	BN	Durham Cathedral
91103	GN	H	IECA	BN	County of Lincolnshire
91104	GN	H	IECA	BN	Grantham
91105	GN	H	IECA	BN	County Durham
91106	GN	H	IECA	BN	East Lothian
91107	GN	H	IECA	BN	Newark on Trent
91108	GN	H	IECA	BN	City of Leeds
91109	GN	H	IECA	BN	The Samaritans
91110	GN	H	IECA	BN	David Livingstone

91111	GN	H	IECA	BN	Terence Cuneo
91112	GN	H	IECA	BN	County of Cambridgeshire
91113	GN	H	IECA	BN	County of North Yorkshire
91114	GN	H	IECA	BN	St. Mungo Cathedral
91115	GN	H	IECA	BN	Holyrood
91116	GN	H	IECA	BN	Strathclyde
91117	GN	H	IECA	BN	Cancer Research UK
91118	GN	H	IECA	BN	Bradford Film Festival
91119	GN	H	IECA	BN	County of Tyne & Wear
91120	GN	H	IECA	BN	Royal Armouries
91121	GN	H	IECA	BN	Archbishop Thomas Cranmer
91122	GN	H	IECA	BN	Double Trigger
91124	GN	H	IECA	BN	Reverend W Awdry
91125	GN	H	IECA	BN	Berwick-upon-Tweed
91126	GN	H	IECA	BN	York Minster
91127	GN	H	IECA	BN	Edinburgh Castle
91128	GN	H	IECA	BN	Peterborough Cathedral
91129	GN	H	IECA	BN	Queen Elizabeth II
91130	GN	H	IECA	BN	City of Newcastle
91131	GN	H	IECA	BN	County of Northumberland
91132	GN	H	IECA	BN	City of Durham

CLASS 92   BRUSH   Co-Co

Built: 1993–1996 by Brush Traction at Loughborough.
Electric Supply System: 25 kV AC 50 HZ overhead or 750 V DC third rail.
Traction Motors: Brush.
Maximum Tractive Effort: 400 kN (90 000 lbf).
Continuous Rating: 5040 kW (6760 h.p.) on AC, 4000 kW (5360 h.p.) on DC.
Maximum Rail Power: **Train Brakes:** Air.
Brake Force: 63 t.   **Dimensions:** 21.34 x 2.67 m.
Weight: 126 t.   **Wheel Diameter:** 1160 mm.
Design Speed: 140 km/h (87 m.p.h.).   **Maximum Speed:** 140 km/h (87 m.p.h.).
Train Supply: Electric, index 108 (AC), 70 (DC).
RA: 7.

92001	E	E	WTAE	CE	Victor Hugo
92002	EP	E	WTAE	CE	H.G. Wells
92003	EP	E	WTAE	CE	Beethoven
92004	EP	E	WNTS	CE	Jane Austen
92005	EP	E	WTAE	CE	Mozart
92006	EP	SF	WTAE	CE	Louis Armand
92007	EP	E	WTAE	CE	Schubert
92008	EP	E	WTAE	CE	Jules Verne
92009	EP	E	WTAE	CE	Elgar
92010	EP	SF	WTAE	CE	Molière
92011	EP	E	WTAE	CE	Handel
92012	EP	E	WTAE	CE	Thomas Hardy
92013	EP	E	WTAE	CE	Puccini
92014	EP	SF	WTAE	CE	Emile Zola
92015	EP	E	WNTR	CE	D.H. Lawrence

92016	**EP**	E	WTAE	CE	Brahms
92017	**EP**	E	WTAE	CE	Shakespeare
92018	**EP**	SF	WTAE	CE	Stendhal
92019	**EP**	E	WNTR	CE	Wagner
92020	**EP**	EU	WNWX	CE	Milton
92021	**EP**	EU	WNWX	CE	Purcell
92022	**EP**	E	WTAE	CE	Charles Dickens
92023	**EP**	SF	WTAE	CE	Ravel
92024	**EP**	E	WNTR	CE	J.S. Bach
92025	**EP**	E	WTAE	CE	Oscar Wilde
92026	**EP**	E	WTAE	CE	Britten
92027	**EP**	E	WTAE	CE	George Eliot
92028	**EP**	SF	WTAE	CE	Saint Saëns
92029	**EP**	E	WTAE	CE	Dante
92030	**EP**	E	WTAE .	CE	Ashford
92031	**E**	E	WTAE	CE	The Institute of Logistics and Transport
92032	**EP**	EU	WNWX	CE	César Franck
92033	**EP**	SF	WTAE	CE	Berlioz
92034	**EP**	E	WNTR	CE	Kipling
92035	**EP**	E	WNTR	CE	Mendelssohn
92036	**EP**	E	WTAE	CE	Bertolt Brecht
92037	**EP**	E	WTAE	CE	Sullivan
92038	**EP**	SF	WTAE	CE	Voltaire
92039	**EP**	E	WTAE	CE	Johann Strauss
92040	**EP**	EU	WNWX	CE	Goethe
92041	**EP**	E	WTAE	CE	Vaughan Williams
92042	**EP**	E	WTAE	CE	Honegger
92043	**EP**	SF	WTAE	CE	Debussy
92044	**EP**	EU	WNWX	CE	Couperin
92045	**EP**	EU	WNWX	CE	Chaucer
92046	**EP**	EU	WNWX	CE	Sweelinck

3. EUROTUNNEL LOCOMOTIVES

DIESEL LOCOMOTIVES

0001–0005   MaK   Bo-Bo

Built: 1992–1993 by MaK at Kiel, Germany (Model DE1004).
Engine: MTU 12V 396 Tc of 1180 kW (1580 h.p.) at 1800 rpm.
Main Alternator: BBC.   **Traction Motors:** BBC.
Maximum Tractive Effort: 305 kN (68600 lbf).
Continuous Tractive Effort: 140 kN (31500 lbf) at 20 mph.
Power At Rail: 750 kW (1012 h.p.).
Brake Force: 120 kN.   **Dimensions:** 16.50 x ?? x ?? m.
Weight: 84 t.   **Wheel Diameter:** 1000 mm.
Design Speed: 120 km/h.   **Maximum Speed:** 120 km/h.
Fuel Capacity: **Train Brakes:** Air.
Train Supply: Not equipped.   **Multiple Working:** Within class.

0001	GY	ET	EU
0002	GY	ET	EU
0003	GY	ET	EU
0004	GY	ET	EU
0005	GY	ET	EU

0031–0042   HUNSLET/SCHÖMA   0-4-0

Built: 1989–1990 by Hunslet Engine Company at Leeds as 900 mm. gauge.
Rebuilt: 1993-1994 by Schöma in Germany to 1435 mm. gauge.
Engine: Deutz of 270 kW (200 h.p.) at ???? rpm.
Transmission: Mechanical.   **Maximum Tractive Effort:**
Cont. Tractive Effort: **Power At Rail:**
Brake Force: **Dimensions:**
Weight: **Wheel Diameter:**
Design Speed: 50 km/h.   **Maximum Speed:** 50 km/h.
Fuel Capacity: **Train Brakes:** Air.
Train Supply: Not equipped.   **Multiple Working:** Not equipped.

0031	Y	ET	EU	FRANCES
0032	Y	ET	EU	ELISABETH
0033	Y	ET	EU	SILKE
0034	Y	ET	EU	AMANDA
0035	Y	ET	EU	MARY
0036	Y	ET	EU	LAWRENCE
0037	Y	ET	EU	LYDIE
0038	Y	ET	EU	JENNY
0039	Y	ET	EU	PACITA
0040	Y	ET	EU	JILL
0041	Y	ET	EU	KIM
0042	Y	ET	EU	NICOLE

ELECTRIC LOCOMOTIVES

9001–9113   BRUSH/ABB   Bo-Bo-Bo

Built: 1993–2001 by Brush Traction at Loughborough.
Supply System: 25 kV AC 50 Hz overhead.
Traction Motors: ABB 6PH.   **Maximum Tractive Effort:** 400 kN (90 000 lbf).
Continuous Rating: 5760 kW (7725 h.p.) giving a TE of 310 kN at 65 km/h.
(* Fleet being progressively upgraded to 7000 kW (9387 h.p.) and are also
being renumbered into the 98xx number series upon refurbishment).
Maximum Rail Power: **Multiple Working:** TDM system.
Brake Force: 50 t.   **Dimensions:** 22.01 x 2.97 x 4.20 m.
Weight: 132 t.   **Wheel Diameter:** 1090 mm.
Design Speed: 175 km/h (100 m.p.h.)   **Maximum Speed:** 160 km/h (87 m.p.h.)
Train Supply: Electric.   **Train Brakes:** Air.

CLASS 9/0 and CLASS 9/8. Mixed traffic locomotives.

9001		**EB**	ET	EU	LESLEY GARRETT
9002		**EB**	ET	EU	STUART BURROWS
9003		**EB**	ET	EU	BENJAMIN LUXON
9804	*	**EB**	ET	EU	VICTORIA DE LOS ANGELES
9005		**EB**	ET	EU	JESSYE NORMAN
9006		**EB**	ET	EU	REGINE CRESPIN
9007		**EB**	ET	EU	DAME JOAN SUTHERLAND
9808	*	**EB**	ET	EU	ELISABETH SODERSTROM
9809	*	**EB**	ET	EU	FRANÇOIS POLLET
9810	*	**EB**	ET	EU	JEAN-PHILIPPE COURTIS
9011		**EB**	ET	EU	JOSÉ VAN DAM
9012		**EB**	ET	EU	LUCIANO PAVAROTTI
9013		**EB**	ET	EU	MARIA CALLAS
9014		**EB**	ET	EU	LUCIA POPP
9015		**EB**	ET	EU	LÖTSCHBERG 1913
9016		**EB**	ET	EU	WILLARD WHITE
9017		**EB**	ET	EU	JOSÉ CARRERAS
9018		**EB**	ET	EU	WILHELMENA FERNANDEZ
9819	*	**EB**	ET	EU	MARIA EWING
9820	*	**EB**	ET	EU	Nicolai Ghiaurov
9821	*	**EB**	ET	EU	TERESA BERGANZA
9022		**EB**	ET	EU	DAME JANET BAKER
9023		**EB**	ET	EU	DAME ELISABETH LEGGE-SCHWARZKOPF
9024		**EB**	ET	EU	GOTTHARD 1882
9825	*	**EB**	ET	EU	JUNGFRAUJOCH 1912
9026		**EB**	ET	EU	FURKATUNNEL 1982
9027		**EB**	ET	EU	BARBARA HENDRICKS
9828	*	**EB**	ET	EU	DAME KIRI TE KANAWA
9029		**EB**	ET	EU	THOMAS ALLEN
9031		**EB**	ET	EU	
9032		**EB**	ET	EU	RENATA TEBALDI
9033		**EB**	ET	EU	MONTSERRAT CABALLE

9034	**EB**	ET	EU	MIRELLA FRENI
9035	**EB**	ET	EU	Nicolai Gedda
9036	**EB**	ET	EU	ALAIN FONDARY
9037	**EB**	ET	EU	GABRIEL BACQUIER
9038	**EB**	ET	EU	HILDEGARD BEHRENS
9040	**EB**	ET	EU	

CLASS 9/1. Freight Shuttle dedicated locomotives.

9101	**EB**	ET	EU
9102	**EB**	ET	EU
9103	**EB**	ET	EU
9104	**EB**	ET	EU
9105	**EB**	ET	EU
9106	**EB**	ET	EU
9107	**EB**	ET	EU
9108	**EB**	ET	EU
9109	**EB**	ET	EU
9110	**EB**	ET	EU
9111	**EB**	ET	EU
9112	**EB**	ET	EU
9113	**EB**	ET	EU

9701–9707 BRUSH/BOMBARDIER Bo-Bo-Bo

CLASS 9/7. Increased power freight shuttle dedicated locomotives.

Built: 2001–2002 by Brush Traction at Loughborough.
Supply System: 25 kV AC 50 Hz overhead.
Traction Motors: ABB 6PH.   **Maximum Tractive Effort:** 400kN (90 000lbf)
Continuous Rating: 7000 kW (9387 h.p.).
Maximum Rail Power: **Multiple Working:** TDM system.
Brake Force: 50 t.   **Dimensions:** 22.01 x 2.97 x 4.20 m.
Weight: 132 t.   **Wheel Diameter:** 1090 mm.
Design Speed: 175 km/h (100 m.p.h.)   **Maximum Speed:** 160 km/h (87 m.p.h.).
Train Supply: Electric.   **Train Brakes:** Air.

9701	**EB**	ET	EU
9702	**EB**	ET	EU
9703	**EB**	ET	EU
9704	**EB**	ET	EU
9705	**EB**	ET	EU
9706	**EB**	ET	EU
9707	**EB**	ET	EU

2. LOCO-HAULED PASSENGER COACHING STOCK

INTRODUCTION

LAYOUT OF INFORMATION

Coaches are listed in numerical order of painted number in batches according to type.

Each coach entry is laid out as in the following example (former number column may be omitted where not applicable):

Number	Old No.	Detail	Livery	Owner	Operator	Depot
10216	(11041)	*	**AR**	P	*1A*	NC

Note that the operator is the organisation which facilitates the use of the coach and may not be the actual train operating company which runs the train. For example coaches operated by Riviera Trains might run in trains which are operated by Arriva Trains Wales.

DETAILED INFORMATION & CODES

Under each type heading, the following details are shown:

- "Mark" of coach (see below).
- Descriptive text.
- Number of first class seats, standard class seats, lavatory compartments and wheelchair spaces shown as F/S nT nW respectively.
- Bogie type (see below).
- Additional features.
- ETH Index.

TOPS TYPE CODES

TOPS type codes are allocated to all coaching stock. For vehicles numbered in the passenger stock number series the code consists of:

(1) Two letters denoting the layout of the vehicle as follows:

AA Gangwayed Corridor
AB Gangwayed Corridor Brake
AC Gangwayed Open (2+2 seating)
AD Gangwayed Open (2+1 seating)
AE Gangwayed Open Brake
AF Gangwayed Driving Open Brake
AG Micro-Buffet
AH Brake Micro-Buffet

AI	As "AC" but with drop-head buckeye and gangway at one end only
AJ	Restaurant Buffet with Kitchen
AK	Kitchen Car
AL	As "AC" but with disabled person's toilet (Mark 4 only)
AN	Miniature Buffet
AP	Pullman First with Kitchen
AQ	Pullman Parlour First
AR	Pullman Brake First
AS	Sleeping Car
AT	Royal Train Coach
AU	Sleeping Car with Pantry
AV	Mark 4 Barrier Vehicle
AW	EMU Translator vehicle
AX	Generator Van (1000 V DC)
AZ	Special Saloon
GS	HST Barrier Vehicle
NW	Desiro Barrier Vehicle

(2) A digit denoting the class of passenger accommodation:

1 First	4 Unclassified
2 Standard (formerly second)	5 None
3 Composite (first & standard)	

(3) A suffix relating to the build of coach.

1	Mark 1	C	Mark 2C	G	Mark 3 or 3A
Z	Mark 2	D	Mark 2D	H	Mark 3B
A	Mark 2A	E	Mark 2E	J	Mark 4
B	Mark 2B	F	Mark 2F		

OPERATING CODES

Operating codes used by train company operating staff (and others) to denote vehicle types in general. These are shown in parentheses adjacent to TOPS type codes. Letters used are:

B Brake	K Side corridor with lavatory
C Composite	O Open
F First Class	S Standard Class (formerly second)

Various other letters are in use and the meaning of these can be ascertained by referring to the titles at the head of each type.

Readers should note the distinction between an SO (Open Standard) and a TSO (Tourist Open Standard) The former has 2+1 seating layout, whilst the latter has 2+2.

BOGIE TYPES

BR Mark 1 (BR1). Double bolster leaf spring bogie. Generally 90 m.p.h., but Mark 1 bogies may be permitted to run at 100 m.p.h. with special maintenance. Weight: 6.1 t.
BR Mark 2 (BR2). Single bolster leaf-spring bogie used on certain types of

non-passenger stock and suburban stock (all now withdrawn). Weight: 5.3 t.

COMMONWEALTH (C). Heavy, cast steel coil spring bogie. 100 m.p.h. Weight: 6.75 t.

B4. Coil spring fabricated bogie. Generally 100 m.p.h., but B4 bogies may be permitted to run at 110 m.p.h. with special maintenance. Weight: 5.2 t.

B5. Heavy duty version of B4. 100 m.p.h. Weight: 5.3 t.

B5 (SR). A bogie originally used on Southern Region EMUs, similar in design to B5. Now also used on locomotive hauled coaches. 100 m.p.h.

BT10. A fabricated bogie designed for 125 m.p.h. Air suspension.

T4. A 125 m.p.h. bogie designed by BREL (now Bombardier Transportation).

BT41. Fitted to Mark 4 vehicles, designed by SIG in Switzerland. At present limited to 125 m.p.h., but designed for 140 m.p.h.

BRAKES

Air braking is now standard on British main line trains. Vehicles with other equipment are denoted:

v   Vacuum braked.
x   Dual braked (air and vacuum).

HEATING & VENTILATION

Electric heating and ventilation is now standard on British main-line trains. Certain coaches for use on charter services may also have steam heating facilities, or be steam heated only.

PUBLIC ADDRESS

It is assumed all coaches are now fitted with public address equipment, although certain stored vehicles may not have this feature. In addition, it is assumed all vehicles with a conductor's compartment have public address transmission facilities, as have catering vehicles.

COOKING EQUIPMENT

It is assumed that Mark 1 catering vehicles have gas powered cooking equipment, whilst Mark 2, 3 and 4 catering vehicles have electric powered cooking equipment unless stated otherwise.

ADDITIONAL FEATURE CODES

d   Secondary door locking.
dg   Driver–Guard communication equipment.
f   Facelifted or fluorescent lighting.
k   Composition brake blocks (instead of cast iron).
n   Day/night lighting.
p   Public telephone.
pg   Public address transmission and driver-guard communication.
pt   Public address transmission facility.

q   Catering staff to shore telephone.
w   Wheelchair space.
z   Disabled persons' toilet.
★   Blue star multiple working cables fitted.

Standard class coaches with wheelchair space also have one tip-up seat per space.

NOTES ON ETH INDICES

The sum of ETH indices in a train must not be more than the ETH index of the locomotive. The normal voltage on British trains is 1000 V. Suffix 'X' denotes 600 amp wiring instead of 400 amp. Trains whose ETH index is higher than 66 must be formed completely of 600 amp wired stock. Class 33 and 73 locomotives cannot provide a suitable electric train supply for Mark 2D, Mark 2E, Mark 2F, Mark 3, Mark 3A, Mark 3B or Mark 4 coaches. Class 55 locomotives provide an e.t.s. directly from one of their traction generators into the train line. Consequently voltage fluctuations can result in motor-alternator flashover. Thus these locomotives are not suitable for use with Mark 2D, Mark 2E, Mark 2F, Mark 3, Mark 3A, Mark 3B or Mark 4 coaches unless modified motor-alternators are fitted. Such motor alternators were fitted to Mark 2D and 2F coaches used on the East Coast main line, but few remain fitted.

BUILD DETAILS

Lot Numbers
Vehicles ordered under the auspices of BR were allocated a lot (batch) number when ordered and these are quoted in class headings and sub-headings.

Builders
These are shown for each lot. Abbreviations used are found in section 7.8.

Information on sub-contracting works which built parts of vehicles e.g. the underframes etc. is not shown.
In addition to the above, certain vintage Pullman cars were built or rebuilt at the following works:

Metropolitan Carriage & Wagon Company, Birmingham (Now Alstom)
Midland Carriage & Wagon Company, Birmingham
Pullman Car Company, Preston Park, Brighton
Conversions have also been carried out at the Railway Technical Centre, Derby, LNWR, Crewe and Blakes Fabrications, Edinburgh.

Vehicle Numbers
Where a coach has been renumbered, the former number is shown in parentheses. If a coach has been renumbered more than once, the original number is shown first in parentheses, followed by the most recent previous number. Where the former number of a coach due to be converted or renumbered is known and the conversion and/or renumbering has not yet taken place, the coach is listed under both current number (with depot allocation) and under new number (without allocation).

Numbering Systems
Seven different numbering systems were in use on BR. These were the BR

series, the four pre-nationalisation companies' series', the Pullman Car Company's series and the UIC (International Union of Railways) series. BR number series coaches and former Pullman Car Company series are listed separately. There is also a separate listing of 'Saloon' type vehicles which are registered to run on National Rail. Please note the Mark 2 Pullman vehicles were ordered after the Pullman Car Company had been nationalised and are therefore numbered in the BR series.

THE DEVELOPMENT OF BR STANDARD COACHES

The standard BR coach built from 1951 to 1963 was the Mark 1. This type features a separate underframe and body. The underframe is normally 64 ft. 6 in. long, but certain vehicles were built on shorter (57 ft.) frames. Tungsten lighting was standard and until 1961, BR Mark 1 bogies were generally provided. In 1959 Lot No. 30525 (TSO) appeared with fluorescent lighting and melamine interior panels, and from 1961 onwards Commonwealth bogies were fitted in an attempt to improve the quality of ride which became very poor when the tyre profiles on the wheels of the BR1 bogies became worn. Later batches of TSO and BSO retained the features of Lot No. 30525, but compartment vehicles – whilst utilising melamine panelling in standard class – still retained tungsten lighting. Wooden interior finish was retained in first class vehicles where the only change was to fluorescent lighting in open vehicles (except Lot No. 30648, which had tungsten lighting). In later years many Mark 1 coaches had BR 1 bogies replaced by B4.

In 1964, a new prototype train was introduced. Known as 'XP64', it featured new seat designs, pressure heating & ventilation, aluminium compartment doors and corridor partitions, foot pedal operated toilets and B4 bogies. The vehicles were built on standard Mark 1 underframes. Folding exterior doors were fitted, but these proved troublesome and were later replaced with hinged doors. All XP64 coaches have been withdrawn, but some have been preserved. The prototype Mark 2 vehicle (W 13252) was produced in 1963. This was an FK of semi-integral construction and had pressure heating & ventilation, tungsten lighting, and was mounted on B4 bogies. This vehicle has been preserved by the National Railway Museum and is currently stored at MoD Kineton DM. The production build was similar, but wider windows were used. The TSO and SO vehicles used a new seat design similar to that in the XP64 and fluorescent lighting was provided. Interior finish reverted to wood. Mark 2 vehicles were built from 1964–66.

The Mark 2A design, built 1967–68, incorporated the remainder of the features first used in the XP64 coaches, i.e. foot pedal operated toilets (except BSO), new first class seat design, aluminium compartment doors and partitions together with fluorescent lighting in first class compartments. Folding gangway doors (lime green coloured) were used instead of the traditional one-piece variety.

The following list summarises the changes made in the later Mark 2 variants:

Mark 2B: Wide wrap around doors at vehicle ends, no centre doors, slightly longer body. In standard class, one toilet at each end instead of two at one end as previously. Red folding gangway doors.

Mark 2C: Lowered ceiling with twin strips of fluorescent lighting and ducting for air conditioning, but air conditioning not fitted.

Mark 2D: Air conditioning. No opening top-lights in windows.

Mark 2E: Smaller toilets with luggage racks opposite. Fawn folding gangway doors.

Mark 2F: Plastic interior panels. Inter-City 70 type seats. Modified air conditioning system.

The Mark 3 design has BT10 bogies, is 75 ft. (23 m.) long and is of fully integral construction with Inter-City 70 type seats. Gangway doors were yellow (red in RFB) when new, although these are being changed on refurbishment. Loco-hauled coaches are classified Mark 3A, Mark 3 being reserved for HST trailers. A new batch of FO and BFO, classified Mark 3B, was built in 1985 with Advanced Passenger Train-style seating and revised lighting. The last vehicles in the Mark 3 series were the driving brake vans built for West Coast Main Line services.

The Mark 4 design was built by Metro-Cammell for use on the East Coast Main Line after electrification and features a body profile suitable for tilting trains, although tilt is not fitted, and is not intended to be. This design is suitable for 140 m.p.h. running, although is restricted to 125 m.p.h. because the signalling system on the route is not suitable for the higher speed. The bogies for these coaches were built by SIG in Switzerland and are designated BT41. Power operated sliding plug exterior doors are standard. These coaches are now being rebuilt with completely new interiors and are referred to as "Mallard stock" by GNER.

2.1. BR NUMBER SERIES STOCK
PASSENGER STOCK

AJ11 (RF) RESTAURANT FIRST

Mark 1. Spent most of its life as a Royal Train vehicle and was numbered 2907 for a time. Built with Commonwealth bogies, but B5 bogies substituted. 24/–. ETH 2.

Lot No. 30633 Swindon 1961. 41 t.

| 325 | **PC** | VS | *VS* | SL | |

AP1Z (PFK) PULLMAN FIRST WITH KITCHEN

Mark 2. Pressure Ventilated. Seating removed and replaced with servery. 2T. B5 bogies. ETH 6.

Lot No. 30755 Derby 1966. 40 t.

| 504 | **PC** | WC | *WC* | CS | ULLSWATER |
| 506 | **PC** | WC | *WC* | CS | WINDERMERE |

AQ1Z (PFP) PULLMAN PARLOUR FIRST

Mark 2. Pressure Ventilated. 36/– 2T. B4 bogies. ETH 5.

Lot No. 30754 Derby 1966. 35 t.

546	**PC**	WC	*WC*	CS	CONISTON WATER
548	**PC**	WC	*WC*	CS	GRASMERE
549	**PC**	WC	*WC*	CS	BASSENTHWAITE
550	**PC**	WC	*WC*	CS	RYDAL WATER
551	**PC**	WC	*WC*	CS	BUTTERMERE
552	**PC**	WC	*WC*	CS	ENNERDALE WATER
553	**PC**	WC	*WC*	CS	CRUMMOCK WATER

AR1Z (PFB) PULLMAN BRAKE FIRST

Mark 2. Pressure Ventilated. 30/– 2T. B4 bogies. ETH 4.

Lot No. 30753 Derby 1966. 35 t.

| 586 | **PC** | WC | *WC* | CS | DERWENTWATER |

AJ21 (RG)   GRIDDLE CAR

Mark 1. Rebuilt from RF. –/30. B5 bogies. ETH 2.

This vehicle was numbered DB975878 for a time when in departmental service for British Railways.

Lot No. 30013 Doncaster 1952. Rebuilt Wolverton 1965. 40 t.

1105	(302)	v	**G**	MH	*MH*	RL

AJ1F (RFB)   BUFFET OPEN FIRST

Mark 2F. Air conditioned. Converted 1988–9/91 at BREL, Derby from Mark 2F FOs. 1200/1/3/6/11/14–16/20/21/50/2/5/6/9 have Stones equipment, others have Temperature Ltd. 25/– 1T 1W (except 1253 which is 26/– 1T). B4 bogies. p. q. d. ETH 6X.

1200/3/6/11/14/16/20/52/5/6. Lot No. 30845 Derby 1973. 33 t.
1201/4/5/7/8/10/12/13/15/18/19/21/50/1/4/8/60. Lot No. 30859 Derby 1973–74. 33 t.
1202/9/53/8. Lot No. 30873 Derby 1974–75. 33 t.

† Fitted with new m.a. sets.

1200	(3287, 6459)	†	**RV**	H	*RV*	CP
1201	(3361, 6445)		**V**	H		TM
1202	(3436, 6456)	†	**V**	H		KT
1203	(3291)	†		H	*RV*	CP
1204	(3401)	†	**V**	H		PY
1205	(3329, 6438)	†	**V**	AE		ZA
1206	(3319)	†	**V**	H		KT
1207	(3328, 6422)	†	**V**	H		KT
1208	(3393)		**V**	H		KT
1209	(3437, 6457)	†	**V**	H		KT
1210	(3405, 6462)	†	**V**	H		KT
1211	(3305)			H	*FM*	OY
1212	(3427, 6453)	†	**V**	H	*RV*	CP
1213	(3419)	†	**V**	H		KT
1214	(3317, 6433)		**AR**	H	*1A*	NC
1215	(3377)		**AR**	H	*1A*	NC
1216	(3302)	†	**V**	H	*RV*	CP
1218	(3332)		**AR**	H	*1A*	NC
1219	(3418)		**AR**	H	*1A*	NC
1220	(3315, 6432)	†	**CS**	H	*SR*	IS
1221	(3371)			H	*FM*	OY
1250	(3372)	†	**V**	H	*RV*	CP
1251	(3383)	†	**V**	H		KT
1252	(3280)	†	**V**	H		KT
1253	(3432)	†	**V**	H		KT
1254	(3391)	†	**V**	H	*FM*	OY
1255	(3284)	†	**V**	H		KT
1256	(3296)	†		H	*FM*	OY

1258	(3322)	†	**V**	H	*RV*	CP
1259	(3439)	†	**V**	H		KT
1260	(3378)	†	**V**	H	*RV*	CP

AK51 (RKB)   KITCHEN BUFFET

Mark 1. No seats. B5 bogies. ETH 1.

Lot No. 30624 Cravens 1960–61. 41 t.

| 1566 | **VN** VS *VS* CP |

AJ41 (RBR)   RESTAURANT BUFFET

Mark 1. Built with 23 loose chairs. All remaining vehicles refurbished with 23 fixed polypropylene chairs and fluorescent lighting. ETH 2 (2X*). 1683/92/99 were further refurbished with 21 chairs, payphone, wheelchair space and carpets.

s Modified for use as servery vehicle with seating removed.

1646–1699. Lot No. 30628 Pressed Steel 1960–61. Commonwealth bogies. 39 t.
1730. Lot No. 30512 BRCW 1960–61. B5 bogies. 37 t.

Non-standard Livery: 1651, 1657, 1683 and 1699 are Oxford blue.

1646			FM		RD		1680	*s	**GC**	E	*E*	OM
1651	**0**		RV		CO		1683	s	**0**	RV	*RV*	CP
1657	**0**		FM	*FM*	OY		1692	s	**CH**	RV	*RV*	CP
1658	**BG**		E	*E*	OM		1696		**G**	E	*E*	OM
1659	s	**PC**	WT	*WT*	OM		1698	s	**GC**	E	*E*	OM
1671	x*	**M**	E	*E*	OM		1699	s	**0**	RV	*RV*	CP
1674			E		BN		1730	x	**M**	BK	*BK*	BT
1679	s	**GC**	E	*E*	OM

AN2F (RSS)   SELF-SERVICE BUFFET CAR

Mark 2F. Air conditioned. Temperature Ltd. equipment. Inter-City 70 seats. Converted 1974 from a Mark 2F TSO as a prototype self-service buffet for APT-P. Sold to Northern Ireland Railways 1983 and regauged to 5'3". Since withdrawn, repatriated to Great Britain and converted back to standard gauge. –/24. B5 bogies. ETH 12X.

Lot No. 30860 Derby 1973–74. 33 t.

| 1800 | (5970, NIR546) | **PC** WT *WT* OM |

AN21 (RMB)   MINIATURE BUFFET CAR

Mark 1. –/44 2T. These vehicles are basically an open standard with two full window spaces removed to accommodate a buffet counter, and four seats removed to allow for a stock cupboard. All remaining vehicles now have fluorescent lighting. Commonwealth bogies. ETH 3.

1813–1832. Lot No. 30520 Wolverton 1960. 38 t.
1840–1842. Lot No. 30507 Wolverton 1960. 37 t.
1859–1863. Lot No. 30670 Wolverton 1961–62. 38 t.
1882. Lot No. 30702 Wolverton 1962. 38 t.

1842 has been refurbished and fitted with a microwave oven and payphone.

1813	x	**M**	E	*E*	OM		1860	x	**M**	WC *WC*	CS
1832	x	**G**	E	*E*	OM		1861	x	**M**	WC *WC*	CS
1840	v	**G**	FM	*FM*	RL		1863	x	**CH**	RV *RV*	CP
1842	x	**CH**	RV	*RV*	CP		1882	x	**M**	WC *WC*	CS
1859	x	**M**	BK	*BK*	BT						

AJ41 (RBR)   RESTAURANT BUFFET

Mark 1. These vehicles were built as unclassified restaurant (RU). They were rebuilt with buffet counters and 23 fixed polypropylene chairs (RBS), then further refurbished by fitting fluorescent lighting and reclassified RBR. ETH 2X.

s Modified for use as servery vehicle with seating removed.

1953. Lot No. 30575 Swindon 1960. B4/B5 bogies. 36.5 t.
1961. Lot No. 30632 Swindon 1961. Commonwealth bogies. 39 t.

1953	s	**VN**	VS	*VS*	CP		1961	v	**G**	FM *FM*	RL

AU51   CHARTER TRAIN STAFF COACHES

Mark 1. Converted from BCKs in 1988. Commonwealth bogies. ETH 2.

Lot No. 30732 Derby 1964. 37 t.

2833	(21270)	**BG**	E	*E*	OM
2834	(21267)	**GC**	E	*E*	OM

AT5G   HM THE QUEEN'S SALOON

Mark 3. Converted from a FO built 1972. Consists of a lounge, bedroom and bathroom for HM The Queen, and a combined bedroom and bathroom for the Queen's dresser. One entrance vestibule has double doors. Air conditioned. BT10 bogies. ETH 9X.

Lot No. 30886 Wolverton 1977. 36 t.

2903	(11001)	**RP**	NR	*RP*	ZN

AT5G HRH THE DUKE OF EDINBURGH'S SALOON

Mark 3. Converted from a TSO built 1972. Consists of a combined lounge/dining room, a bedroom and a shower room for the Duke, a kitchen and a valet's bedroom and bathroom. Air conditioned. BT10 bogies. ETH 15X.

Lot No. 30887 Wolverton 1977. 36 t.

2904	(12001)	**RP**	NR	*RP*	ZN

AT5G   ROYAL HOUSEHOLD SLEEPING CAR

Mark 3A. Built to similar specification as SLE 10646–732. 12 sleeping compartments for use of Royal Household with a fixed lower berth and a hinged upper berth. 2T plus shower room. Air conditioned. BT10 bogies. ETH 11X.

Lot No. 31002 Derby/Wolverton 1985. 44 t.

| 2915 | | **RP** | NR | *RP* | ZN |

AT5G   ROYAL KITCHEN/DINING CAR

Mark 3. Converted from HST TRUK built 1976. Large kitchen retained, but dining area modified for Royal use seating up to 14 at central table(s). Air conditioned. BT10 bogies. ETH 13X.

Lot No. 31059 Wolverton 1988. 43 t.

| 2916 | (40512) | **RP** | NR | *RP* | ZN |

AT5G ROYAL HOUSEHOLD KITCHEN/DINING CAR

Mark 3. Converted from HST TRUK built 1977. Large kitchen retained and dining area slightly modified with seating for 22 Royal Household members. Air conditioned. BT10 bogies. ETH 13X.

Lot No. 31084 Wolverton 1990. 43 t.

| 2917 | (40514) | **RP** | NR | *RP* | ZN |

AT5G   ROYAL HOUSEHOLD CARS

Mark 3. Converted from HST TRUKs built 1976/7. Air conditioned. BT10 bogies. ETH 10X.

Lot Nos. 31083 (31085*) Wolverton 1989. 41.05 t.

| 2918 | (40515) | | **RP** | NR | | ZN |
| 2919 | (40518) | * | **RP** | NR | | ZN |

AT5B   ROYAL HOUSEHOLD COUCHETTES

Mark 2B. Converted from BFK built 1969. Consists of luggage accommodation, guard's compartment, workshop area, 350 kW diesel generator and staff sleeping accommodation. B5 bogies. ETH2X.

Lot No. 31044 Wolverton 1986. 48 t.

| 2920 | (14109, 17109) | **RP** | NR | *RP* | ZN |

Mark 2B. Converted from BFK built 1969. Consists of luggage accommodation, kitchen, brake control equipment and staff accommodation. B5 bogies. ETH7X.

Lot No. 31086 Wolverton 1990. 41.5 t.

| 2921 | (14107, 17107) | **RP** | NR | *RP* | ZN |

AT5G HRH THE PRINCE OF WALES'S SLEEPING CAR

Mark 3B. BT10 bogies. Air conditioned.ETH 7X.

Lot No. 31035 Derby/Wolverton 1987.

2922   **RP**   NR   *RP*   ZN

AT5G   HRH THE PRINCE OF WALES'S SALOON

Mark 3B. BT10 bogies. Air conditioned. ETH 6X.

Lot No. 31036 Derby/Wolverton 1987.

2923   **RP**   NR   *RP*   ZN

AD11 (FO)   OPEN FIRST

Mark 1. 42/– 2T. ETH 3. Many now fitted with table lamps.

3063–3069. Lot No. 30169 Doncaster 1955. B4 bogies. 33 t.
3096–3100. Lot No. 30576 BRCW 1959. B4 bogies. 33 t.

3064 and 3068 were numbered DB 975607 and DB 975606 for a time when in
departmental service for British Railways.

3063	**BG**	VS		SL	3096	x **M**	BK	*BK*	BT
3064	**BG**	VS		SL	3097	x **CH**	RV	*RV*	CP
3066	**RV**	RV	*RV*	CP	3098	x **CH**	RV	*RV*	CP
3068	**RV**	RV	*RV*	CP	3100	x **M**	E	*E*	OM
3069	**RV**	RV	*RV*	CP					

Later design with fluorescent lighting, aluminium window frames and
Commonwealth bogies.

3105–3128. Lot No. 30697 Swindon 1962–63. 36 t.
3130–3150. Lot No. 30717 Swindon 1963. 36 t.

3128/36/41/3/4/6/7/8 were renumbered 1058/60/3/5/6/8/9/70 when reclassified
RUO, then 3600/5/8/9/2/6/4/10 when declassified, but have since regained their
original numbers. 3136 was numbered DB977970 for a time when in use with
Serco Railtest as a Brake Force Runner.

3105	x **M**	WC	*WC*	CS	3123	**GC**	E	*E*	OM
3107	x **CH**	RV	*RV*	CP	3124	**G**	E	*E*	OM
3110	x **M**	E	*E*	OM	3127	**G**	E	*E*	OM
3112	x **CH**	RV	*RV*	CP	3128	x **M**	WC	*WC*	CS
3113	x **M**	WC	*WC*	CS	3130	v **M**	WC	*WC*	CS
3114	**G**	E	*E*	BN	3131	x **M**	E	*E*	OM
3115	x **BG**	E		BN	3132	x **M**	E	*E*	OM
3117	x **M**	WC	*WC*	CS	3133	x **M**	E	*E*	OM
3119	x **GC**	E	*E*	OM	3136	**M**	WC	*WC*	CS
3120	**GC**	E	*E*	OM	3140	x **CH**	RV	*RV*	CP
3121	**GC**	E	*E*	OM	3141	**GC**	E	*E*	OM
3122	x **CH**	RV	*RV*	CP	3143	**M**	WC	*WC*	CS

3144	x	**M**	E	*E*	OM		3148		**BG**	RV	*RV*	CP
3146		**GC**	E	*E*	OM		3149		**GC**	E	*E*	OM
3147		**GC**	E	*E*	OM		3150		**G**	E		BN

AD1D (FO) OPEN FIRST

Mark 2D. Air conditioned. Stones equipment. 42/– 2T. B4 bogies. ETH 5.

† Interior modified to resemble a Pullman Car with new seating, tungsten lighting and table lights for VSOE "Northern Belle".

Lot No. 30821 Derby 1971–72. 34 t.

3174	†	**VN**	VS	*VS*	CP		3186			MA		DY
3181		**RV**	RV	*RV*	CP		3188		**RV**	RV	*RV*	CP
3182	†	**VN**	VS	*VS*	CP							

AD1E (FO) OPEN FIRST

Mark 2E. Air conditioned. Stones equipment. 42/– 2T (41/– 2T 1W w, 36/– 2T p). B4 bogies. ETH 5.

r Refurbished with new seats.
u Fitted with power supply for Mk. 1 RBR.
† Interior modified to resemble a Pullman Car with new seating, tungsten lighting and table lights for VSOE "Northern Belle".

3255 was numbered 3525 for a time when fitted with a pantry.

Lot No. 30843 Derby 1972–73. 32.5 t. (35.8 t. †).

3223		**RV**	RV	*RV*	CP		3246	p	**PC**	RA	*WT*	OM
3228	du	**RV**	H	*RV*	CP		3247	†	**VN**	VS	*VS*	CP
3229	d	**RV**	H	*RV*	CP		3255	dr	**FP**	H	*GW*	OO
3231	p	**PC**	RA	*WT*	OM		3261	dw	**FP**	H	*RV*	CP
3232	dr	**FP**	H	*GW*	OO		3267	†	**VN**	VS	*VS*	CP
3240		**RV**	RV	*RV*	CP		3269	dr	**FP**	H	*GW*	OO
3241	dr	**FP**	H	*GW*	OO		3273	†	**VN**	VS	*VS*	CP
3244	d	**RV**	H	*RV*	CP		3275	†	**VN**	VS	*VS*	CP

AD1F (FO) OPEN FIRST

Mark 2F. Air conditioned. 3277–3318/58–81 have Stones equipment, others have Temperature Ltd. 42/– 2T. All now refurbished with power-operated vestibule doors, new panels and new seat trim. B4 bogies. d. ETH 5X.

3277–3318. Lot No. 30845 Derby 1973. 33.5 t.
3325–3428. Lot No. 30859 Derby 1973–74. 33.5 t.
3429–3438. Lot No. 30873 Derby 1974–75. 33.5 t.

r Further refurbished with table lamps, modified seats with burgundy seat trim and new m.a. sets.
s Further refurbished with table lamps and modified seats with burgundy seat trim.
u Fitted with power supply for Mk. 1 RBR.

3403 was numbered 6450 for a time when declassified.

3277	**AR**	H	*1A*	NC
3278 r	**V**	H		OY
3279 u	**AR**	H	*1A*	NC
3285 s	**V**	H		OY
3290	**AR**	H	*1A*	NC
3292		H	*1A*	NC
3295	**AR**	H	*1A*	NC
3299 r	**V**	H	·	KT
3300 s	**V**	H		OM
3303	**AR**	H	*1A*	NC
3304 r	**V**	H	*RV*	CP
3309		H	*1A*	NC
3312		H	*FM*	OY
3313 r	**V**	H		KT
3314 r	**V**	H	*RV*	CP
3318		H	*1A*	NC
3325 r	**V**	H	*RV*	CP
3326 r	**V**	H		KT
3330 r	**V**	H	*RV*	CP
3331	**AR**	H	*1A*	NC
3333 r	**V**	H	*RV*	CP
3334	**AR**	H	*1A*	NC
3336 u	**AR**	H	*1A*	NC
3337 r	**V**	H		OM
3338 u	**AR**	H	*1A*	NC
3340 r	**V**	H	*RV*	CP
3344 r	**V**	H	*RV*	CP
3345 r	**V**	H	*RV*	CP
3348 r	**V**	H	*RV*	CP
3350 r	**V**	H		KT
3351	**AR**	H	*1A*	NC
3352 r	**V**	H		KT
3353 s	**V**	H		CT
3354 s	**V**	H		CT
3356 r	**V**	H	*RV*	CP
3358	**AR**	H	*1A*	NC
3359 s	**V**	FM	*FM*	OY
3360 s			FM	*FM*	OY
3362 s			FM	*FM*	OY

3363 s	**V**	H		CT
3364 r	**V**	H	*RV*	CP
3366 s	**V**	H	*FM*	OY
3368	**AR**	H	*1A*	NC
3369 s	**V**	H		CT
3373		H		BR
3374		H	*FM*	OY
3375	**AR**	H	*1A*	NC
3379 u	**AR**	H	*1A*	NC
3381		H		Bramley
3384 r	**V**	H	*RV*	CP
3385 r	**V**	H	*FM*	OY
3386 r	**V**	H	*RV*	CP
3387 s	**V**	H		CT
3388	**AR**	H	*1A*	NC
3389 s	**V**	H		CT
3390 r	**V**	H	*RV*	CP
3392 r	**V**	H		KT
3395 r	**V**	H	*FM*	OY
3397 r	**V**	H	*RV*	CP
3399 u	**AR**	H	*1A*	NC
3400	**AR**	H	*1A*	NC
3402 s	**V**	H		CT
3403 s	**V**	H		CT
3408 s	**V**	FM	*FM*	OY
3411 s	**V**	H		CT
3414	**AR**	H	*1A*	NC
3416		H	*1A*	NC
3417	**AR**	H	*1A*	NC
3424	**AR**	H	*1A*	NC
3425 s	**V**	H		CT
3426 r	**V**	H	*RV*	CP
3428 s	**V**	H		CT
3429 r	**V**	H		OM
3431 r	**V**	H		KT
3433 r	**V**	H		PY
3434 s	**V**	H		CT
3438 s	**V**	H		CT

AG1E (FO (T))   OPEN FIRST (PANTRY)

Mark 2E. Air conditioned. Converted from FO. Fitted with pantry containing microwave oven and space for a trolley. 36/– 2T. B4 bogies. p. d. ETH 5X.

Lot No. 30843 Derby 1972–73. 32.5 t.

3520	(3253)	**FP**	H	BR
3521	(3271)	**AR**	H	BR
3522	(3236)	**FP**	H	BR

3523	(3238)		H	BR
3524	(3254)		H	BR

AC21 (TSO) OPEN STANDARD

Mark 1. These vehicles have 2+2 seating and are classified TSO ('Tourist second open'– a former LNER designation). –/64 2T. ETH 4.

3766. Lot No. 30079 York 1953. Commonwealth bogies (originally built with BR Mark 1 bogies). This coach has narrower seats than later vehicles. 36 t.

3766 x   **M**   WC *WC*   CS

AC21 (TSO) OPEN STANDARD

Mark 1. These vehicles are a development of the above with fluorescent lighting and modified design of seat headrest. Built with BR Mark 1 bogies. –/64 2T. ETH 4.

4831–4836. Lot No. 30506 Wolverton 1959. Commonwealth bogies. 33 t.
4856. Lot No. 30525 Wolverton 1959–60. B4 bogies. 33 t.

4831	x	**M**	BK *BK*	BT	4836	x	**M**	BK *BK*	BT
4832	x	**M**	BK *BK*	BT	4856	x	**M**	BK *BK*	BT

Lot No. 30646 Wolverton 1961. Built with Commonwealth bogies, but BR Mark 1 bogies substituted by the SR. All now re-rebogied. 34 t B4, 36 t C.

4902	x B4	**CH**	RV *RV*	CP	4912	x C	**M**	WC *WC*	CS
4905	x C	**M**	WC *WC*	CS					

Lot No. 30690 Wolverton 1961–62. Commonwealth bogies and aluminium window frames. 37 t.

4925		**G**	E	*E*	OM	4996	x **M**	E	*E*	OM
4927	x	**CH**	RV	*RV*	CP	4998	**BG**	E	*E*	OM
4931	v	**M**	WC	*WC*	CS	4999	**BG**	E	*E*	OM
4940	x	**M**	WC	*WC*	CS	5002	**BG**	E	*E*	OM
4946	x	**M**	E	*E*	OM	5005	**BG**	E	*E*	OM
4949	x	**M**	E	*E*	OM	5007	**G**	E	*E*	OM
4951	x	**M**	WC	*WC*	CS	5008	x **M**	E	*E*	OM
4954	v	**M**	WC	*WC*	CS	5009	x **CH**	RV	*RV*	CP
4956		**BG**	E	*E*	OM	5023	**G**	E	*E*	OM
4958	v	**M**	WC	*WC*	CS	5027	**G**	E	*E*	OM
4959		**BG**	E	*E*	OM	5028	x **M**	BK	*BK*	BT
4960	x	**M**	WC	*WC*	CS	5032	x **M**	WC	*WC*	CS
4973	x	**M**	WC	*WC*	CS	5033	x **M**	WC	*WC*	CS
4977		**G**	E		BN	5035	x **M**	WC	*WC*	CS
4984	x	**M**	WC	*WC*	CS	5037	**G**	E	*E*	OM
4986		**G**	E	*E*	OM	5040	x **CH**	RV	*RV*	CP
4991		**BG**	E	*E*	OM	5044	x **M**	WC	*WC*	CS
4994	x	**M**	WC	*WC*	CS					

AC2Z (TSO) OPEN STANDARD

Mark 2. Pressure ventilated. –/64 2T. B4 bogies. ETH 4.

Lot No. 30751 Derby 1965–67. 32 t.

5125	v	**G**	FM	*FM*	RL
5141	f	**G**	FM		RL
5148	v	**RR**	H		TM
5157	v	**CH**	H	*VT*	TM
5171	v	**G**	FM	*FM*	RL
5177	v	**CH**	H	*VT*	TM
5179	v	**RR**	H		TM
5183	v	**RR**	H		TM
5186	v	**RR**	H		TM
5191	v	**CH**	H	*VT*	TM
5193	v	**LN**	H		TM
5194	v	**RR**	H		TM
5198	v	**CH**	H	*VT*	TM
5199	v	**G**	FM		RL
5200	v	**G**	FM	*FM*	RL
5212	v	**LN**	H		TM
5216	v	**G**	FM	*FM*	RL
5221	v	**RR**	H		TM
5222	v	**G**	FM	*FM*	RL

AD2Z (SO) OPEN STANDARD

Mark 2. Pressure ventilated. –/48 2T. B4 bogies. ETH 4.

Lot No. 30752 Derby 1966. 32 t.

5229		**PC**	WT	*WT*	OM
5236	v	**G**	FM	*FM*	RL
5237	v	**G**	FM	*FM*	RL
5239		**PC**	WT	*WT*	OM
5249	v	**G**	FM	*FM*	RL

AC2A (TSO) OPEN STANDARD

Mark 2A. Pressure ventilated. –/64 2T (–/62 2T w). B4 bogies. ETH 4.

5276–5341. Lot No. 30776 Derby 1967–68. 32 t.
5350–5419. Lot No. 30787 Derby 1968. 32 t.

f Facelifted vehicles.

5276	f	**RV**	RV	*RV*	CP
5278		**PC**	WT	*WT*	OM
5292	f	**RV**	RV	*RV*	CP
5299		**M**	WC	*WC*	CS
5309		**CH**	RV	*RV*	CP
5322	f	**RV**	RV	*RV*	CP
5331		**RR**	E		TO
5341	f	**RV**	RV	*RV*	CP
5350		**RV**	RV	*RV*	CP
5365		**RV**	RV	*RV*	CP
5366	f	**RV**	RV	*RV*	CP
5376		**RV**	RV	*RV*	CP
5386	w	**RR**	E		TO
5412	w	**M**	BK		CO
5419	w	**PC**	WT	*WT*	OM

AC2B (TSO) OPEN STANDARD

Mark 2B. Pressure ventilated. –/62 2T. B4 bogies. ETH 4.

Note: 5482 was numbered DB977936 for a time when in departmental service for British Railways.

Lot No. 30791 Derby 1969. 32 t.

5453	d	**M**	WC	*WC*	CS
5463	d	**M**	WC	*WC*	CS

| 5478 | d | **M** | WC | *WC* | CS | 5487 | d | **M** | WC | *WC* | CS |
| 5482 | | **G** | RP | *E* | OM | 5491 | d | **M** | WC | *WC* | CS |

AC2C (TSO)   OPEN STANDARD

Mark 2C. Pressure ventilated. –/62 2T. B4 bogies. ETH 4.

Lot No. 30795 Derby 1969–70. 32 t.

| 5569 | d | **M** | WC | *WC* | CS | 5600 | | **M** | WC | *WC* | CS |

AC2D (TSO)   OPEN STANDARD

Mark 2D. Air conditioned. Stones equipment. –/62 2T. B4 bogies. ETH 5.

r Refurbished with new seats and end luggage stacks. –/58 2T.

Lot No. 30822 Derby 1971. 33 t.

5631	dr	**FP**	H	*GW*	OO	5700	dr	**FP**	H	*GW*	OO
5632	dr	**FP**	H	*GW*	OO	5704		**M**	WC	*WC*	CS
5636	dr	**FP**	H	*GW*	OO	5710	dr	**FP**	H	*GW*	OO
5647		**RV**	RV	*RV*	CP	5714		**M**	WC	*WC*	CS
5657	dr	**FP**	H	*GW*	OO	5727		**M**	WC	*WC*	CS
5669	dr	**FP**	H	*GW*	OO	5737	dr	**FP**	H	*GW*	OO
5679	dr	**FP**	H	*GW*	OO	5740	dr	**FP**	H	*GW*	OO

AC2E (TSO)   OPEN STANDARD

Mark 2E. Air conditioned. Stones equipment. –/64 2T (w –/62 2T 1W). B4 bogies.
d (except 5756). ETH 5.

5744–5801. Lot No. 30837 Derby 1972. 33.5 t.
5810–5906. Lot No. 30844 Derby 1972–73. 33.5 t.

r Refurbished with new interior panelling.
s Refurbished with new interior panelling, modified design of seat headrest
and centre luggage stack. –/60 2T (w –/58 2T 1W).
t Refurbished with new interior panelling and new seats.

5744		**FP**	H		BR	5784	r		**V**	H		KT
5745	s	**V**	H		KT	5787	s		**V**	H		KT
5746	r	**V**	H		KT	5788	r			H	*FM*	OY
5748	r pt		H	*RV*	CP	5789	r pt			H	*FM*	OY
5750	s	**V**	H		KT	5791	wr			H	*RV*	CP
5752	wrpt		H	*RV*	CP	5792	r			H	*RV*	CP
5754	ws	**V**	H		KT	5793	wspt	**V**	H		KT
5756		**M**	WC	*WC*	CS	5794	wr			H	*RV*	CP
5769	r		H	*RV*	CP	5796	wr			H	*RV*	CP
5773	s pt	**V**	H	*RV*	CP	5797	r★			H	*FM*	BH
5775	s	**V**	H		KT	5800		**AR**	H	*1A*	NC
5776	r		H	*RV*	CP	5801	r	**V**	H		KT
5778		**AR**	H	*1A*	NC	5810	s	**V**	H		KT
5779	r		H	*FM*	OY	5812	wr			H	*FM*	OY
5780		**AR**	H	*1A*	NC	5814	r			H		OM

5815	ws	V	H		KT
5816	r pt		H		OM
5821	r pt	V	H		KT
5822	wspt	V	H		KT
5824	rw		H	FM	OY
5827	r		H	FM	OY
5828	ws	V	H		KT
5831		AR	H	1A	NC
5836		AR	H	1A	NC
5843	rw		H	RV	CP
5845	s	V	H		KT
5847	rw	V	H		KT
5852		AR	H	1A	NC
5853	t	M	WC	WC	CS
5859	s	V	H		KT
5863		AR	H	1A	NC
5866	r pt★		H	FM	BH
5868	s pt	V	H		KT
5869	t	M	WC	WC	CS
5874	t	M	WC	WC	CS
5876	s pt	V	H		KT
5881	ws	V	H		KT
5886	s	V	H		KT
5887	wr	AR	H	1A	NC
5888	wr		H	FM	OY
5889	s	V	H		KT
5893	s	V	H		KT
5897	r		H	FM	OY
5899	s	V	H		KT
5900	wspt	V	H		KT
5901	s	V	H		KT
5902	s	V	H		KT
5903	s	V	H		KT
5905	s	V	H	RV	CP
5906	wspt★		H	FM	BH

AC2F (TSO)   OPEN STANDARD

Mark 2F. Air conditioned. Temperature Ltd. equipment. Inter-City 70 seats.
All were refurbished in the 1980s with power-operated vestibule doors, new
panels and new seat trim. –/64 2T. (w –/62 2T 1W) B4 bogies. d. ETH 5X.

5908–5958. Lot No. 30846 Derby 1973. 33 t.
5959–6170. Lot No. 30860 Derby 1973–74. 33 t.
6171–6184. Lot No. 30874 Derby 1974–75. 33 t.

* Early Mark 2 style seats.

These vehicles have undergone a second refurbishment with carpets and
new seat trim .
r Standard refurbished vehicles with new m.a. sets.

Former Cross-Country vehicles:

s Also fitted with centre luggage stack. –/60 2T.
t Also fitted with centre luggage stack and wheelchair space. –/58 2T 1W.

Former West Coast vehicles:

u As 'r' but with two wheelchair spaces. –/60 2T 2W.
† Standard refurbished vehicles with new seat trim.

5908		V	H		KT
5910	u	V	H	RV	CP
5911	s	V	RV	AW	CF
5912	s	V	H	FM	OY
5913	s	M	WC	WC	CS
5914	u	V	H		KT
5915	r	V	H		PY
5916	t		H		KT
5917	s	V	H		KT
5918	t	V	H		KT
5919	s pt	V	H	FM	OY
5920	†	V	H		CT
5921		AR	H	1A	NC
5922		AR	H	1A	NC
5924		AR	H	1A	NC
5925	s pt★		H	FM	BH
5926			H	1A	NC
5927		AR	H	1A	NC
5928		AR	H	1A	NC
5929		AR	H	1A	NC

No.					
5930	t	**V**	H		KT
5931	†w	**V**	H	*RV*	CP
5932	r	**V**	H	*RV*	CP
5933	r	**V**	H		KT
5934	r	**V**	H	*RV*	CP
5935		**AR**	H	*1A*	NC
5936		**AR**	H	*1A*	NC
5937	r	**V**	H	*RV*	CP
5939	r	**V**	H		PY
5940	u	**V**	H		KT
5941	r	**V**	H	*RV*	CP
5943	rw	**V**	H		KT
5944		**AR**	H	*1A*	NC
5945	r	**V**	H	*RV*	CP
5946	r	**V**	H	*RV*	CP
5947	s pt	**V**	H		KT
5948	u	**V**	H	*FM*	OY
5949	u	**V**	H		KT
5950		**AR**	H	*1A*	NC
5951	r	**V**	H		KT
5952	r	**V**	H	*RV*	CP
5954		**AR**	H	*1A*	NC
5955	r	**V**	H	*RV*	CP
5956			H	*1A*	NC
5957	r	**V**	H		KT
5958	s★		H	*FM*	BH
5959	n	**AR**	H	*1A*	NC
5960	s	**V**	H	*FM*	OY
5961	s pt	**V**	RV	*AW*	CF
5962	s pt	**V**	H		KT
5963	r	**V**	H	*RV*	CP
5964		**AR**	H	*1A*	NC
5965	t	**M**	WC	*WC*	CS
5966		**AR**	H	*1A*	NC
5967	t	**V**	H		KT
5968		**AR**	H	*1A*	NC
5969	u	**V**	H	*RV*	CP
5971	s	**V**	RV	*AW*	CF
5973		**AR**	H	*1A*	NC
5975	s	**V**	H		KT
5976	t	**V**	RV	*AW*	CF
5977	r	**V**	H		KT
5978	r	**V**	H		KT
5980	r	**V**	H		KT
5981	s★		H	*FM*	BH
5983	s	**V**	H	*FM*	OY
5984	r	**V**	H	*RV*	CP
5985		**AR**	H	*1A*	NC
5986	r	**V**	H	*RV*	CP
5987	r	**V**	H	*RV*	CP
5988	r	**V**	H		KT
5989	t	**V**	H	*FM*	OY
5991	s	**V**	H	*FM*	OY
5993	*	**AR**	H	*1A*	NC
5994	r	**V**	H		KT
5995	s	**V**	H	*FM*	OY
5996	s pt	**V**	H		KT
5997	r	**V**	H	*RV*	CP
5998		**AR**	H	*1A*	NC
5999	s	**V**	H		KT
6000	t	**V**	H		KT
6001	u	**V**	H	*FM*	OY
6002	†	**V**	H		CT
6005	r	**V**	H		KT
6006		**AR**	H	*1A*	NC
6008	s	**V**	RV	*AW*	CF
6009	r	**V**	H		KT
6010	s	**V**	H		KT
6011	s	**V**	H		KT
6012	r	**V**	H		KT
6013	s	**M**	WC	*WC*	CS
6014	s pt		H		KT
6015	t	**V**	H		KT
6016	r	**V**	H		KT
6018	t	**V**	H		KT
6021	r	**V**	H		KT
6022	s	**V**	H		KT
6024	s	**V**	H		OM
6025	t	**V**	H		KT
6026	s	**V**	H		KT
6027	u	**V**	H	*RV*	CP
6028		**AR**	H	*1A*	NC
6029	r	**V**	H		KT
6030	t	**V**	H		KT
6031	r	**V**	H		KT
6034		**AR**	H	*1A*	NC
6035	t★	**AV**	E		OM
6036	*	**AR**	H	*1A*	NC
6037		**AR**	H	*1A*	NC
6038	s	**V**	H		OM
6041	s	**V**	H		KT
6042		**AR**	H	*1A*	NC
6043	†	**V**	H	*RV*	CP
6045	†w	**V**	H	*FM*	OY
6046	s	**V**	H	*FM*	OY
6047	†n*	**V**	H		CT
6049	r	**V**	H	*FM*	OY
6050	s		H		KT
6051	r	**V**	H	*RV*	CP
6052	tw		H		KT
6053	*	**AR**	H	*1A*	NC
6054	r	**V**	H	*RV*	CP

6055 †	**V**	H		KT		6142 †*	**V**	H	*RV*	CP
6056 †	**V**	H	*RV*	CP		6144 †*	**V**	H		CT
6059 s	**V**	H	*FM*	OY		6145 s pt	**V**	H		KT
6060 u	**V**	H		BH		6146 *	**AR**	H	*1A*	NC
6061 s pt	**V**	H		KT		6147 r	**V**	H		BH
6062 †	**V**	H		KT		6148 s		H		KT
6063 †w	**V**	H		CT		6149 u	**V**	H		PY
6064 s	**V**	RV	*AW*	CF		6150 s		H		KT
6065 r	**V**	H		KT		6151 †*	**V**	H	*FM*	OY
6066 s★	**AV**	E		OM		6152 *	**AR**	H	*1A*	NC
6067 s pt	**V**	RV	*AW*	CF		6153 †	**V**	H		KT
6073 s	**V**	H		KT		6154 r pt		H		KT
6100 †*	**V**	H		CT		6155 *	**AR**	H	*1A*	NC
6101 r	**V**	H	*RV*	CP		6157 s	**V**	H	*RV*	CP
6102 r	**V**	H		BH		6158 r	**V**	H	*RV*	CP
6103	**AR**	H	*1A*	NC		6159 s pt	**V**	H		KT
6104 r	**V**	H	*RV*	CP		6160 *	**AR**	H	*1A*	NC
6105 tpt	**V**	H		KT		6161 †*	**V**	H		CT
6107 r	**V**	H	*RV*	CP		6162 s pt	**V**	RV	*AW*	CF
6110		H	*1A*	NC		6163 r	**V**	H	*RV*	CP
6111 †	**V**	H	*RV*	CP		6164 r	**V**	H	*FM*	OY
6112 s pt	**V**	H		KT		6165 r	**V**	H		KT
6113 †	**V**	H	*RV*	CP		6166		H	*1A*	NC
6115 s		H		KT		6167	**AR**	H	*1A*	NC
6116 †	**V**	H		KT		6168 s★		H	*FM*	BH
6117 t★	**WX**	H	*WX*	PM		6170 s★	**AV**	E		OM
6119 s	**V**	RV	*AW*	CF		6171 †	**V**	H	*RV*	CP
6120 s	**V**	H		KT		6172 s	**V**	H		KT
6121 †	**V**	H	*FM*	OY		6173 s★	**WX**	H	*WX*	PM
6122 s★	**WX**	H	*WX*	PM		6174	**AR**	H	*1A*	NC
6123	**AR**	H	*1A*	NC		6175 r	**V**	H		KT
6124 s pt★	**AV**	E		OM		6176 t	**V**	H		OM
6134 †	**V**	H	*FM*	OY		6177 s	**V**	RV	*AW*	CF
6135 s		H		KT		6179 r	**V**	H		KT
6136 r	**V**	H		KT		6180 †w	**V**	H	*RV*	CP
6137 s pt	**V**	RV	*AW*	CF		6181 †wn	**V**	H		CT
6138 †	**V**	H	*RV*	CP		6182 s	**V**	H		KT
6139 n*		H	*1A*	NC		6183 s	**V**	RV	*AW*	CF
6141 u	**V**	H	*RV*	CP		6184 s	**V**	H		KT

AC2D (TSO)   OPEN STANDARD

Mark 2D. Air conditioned (Stones). Rebuilt from FO with new style 2+2 seats. – /58 2T. (–/58 1T*). B4 bogies. d. ETH 5X.

Lot No. 30821 Derby 1971–72. 33.5 t.

* One toilet converted to store room.

6200	(3198)	**FP**	H		BR		6203 (3180)	**FP** H		BR
6202	(3191)*	**FP**	H		KT		6206 (3183)	**FP** H		BR

6207	(3204)	**FP** H	BR	6219	(3213)	**FP** H	BR
6212	(3176)	**FP** H	BR	6221	(3173)	**FP** H	BR
6213	(3208)	**FP** H	BR	6226	(3203)	**FP** H	BR

AX51   GENERATOR VAN

Mark 1. Converted from NEA/NHA in 2003 to generator vans for use on the Southern Region power upgrade project. B5 bogies.

6260. Lot No. 30400 Pressed Steel 1957–58.
6261. Lot No. 30323 Pressed Steel 1957.
6262. Lot No. 30228 Metro-Cammell 1957–58.
6263. Lot No. 30163 Pressed Steel 1957.
6264. Lot No. 30173 York 1956.

6260	(81450, 92116)	**NR**	NR	*E*	LU
6261	(81284, 92988)	**NR**	NR	*E*	LU
6262	(81064, 92928)	**Y**	NR	*E*	LU
6263	(81231, 92961)	**Y**	NR	*E*	DY
6264	(80971, 92923)	**Y**	NR	*E*	DY

AX51   BRAKE GENERATOR VAN

Mark 1. Renumbered 1989 from BR departmental series. Converted from NDA in 1973 to three-phase supply brake generator van for use with HST trailers. Modified 1999 for use with loco-hauled stock. B5 bogies.

Lot No. 30400 Pressed Steel 1958.

6310	(81448, 975325)	**CH**	RV	*RV*	CP

AX51   GENERATOR VAN

Mark 1. Converted from NDA in 1992 to generator vans for use on Anglo-Scottish sleeping car services. Now normally used on trains hauled by steam locomotives. B4 bogies. ETH75.

6311. Lot No. 30162 Pressed Steel 1958. 37.25 t.
6312. Lot No. 30224 Cravens 1956. 37.25 t.
6313. Lot No. 30484 Pressed Steel 1958. 37.25 t.

Note: 6312 is currently on loan to Bombardier Transportation, Horbury for use in the static testing of Mark 4 stock.

6311	(80903, 92911)	**B**	E	*E*	OM
6312	(81023, 92925)	**PC**	FS		SO
6313	(81553, 92167)	**E**	P	*VS*	SL

NW51   DESIRO EMU BARRIER VEHICLE

Mark 1. Converted from GUVs with bodies removed and B4 bogies for use as Eurostar barrier vehicles but modified in 2003 by LNWR Co., Crewe for current use.

6321. Lot No. 30343 York 1957. 40 t.
6322/23. Lot No. 30616 Pressed Steel 1959–60. 40 t.
6324. Lot No. 30403 Glasgow 1958–60. 40 t.
6325. Lot No. 30417 Pressed Steel 1958–59. 40 t.

6321	(86515, 96385)	**B**	SM	*FL*	CP
6322	(86859, 96386)	**B**	SM	*FL*	CP
6323	(86973, 96387)	**B**	SM	*FL*	CP
6324	(86562, 96388)	**B**	SM	*FL*	CP
6325	(86135, 96389)	**B**	SM	*FL*	CP

GS5 (HSBV)   HST BARRIER VEHICLE

Renumbered from BR departmental series, or converted from various types. B4 bogies (Commonwealth bogies *).

6330. Mark 2A. Lot No. 30786 Derby 1968. 32 t.
6336/38/44. Mark 1. Lot No. 30715 Gloucester 1962. 31 t.
6340. Mark 1. Lot No. 30669 Swindon 1962. 36 t.
6346. Mark 2A. Lot No. 30777 Derby 1967. 31.5 t.
6348. Mark 1. Lot No. 30163 Pressed Steel 1957. 31.5 t.

6330	(14084, 975629)		**G**	A	*GW*	LA
6336	(81591, 92185)		**G**	A	*GW*	LA
6338	(81581, 92180)		**G**	A	*GW*	LA
6340	(21251, 975678)	*	**G**	A	*GW*	LA
6344	(81263, 92080)		**GN**	A	*GN*	EC
6346	(9422)		**GN**	A	*GN*	EC
6348	(81233, 92963)		**G**	A	*GW*	LA

AV5A/AV5C (MFBV) MARK 4 BARRIER VEHICLE

Mark 2A/2C. Converted from FK* or BSO. B4 bogies.

6352/3. Mark 2A. Lot No. 30774 Derby 1968. 33 t.
6354/5. Mark 2C. Lot No. 30820 Derby 1970. 32 t.
6358/9. Mark 2A. Lot No. 30788 Derby 1968. 31.5 t.

6352	(13465, 19465)	*	**GN**	H	*GN*	BN
6353	(13478, 19478)	*	**GN**	H	*GN*	BN
6354	(9459)		**GN**	H	*GN*	BN
6355	(9477)		**GN**	H	*GN*	BN
6358	(9432)		**GN**	H	*GN*	BN
6359	(9429)		**GN**	H	*GN*	BN

AW51   EMU TRANSLATOR VEHICLE

Mark 1. Converted 1992 from BG. BR Mark 1 bogies.

6364. Mark 1. Lot No. 30039 Derby 1954. 32 t.
6365. Mark 1. Lot No. 30323 Pressed Steel 1957. 32 t.

6364	(80565)	**RR**	MA	*CT*	SI
6365	(81296, 84296)	**RR**	MA	*CT*	SI

AW51   EMU TRANSLATOR VEHICLE

Mark 1. Converted 1980 from RUO. Commonwealth bogies.

Lot No. 30647 Wolverton 1959–61. 36 t.

6376	(1021, 975973)	**P**	P	*E*	CJ
6377	(1042, 975975)	**P**	P	*E*	CJ
6378	(1054, 975971)	**P**	P	*E*	CJ
6379	(1059, 975972)	**P**	P	*E*	CJ

GS51 (HSBV)   HST BARRIER VEHICLE

Mark 1. Converted from BG in 1994–5. B4 bogies.

6392. Lot No. 30715 Gloucester 1962. 29.5 t.
6393/96/97. Lot No. 30716 Gloucester 1962. 29.5 t.
6394. Lot No. 30162 Pressed Steel 1956–57. 30.5 t.
6395. Lot No. 30484 Pressed Steel 1958. 30.5 t.
6398/99. Lot No. 30400 Pressed Steel 1957–58. 30.5 t.

Non-Standard Livery: 6399 is **MA** on one side and **P** on the other.

6392	(81588, 92183)	**P**	P	*MM*	NL
6393	(81609, 92196)	**P**	P	*MM*	NL
6394	(80878, 92906)	**P**	P	*MM*	NL
6395	(81506, 92148)	**P**	MA	*MM*	NL
6396	(81607, 92195)	**P**	P	*MM*	NL
6397	(81600, 92190)	**P**	P	*MM*	NL
6398	(81471, 92126)	**P**	MA	*MM*	NL
6399	(81367, 92994)	**0**	MA	*MM*	NL

AG2C (TSOT)   OPEN STANDARD (TROLLEY)

Mark 2C. Converted from TSO by removal of one seating bay and replacing this by a counter with a space for a trolley. Adjacent toilet removed and converted to steward's washing area/store. Pressure ventilated. –/55 1T. B4 bogies. ETH 4.

Lot No. 30795 Derby 1969–70. 32.5 t.

6528	(5592)	**M**	WC	*WC*	CS

AN1F (RLO)   SLEEPER RECEPTION CAR

Mark 2F. Converted from FO, these vehicles consist of pantry, microwave cooking facilities, seating area for passengers, telephone booth and staff toilet. 6703–8 also have a bar. Converted at RTC, Derby (6700), Ilford (6701–5) and Derby (6706–8). Air conditioned. 6700/1/3/5/–8 have Stones equipment and 6702/4 have Temperature Ltd. equipment. 26/– 1T. B4 bogies. p. q. d. ETH 5X.

Advertising Livery: 6703 is "Visit Scotland" – silver with broad blue tartan stripe down one end.

6700–2/4/8. Lot No. 30859 Derby 1973–74. 33.5 t.

6703/5–7. Lot No. 30845 Derby 1973. 33.5 t.

6700	(3347)	**CS**	H	*SR*	IS
6701	(3346)	**CS**	H	*SR*	IS
6702	(3421)	**CS**	H	*SR*	IS
6703	(3308)	**AL**	H	*SR*	IS
6704	(3341)	**CS**	H	*SR*	IS
6705	(3310, 6430)	**CS**	H	*SR*	IS
6706	(3283, 6421)	**CS**	H	*SR*	IS
6707	(3276, 6418)	**CS**	H	*SR*	IS
6708	(3370)	**CS**	H	*SR*	IS

AN1D (RMBF)   MINIATURE BUFFET CAR

Mark 2D. Converted from TSOT by the removal of another seating bay and fitting a proper buffet counter with boiler and microwave oven. Now converted to first class with new seating and end luggage stacks. Air conditioned. Stones equipment. 30/– 1T. B4 bogies. p. q. d. ETH 5.

Lot No. 30822 Derby 1971. 33 t.

6720	(5622, 6652)	**FP**	H	*GW*	OO
6721	(5627, 6660)	**FP**	H	*GW*	OO
6722	(5736, 6661)	**FP**	H	*GW*	OO
6723	(5641, 6662)	**FP**	H	*GW*	OO
6724	(5721, 6665)	**FP**	H	*GW*	OO

AC2F (TSO)   OPEN STANDARD

Mark 2F. Renumbered from FO and declassified in 1985–6. Converted 1990 to TSO with mainly unidirectional seating and power-operated sliding doors. Air conditioned. 6800–14 were converted by BREL Derby and have Temperature Ltd. air conditioning. 6815–29 were converted by RFS Industries Doncaster and have Stones air conditioning. –/74 2T. B4 bogies. d. ETH 5X.

6800–07. 6810–12. 6813–14. 6819/22/28. Lot No. 30859 Derby 1973–74. 33 t.
6808–6809. Lot No. 30873 Derby 1974–75. 33.5 t.
6815–18. 6820–21. 6823–27. 6829. Lot No. 30845 Derby 1973. 33 t.

6800	(3323, 6435)	**AR**	H	*1A*	NC
6801	(3349, 6442)	**AR**	H	*1A*	NC
6802	(3339, 6439)	**AR**	H	*1A*	NC
6803	(3355, 6443)	**AR**	H	*1A*	NC
6804	(3396, 6449)		H	*1A*	NC
6805	(3324, 6436)	**AR**	H	*1A*	NC
6806	(3342, 6440)	**AR**	H	*1A*	NC
6807	(3423, 6452)		H	*1A*	NC
6808	(3430, 6454)	**AR**	H	*1A*	NC
6809	(3435, 6455)	**AR**	H	*1A*	NC
6810	(3404, 6451)	**AR**	H	*1A*	NC
6811	(3327, 6437)	**AR**	H	*1A*	NC
6812	(3394, 6448)	**AR**	H	*1A*	NC
6813	(3410, 6463)		H	*1A*	NC

6814	(3422, 6465)	**AR**	H	*1A*	NC
6815	(3282, 6420)	**AR**	H	*1A*	NC
6816	(3316, 6461)	**AR**	H	*1A*	NC
6817	(3311, 6431)	**AR**	H	*1A*	NC
6818	(3298, 6427)	**AR**	H	*1A*	NC
6819	(3365, 6446)	**AR**	H	*1A*	NC
6820	(3320, 6434)	**AR**	H	*1A*	NC
6821	(3281, 6458)	**AR**	H	*1A*	NC
6822	(3376, 6447)	**AR**	H	*1A*	NC
6823	(3289, 6424)	**AR**	H	*1A*	NC
6824	(3307, 6429)	**AR**	H	*1A*	NC
6825	(3301, 6460)	**AR**	H	*1A*	NC
6826	(3294, 6425)	**AR**	H	*1A*	NC
6827	(3306, 6428)	**AR**	H	*1A*	NC
6828	(3380, 6464)	**AR**	H	*1A*	NC
6829	(3288, 6423)	**AR**	H	*1A*	NC

AH2Z (BSOT)
OPEN BRAKE STANDARD (MICRO-BUFFET)

Mark 2. Converted from BSO by removal of one seating bay and replacing this by a counter with a space for a trolley. Adjacent toilet removed and converted to a steward's washing area/store. –/23 0T. B4 bogies. ETH 4.

Lot No. 30757 Derby 1966. 31 t.

| 9101 | (9398) | v | **CH** | H | *VT* | TM |
| 9104 | (9401) | v | **G** | FM | *FM* | RL |

AE2Z (BSO)   OPEN BRAKE STANDARD

Mark 2. These vehicles use the same body shell as the Mark 2 BFK and have first class seat spacing and wider tables. Pressure ventilated. –/31 1T. B4 bogies. ETH 4.

Lot No. 30757 Derby 1966. 31.5 t.

| 9391 | **PC** WT *WT* | OM | | 9392 | v | **G** | FM *FM* | RL |

AE2A (BSO)   OPEN BRAKE STANDARD

Mark 2A. These vehicles use the same body shell as the Mark 2A BFK and have first class seat spacing and wider tables. Pressure ventilated. –/31 1T. B4 bogies. ETH 4.

9419. Lot No. 30777 Derby 1970. 31.5 t.
9428. Lot No. 30820 Derby 1970. 31.5 t.

| 9419 | **DR** DR *DR* | KM | | 9428 | **DR** DR *DR* | KM |

AE2C (BSO)   OPEN BRAKE STANDARD

Mark 2C. Pressure ventilated. –/31 1T. B4 bogies. ETH 4.

Lot No. 30798 Derby 1970. 32 t.

9440	d	**M**	WC	*WC*	CS		9448	d	**M**	WC	*WC*	CS

AE2D (BSO)   OPEN BRAKE STANDARD

Mark 2D. Air conditioned (Stones). –/31 1T. B4 bogies. d. pg. ETH 5.

r Refurbished with new interior panelling.
s Refurbished with new seating –/22 1TD.
w Facelifted –/28 1W 1T.

Lot No. 30824 Derby 1971. 33 t.

9479	r		H	*FM*	OY		9490	s	**FP**	H	*GW*	OO
9480		**FP**	H		KT		9492	w	**FP**	H		OM
9481	s	**FP**	H	*GW*	OO		9493	s	**FP**	H	*GW*	OO
9488	s	**FP**	H	*GW*	OO		9494	s	**FP**	H	*GW*	OO
9489	r	**V**	H		KT							

AE2E (BSO)   OPEN BRAKE STANDARD

Mark 2E. Air conditioned (Stones). –/32 1T. B4 bogies. d. pg. ETH 5.

Lot No. 30838 Derby 1972. 33 t.

r Refurbished with new interior panelling.
s Refurbished with modified design of seat headrest and new interior panelling.
w Facelifted –/28 1W 1T.

9496	r		H	*FM*	OY		9504	s	**V**	H	*RV*	CP
9497	r★		H	*FM*	BH		9505	s★		H	*FM*	BH
9498	r	**V**	H		KT		9506	s★	**WX**	H	*WX*	PM
9500	r		H	*FM*	OY		9507	s	**V**	H	*RV*	CP
9501	w	**FP**	H		OM		9508	s	**V**	H		KT
9502	s	**V**	H		KT		9509	s	**V**	H	*RV*	CP
9503	s	**V**	H	*RV*	CP							

AE2F (BSO)   OPEN BRAKE STANDARD

Mark 2F. Air conditioned (Temperature Ltd.). All now refurbished with power-operated vestibule doors, new panels and seat trim. All now further refurbished with carpets and new m.a. sets. –/32 1T. B4 bogies. d. pg. ETH5X.

Lot No. 30861 Derby 1974. 34 t.

9513		**V**	H	*FM*	OY		9526	n★		H	*RV*	CP
9516	n	**V**	H	*FM*	OY		9527	n	**V**	RV	*AW*	CF
9520	n	**V**	RV	*AW*	CF		9529	n	**V**	RV	*AW*	CF
9521	★	**AV**	E		OM		9531		**V**	RV	*AW*	CF
9522		**V**	H	*FM*	OY		9537	n	**V**	H	*RV*	CP
9523		**V**	H		KT		9538		**V**	H		KT
9524	n★	**AV**	E		OM		9539		**M**	WC	*WC*	CS
9525		**WX**	H	*WX*	PM							

AF2F (DBSO) DRIVING OPEN BRAKE STANDARD

Mark 2F. Air conditioned (Temperature Ltd.). Push & pull (t.d.m. system). Converted from BSO, these vehicles originally had half cabs at the brake end. They have since been refurbished and have had their cabs widened and the cab-end gangways removed. –/30 1W 1T. B4 bogies. d. pg. Cowcatchers. ETH 5X.

9701–9710. Lot No. 30861 Derby 1974. Converted Glasgow 1979. Disc brakes. 34 t.
9711–9713. Lot No. 30861 Derby 1974. Converted Glasgow 1985. 34 t.
9714. Lot No. 30861 Derby 1974. Converted Glasgow 1986. Disc brakes. 34 t.

9701	(9528)	**AR**	H	1A	NC		9709	(9515)	**AR**	H	1A	NC
9702	(9510)	**AR**	H	1A	NC		9710	(9518)	1	H	1A	NC
9703	(9517)	**AR**	H	1A	NC		9711	(9532)	**AR**	H	1A	NC
9704	(9512)	**AR**	H	1A	NC		9712	(9534)	**AR**	H	1A	NC
9705	(9519)	**AR**	H	1A	NC		9713	(9535)	**AR**	H	1A	NC
9707	(9511)	**AR**	H	1A	NC		9714	(9536)	**AR**	H	1A	NC
9708	(9530)	**AR**	H	1A	NC							

AE4E (BUO)   UNCLASSIFIED OPEN BRAKE

Mark 2E. Converted from TSO with new seating for use on Anglo-Scottish overnight services by Railcare, Wolverton. Air conditioned. Stones equipment. B4 bogies. d. –/31 2T. B4 bogies. ETH 4X.

9801–9803. Lot No. 30837 Derby 1972. 33.5 t.
9804–9810. Lot No. 30844 Derby 1972–73. 33.5 t.

9800	(5751)	**CS**	H	SR	IS		9806	(5840)	**CS**	H	SR	IS
9801	(5760)	**CS**	H	SR	IS		9807	(5851)	**CS**	H	SR	IS
9802	(5772)	**CS**	H	SR	IS		9808	(5871)	**CS**	H	SR	IS
9803	(5799)	**CS**	H	SR	IS		9809	(5890)	**CS**	H	SR	IS
9804	(5826)	**CS**	H	SR	IS		9810	(5892)	**CS**	H	SR	IS
9805	(5833)	**CS**	H	SR	IS							

AJ1G (RFM)
RESTAURANT BUFFET FIRST (MODULAR)

Mark 3A. Air conditioned. Converted from HST TRFKs, RFBs and FOs. Refurbished with table lamps and burgundy seat trim (except *). 18/– plus two seats for staff use (*24/–). BT10 bogies. p. q. d. ETH 14X.

10200–10211. Lot No. 30884 Derby 1977. 39.8 t.
10212–10229. Lot No. 30878 Derby 1975–76. 39.8 t.
10230–10260. Lot No. 30890 Derby 1979. 39.8 t.

Non-standard Livery: 10211 is EWS dark maroon.

10200	(40519)	*		P	1A	NC		10203	(40506)	* **AR**	P	1A	NC
10201	(40520)	**V**		P		LT		10204	(40502)	**V**	P		PC
10202	(40504)	**V**		P	VW	MA		10205	(40503)	**V**	P		LT

10206	(40507)	**V**	P	*VW*	MA	10232	(10027)	**V**	P		WI
10207	(40516)	**V**	P		LT	10233	(10013)	**V**	P		WI
10208	(40517)	**V**	P		WI	10234	(10004)	**V**	P		LT
10209	(40508)	**V**	P		LT	10235	(10015)	**V**	P	*CD*	OY
10210	(40509)	**V**	P		LT	10236	(10018)	**V**	P		WI
10211	(40510)	**0**	E	*E*	TO	10237	(10022)	**V**	P	*VW*	MA
10212	(11049)	**V**	P	*VW*	MA	10238	(10017)	**V**	P		LT
10213	(11050)	**V**	P		LT	10240	(10003)	**V**	P	*1A*	NC
10214	(11034)	* **AR**	P	*1A*	NC	10241	(10009)	* **AR**	P	*1A*	NC
10215	(11032)	**V**	P		WI	10242	(10002)	**V**	P		PC
10216	(11041)	* **AR**	P	*1A*	NC	10245	(10019)	**V**	P		PC
10217	(11051)	**V**	P	*VW*	MA	10246	(10014)	**V**	P		WI
10218	(11053)	**V**	P		WI	10247	(10011)	* **AR**	P	*1A*	NC
10219	(11047)	**V**	P		MA	10248	(10005)	**V**	P	*E*	OM
10220	(11056)	**V**	P		LT	10249	(10012)	**V**	P		WI
10221	(11012)	**V**	P		LT	10250	(10020)	**V**	P		LT
10222	(11063)	**V**	P		MA	10251	(10024)	**V**	P	*E*	OM
10223	(11043)	* **AR**	P	*1A*	NC	10252	(10008)	**V**	P		LT
10224	(11062)	**V**	P		LT	10253	(10026)	**V**	P		WI
10225	(11014)	**V**	P		WI	10254	(10006)	**V**	P		LT
10226	(11015)	**V**	P	*VW*	MA	10255	(10010)	**V**	P		WI
10227	(11057)	**V**	P		WI	10256	(10028)	**V**	P		LT
10228	(11035)	* **AR**	P	*1A*	NC	10257	(10007)	**V**	P	*E*	OM
10229	(11059)	**V**	P		PC	10258	(10023)	**V**	P		WI
10230	(10021)	**1**	P	*1A*	NC	10259	(10025)	**V**	P		LT
10231	(10016)	**V**	P	*FM*	OY	10260	(10001)	**V**	P		LT

AJ1J/AG2J (RFM/RSB) RESTAURANT BUFFET

Mark 4. Air conditioned. 20/– 1T. BT41 bogies. ETH 6X.

m "Mallard" vehicles. Rebuilt with standard class seating with bar adjacent to seating area instead of adjacent to end of coach. –/30 1T.

Lot No. 31045 Metro-Cammell 1989 onwards. 45.5 t (43.2 t m).

10300 m	**GN**	H	*GN*	BN	10316	**GN**	H	*GN*	BN
10301	**GN**	H	*GN*	BN	10317	**GN**	H	*GN*	BN
10302	**GN**	H	*GN*	BN	10318	**GN**	H	*GN*	BN
10303 m	**GN**	H	*GN*	BN	10319	**GN**	H	*GN*	BN
10304 m	**GN**	H	*GN*	BN	10320 m	**GN**	H	*GN*	BN
10305 m	**GN**	H	*GN*	BN	10321	**GN**	H	*GN*	BN
10306 m	**GN**	H	*GN*	BN	10323 m	**GN**	H	*GN*	BN
10307	**GN**	H	*GN*	BN	10324 m	**GN**	H	*GN*	BN
10308 m	**GN**	H	*GN*	BN	10325	**GN**	H	*GN*	BN
10309 m	**GN**	H	*GN*	BN	10326	**GN**	H	*GN*	BN
10310	**GN**	H	*GN*	BN	10328	**GN**	H	*GN*	BN
10311	**GN**	H	*GN*	BN	10329	**GN**	H	*GN*	BN
10312	**GN**	H	*GN*	BN	10330	**GN**	H	*GN*	BN
10313 m	**GN**	H	*GN*	BN	10331 m	**GN**	H	*GN*	BN
10314	**GN**	H	*GN*	BN	10332 m	**GN**	H	*GN*	BN
10315 m	**GN**	H	*GN*	BN	10333	**GN**	H	*GN*	BN

AU4G (SLEP)   SLEEPING CAR WITH PANTRY

Mark 3A. Air conditioned. Retention toilets. 12 compartments with a fixed lower berth and a hinged upper berth, plus an attendants compartment. 2T BT10 bogies. ETH 7X.

Non-standard Livery: 10546 is EWS dark maroon.

Lot No. 30960 Derby 1981–83. 41 t.

10501	d	**CS**	P	*SR*	IS	10551	d	**CS**	P	*SR*	IS
10502	d	**CS**	P	*SR*	IS	10553	d	**CS**	P	*SR*	IS
10504	d	**CS**	P	*SR*	IS	10555	d		P		KT
10506	d	**CS**	P	*SR*	IS	10559	d		P		KT
10507	d	**CS**	P	*SR*	IS	10561	d	**CS**	P	*SR*	IS
10508	d	**CS**	P	*SR*	IS	10562	d	**CS**	P	*SR*	IS
10510	d		P		ZH	10563	d	**FP**	P	*GW*	PZ
10513	d	**CS**	P	*SR*	IS	10565	d	**CS**	P	*SR*	IS
10515	d		P		IS	10569	d	**PC**	VS	*VS*	SL
10516	d	**CS**	P	*SR*	IS	10580	d	**CS**	P	*SR*	IS
10519	d	**CS**	P	*SR*	IS	10584	d	**FP**	P	*GW*	PZ
10520	d	**CS**	P	*SR*	IS	10588	d	**FP**	P	*GW*	PZ
10522	d	**CS**	P	*SR*	IS	10589	d	**FP**	P	*GW*	PZ
10523	d	**CS**	P	*SR*	IS	10590	d	**FP**	P	*GW*	PZ
10526	d	**CS**	P	*SR*	IS	10594	d	**FP**	P	*GW*	PZ
10527	d	**CS**	P	*SR*	IS	10596	d		P		KT
10529	d	**CS**	P	*SR*	IS	10597	d	**CS**	P	*SR*	IS
10531	d	**CS**	P	*SR*	IS	10598	d	**CS**	P	*SR*	IS
10532	d	**FP**	P	*GW*	PZ	10600	d	**CS**	P	*SR*	IS
10534	d	**FP**	P	*GW*	PZ	10601	d	**FP**	P	*GW*	PZ
10538	d		P		KT	10605	d	**CS**	P	*SR*	IS
10539	d		P		KT	10607	d	**CS**	P	*SR*	IS
10542	d	**CS**	P	*SR*	IS	10610	d	**CS**	P	*SR*	IS
10543	d	**CS**	P	*SR*	IS	10612	d	**FP**	P	*GW*	PZ
10544	d	**CS**	P	*SR*	IS	10613	d	**CS**	P	*SR*	IS
10546	d	**O**	E	*E*	TO	10614	d	**CS**	P	*SR*	IS
10547	d		P		IS	10616	d	**FP**	P	*GW*	PZ
10548	d	**CS**	P	*SR*	IS	10617	d	**CS**	P	*SR*	IS

AS4G/AQ4G* (SLE/SLED*)   SLEEPING CAR

Mark 3A. Air conditioned. Retention toilets. 13 compartments with a fixed lower berth and a hinged upper berth (* 11 compartments with a fixed lower berth and a hinged upper berth + one compartment for a disabled person). 2T. BT10 bogies. ETH 6X.

Notes:

10704 has Siemens bogies.
10734 was originally 2914 and used as a Royal Train staff sleeping car. It has 12 berths and a shower room and is ETH11X.

10647–10732. Lot No. 30961 Derby 1980–84. 43.5 t.

10734. Lot No. 31002 Derby/Wolverton 1985. 42.5 t.

10647	d		P		KT			
10648	d* **CS**	P		*SR*	IS			
10649	d		P		KT			
10650	d* **CS**	P		*SR*	IS			
10658	d		P		KT			
10663	d		P		IS			
10666	d* **CS**	P		*SR*	IS			
10675	d **CS**	P		*SR*	IS			
10680	d* **CS**	P		*SR*	IS			
10683	d **CS**	P		*SR*	IS			
10688	d **CS**	P		*SR*	IS			
10689	d* **CS**	P		*SR*	IS			
10690	d **CS**	P		*SR*	IS			
10693	d **CS**	P		*SR*	IS			
10697	d		P		KT			

10699	d* **CS**	P	*SR*	IS
10701	d	P		KT
10703	d **CS**	P	*SR*	IS
10704	d	AE		ZA
10706	d* **CS**	P	*SR*	IS
10710	d	P		KT
10714	d* **CS**	P	*SR*	IS
10718	d* **CS**	P	*SR*	IS
10719	d* **CS**	P	*SR*	IS
10722	d* **CS**	P	*SR*	IS
10723	d* **CS**	P	*SR*	IS
10729	**VN**	SA	*VS*	CP
10732	d	P		KT
10734	**RP**	VS		CP

AD1G (FO)   OPEN FIRST

Mark 3A. Air conditioned. All now refurbished with table lamps and new seat cushions and trim. 48/– 2T (* 48/– 1T 1TD). BT10 bogies. d. ETH 6X.

11005–7 were open composites 11905–7 for a time.

Non-standard Livery: 11039 is EWS dark maroon.

Lot No. 30878 Derby 1975–76. 34.3 t.

11005	**V**	P		LT		11031	**V**	P		MA
11006	**V**	P		LT		11033	**V**	P *CD*		OY
11007	**V**	P		LT		11036	**V**	P *VW*		MA
11011	* **V**	P *VW*		MA		11037	**V**	P		ZD
11013	**V**	P *CD*		OY		11038	**1**	P *1A*		NC
11016	**V**	P *E*		OM		11039	**0**	E *E*		TO
11017	**V**	P		PC		11040	**V**	P		PC
11018	**V**	P *VW*		MA		11042	**V**	P		WI
11019	**V**	P		PC		11044	**V**	P *VW*		MA
11020	**V**	P *VW*		MA		11045	**V**	P *E*		OM
11021	**V**	P *E*		OM		11046	**V**	P		PC
11023	**1**	P *1A*		NC		11048	**V**	P *VW*		MA
11024	**V**	P *VW*		MA		11052	**V**	P		WI
11026	**V**	P *VW*		MA		11054	**V**	P		PC
11027	**V**	P *VW*		MA		11055	**V**	P		PC
11028	**V**	P *VW*		MA		11058	**V**	P		PC
11029	**V**	P *VW*		MA		11060	**V**	P *VW*		MA
11030	**V**	P *VW*		MA						

AD1H (FO)   OPEN FIRST

Mark 3B. Air conditioned. Inter-City 80 seats. All now refurbished with table lamps and new seat cushions and trim. 48/– 2T. BT10 bogies. d. ETH 6X.

Lot No. 30982 Derby 1985. 36.5 t.

11064	**V**	P	*VW*	MA	11083 p	**V**	P	*VW*	MA
11065	**V**	P		PC	11084 p	**V**	P	*1A*	NC
11066	**V**	P	*CD*	OY	11085 p	**V**	P		LT
11067	**V**	P		PC	11086 p	**V**	P	*VW*	MA
11068	**V**	P		PC	11087 p	**V**	P	*1A*	NC
11069	**V**	P		MA	11088 p	**V**	P		PC
11070	**V**	P		ZD	11089 p	**V**	P	*VW*	MA
11071	**V**	P		MA	11090 p	**V**	P		PC
11072	**V**	P		LT	11091 p	**V**	P		WB
11073	**V**	P		OM	11092 p	**V**	P		PC
11074	**V**	P	*VW*	MA	11093 p	**V**	P		ZD
11075	**V**	P		LT	11094 p	**V**	P		LT
11076	**V**	P		ZD	11095 p	**V**	P	*1A*	NC
11077	**V**	P		WB	11096 p	**V**	P		ZD
11078	**V**	P		ZD	11097 p	**V**	P	*1A*	NC
11079	**V**	P	*VW*	MA	11098 p	**V**	P		PC
11080	**V**	P		PC	11099 p	**V**	P		PC
11081	**V**	P	*E*	OM	11100 p	**V**	P		LT
11082	**V**	P	*E*	OM	11101 p	**V**	P		ZD

AD1J (FO)   OPEN FIRST

Mark 4. Air conditioned. 46/– 1T. BT41 bogies. ETH 6X.

m "Mallard" vehicles. Rebuilt with new interior Bombardier Wakefield 2003–05 (some converted from standard class vehicles).

Note: 11264–11271 were cancelled.

Lot No. 31046 Metro-Cammell 1989–92. 39.7 t. (41.3 t. m).

11200		**GN** H *GN* BN	11242	p	**GN** H *GN* BN
11201	m	**GN** H *GN* BN	11243		**GN** H *GN* BN
11203	p	**GN** H *GN* BN	11244		**GN** H *GN* BN
11204	p	**GN** H *GN* BN	11245	p	**GN** H *GN* BN
11206		**GN** H *GN* BN	11247	p	**GN** H *GN* BN
11214	p	**GN** H *GN* BN	11248		**GN** H *GN* BN
11215		**GN** H *GN* BN	11249	p	**GN** H *GN* BN
11216		**GN** H *GN* BN	11250		**GN** H *GN* BN
11219	p	**GN** H *GN* BN	11252		**GN** H *GN* BN
11220		**GN** H *GN* BN	11253	p	**GN** H *GN* BN
11228	p	**GN** H *GN* BN	11255	p	**GN** H *GN* BN
11229	m	**GN** H *GN* BN	11261	p	**GN** H *GN* BN
11230		**GN** H *GN* BN	11273		**GN** H *GN* BN
11231	p	**GN** H *GN* BN	11274		**GN** H *GN* BN
11232		**GN** H *GN* BN	11275		**GN** H *GN* BN
11233	p	**GN** H *GN* BN	11277 (12408)	m	**GN** H *GN* BN
11234		**GN** H *GN* BN	11278 (12479)	m	**GN** H *GN* BN
11235	p	**GN** H *GN* BN	11279 (12521)	m	**GN** H *GN* BN
11236		**GN** H *GN* BN	11280 (12523)	m	**GN** H *GN* BN
11237	p	**GN** H *GN* BN	11281 (12418)	m	**GN** H *GN* BN
11239	p	**GN** H *GN* BN	11282 (12524)	m	**GN** H *GN* BN
11241		**GN** H *GN* BN	11283 (12435)	m	**GN** H *GN* BN

11284 (12487) m **GN** H *GN* BN	11292 ( ) m **GN** H
11285 (12537) m **GN** H *GN* BN	11293 ( ) m **GN** H
11286 (12482) m **GN** H *GN* BN	11294 ( ) m **GN** H
11287 (12527) m **GN** H *GN* BN	11295 ( ) m **GN** H
11288 (12517) m **GN** H *GN* BN	11296 ( ) m **GN** H
11289 (12528) m **GN** H *GN* BN	11297 ( ) m **GN** H
11290 ( ) m **GN** H	11298 ( ) m **GN** H
11291 ( ) m **GN** H	11299 ( ) m **GN** H

AD1J (FOD)   OPEN FIRST (DISABLED)

Mark 4. Air conditioned. "Mallard" vehicles. Rebuilt from FO by Bombardier Wakefield 2003–05. 42/– 1W 1TD. BT41 bogies. ETH 6X.

Lot No. 31046 Metro-Cammell 1989–92. 40.7 t.

11301 ( ) **GN** H	11316 (11227) **GN** H *GN* BN
11302 ( ) **GN** H	11317 (11223) **GN** H *GN* BN
11303 (11211) **GN** H *GN* BN	11318 (11251) **GN** H *GN* BN
11304 (11257) **GN** H *GN* BN	11319 ( ) **GN** H
11305 ( ) **GN** H	11320 ( ) **GN** H
11306 (11276) **GN** H *GN* BN	11321 ( ) **GN** H
11307 (11217) **GN** H *GN* BN	11322 ( ) **GN** H
11308 (11263) **GN** H *GN* BN	11323 ( ) **GN** H
11309 (11259) **GN** H *GN* BN	11324 ( ) **GN** H
11310 (11272) **GN** H *GN* BN	11325 ( ) **GN** H
11311 (11221) **GN** H *GN* BN	11326 ( ) **GN** H
11312 (11225) **GN** H *GN* BN	11327 ( ) **GN** H
11313 (11210) **GN** H *GN* BN	11328 ( ) **GN** H
11314 (11207) **GN** H *GN* BN	11329 ( ) **GN** H
11315 (11238) **GN** H *GN* BN	11330 ( ) **GN** H

AD1J (FOS)   OPEN FIRST (SMOKING)

Mark 4. Air conditioned. "Mallard" vehicles. Rebuilt from FO by Bombardier Wakefield 2003–05. 46/– 1W 1TD. Partitioned off area for 7 smokers. BT41 bogies. ETH 6X.

Lot Nos. 31046/31049 Metro-Cammell 1989–92. 42.1 t.

11401 ( ) **GN** H	11414 (11246) **GN** H *GN* BN
11402 ( ) **GN** H	11415 (11208) **GN** H *GN* BN
11403 (11258) **GN** H *GN* BN	11416 (11254) **GN** H *GN* BN
11404 (11202) **GN** H *GN* BN	11417 (11226) **GN** H *GN* BN
11405 ( ) **GN** H	11418 (11222) **GN** H *GN* BN
11406 (11205) **GN** H *GN* BN	11419 ( ) **GN** H
11407 (11256) **GN** H *GN* BN	11420 ( ) **GN** H
11408 (11218) **GN** H *GN* BN	11421 ( ) **GN** H
11409 (11262) **GN** H *GN* BN	11422 ( ) **GN** H
11410 (11260) **GN** H *GN* BN	11423 ( ) **GN** H
11411 (11240) **GN** H *GN* BN	11424 ( ) **GN** H
11412 (11209) **GN** H *GN* BN	11425 ( ) **GN** H
11413 (11212) **GN** H *GN* BN	11426 ( ) **GN** H

| 11427 (|) | **GN** H | | 11429 (|) | **GN** H |
| 11428 (|) | **GN** H | | 11430 (|) | **GN** H |

AC2G (TSO)   OPEN STANDARD

Mark 3A. Air conditioned. All refurbished with modified seat backs and new layout and now further refurbished with new seat trim. –/76 2T (s –/70 2T 2W, z –/70 1TD 1T 2W). BT10 bogies. d. ETH 6X.

Note: 12169–72 were converted from open composites 11908–10/22, formerly FOs 11008–10/22.

Lot No. 30877 Derby 1975–77. 34.3 t.

12004		**V**	P	*SR*	PC		12045		**V**	P	*VW*	MA
12005		**V**	P		WB		12046		**V**	P	*SR*	PC
12007		**V**	P		MA		12047	z	**V**	P		WI
12008		**V**	P		MA		12048		**V**	P	*1A*	NC
12009		**V**	P		LT		12049		**V**	P		PC
12010		**V**	P	*VW*	MA		12050	s	**V**	P	*VW*	MA
12011		**V**	P	*VW*	MA		12051		**V**	P	*1A*	NC
12012		**V**	P	*1A*	NC		12052		**V**	P	*CD*	OY
12013		**V**	P	*VW*	MA		12053		**V**	P	*VW*	MA
12014		**V**	P	*SR*	PC		12054	s	**V**	P	*VW*	MA
12015		**V**	P		LT		12055		**V**	P		MA
12016		**V**	P		LT		12056		**V**	P		MA
12017		**V**	P		WI		12057		**V**	P	*VW*	MA
12019		**V**	P	*SR*	PC		12058		**V**	P	*1A*	NC
12020		**V**	P		LT		12059	s	**V**	P		PC
12021		**V**	P	*1A*	NC		12060		**V**	P		LT
12022		**V**	P		WI		12061	s	**V**	P	*1A*	NC
12023		**V**	P		ZD		12062		**V**	P		ZD
12024	s	**V**	P		ZD		12063		**V**	P	*VW*	MA
12025		**V**	P	*VW*	MA		12064		**V**	P	*1A*	NC
12026		**V**	P		ZD		12065		**V**	P	*SR*	PC
12027		**V**	P	*VW*	MA		12066		**V**	P	*VW*	MA
12028		**V**	P	*VW*	MA		12067		**V**	P	*VW*	MA
12029		**V**	P		PC		12068		**V**	P		MA
12030		**V**	P		LT		12069		**V**	P	*VW*	MA
12031		**V**	P		ZD		12070		**V**	P	*CD*	OY
12032		**V**	P	*SR*	PC		12071		**V**	P		WI
12033	z	**V**	P	*VW*	MA		12072		**V**	P		WI
12034		**V**	P		LT		12073		**V**	P	*VW*	MA
12035		**V**	P	*1A*	NC		12075		**V**	P	*VW*	MA
12036	s	**V**	P	*SR*	PC		12076		**V**	P		WI
12037		**V**	P		ZD		12077		**V**	P	*E*	OM
12038		**V**	P	*SR*	PC		12078		**V**	P	*VW*	MA
12040		**V**	P	*SR*	PC		12079		**V**	P		ZD
12041		**V**	P	*SR*	PC		12080		**V**	P		WI
12042	s	**V**	P		LT		12081		**V**	P		LT
12043		**V**	P	*VW*	MA		12082		**1**	P	*1A*	NC
12044		**V**	P	*VW*	MA		12083		**V**	P		WI

12084		**V**	P		PC	12128 s	**V**	P *SR*	PC
12085 s		**V**	P *VW*	MA	12129	**V**	P *CD*	OY
12086 s		**V**	P	WI	12130	**V**	P *VW*	MA
12087 s		**V**	P *VW*	MA	12131	**V**	P *VW*	MA
12088 z	1	P *1A*	NC	12132	**V**	P	WB
12089		**V**	P *1A*	NC	12133	**V**	P *VW*	MA
12090		**V**	P	PC	12134	**V**	P *SR*	PC
12091		**V**	P	LT	12135	**V**	P *CD*	OY
12092		**V**	P *SR*	PC	12136	**V**	P *1A*	NC
12093		**V**	P	LT	12137	**V**	P *SR*	PC
12094		**V**	P	MA	12138	**V**	P *VW*	MA
12095		**V**	P	WI	12139	**V**	P *SR*	PC
12096		**V**	P *VW*	MA	12141	**V**	P *1A*	NC
12097		**V**	P	MA	12142 z	**V**	P	MA
12098		**V**	P	PC	12143	**V**	P	LT
12099		**V**	P	LT	12144 s	**V**	P	WI
12100 z		**V**	P *SR*	PC	12145	**V**	P *VW*	MA
12101 s		**V**	P *VW*	MA	12146	**V**	P	LT
12102 s		**V**	P *VW*	MA	12147	**V**	P *SR*	PC
12103 s		**V**	P	ZD	12148	1	P *1A*	NC
12104		**V**	P *VW*	MA	12149	**V**	P *VW*	MA
12105		**V**	P	ZD	12150	**V**	P *VW*	MA
12106		**V**	P	MA	12151	**V**	P *SR*	PC
12107		**V**	P	LT	12152	**V**	P	MA
12108 s		**V**	P	LT	12153	**V**	P	LT
12109 s		**V**	P	ZD	12154	1	P *1A*	NC
12110		**V**	P *CD*	OY	12155 s	**V**	P	PC
12111		**V**	P *VW*	MA	12156	**V**	P *VW*	MA
12112 z		**V**	P *VW*	MA	12157	**V**	P *1A*	NC
12113		**V**	P	WI	12158	**V**	P	PC
12114		**V**	P *VW*	MA	12159	**V**	P	LT
12115		**V**	P	LT	12160 s	**V**	P	PC
12116	1	P *1A*	NC	12161 z	**V**	P *VW*	MA
12117		**V**	P *VW*	MA	12163	**V**	P *VW*	MA
12118		**V**	P	LT	12164	**V**	P *VW*	MA
12119		**V**	P *VW*	MA	12165	**V**	P *VW*	MA
12120		**V**	P	ZD	12166	**V**	P *SR*	PC
12121		**V**	P *VW*	MA	12167	**V**	P	WB
12122 z		**V**	P *VW*	MA	12168 s	**V**	P	LT
12123		**V**	P *1A*	NC	12169 s	**V**	P	WI
12124		**V**	P *CD*	OY	12170 s	**V**	P *VW*	MA
12125		**V**	P	WB	12171 s	**V**	P	LT
12126		**V**	P	MA	12172 s	**V**	P *SR*	PC
12127		**V**	P *1A*	NC				

AI2J (TSOE)   OPEN STANDARD (END)

Mark 4. Air conditioned. –/74 2T. BT41 bogies. ETH 6X.

m "Mallard" vehicles. Rebuilt with new interior Bombardier Wakefield 2003–05.
Partitioned off area for 26 smokers. –/76 1T.
Lot No. 31047 Metro-Cammell 1989–91. 39.5 t.

Note: 12232 was converted from the original 12405.

12200	**GN**	H *GN*	BN		12217	**GN**	H *GN*	BN
12201	m **GN**	H *GN*	BN		12218	**GN**	H *GN*	BN
12202	m **GN**	H *GN*	BN		12219	**GN**	H *GN*	BN
12203	m **GN**	H *GN*	BN		12220	**GN**	H *GN*	BN
12204	**GN**	H *GN*	BN		12222	**GN**	H *GN*	BN
12205	m **GN**	H *GN*	BN		12223	m **GN**	H *GN*	BN
12207	**GN**	H *GN*	BN		12224	**GN**	H *GN*	BN
12208	m **GN**	H *GN*	BN		12225	**GN**	H *GN*	BN
12209	**GN**	H *GN*	BN		12226	m **GN**	H *GN*	BN
12210	**GN**	H *GN*	BN		12227	**GN**	H *GN*	BN
12211	**GN**	H *GN*	BN		12228	m **GN**	H *GN*	BN
12212	m **GN**	H *GN*	BN		12229	m **GN**	H *GN*	BN
12213	m **GN**	H *GN*	BN		12230	m **GN**	H *GN*	BN
12214	m **GN**	H *GN*	BN		12231	m **GN**	H *GN*	BN
12215	m **GN**	H *GN*	BN		12232	**GN**	H *GN*	BN
12216	**GN**	H *GN*	BN					

AL2J (TSOD) OPEN STANDARD (DISABLED ACCESS)

Mark 4. Air conditioned. –/72 1W 1TD. BT41 bogies. p. ETH 6X.

m "Mallard" vehicles. Rebuilt with new interior Bombardier Wakefield 2003–05.
–/68 2W 1TD.

Lot No. 31048 Metro-Cammell 1989–91. 39.4 t.

12300	**GN**	H *GN*	BN		12317	**GN**	H *GN*	BN
12301	m **GN**	H *GN*	BN		12318	**GN**	H *GN*	BN
12302	**GN**	H *GN*	BN		12319	**GN**	H *GN*	BN
12303	m **GN**	H *GN*	BN		12320	**GN**	H *GN*	BN
12304	m **GN**	H *GN*	BN		12321	**GN**	H *GN*	BN
12305	m **GN**	H *GN*	BN		12322	**GN**	H *GN*	BN
12307	**GN**	H *GN*	BN		12323	**GN**	H *GN*	BN
12308	m **GN**	H *GN*	BN		12324	m **GN**	H *GN*	BN
12309	m **GN**	H *GN*	BN		12325	**GN**	H *GN*	BN
12310	**GN**	H *GN*	BN		12326	**GN**	H *GN*	BN
12311	m **GN**	H *GN*	BN		12327	m **GN**	H *GN*	BN
12312	m **GN**	H *GN*	BN		12328	m **GN**	H *GN*	BN
12313	m **GN**	H *GN*	BN		12329	m **GN**	H *GN*	BN
12315	m **GN**	H *GN*	BN		12330	m **GN**	H *GN*	BN
12316	**GN**	H *GN*	BN					

AC2J (TSO)   OPEN STANDARD

Mark 4. Air conditioned. –/74 2T. BT41 bogies. ETH 6X.

m "Mallard" vehicles. Rebuilt with new interior Bombardier Wakefield 2003–05. –/76 1T.

Lot No. 31049 Metro-Cammell 1989–92. 39.9 t. (40.8 t. m).

Note: 12405 is the second coach to carry that number. It was built from the bodyshell originally intended for 12221. The original 12405 is now 12232. 12490–12512 were cancelled.

12400	**GN**	H *GN*	BN	12444 m **GN**	H *GN*	BN
12401 m **GN**	H *GN*	BN	12445 m **GN**	H *GN*	BN
12402	**GN**	H *GN*	BN	12446	**GN**	H *GN*	BN
12403	**GN**	H *GN*	BN	12447	**GN**	H *GN*	BN
12404 m **GN**	H *GN*	BN	12448	**GN**	H *GN*	BN
12405 m **GN**	H *GN*	BN	12449	**GN**	H *GN*	BN
12406 m **GN**	H *GN*	BN	12450	**GN**	H *GN*	BN
12407 m **GN**	H *GN*	BN	12451	**GN**	H *GN*	BN
12409 m **GN**	H *GN*	BN	12452	**GN**	H *GN*	BN
12410 m **GN**	H *GN*	BN	12453 m **GN**	H *GN*	BN
12411 m **GN**	H *GN*	BN	12454	**GN**	H *GN*	BN
12414	**GN**	H *GN*	BN	12455	**GN**	H *GN*	BN
12415	**GN**	H *GN*	BN	12456	**GN**	H *GN*	BN
12416	**GN**	H *GN*	BN	12457	**GN**	H *GN*	BN
12417	**GN**	H *GN*	BN	12458	**GN**	H *GN*	BN
12419 m **GN**	H *GN*	BN	12459 m **GN**	H *GN*	BN
12420 m **GN**	H *GN*	BN	12460	**GN**	H *GN*	BN
12421 m **GN**	H *GN*	BN	12461	**GN**	H *GN*	BN
12422 m **GN**	H *GN*	BN	12462	**GN**	H *GN*	BN
12423 m **GN**	H *GN*	BN	12463	**GN**	H *GN*	BN
12424 m **GN**	H *GN*	BN	12464	**GN**	H *GN*	BN
12425	**GN**	H *GN*	BN	12465	**GN**	H *GN*	BN
12426 m **GN**	H *GN*	BN	12466	**GN**	H *GN*	BN
12427 m **GN**	H *GN*	BN	12467 m **GN**	H *GN*	BN
12428 m **GN**	H *GN*	BN	12468 m **GN**	H *GN*	BN
12429	**GN**	H *GN*	BN	12469 m **GN**	H *GN*	BN
12430 m **GN**	H *GN*	BN	12470	**GN**	H *GN*	BN
12431 m **GN**	H *GN*	BN	12471	**GN**	H *GN*	BN
12432 m **GN**	H *GN*	BN	12472	**GN**	H *GN*	BN
12433 m **GN**	H *GN*	BN	12473	**GN**	H *GN*	BN
12434	**GN**	H *GN*	BN	12474	**GN**	H *GN*	BN
12436 m **GN**	H *GN*	BN	12475	**GN**	H *GN*	BN
12437 m **GN**	H *GN*	BN	12476	**GN**	H *GN*	BN
12438	**GN**	H *GN*	BN	12477	**GN**	H *GN*	BN
12439	**GN**	H *GN*	BN	12478 m **GN**	H *GN*	BN
12440	**GN**	H *GN*	BN	12480 m **GN**	H *GN*	BN
12441	**GN**	H *GN*	BN	12481 m **GN**	H *GN*	BN
12442 m **GN**	H *GN*	BN	12483 m **GN**	H *GN*	BN
12443 m **GN**	H *GN*	BN	12484 m **GN**	H *GN*	BN

12485	m	**GN**	H	*GN*	BN	12526	m	**GN**	H *GN* BN
12486		**GN**	H	*GN*	BN	12529		**GN**	H *GN* BN
12488	m	**GN**	H	*GN*	BN	12530		**GN**	H *GN* BN
12489	m	**GN**	H	*GN*	BN	12531		**GN**	H *GN* BN
12513	m	**GN**	H	*GN*	BN	12532		**GN**	H *GN* BN
12514	m	**GN**	H	*GN*	BN	12533		**GN**	H *GN* BN
12515	m	**GN**	H	*GN*	BN	12534		**GN**	H *GN* BN
12518	m	**GN**	H	*GN*	BN	12535		**GN**	H *GN* BN
12519		**GN**	H	*GN*	BN	12536		**GN**	H *GN* BN
12520		**GN**	H	*GN*	BN	12538		**GN**	H *GN* BN
12522		**GN**	H	*GN*	BN				

AA11 (FK)   CORRIDOR FIRST

Mark 1. 42/– 2T. ETH 3.

13229–13230. Lot No. 30381 Swindon 1959. B4 bogies. 33 t.
13321. Lot No. 30667 Swindon 1962. Commonwealth bogies. 36 t.

13229	xk	**M**	BK	*BK*	BT		13321	x	**M**	WC	*WC*	CS
13230	xk	**M**	BK	*BK*	BT							

AA1A (FK)   CORRIDOR FIRST

Mark 2A. Pressure ventilated. 42/– 2T. B4 bogies. ETH 4.

13440. Lot No. 30774 Derby 1968. 33 t.
13474. Lot No. 30785 Derby 1968. 33 t.

13440	v	**G**	FM	*FM*	RL		13474	v	**G**	FM	*FM*	RL

AD1B (FO)   OPEN FIRST

Mark 2B. Pressure ventilated. 42/– 2T. B4 bogies. ETH 4.

Lot No. 30789 Derby 1968. 33 t.

These two vehicles were built as FKs, sold to Northern Ireland Railways 1980 and regauged to 5'3". NIR converted them to 56-seater TSOs. Since withdrawn, repatriated to Britain and converted back to standard gauge 2002/3. Under conversion to FO.

13498	(13498, NIR926)	**PC**	WT	LC
13508	(13508, NIR924)	**PC**	WT	LC

AB11 (BFK)   CORRIDOR BRAKE FIRST

Mark 1. 24/– 1T. Commonwealth bogies. ETH 2.

14007. Lot No. 30382 Swindon 1959. 35 t.
17013–17019. Lot No. 30668 Swindon 1961. 36 t.
17023. Lot No. 30718 Swindon 1963. Metal window frames. 36 t.

Originally numbered in 14xxx series and then renumbered in 17xxx series.

14007	x	**M**	B1	*LS*	RD
17013		**PC**	NM	*LS*	YK
17015	x	**G**	E	*E*	OM

17018	v	**CH**	VT	*VT*	TM
17019	x	**M**	NE	*LS*	BQ
17023	x	**G**	E		BN

AB1Z (BFK)   CORRIDOR BRAKE FIRST

Mark 2. Pressure ventilated. 24/– 1T. B4 bogies. ETH 4.

Lot No. 30756 Derby 1966. 31.5 t.
Originally numbered 14041.

| 17041 | **M** | DG | *LS* | BQ |

AB1A (BFK)   CORRIDOR BRAKE FIRST

Mark 2A. Pressure ventilated. 24/– 1T. B4 bogies. ETH 4.

17056–17077. Lot No. 30775 Derby 1967–8. 32 t.
17086–17102. Lot No. 30786 Derby 1968. 32 t.

Originally numbered 14056–102. 17089 and 17090 were numbered 35502 and 35503 for a time when declassified.

17056		**CH**	RV	*RV*	CP
17077		**RV**	RV	*RV*	CP
17086		**RV**	RV	*RV*	CP
17089	v	**G**	FM		RL

17090	v	**CH**	H	*VT*	TM
17096		**G**	MN	*LS*	SL
17102		**M**	WC	*WC*	CS

AX5B   COUCHETTE/GENERATOR COACH

Mark 2B. Formerly part of Royal Train. Converted from a BFK built 1969. Consists of luggage accommodation, guard's compartment, 350 kW diesel generator and staff sleeping accommodation. Pressure ventilated. B5 bogies. ETH 5X.

Non-standard Livery: 17105 is Oxford blue.

Lot No. 30888 Wolverton 1977. 46 t.

| 17105 | (14105, 2905) | **0** | RV | *RV* | CP |

AB1D (BFK)   CORRIDOR BRAKE FIRST

Mark 2D. Air conditioned (Stones equipment). 24/– 1T. B4 Bogies. ETH 5.

Lot No. 30823 Derby 1971–72. 33.5 t.

Non-Standard Livery: 17141 is purple.
Originally numbered 14141–72.

17141		**0**	E		FP
17144			FM		BH
17153		**WR**	E		CS
17156			MA		DY
17159		**CH**	RV		OM
17161			E		OM
17163			VS		CO

17165			E		FP
17167		**VN**	VS	*VS*	CP
17168	d	**M**	WC	*WC*	CS
17169			E		CS
17170			FM		BH
17172			E		FP

AE1G (BFO)   OPEN BRAKE FIRST

Mark 3B. Air conditioned. Fitted with hydraulic handbrake. Refurbished with table lamps and burgundy seat trim. 36/– 1T (w 35/– 1T) BT10 bogies. pg. d. ETH 5X.

Lot No. 30990 Derby 1986. 35.81 t.

| 17173 | | **V** | P | *CD* | OY | | 17175 w | **V** | P | *E* | OM |
| 17174 | | **V** | P | | WI | | | | | | |

AA21 (SK)   CORRIDOR STANDARD

Mark 1. Each vehicle has eight compartments. All remaining vehicles have metal window frames and melamine interior panelling. Commonwealth bogies. –/48 2T. ETH 4.

18756–18893. Lot No. 30685 Derby 1961–62. 36 t.
19013. Lot No. 30719 Derby 1962. 37 t.

Non-Standard Livery: 19013 is Pilkington's K (green with white/red chevron and light blue block).

t Rebuilt internally as TSO using components from 4936. –/64 2T.

Originally numbered 25756–26013.

18756	x	**M**	WC	*WC*	CS		18862	x	**M**	WC	*WC*	CS
18767	x	**M**	WC	*WC*	CS		18893	x	**CH**	WC	*WC*	CS
18806	xt	**M**	WC	*WC*	CS		19013	x	**O**	WC	*WC*	CS
18808	x	**M**	WC	*WC*	CS							

AB31 (BCK)   CORRIDOR BRAKE COMPOSITE

Mark 1. There are two variants depending upon whether the standard class compartments have armrests. Each vehicle has two first class and three standard class compartments. 12/18 2T (12/24 2T *). ETH 2.

21232. Lot No. 30574 GRCW 1960. B4 bogies. 34 t.
21241–21246. Lot No. 30669 Swindon 1961–62. Commonwealth bogies. 36 t.
21252–21256. Lot No. 30731 Derby 1963. Commonwealth bogies. 37 t.
21266–21272. Lot No. 30732 Derby 1964. Commonwealth bogies. 37 t.

Non-Standard Livery: 21232 is in BR Carmine & Cream lined out in black and gold.

21232	x	**O**	62	*LS*	SK		21256	x	**M**	WC	*WC*	CS
21241	x	**M**	BK	*BK*	BT		21266	x*	**M**	WC	*WC*	CS
21245	x	**M**	E	*E*	OM		21268	*		FS		SO
21246		**BG**	E	*E*	OM		21269	*	**GC**	E	*E*	OM
21252	v	**G**	MH	*MH*	RL		21272	x*	**CH**	RV	*RV*	CP

AB21 (BSK)   CORRIDOR BRAKE STANDARD

Mark 1. There are two variants depending upon whether the compartments have armrests. Each vehicle has four compartments. Lots 30699 and 30721 have metal window frames and melamine interior panelling. –/24 1T (–/32 1T*). ETH2.

b In use as a Pendolino barrier vehicle.
g Fitted with an e.t.s. generator.

34991. Lot No. 30229 Metro-Cammell 1956–57. Commonwealth bogies. 36 t.
35185. Lot No. 30427 Wolverton 1959. B4 bogies. 33 t.
35317–35333. Lot No. 30699 Wolverton 1962–63. Commonwealth bogies. 37 t.
35452–35486. Lot No. 30721 Wolverton 1963. Commonwealth bogies. 37 t.

Non-Standard Livery: 35465 is in BR Carmine & Cream lined out in black and gold.

34991	*	PC	VS	VS	SL	35463	v	M	WC	LS	CS
35185	x	M	BK	BK	BT	35465	x	O	LW	LS	CP
35317	x	G	WT	LS	OM	35468	v	M	NM	LS	YK
35329	v	G	MH	LS	RL	35469	xg	M	E	E	OM
35333	x	CH	24	LS	DI	35470	x	CH	VT	LS	TM
35452	xb	RR	LW	FL	CP	35476	x	M	62	LS	SK
35453	x	CH	GW	LS	DI	35479	v	M	SV	LS	KR
35459	x	M	WC	WC	CS	35486	x	M	SV	LS	KR
35461	x	CH	RV	LS	OM						

AB1C (BFK)   CORRIDOR BRAKE FIRST

Mark 2C. Pressure ventilated. Renumbered when declassified. –/24 1T. B4 bogies. ETH 4.

Lot No. 30796 Derby 1969–70. 32.5 t.

| 35508 | (14128, 17128) | **RR** | IR | LS | BQ |

AB5C   BRAKE/POWER KITCHEN

Mark 2C. Pressure ventilated. Converted from BFK (declassified to BSK) built 1970. Converted at West Coast Railway Company 2000–01. Consists of 60 kVA generator, guard's compartment and electric kitchen. B5 bogies. ETH 4.

Non-Standard Livery: British Racing Green with gold lining.

Lot No. 30796 Derby 1969–70. 32.5 t.

| 35511 | (14130, 17130) | **O** | RA | | CP |

AB1A (BFK)   CORRIDOR BRAKE FIRST

Mark 2A. Pressure ventilated. Renumbered when declassified. –/24 1T. B4 bogies.
Cage removed from brake compartment. ETH 4.

Lot No. 30786 Derby 1968. 32 t.

35517	(14088, 17088)	**M**	IR	*LS*	BQ
35518	(14097, 17097)	**PC**	WT	*LS*	OM

NAMED COACHES

The following miscellaneous coaches carry names:¶

1200	AMBER	3247	CHATSWORTH
1659	CAMELOT	3267	BELVOIR
1800	TINTAGEL	3273	ALNWICK
3105	JULIA	3275	HARLECH
3113	JESSICA	5193	CLAN MACLEOD
3117	CHRISTINA	5212	CAPERKAILZIE
3128	VICTORIA	5229	THE GREEN KNIGHT
3130	PAMELA	5239	THE RED KNIGHT
3136	DIANA	5278	MELISANDE
3143	PATRICIA	5350	Dawn
3174	GLAMIS	5365	Deborah
3181	TOPAZ	5376	Michaela
3182	WARWICK	5419	SIR LAUNCELOT
3188	ONYX	9391	PENDRAGON
3223	DIAMOND	10569	LEVIATHAN
3228	AMETHYST	10729	CREWE
3229	JADE	10734	BALMORAL
3231	Apollo	13508	EXCALIBUR
3240	SAPPHIRE	17013	ALBANNACH SGIATHACH
3244	EMERALD	17086	Georgina
3246	Aphrodite	35518	MERLIN

2.2. HIGH SPEED TRAIN TRAILER CARS

HSTs consist of a number of trailer cars (usually seven to nine) with a power car at each end. All trailer cars are classified Mark 3 and have BT10 bogies with disc brakes and central door locking. Heating is by a 415 V three-phase supply and vehicles have air conditioning. Max. Speed is 125 m.p.h.

All vehicles underwent a mid-life refurbishment in the 1980s, and a further refurbishment programme was completed in November 2000, with each train operating company having a different scheme as follows:

First Great Western. Green seat covers and extra partitions between seat bays.
Great North Eastern Railway. New ceiling lighting panels and brown seat covers. First class vehicles have table lamps and imitation walnut plastic end panels.
Virgin Cross-Country. Green seat covers. Standard class vehicles had four seats in the centre of each carriage replaced with a luggage stack. All have now passed to other operators or are in store.
Midland Mainline. Grey seat covers, redesigned seat squabs, side carpeting and two seats in the centre of each carriage replaced with a luggage stack.

Midland Mainline vehicles underwent a further refurbishment programme during 2003/04. This involved fitting new fluorescent and halogen ceiling lighting panels and a new design of seat squab with blue upholstery in standard and first class.

In addition, **GNER** buffet cars have been modernised with new corner bars and each set had an extra vehicle added with a disabled persons toilet.

Ten sets ex-Virgin Cross-Country, and some spare vehicles, were temporarily allocated to Midland Mainline for the temporary service to Manchester during 2003/04 and had a facelift. Buffet cars were converted from TRSB to TRFB and renumbered in the 408xx series. Midland Mainline retain one of these sets in use whilst five have moved to First Great Western and the remainder are in store.

Tops Type Codes

TOPS type codes for HST trailer cars are made up as follows:

(1) Two letters denoting the layout of the vehicle as follows:

GH	Open	GL	Kitchen
GJ	Open with Guard's compartment.	GN	Buffet
GK	Buffet		

(2) A digit for the class of passenger accommodation

1	First	4	Unclassified
2	Standard (formerly second)		

(3) A suffix relating to the build of coach.

G   Mark 3

Operator Codes

The normal operator codes are given in brackets after the TOPS codes. These are as follows:

TF	Trailer First	TGS	Trailer Guard's Standard
TRB	Trailer Buffet First	TRSB	Trailer Buffet Standard
TRFB	Trailer Buffet First	TS	Trailer Standard
TRFM	Trailer Modular Buffet First		

GN4G (TRB) TRAILER BUFFET FIRST

Converted from TRSB by fitting first class seats. Renumbered from 404xx series by subtracting 200. 23/–. p. q.

40204–40228. Lot No. 30883 Derby 1976–77. 36.12 t.
40231. Lot No. 30899 Derby 1978–79. 36.12 t.

40204	**FG**	A	*GW*	PM	40209	**FG**	A	*GW*	PM
40205	**FG**	A	*GW*	PM	40210	**FG**	A	*GW*	PM
40206	**FG**	A		ZC	40221	**FG**	A	*GW*	PM
40207	**FG**	A	*GW*	PM	40228	**FG**	A	*GW*	PM
40208	**FG**	A	*GW*	PM	40231	**FG**	A	*GW*	PM

GK2G (TRSB) TRAILER BUFFET STANDARD

Renumbered from 400xx series by adding 400. –/33 1W. p. q.

40401–40426. Lot No. 30883 Derby 1976–77. 36.12 t.
40433–40437. Lot No. 30899 Derby 1978–79. 36.12 t.

Note: 40433–40434 were numbered 40233–40234 for a time when fitted with 23 first class seats.

40401	**V**	FG	BR	40424	**V**	P	BR
40402	**V**	P	BR	40425	**V**	P	BR
40403	**V**	P	BR	40426	**V**	P	BR
40416	**V**	P	BR	40433	**V**	P	BR
40417	**V**	P	BR	40434	**V**	P	BR
40419	**V**	P	ZC	40436	**V**	P	EC
40422	**V**	FG	WS	40437	**V**	FG	BR
40423	**V**	FG	OO				

GK1G (TRFM) TRAILER MODULAR BUFFET FIRST

Converted to modular catering from TRFB 40719. 17/–. p. q. To be converted as a test coach for the Network Rail New Measurement Train.
 Lot No. 30921 Derby 1978–79. 38.16 t.

40619	P	ZA

GK1G (TRFB) TRAILER BUFFET FIRST

These vehicles have larger kitchens than the 402xx and 404xx series vehicles, and are used in trains where full meal service is required. They were renumbered from the 403xx series (in which the seats were unclassified) by adding 400 to previous number. 17/–. p. q.

40700–40721. Lot No. 30921 Derby 1978–79. 38.16 t.
40722–40735. Lot No. 30940 Derby 1979–80. 38.16 t.
40736–40753. Lot No. 30948 Derby 1980–81. 38.16 t.
40754–40757. Lot No. 30966 Derby 1982. 38.16 t.

r Modified with new corner bar.

40700	**MN**	P	*MM*	NL		40730	**MN**	P	*MM*	NL
40701	**MN**	P	*MM*	NL		40731	**FG**	A	*GW*	LA
40702	**MN**	P	*MM*	NL		40732	**MN**	A	*MM*	NL
40703	**FG**	A	*GW*	LA		40733	**FG**	A	*GW*	LA
40704 r	**GN**	A	*GN*	EC		40734	**FG**	A	*GW*	LA
40705 r	**GN**	A	*GN*	EC		40735 r	**GN**	A	*GN*	EC
40706 r	**GN**	A	*GN*	EC		40736	**FG**	A	*GW*	LA
40707	**FG**	A	*GW*	LA		40737 r	**GN**	A	*GN*	EC
40708	**MN**	P	*MM*	NL		40738	**FG**	A	*GW*	LA
40709	**FG**	A	*GW*	LA		40739	**FG**	A	*GW*	PM
40710	**FG**	A	*GW*	LA		40740 r	**GN**	A	*GN*	EC
40711 r	**GN**	A	*GN*	EC		40741	**MN**	P	*MM*	NL
40712	**FG**	A	*GW*	LA		40742 r	**GN**	A	*GN*	EC
40713	**FG**	A	*GW*	LA		40743	**FG**	A	*GW*	LA
40714	**FG**	A	*GW*	PM		40744	**FG**	A	*GW*	LA
40715	**FG**	A	*GW*	LA		40745	**FG**	A	*GW*	LA
40716	**FG**	A	*GW*	PM		40746	**MN**	P	*MM*	NL
40717	**FG**	A	*GW*	LA		40747	**FG**	A	*GW*	PM
40718	**FG**	A	*GW*	LA		40748 r	**GN**	A	*GN*	EC
40720 r	**GN**	A	*GN*	EC		40749	**MN**	P	*MM*	NL
40721	**FG**	A	*GW*	LA		40750 r	**GN**	A	*GN*	EC
40722	**FG**	A	*GW*	LA		40751	**MN**	P	*MM*	NL
40723	**MN**	A	*MM*	NL		40752	**FG**	A	*GW*	LA
40724	**FG**	A	*GW*	LA		40753	**MN**	P	*MM*	NL
40725	**FG**	A	*GW*	LA		40754	**MN**	P	*MM*	NL
40726	**FG**	A	*GW*	LA		40755	**FG**	A	*GW*	LA
40727	**FG**	A	*GW*	LA		40756	**MN**	P	*MM*	NL
40728	**MN**	P	*MM*	NL		40757	**FG**	A	*GW*	LA
40729	**MN**	P	*MM*	NL						

GK1G (TRFB)   TRAILER BUFFET FIRST

These vehicles have been converted from TRSBs in the 404xx series to be similar to the 407xx series vehicles. 17/– .

40801–40803/40805/40808/40809/40811. Lot No. 30883 Derby 1976–77. 38.16 t.
40804/40806/40807/40810. Lot No. 30899 Derby 1978–79. 38.16 t.

Note: 40802/40804/40811 were numbered 40212/40232/40211 for a time when fitted with 23 first class seats.

40801	(40027, 40427)	**FG**	P	*GW*	LA
40802	(40012, 40412)	**FG**	P	*GW*	LA
40803	(40018, 40418)	**FG**	P	*GW*	LA
40804	(40032, 40432)	**MN**	P	*MM*	NL
40805	(40020, 40420)	**MN**	P	*MM*	NL

40806	(40029, 40429)	**FG**	P	*GW*	LA
40807	(40035, 40435)	**MN**	P	*MM*	NL
40808	(40015, 40415)	**FG**	P	*GW*	LA
40809	(40014, 40414)	**MN**	P	*MM*	NL
40810	(40030, 40430)	**MN**	P	*MM*	NL
40811	(40011, 40411)	**GN**	P	*GN*	EC

GH1G (TF)   TRAILER FIRST

41003–41056. Lot No. 30881 Derby 1976–77. 33.66 t.
41057–41120. Lot No. 30896 Derby 1977–78. 33.66 t.
41121–41148. Lot No. 30938 Derby 1979–80. 33.66 t.
41149–41166. Lot No. 30947 Derby 1980. 33.66 t.
41167–41169. Lot No. 30963 Derby 1982. 33.66 t.
41170. Lot No. 30967 Derby 1982. Former prototype vehicle. 33.66 t.
41179/80. Lot No. 30884 Derby 1976–77. 33.66 t.
41181–41184/41189. Lot No. 30939 Derby 1979–80. 33.66 t.
41185–41188. Lot No. 30969 Derby 1982. 33.66 t.

As built 48/– 2T. (w 47/– 2T 1W).
s Fitted with centre luggage stack. 46/– 1T 1TD 1W.

41003 p	**FG**	A	*GW*	LA		41033 p	**FG**	A	*GW*	LA
41004	**FG**	A	*GW*	PM		41034	**FG**	A	*GW*	LA
41005 p	**FG**	A	*GW*	LA		41035 p	**MN**	A	*MM*	NL
41006	**FG**	A	*GW*	LA		41036 w	**MN**	A	*MM*	NL
41007 p	**FG**	A	*GW*	PM		41037 p	**FG**	A	*GW*	LA
41008	**FG**	A	*GW*	PM		41038	**FG**	A	*GW*	LA
41009 p	**FG**	A	*GW*	PM		41039	**GN**	A	*GN*	EC
41010	**FG**	A	*GW*	PM		41040 w	**GN**	A	*GN*	EC
41011 p	**FG**	A	*GW*	PM		41041 ps	**MN**	P	*MM*	NL
41012	**FG**	A	*GW*	PM		41043	**GN**	A	*GN*	EC
41013 p	**FG**	A		ZC		41044 w	**GN**	A	*GN*	EC
41014	**FG**	A		ZC		41045 w	**V**	FG		BR
41015 p	**FG**	A	*GW*	PM		41046 s	**MN**	P	*MM*	NL
41016	**FG**	A	*GW*	PM		41051	**FG**	A	*GW*	LA
41017 p	**FG**	A	*GW*	PM		41052	**FG**	A	*GW*	LA
41018	**FG**	A	*GW*	PM		41055	**FG**	A	*GW*	LA
41019 p	**FG**	A	*GW*	PM		41056	**FG**	A	*GW*	LA
41020	**FG**	A	*GW*	PM		41057	**MN**	P	*MM*	NL
41021 p	**FG**	A	*GW*	PM		41058 s	**MN**	P	*MM*	NL
41022	**FG**	A	*GW*	PM		41059 w	**V**	FG		BR
41023 p	**FG**	A	*GW*	LA		41061	**MN**	P	*MM*	NL
41024	**FG**	A	*GW*	LA		41062 rw	**MN**	P	*MM*	NL
41025 p	**MN**	A	*MM*	NL		41063	**MN**	P	*MM*	NL
41026	**MN**	A	*MM*	NL		41064 s	**MN**	P	*MM*	NL
41027 p	**FG**	A	*GW*	LA		41065	**FG**	A	*GW*	LA
41028	**FG**	A	*GW*	LA		41066 p	**GN**	A	*GN*	EC
41029 p	**FG**	A	*GW*	LA		41067 s	**MN**	P	*MM*	NL
41030	**FG**	A	*GW*	LA		41068 s	**MN**	P	*MM*	NL
41031 p	**FG**	A	*GW*	LA		41069 s	**MN**	P	*MM*	NL
41032	**FG**	A	*GW*	LA		41070 s	**MN**	P	*MM*	NL

41071		**MN**	P	*MM*	NL	41122		**FG**	A	*GW*	LA
41072	s	**MN**	P	*MM*	NL	41123	p	**FG**	A	*GW*	PM
41075		**MN**	P	*MM*	NL	41124		**FG**	A	*GW*	PM
41076	s	**MN**	P	*MM*	NL	41125		**FG**	A	*GW*	LA
41077		**MN**	P	*MM*	NL	41126	p	**FG**	A	*GW*	LA
41078		**MN**	P	*MM*	NL	41127	p	**FG**	A	*GW*	LA
41079		**MN**	P	*MM*	NL	41128		**FG**	A	*GW*	LA
41080	s	**MN**	P	*MM*	NL	41129	p	**FG**	A	*GW*	PM
41081	w	**MN**	P		ZD	41130		**FG**	A	*GW*	PM
41083		**MN**	P	*MM*	NL	41131	p	**FG**	A	*GW*	LA
41084	s	**MN**	P	*MM*	NL	41132		**FG**	A	*GW*	LA
41085		**GN**	P	*GN*	EC	41133	p	**FG**	A	*GW*	LA
41086	w	**V**	FG		OO	41134		**FG**	A	*GW*	LA
41087		**GN**	A	*GN*	EC	41135	p	**FG**	A	*GW*	LA
41088	w	**GN**	A	*GN*	EC	41136		**FG**	A	*GW*	LA
41089		**FG**	A	*GW*	LA	41137		**FG**	A	*GW*	PM
41090	w	**GN**	A	*GN*	EC	41138		**FG**	A	*GW*	PM
41091		**GN**	A	*GN*	EC	41139	p	**FG**	A	*GW*	LA
41092	w	**GN**	A	*GN*	EC	41140		**FG**	A	*GW*	LA
41093		**FG**	A	*GW*	LA	41141	p	**FG**	A	*GW*	LA
41094		**FG**	A	*GW*	LA	41142		**FG**	A	*GW*	LA
41095	w	**MN**	P		ZD	41143	p	**FG**	A	*GW*	LA
41096	w	**MN**	P		ZD	41144		**FG**	A	*GW*	LA
41097		**GN**	A	*GN*	EC	41145	p	**FG**	A	*GW*	LA
41098	w	**GN**	A	*GN*	EC	41146		**FG**	A	*GW*	LA
41099		**GN**	A	*GN*	EC	41147	w	**FG**	P	*GW*	LA
41100	w	**GN**	A	*GN*	EC	41148	w	**V**	P		BR
41101		**FG**	A	*GW*	LA	41149	w	**FG**	P	*GW*	LA
41102		**FG**	A	*GW*	LA	41150	w	**GN**	A	*GN*	EC
41103		**FG**	A	*GW*	LA	41151		**GN**	A	*GN*	EC
41104		**FG**	A	*GW*	LA	41152		**GN**	A	*GN*	EC
41105		**FG**	A	*GW*	PM	41153		**MN**	P	*MM*	NL
41106		**FG**	A	*GW*	PM	41154	s	**MN**	P	*MM*	NL
41107	w	**FG**	P	*GW*	LA	41155		**MN**	P	*MM*	NL
41108	w	**MN**	P		ZD	41156		**MN**	P	*MM*	NL
41109	w	**FG**	P	*GW*	LA	41157		**FG**	A	*GW*	LA
41110		**FG**	A	*GW*	PM	41158		**FG**	A	*GW*	LA
41111		**MN**	P	*MM*	NL	41159	w	**V**	P		BR
41112		**MN**	P	*MM*	NL	41160	w	**V**	FG		OO
41113	s	**MN**	P	*MM*	NL	41161	w	**MN**	P		ZD
41114	w	**V**	FG		WS	41162	w	**V**	FG		WS
41115	w	**V**	P		BR	41163	w	**V**	FG		BR
41116		**FG**	A	*GW*	LA	41164	w	**GN**	A	*GN*	EC
41117		**MN**	P	*MM*	NL	41165	w	**V**	P		BR
41118	w	**GN**	A	*GN*	EC	41166	w	**V**	FG		BR
41119	w	**MN**	P	*MM*	NL	41167		**GN**	P	*GN*	EC
41120		**GN**	A	*GN*	EC	41168	w	**FG**	P	*GW*	LA
41121	p	**FG**	A	*GW*	LA	41169	w	**V**	P		BR

41170	(41001)	**GN**	A	*GN*	EC		
41179	(40505)	**FG**	A	*GW*	PM		
41180	(40511)	**FG**	A	*GW*	LA		
41181	(42282)	**FG**	P	*GW*	LA		
41182	(42278)	**FG**	P	*GW*	LA		
41183	(42274)	**FG**	P	*GW*	LA		
41184	(42270)	**MN**	P		BR		
41185	(42313)	**MN**	P		ZD		
41186	(42312)	**FG**	P	*GW*	LA		
41187	(42311)	**MN**	P	*MM*	NL		
41188	(42310)	**FG**	P	*GW*	LA		
41189	(42298)	**MN**	P		ZD		

GH2G (TS)   TRAILER STANDARD

42003–42090/42362. Lot No. 30882 Derby 1976–77. 33.60 t.
42091–42250. Lot No. 30897 Derby 1977–79. 33.60 t.
42251–42305. Lot No. 30939 Derby 1979–80. 33.60 t.
42306–42322. Lot No. 30969 Derby 1982. 33.60 t.
42323–42341. Lot No. 30983 Derby 1984–85. 33.60 t.
42342/42360. Lot No. 30949 Derby 1982. 33.47 t. Converted from TGS.
42343/42361. Lot No. 30970 Derby 1982. 33.47 t. Converted from TGS.
42344/42361. Lot No. 30964 Derby 1982. 33.47 t. Converted from TGS.
42346/42347/42350/42351. Lot No. 30881 Derby 1976–77. 33.66 t. Converted from TF.
42348/42349/42363. Lot No. 30896 Derby 1977–78. 33.66 t. Converted from TF.
42352/42354. Lot No. 30897 Derby 1977. Were TF from 1983 to 1992. 33.66 t.
42353/42355–42357. Lot No. 30967 Derby 1982. Ex-prototype vehicles. 33.66 t.

As built –/76 2T.
s Centre luggage stack –/72 2T.
t Centre luggage stack –/72 2T. Fitted with pt.
u Centre luggage stack –/74 2T.
w Centre luggage stack –72 2T 1W.
z Seats removed for wheelchair spaces –/70 2T 2W.
* disabled persons toilet and 5 tip-up seats. –/65 1T 1TD.
† disabled persons toilet. –/62 1T 1TD 1W.

42158 was also numbered 41177 for a time when fitted with first class seats.

42003		**FG**	A	*GW*	PM	42022		**FG**	A		ZC
42004	*	**FG**	A	*GW*	LA	42023		**FG**	A	*GW*	PM
42005		**FG**	A	*GW*	PM	42024	*	**FG**	A	*GW*	PM
42006		**FG**	A	*GW*	PM	42025		**FG**	A	*GW*	PM
42007	*	**FG**	A	*GW*	LA	42026		**FG**	A	*GW*	PM
42008	*	**FG**	A	*GW*	PM	42027		**FG**	A	*GW*	PM
42009		**FG**	A	*GW*	PM	42028		**FG**	A	*GW*	PM
42012	*	**FG**	A	*GW*	PM	42029	*	**FG**	A	*GW*	PM
42013		**FG**	A	*GW*	PM	42030	*	**FG**	A	*GW*	PM
42014		**FG**	A	*GW*	PM	42031		**FG**	A	*GW*	PM
42015	*	**FG**	A	*GW*	PM	42032		**FG**	A	*GW*	PM
42016		**FG**	A	*GW*	PM	42033		**FG**	A	*GW*	LA
42017		**FG**	A		ZC	42034		**FG**	A	*GW*	LA
42018	*	**FG**	A		ZC	42035		**FG**	A	*GW*	LA
42019		**FG**	A	*GW*	PM	42036	u	**MN**	A	*MM*	NL
42020		**FG**	A		ZC	42037	u	**MN**	A	*MM*	NL
42021	*	**FG**	A	*GW*	PM	42038	u	**MN**	A	*MM*	NL
						42039		**FG**	A	*GW*	LA

No.		C1	C2	C3	C4
42040		**FG**	A	*GW*	LA
42041		**FG**	A	*GW*	LA
42042		**FG**	A	*GW*	LA
42043		**FG**	A	*GW*	LA
42044		**FG**	A	*GW*	LA
42045		**FG**	A	*GW*	LA
42046		**FG**	A	*GW*	LA
42047		**FG**	A	*GW*	LA
42048		**FG**	A	*GW*	LA
42049		**FG**	A	*GW*	LA
42050		**FG**	A	*GW*	LA
42051	u	**MN**	A	*MM*	NL
42052	u	**MN**	A	*MM*	NL
42053	u	**MN**	A	*MM*	NL
42054		**FG**	A	*GW*	LA
42055		**FG**	A	*GW*	LA
42056		**FG**	A	*GW*	LA
42057		**GN**	A	*GN*	EC
42058		**GN**	A	*GN*	EC
42059		**GN**	A	*GN*	EC
42060		**FG**	A	*GW*	LA
42061		**FG**	A	*GW*	PM
42062	*	**FG**	A	*GW*	LA
42063		**GN**	A	*GN*	EC
42064		**GN**	A	*GN*	EC
42065		**GN**	A	*GN*	EC
42066	*	**FG**	A	*GW*	LA
42067		**FG**	A	*GW*	LA
42068		**FG**	A	*GW*	LA
42069	*	**FG**	A	*GW*	LA
42070		**FG**	A	*GW*	LA
42071		**FG**	A	*GW*	LA
42072		**FG**	A	*GW*	PM
42073		**FG**	A	*GW*	LA
42074		**FG**	A	*GW*	LA
42075		**FG**	A	*GW*	PM
42076		**FG**	A	*GW*	LA
42077		**FG**	A	*GW*	LA
42078		**FG**	A	*GW*	LA
42079		**FG**	A	*GW*	PM
42080		**FG**	A	*GW*	PM
42081	*	**FG**	A	*GW*	LA
42083		**FG**	A	*GW*	LA
42084	s	**MN**	P		ZD
42085	t	**MN**	P		ZD
42086	s	**MN**	P		ZD
42087	s	**MN**	P		ZD
42088		**V**	P		BR
42089		**FG**	A	*GW*	PM
42090	s	**V**	P		BR
42091	†	**GN**	A	*GN*	EC
42092	s	**V**	FG		BR
42093	s	**V**	FG		BR
42094	s	**V**	FG		BR
42095	s	**V**	FG		WS
42096		**FG**	A	*GW*	LA
42097	w	**MN**	A	*MM*	NL
42098		**FG**	A	*GW*	PM
42099		**FG**	A	*GW*	LA
42100	u	**MN**	P	*MM*	NL
42101	w	**MN**	P	*MM*	NL
42102	u	**MN**	P	*MM*	NL
42103	z	**GN**	P	*GN*	EC
42104		**GN**	A	*GN*	EC
42105	s	**V**	FG		BR
42106		**GN**	A	*GN*	EC
42107		**FG**	A	*GW*	LA
42108	s	**V**	FG		BR
42109	s	**V**	P		BR
42110	s	**V**	P		BR
42111	u	**MN**	P	*MM*	NL
42112	u	**MN**	P	*MM*	NL
42113	u	**MN**	P	*MM*	NL
42115	t	**MN**	P		ZD
42116	†	**GN**	A	*GN*	EC
42117		**GN**	P	*GN*	EC
42118		**FG**	A	*GW*	LA
42119	u	**MN**	P	*MM*	NL
42120	u	**MN**	P	*MM*	NL
42121	u	**MN**	P	*MM*	NL
42122		**GN**	A	*GN*	EC
42123	u	**MN**	P	*MM*	NL
42124	u	**MN**	P	*MM*	NL
42125	u	**MN**	P	*MM*	NL
42126		**FG**	A	*GW*	LA
42127	†	**GN**	A	*GN*	EC
42128	†	**GN**	A	*GN*	EC
42129		**FG**	A	*GW*	LA
42130	t	**V**	P		BR
42131	u	**MN**	P	*MM*	NL
42132	u	**MN**	P	*MM*	NL
42133	u	**MN**	P	*MM*	NL
42134		**GN**	A	*GN*	EC
42135	u	**MN**	P	*MM*	NL
42136	u	**MN**	P	*MM*	NL
42137	u	**MN**	P	*MM*	NL
42138	*	**FG**	A	*GW*	PM
42139	u	**MN**	P	*MM*	NL
42140	u	**MN**	P	*MM*	NL
42141	u	**MN**	P	*MM*	NL
42143		**FG**	A	*GW*	LA
42144		**FG**	A	*GW*	LA

42145	**FG**	A	*GW*	LA
42146	**GN**	A	*GN*	EC
42147 u	**MN**	P	*MM*	NL
42148 u	**MN**	P	*MM*	NL
42149 u	**MN**	P	*MM*	NL
42150	**GN**	A	*GN*	EC
42151 w	**MN**	P	*MM*	NL
42152 u	**MN**	P	*MM*	NL
42153 u	**MN**	P	*MM*	NL
42154	**GN**	A	*GN*	EC
42155 w	**MN**	P	*MM*	NL
42156 u	**MN**	P	*MM*	NL
42157 u	**MN**	P	*MM*	NL
42158	**GN**	A	*GN*	EC
42159 s	**V**	P		BR
42160 s	**V**	P		BR
42161 †	**GN**	A	*GN*	EC
42162	**FG**	P	*GW*	LA
42163 w	**MN**	P	*MM*	NL
42164 u	**MN**	P	*MM*	NL
42165 u	**MN**	P	*MM*	NL
42166	**FG**	P	*GW*	LA
42167	**GN**	P	*GN*	EC
42168	**GN**	P	*GN*	EC
42169	**GN**	P	*GN*	EC
42170	**FG**	P	*GW*	LA
42171	**GN**	A	*GN*	EC
42172	**GN**	A	*GN*	EC
42173	**FG**	P	*GW*	LA
42174	**FG**	P	*GW*	LA
42175 s	**V**	FG		BR
42176 t	**V**	FG		BR
42177 s	**V**	FG		BR
42178 t	**MN**	P		ZD
42179	**GN**	A	*GN*	EC
42180	**GN**	A	*GN*	EC
42181	**GN**	A	*GN*	EC
42182	**GN**	A	*GN*	EC
42183 *	**FG**	A	*GW*	LA
42184	**FG**	A	*GW*	LA
42185	**FG**	A	*GW*	LA
42186	**GN**	A	*GN*	EC
42187 t	**MN**	P		BR
42188 †	**GN**	A	*GN*	EC
42189 †	**GN**	A	*GN*	EC
42190	**GN**	A	*GN*	EC
42191	**GN**	A	*GN*	EC
42192	**GN**	A	*GN*	EC
42193	**GN**	A	*GN*	EC
42194 w	**MN**	P	*MM*	NL
42195	**FG**	P	*GW*	LA
42196	**FG**	A	*GW*	LA
42197	**FG**	A	*GW*	LA
42198	**GN**	A	*GN*	EC
42199	**GN**	A	*GN*	EC
42200 *	**FG**	A	*GW*	LA
42201 *	**FG**	A	*GW*	LA
42202 *	**FG**	A	*GW*	LA
42203	**FG**	A	*GW*	LA
42204	**FG**	A	*GW*	LA
42205 u	**MN**	P	*MM*	NL
42206 *	**FG**	A	*GW*	LA
42207 *	**FG**	A	*GW*	LA
42208	**FG**	A	*GW*	LA
42209	**FG**	A	*GW*	LA
42210 u	**MN**	P	*MM*	NL
42211 *	**FG**	A	*GW*	PM
42212	**FG**	A	*GW*	PM
42213	**FG**	A	*GW*	PM
42214	**FG**	A	*GW*	PM
42215	**GN**	A	*GN*	EC
42216	**FG**	A	*GW*	LA
42217	**FG**	P	*GW*	LA
42218	**FG**	P	*GW*	LA
42219	**GN**	A	*GN*	EC
42220 w	**MN**	P	*MM*	NL
42221	**FG**	A	*GW*	LA
42222	**FG**	P	*GW*	LA
42223	**FG**	P	*GW*	LA
42224	**FG**	P	*GW*	LA
42225 u	**MN**	P	*MM*	NL
42226	**GN**	A	*GN*	EC
42227 u	**MN**	P	*MM*	NL
42228 u	**MN**	P	*MM*	NL
42229 u	**MN**	P	*MM*	NL
42230 u	**MN**	P	*MM*	NL
42231 s	**V**	FG		WS
42232 t	**V**	FG		WS
42233 s	**V**	FG		WS
42234 s	**V**	P		BR
42235	**GN**	A	*GN*	EC
42236	**FG**	A	*GW*	PM
42237 s	**MN**	P		ZD
42238 †	**GN**	A	*GN*	EC
42239 †	**GN**	A	*GN*	EC
42240	**GN**	A	*GN*	EC
42241	**GN**	A	*GN*	EC
42242	**GN**	A	*GN*	EC
42243	**GN**	A	*GN*	EC
42244	**GN**	A	*GN*	EC
42245	**FG**	A	*GW*	LA
42246 s	**MN**	P	*MM*	NL

42247	t	**MN**	P	*MM*	NL	42294	s	**V**	P		BR
42248	s	**MN**	P	*MM*	NL	42295	*	**FG**	A	*GW*	LA
42249	s	**MN**	P	*MM*	NL	42296		**FG**	A	*GW*	LA
42250		**FG**	A	*GW*	LA	42297		**FG**	A	*GW*	LA
42251	*	**FG**	A	*GW*	PM	42299	*	**FG**	A	*GW*	LA
42252		**FG**	A	*GW*	LA	42300		**FG**	A	*GW*	LA
42253		**FG**	A	*GW*	LA	42301		**FG**	A	*GW*	LA
42254		**FG**	P	*GW*	LA	42302	s	**V**	FG		OO
42255	*	**FG**	A	*GW*	PM	42303	t	**V**	FG		OO
42256		**FG**	A	*GW*	PM	42304	s	**V**	FG		OO
42257		**FG**	A	*GW*	PM	42305	s	**V**	FG		OO
42258		**FG**	P	*GW*	LA	42306	s	**MN**	P		ZD
42259	*	**FG**	A	*GW*	PM	42307	s	**MN**	P		ZD
42260		**FG**	A	*GW*	LA	42308	s	**MN**	P		BR
42261		**FG**	A	*GW*	LA	42309	s	**MN**	P		BR
42262		**FG**	P	*GW*	LA	42314		**FG**	P	*GW*	LA
42263		**FG**	A	*GW*	PM	42315		**FG**	P	*GW*	LA
42264	*	**FG**	A	*GW*	PM	42316		**FG**	P	*GW*	LA
42265		**FG**	A	*GW*	LA	42317		**FG**	P	*GW*	LA
42266		**FG**	P	*GW*	LA	42318	s	**V**	P		NL
42267	*	**FG**	A	*GW*	PM	42319	t	**V**	P		NL
42268	*	**FG**	A	*GW*	LA	42320	s	**V**	P		BR
42269		**FG**	A	*GW*	PM	42321	s	**V**	P		BR
42271	*	**FG**	A	*GW*	LA	42322	s	**V**	P		BR
42272		**FG**	A	*GW*	LA	42323		**GN**	A	*GN*	EC
42273		**FG**	A	*GW*	LA	42324	w	**MN**	P	*MM*	NL
42275	*	**FG**	A	*GW*	LA	42325		**FG**	A	*GW*	LA
42276		**FG**	A	*GW*	LA	42326	s	**MN**	P		BR
42277		**FG**	A	*GW*	LA	42327	w	**MN**	P	*MM*	NL
42279	*	**FG**	A	*GW*	LA	42328	w	**MN**	P	*MM*	NL
42280		**FG**	A	*GW*	LA	42329	w	**MN**	P	*MM*	NL
42281		**FG**	A	*GW*	LA	42330	s	**MN**	P		ZD
42283		**FG**	A	*GW*	LA	42331	w	**MN**	P	*MM*	NL
42284		**FG**	A	*GW*	PM	42332		**FG**	A	*GW*	PM
42285		**FG**	A	*GW*	PM	42333		**FG**	A	*GW*	LA
42286	s	**V**	P		BR	42334		**FG**	P	*GW*	LA
42287	*	**FG**	A	*GW*	LA	42335	u	**MN**	P	*MM*	NL
42288		**FG**	A	*GW*	LA	42336	s	**MN**	P		ZD
42289		**FG**	A	*GW*	LA	42337	w	**MN**	P	*MM*	NL
42290	t	**V**	P		BR	42338	s	**MN**	P		ZD
42291	*	**FG**	A	*GW*	LA	42339	w	**MN**	P	*MM*	NL
42292	*	**FG**	A	*GW*	LA	42340		**GN**	A	*GN*	EC
42293		**FG**	A	*GW*	LA	42341	u	**MN**	P	*MM*	NL

42342	(44082)	u	**MN**	A	*MM*	NL
42343	(44095)		**FG**	A	*GW*	LA
42344	(44092)	*	**FG**	A	*GW*	LA
42345	(44096)	*	**FG**	A	*GW*	LA
42346	(41053)		**FG**	A	*GW*	PM
42347	(41054)		**FG**	A	*GW*	LA
42348	(41073)	*	**FG**	A	*GW*	LA

42349	(41074)		**FG**	A *GW*	PM
42350	(41047)		**FG**	A *GW*	LA
42351	(41048)		**FG**	A *GW*	LA
42352	(42142, 41176)	u	**MN**	P *MM*	NL
42353	(42001, 41171)	s	**V**	FG	PM
42354	(42114, 41175)		**GN**	A *GN*	EC
42355	(42000, 41172)		**GN**	A *GN*	EC
42356	(42002, 41173)		**FG**	A *GW*	PM
42357	(41002, 41174)		**GN**	A *GN*	EC
42360	(44084, 45084)		**FG**	A *GW*	PM
42361	(44099, 42000)		**FG**	A *GW*	PM
42362	(42011, 41178)		**FG**	A *GW*	LA
42363	(41082)	†	**GN**	A *GN*	EC

GJ2G (TGS)   TRAILER GUARD'S STANDARD

44000. Lot No. 30953 Derby 1980. 33.47 t.
44001–44090. Lot No. 30949 Derby 1980–82. 33.47 t.
44091–44094. Lot No. 30964 Derby 1982. 33.47 t.
44097–44101. Lot No. 30970 Derby 1982. 33.47 t.

As built –/65 1T (w –/63 1T 1W). pg.
s t Fitted with centre luggage stack s –/63 1T, t –/61 1T.

44000	w	**FG**	P	*GW*	LA	44028	w	**FG**	A	*GW*	LA
44001	w	**FG**	A	*GW*	LA	44029	w	**FG**	A	*GW*	PM
44002	w	**FG**	A	*GW*	PM	44030	w	**FG**	A	*GW*	LA
44003	w	**FG**	A	*GW*	PM	44031	w	**GN**	A	*GN*	EC
44004	w	**FG**	A	*GW*	PM	44032	w	**FG**	A	*GW*	PM
44005	w	**FG**	A	*GW*	PM	44033	w	**FG**	A	*GW*	LA
44006	w	**FG**	A		ZC	44034	w	**FG**	A	*GW*	LA
44007	w	**FG**	A	*GW*	PM	44035	w	**FG**	A	*GW*	LA
44008	w	**FG**	A	*GW*	PM	44036	w	**FG**	A	*GW*	PM
44009	w	**FG**	A	*GW*	PM	44037	w	**FG**	A	*GW*	LA
44010	w	**FG**	A	*GW*	PM	44038	w	**FG**	A	*GW*	LA
44011	w	**FG**	A	*GW*	LA	44039	w	**FG**	A	*GW*	LA
44012	s	**MN**	A	*MM*	NL	44040	w	**FG**	A	*GW*	LA
44013	w	**FG**	A	*GW*	LA	44041	s	**MN**	P	*MM*	NL
44014	w	**FG**	A	*GW*	LA	44042	t	**MN**	P		ZD
44015	w	**FG**	A	*GW*	LA	44043	w	**FG**	A	*GW*	LA
44016	w	**FG**	A	*GW*	LA	44044	s	**MN**	P	*MM*	NL
44017	s	**MN**	A	*MM*	NL	44045	w	**GN**	A	*GN*	EC
44018	w	**FG**	A	*GW*	LA	44046	s	**MN**	P	*MM*	NL
44019	w	**GN**	A	*GN*	EC	44047	s	**MN**	P	*MM*	NL
44020	w	**FG**	A	*GW*	LA	44048	s	**MN**	P	*MM*	NL
44021	t	**V**	P		ZC	44049	w	**FG**	A	*GW*	LA
44022	w	**FG**	A	*GW*	LA	44050	s	**MN**	P	*MM*	NL
44023	w	**FG**	A	*GW*	LA	44051	s	**MN**	P	*MM*	NL
44024	w	**FG**	A	*GW*	LA	44052	s	**MN**	P	*MM*	NL
44025	w	**FG**	A	*GW*	LA	44053	t	**V**	P		DY
44026	w	**FG**	A	*GW*	PM	44054	s	**MN**	P	*MM*	NL
44027	s	**MN**	P	*MM*	NL	44055	w	**GN**	P	*GN*	EC

44056	w	**GN**	A	*GN*	EC	44076	t	**V**	FG	BR
44057	t	**V**	P		BR	44077	w	**GN**	A	*GN*	EC
44058	w	**GN**	A	*GN*	EC	44078	t	**MN**	P	*MM*	NL
44059	w	**FG**	A	*GW*	LA	44079	w	**FG**	P	*GW*	LA
44060	t	**MN**	P		BR	44080	w	**GN**	A	*GN*	EC
44061	w	**GN**	A	*GN*	EC	44081	t	**V**	FG		BR
44062	t	**MN**	P		NL	44083	s	**MN**	P	*MM*	NL
44063	w	**GN**	A	*GN*	EC	44085	s	**MN**	P	*MM*	NL
44064	w	**FG**	A	*GW*	LA	44086	w	**FG**	A	*GW*	LA
44065	t	**V**	P		BR	44088	t	**V**	P		MA
44066	w	**FG**	A	*GW*	LA	44089	t	**V**	P		BR
44067	w	**FG**	A	*GW*	PM	44090	w	**FG**	P	*GW*	LA
44068	t	**V**	FG		OO	44091	t	**V**	P		BR
44069	t	**MN**	P		ZD	44093	w	**FG**	A	*GW*	LA
44070	s	**MN**	P	*MM*	NL	44094	w	**GN**	A	*GN*	EC
44071	s	**MN**	P	*MM*	NL	44097	w	**FG**	P	*GW*	LA
44072	t	**V**	P		BR	44098	w	**GN**	A	*GN*	EC
44073	w	**MN**	P	*MM*	NL	44100	t	**V**	FG		OO
44074	t	**V**	FG		WS	44101	w	**FG**	P	*GW*	LA
44075	t	**MN**	P		ZD						

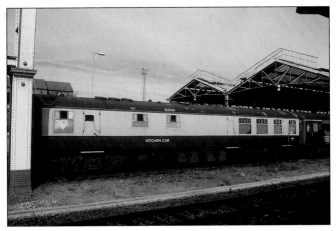

▲ BR blue & grey-liveried Mark 1 RBR 1658 is seen at Chester on 21/08/04.
It is now used as a kitchen car. **Robert Pritchard**

▼ BR maroon-liveried Mark 1 FO 3100 is seen at Holyhead on 30/08/04. This
vehicle has B4 bogies. **Bob Sweet**

▲ Mark 1 BFK 17018 with Commonwealth bogies, in BR Western Region chocolate and cream livery, is seen at Crewe Works during the open day of 31/05/03.
Mark Beal

▼ Mark 1 BCK 21269 is seen at Plymouth on 06/09/03. This coach is part of a rake in British racing green and cream-livery owned by EWS.   **Robert Pritchard**

BR Pullman First (PFK) 506 "WINDERMERE" is seen at Chester on 05/06/04. These vehicles were built for the Manchester Pullman and originally painted in grey and blue livery. They have been repainted into Pullman livery by their present owners West Coast Railway Company. Note the B5 bogies.

Ivor Bufton

▲ BR Southern Region green-liveried Mark 2 BSO 9104 is seen at Ropley, Mid-Hants Railway on 22/05/04. This coach is used both on this preserved line and on main line charters and should be sold to Fragonset on 01/01/2005. **Mark Beal**

▼ Mark 2 BFK 17041 is seen at Holyhead on 30/08/04. This coach has recently been reinstated for main line use as the support coach for 71000 "DUKE OF GLOUCESTER". **Bob Sweet**

▲ Mark 2A TSO 5278 "MELISANDE" in Pulman livery is seen at Newport on 22/05/04. **Simon Wright**

▼ First Great Western green-liveried Mark 2D TSO 5737 at Holyhead on 27/03/04. **Ivor Bufton**

▲ Unclassified Mark 2E Brake 9810 (converted from a TSO) in ScotRail Caledonian Sleepers livery at Fort William on 19/07/04. **Ivor Bufton**

▼ Mark 2F FO 3360, in Inter-City livery and operated by Fragonset, is seen at Chester on 21/08/04. **Robert Pritchard**

▲ Heart of Wessex Line promotional-livery Mark 2F TSO 9525 is seen at Bath Spa on 07/08/04. This coach is operated by Wessex Trains (TOC). **John Chalcraft**

▼ "One"-liveried Mark 2F DBSO 9710 is seen passing Pudding Mill Lane heading the 07.30 Liverpool Street–Norwich on 28/06/04. This is the only DBSO in this livery. **Alex Dasi-Sutton**

▲ Royal Household Kitchen/Dining Car 2917 at York on 21/02/03.
Robert Pritchard

▼ Anglia Railways-liveried Mark 3 RFM buffet 10223 is seen at Colchester on 25/09/03.
Mark Beal

▲ One Anglia introduced their first Mark 3 set into service in April 2004. This set was repainted in "One" livery but not altered internally. Here FO 11023 is seen at Norwich in the new livery on 01/04/04.   **Darren Ford**

▼ Mark 3 TSO 12128 is seen at Drem Jn. on 06/07/04 on an Edinburgh–North Berwick service. This is in Virgin Trains livery but with ScotRail logos.
                                                              Robert Pritchard

▲ First Great Western (green)-liveried Mark 3 SLEP 10601 at Penzance on 05/07/04. **Robert Pritchard**

▼ Midland Mainline-liveried HST TRFB 40741 at Sheffield on 01/03/04.
Robert Pritchard

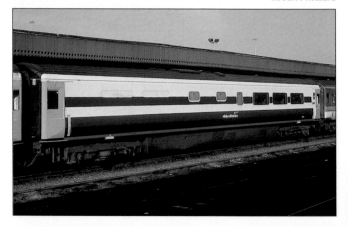

▲ GNER-liveried HST TS 42171 on the Lickey Incline forming part of the 09.25 Newquay–Newcastle Virgin XC service on 31/07/04. **Bob Sweet**

▼ First Great Western-liveried HST TGS 44011 at Castle Cary on 06/08/04.
John Chalcraft

▲ GNER-liveried "Mallard" Mark 4 FOS 11409 is seen at Newcastle Central on 16/10/04. The rebuilt "Mallard" Mark 4 sets are recognisable from unrefurbished sets by their orange doors. **Robert Pritchard**

▼ London & North Western Railway-liveried generator coach 35407 (99886) at Cardiff Central on 22/02/03. **Ivor Bufton**

▲ VSOE Pullman Parlour First No. 301 "PERSEUS", with Gresley bogies, is seen at London Victoria on 21/05/04. **Robert Pritchard**

▼ Virgin-liveried DVT 82106, minus Virgin branding, is seen at Edinburgh Waverley on 31/07/04. **Adrian Sumner**

▲ GNER DVT 82219 "Duke of Edinburgh" leads a rebuilt "Mallard" Mark 4 rake into London King's Cross on 16/06/04.   **Robert Pritchard**

▼ Mark 1 Courier Vehicle 80204 now used by West Coast Railway Company as a locomotive support coach is seen at Wabtec Doncaster during the open day of 26/07/03.   **Mark Beal**

▲ Network Rail-liveried BG 92114 is seen at Derby Etches Park on 18/01/04.
Paul Robertson

▼ Inter-City-liveried BG 92929 is seen at Crewe on 14/02/04. This vehicle is regularly used as a Pendolino Barrier Vehicle, with 92111 (seen, left).
Robert Pritchard

▲ Railtrack blue & green-liveried Ultrasonic Test Coach 99666 is seen at Derby RTC on 17/01/04.   **Paul Robertson**

▼ FGW Motorail Van 96605 at Long Rock depot, Penzance on 02/08/04.
                                                                                          Paul Shannon

2.3. SALOONS

Several specialist passenger carrying vehicles, normally referred to as saloons are permitted to run on the National Rail system. Many of these are to pre-nationalisation designs.

WCJS FIRST SALOON

Built 1892 by LNWR, Wolverton. Originally dining saloon mounted on six-wheel bogies. Rebuilt with new underframe with four-wheel bogies in 1927. Rebuilt 1960 as observation saloon with DMU end. Gangwayed at other end. The interior has a saloon, kitchen, guards vestibule and observation lounge. Gresley bogies. 19/– 1T. 28.5 t. 75 m.p.h.

Non-Standard Livery: London & North Western Railway.

| 41 | (484, 45018) | x | **0** | SH | *SH* | CJ |

LNWR DINING SALOON

Built 1890 by LNWR, Wolverton. Mounted on the underframe of LMS GUV 37908 in the 1980s. Contains kitchen and dining area seating 12 at tables for two. Gresley bogies. 10/–. 75 m.p.h. 25.4 t.

Non-Standard Livery: London & North Western Railway.

| 159 | (5159) | x | **0** | SH | *SH* | CJ |

GNR FIRST CLASS SALOON

Built 1912 by GNR, Doncaster. Contains entrance vestibule, lavatory, two seperate saloons, library and luggage space. Gresley bogies. 19/– 1T. 75 m.p.h. 29.4 t.

Non-Standard Livery: Teak.

| 807 | (4807) | x | **0** | SH | *SH* | CJ |

LNER GENERAL MANAGERS SALOON

Built 1945 by LNER, York. Gangwayed at one end with a verandah at the other. The interior has a dining saloon seating twelve, kitchen, toilet, office and nine seat lounge. 21/– 1T. B4 bogies. 75 m.p.h. ETH3. 35.7 t.

| 1999 | (902260) | **M** | GS | *GS* | CS | DINING CAR No. 2 |

GENERAL MANAGER'S SALOON

Renumbered 1989 from London Midland Region departmental series. Formerly the LMR General Manager's saloon. Rebuilt from LMS period 1 BFK M 5033 M to dia. 1654 and mounted on the underframe of BR suburban BS M 43232. Screw couplings have been removed. B4 bogies. 100 m.p.h. ETH2X.

LMS Lot No. 326 Derby 1927. 27.5 t.

| 6320 | (5033, DM 395707) | x | **M** | 62 | *62* | SK |

GWR FIRST CLASS SALOON

Built 1930 by GWR, Swindon. Contains saloons at either end with body end observation windows, staff compartment, central kitchen and pantry/bar. Numbered DE321011 when in departmental service with British Railways. 20/– 1T. GWR bogies. 75 m.p.h. 34 t.

GWR Lot No. 1431 1930.

9004	**CH**	RA	*SH*	CJ

LMS INSPECTION SALOONS

Built as engineers inspection saloons. Non-gangwayed. Observation windows at each end. The interior layout consists of two saloons interspersed by a central lavatory/kitchen/guards section. BR Mark 1 bogies. 80 m.p.h. 31.5 t.

45020–45026. Lot No. LMS 1356 Wolverton 1944.
45029. Lot No. LMS 1327 Wolverton 1942.
999503–999504. Lot No. BR Wagon Lot. 3093 Wolverton 1957.

45020		**E**	E	*E*	ML
45026	v	**M**	HN		CS
45029	v	**E**	E	*E*	ML
999503	v	**M**	E		OM
999504	v	**E**	E	*E*	TO

"QUEEN OF SCOTS" SERVICE CARS

Converted from BR Mark 1 BSKs. Commonwealth bogies. 100 m.p.h. ETH2.

Non-Standard Livery: London & North Western Railway.

99035. Lot No. 30699 Wolverton 1962–63.
99886. Lot No. 30721 Wolverton 1963.

99035 (35322)	x	**0**	SH	*SH*	CJ	SERVICE CAR No. 2
99886 (35407)	x	**0**	SH	*SH*	CJ	SERVICE CAR No. 1

RAILFILMS KITCHEN/SLEEPING SALOON

Converted from BR Mark 1 SK. Contains three sleeping cabins with showers and toilets and a large kitchen/pantry. Commonwealth bogies. 100 m.p.h. ETH 4.

Non-standard Livery: London & North Western Railway.

99884 (26208, 19208)	**0**	RA		CS	State Car No. 84

ROYAL SCOTSMAN SALOONS

Built 1960 by Metro-Cammell as Pullman Parlour First (§Pullman Kitchen First) for East Coast Main Line services. Rebuilt 1990 as sleeping cars with four twin sleeping rooms (*§ three twin sleeping rooms and two single sleeping rooms at each end). Commonwealth bogies. 38.5 t.

99961 (324 AMBER) * **M**	GS	*GS*	CS	STATE CAR 1
99962 (329 PEARL) **M**	GS	*GS*	CS	STATE CAR 2
99963 (331 TOPAZ) **M**	GS	*GS*	CS	STATE CAR 3
99964 (313 FINCH) § **M**	GS	*GS*	CS	STATE CAR 4

Built 1960 by Metro-Cammell as Pullman Kitchen First for East Coast Main Line services. Rebuilt 1990 as observation car with open verandah seating 32. Commonwealth bogies. 38.5 t.

99965 (319 SNIPE) **M**	GS	*GS*	CS	OBSERVATION CAR

Built 1960 by Metro-Cammell as Pullman Kitchen First for East Coast Main Line services. Rebuilt 1993 as dining car. Commonwealth bogies. 38.5 t.

99967 (317 RAVEN) **M**	GS	*GS*	CS	DINING CAR

Mark 3A. Converted from SLEP at Carnforth Railway Restoration and Engineering Services in 1997. BT10 bogies. Attendant's and adjacent two sleeping compartments converted to generator room containing a 160 kW Volvo unit. In 99968 four sleeping compartments remain for staff use with another converted for use as a staff shower and toilet. The remaining five sleeping compartments have been replaced by two passenger cabins. In 99969 seven sleeping compartments remain for staff use. A further sleeping compartment, along with one toilet, have been converted to store rooms. The other two sleeping compartments have been combined to form a crew mess. ETH7X. 41.5 t.

Lot. No. 30960 Derby 1981–3.

99968 (10541)	**M**	GS	*GS*	CS	STATE CAR 5
99969 (10556)	**M**	GS	*GS*	CS	SERVICE CAR

RAILFILMS 'LMS CLUB CAR'

Converted from BR Mark 1 TSO at Carnforth Railway Restoration and Engineering Services in 1994. Contains kitchenette, pantry, coupé, lounge/reception area with two settees and two dining saloons. 24/– 1T. Commonwealth bogies. 100 m.p.h. ETH 4.

Lot. No. 30724 York 1963. 37 t.

99993 (5067)	**M**	RA	*VT*	TM	LMS CLUB CAR

BR INSPECTION SALOON

Mark 1. Short frames. Non-gangwayed. Observation windows at each end. The interior layout consists of two saloons interspersed by a central lavatory/kitchen/guards/luggage section. BR Mark 1 bogies. 90 m.p.h.

Lot No. BR Wagon Lot. 3379 Swindon 1960. 30.5 t.

999509	**E**	E	*E*	ML

2.4. PULLMAN CAR COMPANY SERIES

Pullman cars have never generally been numbered as such, although many have carried numbers, instead they have carried titles. However, a scheme of schedule numbers exists which generally lists cars in chronological order. In this section those numbers are shown followed by the car's title. Cars described as 'kitchen' contain a kitchen in addition to passenger accommodation and have gas cooking unless otherwise stated. Cars described as 'parlour' consist entirely of passenger accomodation. Cars described as 'brake' contain a compartment for the use of the guard and a luggage compartment in addition to passenger accommodation.

PULLMAN PARLOUR FIRST

Built 1927 by Midland Carriage and Wagon Company. Gresley bogies. 26/– 2T. ETH 2. 41 t.

| 213 MINERVA | **PC** | VS | *VS* | SL |

PULLMAN PARLOUR FIRST

Built 1928 by Metropolitan Carriage and Wagon Company. Gresley bogies. 24/– 2T. ETH 4. 40 t.

| 239 AGATHA | **PC** | VS | | SL |
| 243 LUCILLE | **PC** | VS | *VS* | SL |

PULLMAN KITCHEN FIRST

Built 1925 by BRCW. Rebuilt by Midland Carriage & Wagon Company in 1928. Gresley bogies. 20/– 1T. ETH 4. 41 t.

| 245 IBIS | **PC** | VS | *VS* | SL |

PULLMAN PARLOUR FIRST

Built 1928 by Metropolitan Carriage and Wagon Company. Gresley bogies. 24/– 2T. ETH 4.

| 254 ZENA | **PC** | VS | *VS* | SL |

PULLMAN KITCHEN FIRST

Built 1928 by Metropolitan Carriage and Wagon Company. Gresley bogies. 20/– 1T. ETH 4. 42 t.

| 255 IONE | **PC** | VS | *VS* | SL |

PULLMAN KITCHEN COMPOSITE

Built 1932 by Metropolitan Carriage and Wagon Company. Originally included in '6-Pul EMU. Electric cooking. EMU bogies. 12/16 1T.

264	RUTH	**PC**	VS		SL

PULLMAN KITCHEN FIRST

Built 1932 by Metopolitan Carriage and Wagon Company. Originally included in 'Brighton Belle' EMUs but now used as hauled stock. Electric cooking. B5 (SR) bogies (§ EMU bogies). 20/- 1T. ETH 2. 44 t.

280	AUDREY	**PC**	VS	*VS*	SL
281	GWEN	**PC**	VS	*VS*	SL
283	MONA	§ **PC**	VS		SL
284	VERA	**PC**	VS	*VS*	SL

PULLMAN PARLOUR THIRD

Built 1932 by Metropolitan Carriage and Wagon Company. Originally included in 'Brighton Belle' EMUs. EMU bogies. –/56 2T.

285	CAR No. 85	**PC**	VS		SL
286	CAR No. 86	**PC**	VS		SL

PULLMAN BRAKE THIRD

Built 1932 by Metropolitan Carriage and Wagon Company. Originally driving motor cars in 'Brighton Belle' EMUs. Traction and control equipment removed for use as hauled stock. EMU bogies. –/48 1T.

288	CAR No. 88	**PC**	VS		SL
292	CAR No. 92	**PC**	VS		SL
293	CAR No. 93	**PC**	VS		SL

PULLMAN PARLOUR FIRST

Built 1951 by Birmingham Railway Carriage and Wagon Company. Gresley bogies. 32/- 2T. ETH 3. 39 t.

301	PERSEUS	**PC**	VS	*VS*	SL

Built 1952 by Pullman Car Company, Preston Park using underframe and bogies from 176 RAINBOW, the body of which had been destroyed by fire. Gresley bogies. 26/- 2T. ETH 4. 38 t.

302	PHOENIX	**PC**	VS	*VS*	SL

PULLMAN PARLOUR FIRST

Built 1951 by Birmingham Railway Carriage & Wagon Company. Gresley bogies.
32/– 2T. ETH 3. 39 t.

308 CYGNUS   **PC** VS   *VS*   SL

PULLMAN FIRST BAR

Built 1951 by Birmingham Railway Carriage & Wagon Company. Rebuilt 1999
by Blake Fabrications, Edinburgh with original timber-framed body replaced
by a new fabricated steel body. Contains kitchen, bar, dining saloon and coupé.
Electric cooking. Gresley bogies. 14/– 1T. ETH 3.

310 PEGASUS   **PC** RA   *VS*   CP

Also carries "THE TRIANON BAR" branding.

PULLMAN KITCHEN SECOND

Built 1960–1961 by Metro-Cammell for East Coast Main Line services.
Commonwealth bogies. –/30 1T. 40 t.

335 CAR No. 335   x **PC** WC   *WC*   CS

PULLMAN PARLOUR SECOND

Built 1960–1961 by Metro-Cammell for East Coast Main Line services.
Commonwealth bogies. –/42 2T. 38.5 t.

348 CAR No. 348   **PC** WC   *WC*   CS
353 CAR No. 353   **PC** WC   *WC*   CS

PULLMAN SECOND BAR

Built 1960–1961 by Metro-Cammell for East Coast Main Line services.
Commonwealth bogies. –/24 + 17 bar seats. 38.5 t.

354 CAR No. 354   **PC** WC   *WC*   CS

Formerly also known as "THE HADRIAN BAR".

2.5. PASSENGER COACHING STOCK AWAITING DISPOSAL

This list contains the last known locations of coaching stock awaiting disposal. The definition of which vehicles are "awaiting disposal" is somewhat vague, but generally speaking these are vehicles of types not now in normal service or vehicles which have been damaged by fire, vandalism or collision.

1644 CS	5454 KT	10571 BN
1650 CS	5471 KT	10572 OM
1652 CS	5475 KT	10574 TO
1653 FP	5480 KT	10604 OM
1655 CS	5505 KT	10646 TO
1663 CS	5616 FP	10653 OM
1670 CS	5645 CS	10654 OM
1684 CS	5709 CS	10664 ZN
1688 CS	5712 CS	10669 OM
1981 OM	5781 NC	10677 ZN
2127 CS	6178 HM	10682 OM
3225 KT	6335 LA	10686 OM
3226 KT	6339 EC	10695 ZN
3258 KT	6345 EC	10709 ZN
4849 KT	6356 BH	10711 OM
4854 KT	6357 BH	10712 OM
4860 CS	6360 NL	10713 OM
4866 KT	6361 NL	10721 ZN
4880 KT	6390 ZB	10724 BN
4932 CS	6523 CS	10730 OM
4938 DR	6900 Cambridge Station Yard	13306 CS
4997 CS	6901 Cambridge Station Yard	13320 CS
5042 FP	9385 LT	13323 CS
5226 LT	9458 ZB	13582 KT
5265 KT	9482 NL	13604 FP
5267 KT	9483 PY	13607 FP
5354 PY	9486 PY	17039 CD
5389 OM	10327 ZC	17058 KT
5410 KT	10533 MM	18837 CS
5420 OM	10540 OM	34525 CS
5433 TM	10549 MM	35509 ZH
5443 KT	10554 OM	35513 KT
5446 KT	10557 MM	35516 KT

2.6. 99xxx RANGE NUMBER CONVERSION TABLE

The following table is presented to help readers identify vehicles which may carry numbers in the 99xxx range, the former private owner number series which is no longer in general use.

99xxx	BR No.	99xxx	BR No.	99xxx	BR No.	99xxx	BR No.
99040	21232	99323	5704	99535	Pullman 213	99677	586
99041	35476	99324	5714	99536	Pullman 254	99678	504
99052	Saloon 41	99325	5727	99537	Pullman 280	99679	506
99121	3105	99326	4954	99538	34991	99680	17102
99125	3113	99327	5044	99539	Pullman 255	99710	18767
99127	3117	99328	5033	99541	Pullman 243	99712	18893
99128	3130	99329	4931	99542	889202	99713	19013
99131	1999	99348	Pullman 348	99543	Pullman 284	99716	18808
99304	21256	99353	Pullman 353	99545	80207	99718	18862
99311	1882	99354	Pullman 354	99546	Pullman 281	99721	18756
99312	35463	99361	Pullman 335	99670	546	99722	18806
99316	13321	99371	3128	99671	548	99723	35459
99317	3766	99405	35486	99672	549	99792	17019
99318	4912	99530	Pullman 301	99673	550	99880	159
99319	17168	99531	Pullman 302	99674	551	99881	807
99321	5299	99532	Pullman 308	99675	552	99953	35468
99322	5600	99534	Pullman 245	99676	553		

2.7. PRESERVED LOCOMOTIVE SUPPORT COACHES TABLE

The following table lists support coaches and the BR numbers of the locomotives which they normally support at present. These coaches can spend considerable periods of time off the National Rail system when the locomotives they support are not being used on that system.

14007	61264	35317	34067	35465	46035	35486	SV locos
17013	NM locos	35329	RL locos	35468	NM locos	35517	BQ locos
17019	46201	35333	6024	35470	TM locos	35518	34067
17041	71000	35453	5051	35476	46233	80204	WC locos
17096	35028	35461	5029	35479	SV locos	80220	62005
21232	46233	35463	WC locos				

3. DIESEL MULTIPLE UNITS

INTRODUCTION

DMU CLASSES

DMU Classes are listed in class number order. Principal details and dimensions are quoted for each class in metric and/or imperial units as considered appropriate bearing in mind common usage in the UK.

All dimensions and weights are quoted for vehicles in an "as new" condition with all necessary supplies (e.g. oil, water, sand) on board. Dimensions are quoted in the order Length – Width. All lengths quoted are over buffers or couplers as appropriate. Where two lengths are quoted, the first refers to outer vehicles in a set and the second to inner vehicles. All width dimensions quoted are maxima.

NUMERICAL LISTINGS

DMUs are listed in numerical order of set – using current numbers as allocated by the RSL. Individual "loose" vehicles are listed in numerical order after vehicles formed into fixed formations. Where numbers carried are different from those officially allocated these are noted in class headings where appropriate. Where sets or vehicles have been renumbered in recent years, former numbering detail is shown in parentheses. Each entry is laid out as in the following example:

Set No.	Detail	Livery	Owner	Operator	Depot	Formation	Name
156 433	t	**SC**	A	*SR*	CK	52433 57433	The Kilmarnock Edition

Detail Differences. Detail differences which currently affect the areas and types of train which vehicles may work are shown, plus differences in interior layout. Where such differences occur within a class, these are shown either in the heading information or alongside the individual set or vehicle number. The following standard abbreviation is used:

r   Radio Electronic Token Block (RETB) equipment.

In all cases use of the above abbreviation indicates the equipment indicated is normally operable. Meaning of non-standard abbreviations is detailed in individual class headings.

Set Formations. Regular set formations are shown where these are normally maintained. Readers should note set formations might be temporarily varied from time to time to suit maintenance and/or operational requirements. Vehicles shown as "spare" are not formed in any regular set formation.

Codes. Codes are used to denote the livery, owner, operator and depot of each unit. Details of these will be found in section 7 of this book. Where a unit or spare car is off-lease, the operator column will be left blank.

Names. Only names carried with official sanction are listed. As far as possible names are shown in UPPER/lower case characters as actually shown on the name carried on the vehicle(s). Unless otherwise shown, complete units are regarded as named rather than just the individual car(s) which carry the name.

GENERAL INFORMATION

CLASSIFICATION AND NUMBERING

First generation ("Heritage") DMUs are classified in the series 100–139.
Second generation DMUs are classified in the series 140–199.
Diesel-electric multiple units are classified in the series 200–249.
Service units are classified in the series 930–999.
First and second generation individual cars are numbered in the series 50000–59999 and 79000–79999.

DEMU individual cars are numbered in the series 60000–60999, except for a few former EMU vehicles which retain their EMU numbers.

Service stock individual cars are numbered in the series 975000–975999 and 977000–977999, although this series is not exclusively used for DMU vehicles.

OPERATING CODES

These codes are used by train operating company staff to describe the various different types of vehicles and normally appear on data panels on the inner (i.e. non driving) ends of vehicles.

The first part of the code describes whether or not the car has a motor or a driving cab as follows:

DM Driving motor.
M   Motor
DT   Driving trailer
T   Trailer

The next letter is a "B" for cars with a brake compartment.

This is followed by the saloon details:

F   First
S   Standard
C   Composite
so denotes a semi-open vehicle (part compartments, part open). All other vehicles are assumed to consist solely of open saloons.

L denotes a vehicle with a lavatory compartment.

Finally vehicles with a buffet are suffixed RB or RMB for a miniature buffet.

Where two vehicles of the same type are formed within the same unit, the above codes may be suffixed by (A) and (B) to differentiate between the vehicles.

A composite is a vehicle containing both first and standard class accommodation, whilst a brake vehicle is a vehicle containing separate specific accommodation for the conductor.

Special Note: Where vehicles have been declassified, the correct operating code which describes the actual vehicle layout is quoted in this publication.

BUILD DETAILS

Lot Numbers
Vehicles ordered under the auspices of BR were allocated a lot (batch) number when ordered and these are quoted in class headings and sub-headings.

Builders
These are shown in class headings. Abbreviations used are found in section 7.8.

Information on sub-contracting works which built parts of vehicles e.g. the underframes etc. is not shown.

ACCOMMODATION

The information given in class headings and sub-headings is in the form F/S nT (or TD) nW. For example 12/54 1T 1W denotes 12 first class and 54 standard class seats, one toilet and one space for a wheelchair. The seating layout of open saloons is shown as 2+1, 2+2 or 3+2 as the case may be. Where units have first class accommodation as well as standard and the layout is different for each class then these are shown separately prefixed by "1:" and "2:". TD denotes a toilet suitable for use by a disabled person.

3.1. DIESEL MECHANICAL & DIESEL HYDRAULIC UNITS

3.1.1. FIRST GENERATION UNIT

CLASS 121   PRESSED STEEL SUBURBAN

First generation unit used by Chiltern Railways on selected Aylesbury–Princes Risborough services.
Construction: Steel.
Engines: Two Leyland 1595 of 112 kW (150 h.p.) at 1800 r.p.m.
Transmission: Mechanical. Cardan shaft and freewheel to a four-speed epicyclic gearbox and final drive.
Brakes: Vacuum.
Gangways: Non gangwayed single cars with cabs at each end.
Bogies: DD10.   **Couplers:** Screw couplings.
Dimensions: 20.45 x 2.82 m.   **Seating Layout:** 3+2 facing.
Doors: Manually-operated slam.   **Maximum Speed:** 70 m.p.h.
Multiple Working: "Blue Square" coupling code. First Generation vehicles cannot be coupled to Second Generation units.

55020. DMBS. Lot No. 30518 1960. –/65. 38.0 t.

Non-standard livery: All over Chiltern blue with a silver stripe.

Notes: Fitted with central door locking.

Also formerly in departmental use as unit 960 002 (977722).

| 121 020 | **0** | CR | *CR* | AL | 55020 |

3.1.2. SECOND GENERATION UNITS

All units in this section have air brakes and are equipped with public address, with transmission equipment on driving vehicles and flexible diaphragm gangways. Except where otherwise stated, transmission is Voith 211r hydraulic with a cardan shaft to a Gmeinder GM190 final drive.

CLASS 142   PACER   BREL DERBY/LEYLAND

DMS–DMSL.

Construction: Steel. Built from Leyland National bus parts on four-wheeled underframes.
Engines: One Cummins LTA10-R of 172 kW (230 h.p.) at 2100 r.p.m.
(* One Perkins 2006-TWH of 172 kW (230 h.p.) at 2100 r.p.m.).
Couplers: BSI at outer ends, bar within unit.
Seating Layout: 3+2 mainly unidirectional bus/bench style unless stated.
Dimensions: 15.44 x 2.80 m.

Gangways: Within unit only.   **Wheel Arrangement:** 1-A A-1.
Doors: Twin-leaf inward pivoting.   **Maximum Speed:** 75 m.p.h.
Multiple Working: Within class and with Classes 143, 144, 150, 153, 155, 156, 158, 159.

55542–55591. DMS. Lot No. 31003 1985–1986. –/62 (s –/56, t –/53 or 55 1W, u –/52 or 54 1W, v –/52 1W) 24.5 t.
55592–55641. DMSL. Lot No. 31004 1985–1986. –/59 1T (s –/50 1T, u –/60 1T, v –/50 1T) 25.0 t.
55701–55746. DMS. Lot No. 31013 1986–1987. –/62 (s –/56, t –/53 or 55 1W, u –/52 or 54 1W, v–/52 1W) 24.5 t.
55747–55792. DMSL. Lot No. 31014 1986–1987. –/59 1T (s –/50 1T, u –/60 1T, v–/50 1T) 25.0 t.

s Fitted with 2+2 individual high-backed seating.

t Northern facelifted units – DMS fitted with luggage rack and wheelchair space.

u Merseytravel units – Fitted with 3+2 individual low-back seating.

v Refurbished Arriva Trains Wales units. Fitted with 2+2 individual Chapman seating.

142 001	t	**NW**	A	*NO*	NH	55542	55592
142 002	v	**VL**	A	*AW*	CF	55543	55593
142 003	t	**NW**	A	*NO*	NH	55544	55594
142 004	t	**NW**	A	*NO*	NH	55545	55595
142 005	t	**NW**	A	*NO*	NH	55546	55596
142 006	v	**VL**	A	*AW*	CF	55547	55597
142 007	t	**NW**	A	*NO*	NH	55548	55598
142 009	t	**NW**	A	*NO*	NH	55550	55600	Newton Heath 125 1876–2001
142 010	v	**VL**	A	*AW*	CF	55551	55601
142 011	t	**NW**	A	*NO*	NH	55552	55602
142 012	t	**NW**	A	*NO*	NH	55553	55603
142 013	t	**NW**	A	*NO*	NH	55554	55604
142 014	t	**NW**	A	*NO*	NH	55555	55605
142 015	s	**AV**	A	*NO*	HT	55556	55606
142 016	s	**AV**	A	*NO*	HT	55557	55607
142 017	s	**AV**	A	*NO*	HT	55558	55608
142 018	s	**AV**	A	*NO*	HT	55559	55609
142 019	s	**AV**	A	*NO*	HT	55560	55610
142 020	s	**AV**	A	*NO*	HT	55561	55611
142 021	s	**AV**	A	*NO*	HT	55562	55612
142 022	s	**AV**	A	*NO*	HT	55563	55613
142 023	t	**NW**	A	*NO*	NH	55564	55614
142 024	s	**AV**	A	*NO*	HT	55565	55615
142 025	s	**NS**	A	*NO*	HT	55566	55616
142 026	s	**AV**	A	*NO*	HT	55567	55617
142 027	t	**NW**	A	*NO*	NH	55568	55618
142 028	t	**NW**	A	*NO*	NH	55569	55619
142 029	t	**NW**	A	*NO*	NH	55570	55620
142 030	t	**NW**	A	*NO*	NH	55571	55621
142 031	t	**NW**	A	*NO*	NH	55572	55622
142 032	t	**NW**	A	*NO*	NH	55573	55623

142 033	t	**NW**	A	*NO*	NH	55574	55624	
142 034	t	**NW**	A	*NO*	NH	55575	55625	
142 035	t	**NW**	A	*NO*	NH	55576	55626	
142 036	t	**NW**	A	*NO*	NH	55577	55627	
142 037	t	**NW**	A	*NO*	NH	55578	55628	
142 038	t	**NW**	A	*NO*	NH	55579	55629	
142 039	t	**NW**	A	*NO*	NH	55580	55630	
142 040	t	**NW**	A	*NO*	NH	55581	55631	
142 041	u	**MY**	A	*NO*	NH	55582	55632	
142 042	u	**MY**	A	*NO*	NH	55583	55633	
142 043	u	**MY**	A	*NO*	NH	55584	55634	
142 044	u	**MY**	A	*NO*	NH	55585	55635	
142 045	u	**MY**	A	*NO*	NH	55586	55636	
142 046	u	**MY**	A	*NO*	NH	55587	55637	
142 047	u	**MY**	A	*NO*	NH	55588	55638	
142 048	u	**MY**	A	*NO*	NH	55589	55639	
142 049	u	**MY**	A	*NO*	NH	55590	55640	
142 050	s	**NS**	A	*NO*	HT	55591	55641	
142 051	u	**MY**	A	*NO*	NH	55701	55747	
142 052	u	**MY**	A	*NO*	NH	55702	55748	
142 053	u	**MY**	A	*NO*	NH	55703	55749	
142 054	u	**MY**	A	*NO*	NH	55704	55750	
142 055	u	**MY**	A	*NO*	NH	55705	55751	
142 056	u	**MY**	A	*NO*	NH	55706	55752	
142 057	u	**MY**	A	*NO*	NH	55707	55753	
142 058	u	**MY**	A	*NO*	NH	55708	55754	
142 060	t	**NW**	A	*NO*	NH	55710	55756	
142 061	t	**NW**	A	*NO*	NH	55711	55757	
142 062	t	**NW**	A	*NO*	NH	55712	55758	
142 063	t	**NW**	A	*NO*	NH	55713	55759	
142 064	t	**NW**	A	*NO*	NH	55714	55760	
142 065	s	**NS**	A	*NO*	HT	55715	55761	
142 066	s	**NS**	A	*NO*	HT	55716	55762	
142 067	t	**NW**	A	*NO*	NH	55717	55763	
142 068	t	**NW**	A	*NO*	NH	55718	55764	
142 069	v	**VL**	A	*AW*	CF	55719	55765	
142 070	t	**NW**	A	*NO*	NH	55720	55766	
142 071	s	**AV**	A	*NO*	HT	55721	55767	
142 072	v	**VL**	A	*AW*	CF	55722	55768	
142 073	v	**VL**	A	*AW*	CF	55723	55769	Myfanwy
142 074	v	**VL**	A	*AW*	CF	55724	55770	
142 075	v	**VL**	A	*AW*	CF	55725	55771	
142 076	v	**VL**	A	*AW*	CF	55726	55772	
142 077	v	**VL**	A	*AW*	CF	55727	55773	
142 078	s	**AV**	A	*NO*	HT	55728	55774	
142 079	s	**AV**	A	*NO*	HT	55729	55775	
142 080	v	**VL**	A	*AW*	CF	55730	55776	Caerphilly R.F.C.
142 081	v	**VW**	A	*AW*	CF	55731	55777	
142 082	v	**VL**	A	*AW*	CF	55732	55778	
142 083	v	**VL**	A	*AW*	CF	55733	55779	
142 084	s*	**AV**	A	*NO*	HT	55734	55780	

142 085	v	**VL**	A	*AW*	CF	55735 55781
142 086	s	**AV**	A	*NO*	HT	55736 55782
142 087	s	**AV**	A	*NO*	HT	55737 55783
142 088	s	**AV**	A	*NO*	HT	55738 55784
142 089	s	**AV**	A	*NO*	HT	55739 55785
142 090	s	**AV**	A	*NO*	HT	55740 55786
142 091	s	**AV**	A	*NO*	HT	55741 55787
142 092	s	**AV**	A	*NO*	HT	55742 55788
142 093	s	**AV**	A	*NO*	HT	55743 55789
142 094	s	**AV**	A	*NO*	HT	55744 55790
142 095	s	**AV**	A	*NO*	HT	55745 55791
142 096	s	**AV**	A	*NO*	HT	55746 55792

CLASS 143   PACER   ALEXANDER/BARCLAY

DMS–DMSL. Similar design to Class 142, but bodies built by W. Alexander with Barclay underframes.

Construction: Steel. Alexander bus bodywork on four-wheeled underframes.
Engines: One Cummins LTA10-R of 172 kW (230 h.p.) at 2100 r.p.m.
Couplers: BSI at outer ends, bar couplers within unit.
Seating Layout: All units are now fitted with 2+2 high-back Chapman seating, mainly unidirectional.
Dimensions: 15.44 x 2.80 m.
Gangways: Within unit only.   **Wheel Arrangement:** 1-A A-1.
Doors: Twin-leaf inward pivoting.   **Maximum Speed:** 75 m.p.h.
Multiple Working: Within class and with Classes 142, 144, 150, 153, 155, 156, 158, 159.

DMS. Lot No. 31005 Andrew Barclay 1985–1986. –/54. 24.0 t.
DMSL. Lot No. 31006 Andrew Barclay 1985–1986. –/50 1T. 24.5 t.

143 601	**VL**	RD	*AW*	CF	55642 55667	
143 602	**VL**	P	*AW*	CF	55651 55668	
143 603	**BI**	P	*WX*	EX	55658 55669	
143 604	**VL**	P	*AW*	CF	55645 55670	
143 605	**VL**	P	*AW*	CF	55646 55671	Crimestoppers
143 606	**VL**	P	*AW*	CF	55647 55672	
143 607	**VL**	P	*AW*	CF	55648 55673	
143 608	**VL**	P	*AW*	CF	55649 55674	
143 609	**VL**	BC	*AW*	CF	55650 55675	Tom Jones
143 610	**VL**	RD	*AW*	CF	55643 55676	
143 611	**BI**	P	*WX*	EX	55652 55677	
143 612	**BI**	P	*WX*	EX	55653 55678	
143 613	**BI**	P		PM	55654 55679	
143 614	**VL**	RD	*AW*	CF	55655 55680	
143 615	**VL**	P		CF	55656 55681	
143 616	**VL**	P	*AW*	CF	55657 55682	
143 617	**BI**	RI	*WX*	EX	55644 55683	
143 618	**BI**	RI	*WX*	EX	55659 55684	
143 619	**BI**	RI	*WX*	EX	55660 55685	
143 620	**BI**	P	*WX*	EX	55661 55686	

143 621	BI	P	WX	EX	55662	55687	
143 622	BI	P	AW	CF	55663	55688	
143 623	BI	P	AW	CF	55664	55689	
143 624	VL	P	AW	CF	55665	55690	
143 625	VL	P	AW	CF	55666	55691	Valleys Kids

CLASS 144 PACER ALEXANDER/BREL DERBY

DMS–DMSL or DMS–MS–DMSL. As Class 143, but underframes built by BREL.

Construction: Steel. Alexander bus bodywork on four-wheeled underframes.
Engines: One Cummins LTA10-R of 172 kW (230 h.p.) at 2100 r.p.m.
Couplers: BSI at outer ends, bar couplers within unit.
Seating Layout: All units now fitted with 2+2 high-back Richmond seating, mainly unidirectional.
Dimensions: 15.44/15.42 x 2.80 m.
Gangways: Within unit only.   **Wheel Arrangement:** 1-A A-1.
Doors: Twin-leaf inward pivoting.   **Maximum Speed:** 75 m.p.h.
Multiple Working: Within class and with Classes 142, 143, 150, 153, 155, 156, 158, 159.

DMS. Lot No. 31015 BREL Derby 1986–1987. –/48 1W 24.0 t.
MS. Lot No. BREL Derby 31037 1987. –/58 23.5 t.
DMSL. Lot No. BREL Derby 31016 1986–1987. –/45 1T 24.5 t.

Note: The centre cars of the 3-car units are owned by West Yorkshire PTE, although managed by Porterbrook Leasing Company.

144 001	YP	P	NO	NL	55801		55824
144 002	YP	P	NO	NL	55802		55825
144 003	YP	P	NO	NL	55803		55826
144 004	YP	P	NO	NL	55804		55827
144 005	YP	P	NO	NL	55805		55828
144 006	YP	P	NO	NL	55806		55829
144 007	YP	P	NO	NL	55807		55830
144 008	YP	P	NO	NL	55808		55831
144 009	YP	P	NO	NL	55809		55832
144 010	YP	P	NO	NL	55810		55833
144 011	YP	P	NO	NL	55811		55834
144 012	YP	P	NO	NL	55812		55835
144 013	YP	P	NO	NL	55813		55836
144 014	YP	P	NO	NL	55814	55850	55837
144 015	YP	P	NO	NL	55815	55851	55838
144 016	YP	P	NO	NL	55816	55852	55839
144 017	YP	P	NO	NL	55817	55853	55840
144 018	YP	P	NO	NL	55818	55854	55841
144 019	YP	P	NO	NL	55819	55855	55842
144 020	YP	P	NO	NL	55820	55856	55843
144 021	YP	P	NO	NL	55821	55857	55844
144 022	YP	P	NO	NL	55822	55858	55845
144 023	YP	P	NO	NL	55823	55859	55846

Name (carried on DMSL): 144 001 THE PENISTONE LINE PARTNERSHIP

CLASS 150/0   SPRINTER   BREL YORK

DMSL–MS–DMS. Prototype Sprinter.

Construction: Steel.
Engines: One Cummins NT-855-R4 of 213 kW (285 h.p.) at 2100 r.p.m.
Bogies: BX8P (powered), BX8T (non-powered).
Couplers: BSI at outer end of driving vehicles, bar non-driving ends.
Seating Layout: 3+2 (mainly unidirectional).
Dimensions: 20.06/20.18 x 2.82 m.
Gangways: Within unit only.   **Wheel Arrangement:** 2-B – 2-B – B-2.
Doors: Twin-leaf sliding.   **Maximum Speed:** 75 m.p.h.
Multiple Working: Within class and with Classes 142, 143, 144, 153, 155, 156, 158, 159, 170.

DMSL. Lot No. 30984 1984. –/72 1T. 35.4 t.
MS. Lot No. 30986 1984. –/92. 34.1 t.
DMS. Lot No. 30985 1984. –/76. 29.5 t.

| 150 001 | r | **CO** | A | *CT* | TS | 55200 | 55400 | 55300 |
| 150 002 | r | **CO** | A | *CT* | TS | 55201 | 55401 | 55301 |

CLASS 150/1   SPRINTER   BREL YORK

DMSL–DMS or DMSL–DMSL–DMS or DMSL–DMS–DMS.

Construction: Steel.
Engines: One Cummins NT855R5 of 213 kW (285 h.p.) at 2100 r.p.m.
Bogies: BP38 (powered), BT38 (non-powered).
Couplers: BSI.
Seating Layout: 3+2 facing as built but Centro units were reseated with mainly unidirectional seating.
Dimensions: 20.06 x 2.82 m.
Gangways: Within unit only.   **Wheel Arrangement:** 2-B (– 2–B) – B-2.
Doors: Twin-leaf sliding.   **Maximum Speed:** 75 m.p.h.
Multiple Working: Within class and with Classes 142, 143, 144, 153, 155, 156, 158, 159, 170.

DMSL. Lot No. 31011 1985–1986. –/72 1T (s –/59 1TD, t –/71 1W 1T, u –/71 1T). 38.3 t.
DMS. Lot No. 31012 1985–1986. –/76 (s –/65, u –/70). 38.1 t.

Non-standard livery: 150 134 is in plain dark blue.

Notes: The centre cars of 3-car units are Class 150/2 vehicles. For details see Class 150/2.
Units in **NW** livery have been refurbished with new Chapman seating.

150 003	ru	**CO**	A	*CT*	TS	52103	57210	57103
150 004	ru	**CO**	A	*CT*	TS	52104	52216	57104
150 005	ru	**CO**	A	*CT*	TS	52105	52210	57105
150 006	ru	**CO**	A	*CT*	TS	52106	57214	57106
150 008	ru	**CO**	A	*CT*	TS	52108	57216	57108

150 010	ru	**CO**	A	*CT*	TS	52110	57226	57110
150 011	ru	**CO**	A	*CT*	TS	52111	52204	57111
150 012	ru	**CO**	A	*CT*	TS	52112	57206	57112
150 013	ru	**CO**	A	*CT*	TS	52113	52226	57113
150 014	ru	**CO**	A	*CT*	TS	52114	57204	57114
150 015	ru	**CO**	A	*CT*	TS	52115	52206	57115
150 016	ru	**CO**	A	*CT*	TS	52116	57212	57116
150 017	ru	**CO**	A	*CT*	TS	52117	57209	57117
150 018	ru	**CO**	A	*CT*	TS	52118	52220	57118
150 019	ru	**CO**	A	*CT*	TS	52119	57220	57119
150 022	ru	**CO**	A	*CT*	TS	52122	52214	57122
150 101	ru	**CO**	A	*CT*	TS	52101	57101	
150 102	ru	**CO**	A	*CT*	TS	52102	57102	
150 107	r	**CO**	A	*CT*	TS	52107	57107	
150 109	ru	**CO**	A	*CT*	TS	52109	57109	
150 120	t	**SL**	A	*SL*	BY	52120	57120	Gospel Oak–Barking 2000
150 121	ru	**CO**	A	*CT*	TS	52121	57121	
150 123	t	**SL**	A	*SL*	BY	52123	57123	Bletchley Seven
150 124	ru	**CO**	A	*CT*	TS	52124	57124	
150 125	ru	**CO**	A	*CT*	TS	52125	57125	
150 126	ru	**CO**	A	*CT*	TS	52126	57126	
150 127	t	**SL**	A	*SL*	BY	52127	57127	Bletchley TMD
150 128	t	**SL**	A	*SL*	BY	52128	57128	Community Forest
150 129	t	**SL**	A	*SL*	BY	52129	57129	MARSTON VALE
150 130	t	**SL**	A	*SL*	BY	52130	57130	Bedford–Bletchley 150
150 131	t	**SL**	A	*SL*	BY	52131	57131	LESLIE CRABBE
150 132	r	**CO**	A	*CT*	TS	52132	57132	
150 133	s	**NW**	A	*NO*	NH	52133	57133	
150 134	s	**0**	A	*NO*	NH	52134	57134	
150 135	s	**NW**	A	*NO*	NH	52135	57135	
150 136	s	**NW**	A	*NO*	NH	52136	57136	
150 137	s	**NW**	A	*NO*	NH	52137	57137	
150 138	s	**NW**	A	*NO*	NH	52138	57138	
150 139	s	**NW**	A	*NO*	NH	52139	57139	
150 140	s	**NW**	A	*NO*	NH	52140	57140	
150 141	s	**NW**	A	*NO*	NH	52141	57141	
150 142	s	**NW**	A	*NO*	NH	52142	57142	
150 143	s	**NW**	A	*NO*	NH	52143	57143	
150 144	s	**NW**	A	*NO*	NH	52144	57144	
150 145	s	**NW**	A	*NO*	NH	52145	57145	
150 146	s	**NW**	A	*NO*	NH	52146	57146	
150 147	s	**NW**	A	*NO*	NH	52147	57147	
150 148	s	**NW**	A	*NO*	NH	52148	57148	
150 149	s	**NW**	A	*NO*	NH	52149	57149	
150 150	s	**NW**	A	*NO*	NH	52150	57150	

CLASS 150/2   SPRINTER   BREL YORK

DMSL–DMS.

Construction: Steel.
Engines: One Cummins NT855R5 of 213 kW (285 h.p.) at 2100 r.p.m.
Bogies: BP38 (powered), BT38 (non-powered).
Couplers: BSI.
Seating Layout: 3+2 mainly unidirectional seating as built, but many units have now been refurbished with 2+2 seating.
Dimensions: 20.06 x 2.82 m.
Gangways: Throughout.   **Wheel Arrangement:** 2-B – B-2.
Doors: Twin-leaf sliding.   **Maximum Speed:** 75 m.p.h.
Multiple Working: Within class and with Classes 142, 143, 144, 153, 155, 156, 158, 159, 170.

DMSL. Lot No. 31017 1986–1987. –/73 1T (s –/62 1TD, v –/68 1T, w –/68 1T). 37.5 t.
DMS. Lot No. 31018 1986–1987. –/76 (* –/68, s –/70, v –/71, w –/73). 36.5 t.

Notes:

Units in **NW** livery have been refurbished with Chapman seating.
v Refurbished Arriva Trains Wales units with 2+2 individual Chapman seating.
w Refurbished Wessex Trains units with 2+2 individual Chapman seating.
One Anglia units have Chapman seating.

150 201	s	**NW**	A	*NO*	NH	52201	57201
150 202		**CO**	A	*CT*	TS	52202	57202
150 203	s	**NW**	A	*NO*	NH	52203	57203
150 205	s	**NW**	A	*NO*	NH	52205	57205
150 207	s	**NW**	A	*NO*	NH	52207	57207
150 208		**SR**	P	*AW*	CF	52208	57208
150 211	s	**NW**	A	*NO*	NH	52211	57211
150 213	r*	**AR**	P	*1A*	NC	52213	57213	LORD NELSON
150 215	s	**NW**	A	*NO*	NH	52215	57215
150 217	r*	**AR**	P	*1A*	NC	52217	57217	OLIVER CROMWELL
150 218	s	**NW**	A	*NO*	NH	52218	57218
150 219	rw	**WZ**	P	*WX*	EX	52219	57219
150 221	rw	**WZ**	P	*WX*	EX	52221	57221
150 222	s	**NW**	A	*NO*	NH	52222	57222
150 223	s	**NW**	A	*NO*	NH	52223	57223
150 224	s	**NW**	A	*NO*	NH	52224	57224
150 225	s	**NW**	A	*NO*	NH	52225	57225
150 227	r*	**AR**	P	*1A*	NC	52227	57227	SIR ALF RAMSEY
150 228		**RR**		*NO*	NL	52228	57228
150 229	r*	**AR**	P	*1A*	NC	52229	57229	GEORGE BORROW
150 230	rw	**WZ**	P	*WX*	EX	52230	57230	The Tamar Kingfisher
150 231	r*	**AR**	P	*1A*	NC	52231	57231	KING EDMUND
150 232	rw	**WZ**	P	*WX*	EX	52232	57232	The Coastal Connection
150 233	rw	**WZ**	P	*WX*	EX	52233	57233	The Lady Margaret of Looe Valley
150 234	rw	**WZ**	P	*WX*	EX	52234	57234	The National Trust

150 235	r*	**AR**	P	*CT*	TS	52235	57235	
150 236	rw	**WZ**	P	*WX*	EX	52236	57236	The Lord Clinton
150 237	r*	**AR**	P	*1A*	NC	52237	57237	HEREWARD THE WAKE
150 238	rw	**WZ**	P	*WX*	EX	52238	57238	Exeter Explorer
150 239	rw	**WZ**	P	*WX*	EX	52239	57239	
150 240	rw	**WZ**	P	*WX*	EX	52240	57240	
150 241	rw	**WZ**	P	*WX*	EX	52241	57241	The Tarka Belle
150 242	rw	**WZ**	P	*WX*	EX	52242	57242	
150 243	rw	**WZ**	P	*WX*	EX	52243	57243	The Filton Partnership
150 244	rw	**WZ**	P	*WX*	EX	52244	57244	The West Cornwall Experience
150 245	r	**AR**	P	*1A*	NC	52245	57245	
150 246	rw	**WZ**	P	*WX*	EX	52246	57246	
150 247	rw	**WZ**	P	*WX*	EX	52247	57247	
150 248	rw	**WZ**	P	*WX*	EX	52248	57248	The Great Gardens of Cornwall
150 249	rw	**WZ**	P	*WX*	EX	52249	57249	
150 250		**SR**	P	*AW*	CF	52250	57250	
150 251	rw	**WZ**	P	*WX*	EX	52251	57251	
150 252		**SR**	P	*AW*	CF	52252	57252	
150 253	rw	**WZ**	P	*WX*	EX	52253	57253	The Exmouth Avocet
150 254	rw	**WZ**	P	*WX*	EX	52254	57254	
150 255	r*	**AR**	P	*1A*	NC	52255	57255	HENRY BLOGG
150 256		**SR**	P	*AW*	CF	52256	57256	
150 257	r*	**AR**	P	*1A*	NC	52257	57257	QUEEN BOADICEA
150 258		**SR**	P	*SR*	HA	52258	57258	
150 259		**SR**	P	*AW*	CF	52259	57259	
150 260		**SR**	P	*AW*	CF	52260	57260	
150 261	rw	**WZ**	P	*WX*	EX	52261	57261	The Riviera Flyer
150 262		**SR**	P	*AW*	CF	52262	57262	
150 263	rw	**WZ**	P	*WX*	EX	52263	57263	The Castles of Cornwall
150 264		**SR**	P	*AW*	CF	52264	57264	
150 265	rw	**WZ**	P	*WX*	EX	52265	57265	The Falmouth Flyer
150 266	rw	**WZ**	P	*WX*	EX	52266	57266	The Whitley Wonder
150 267	rv	**VW**	P	*AW*	CF	52267	57267	
150 268		**RR**	P	*NO*	NL	52268	57268	
150 269		**RR**	P	*NO*	NL	52269	57269	
150 270		**RR**	P	*NO*	NL	52270	57270	
150 271		**RR**	P	*NO*	NL	52271	57271	
150 272		**RR**	P	*NO*	NL	52272	57272	
150 273		**RR**	P	*NO*	NL	52273	57273	
150 274		**RR**	P	*NO*	NL	52274	57274	
150 275		**RR**	P	*NO*	NL	52275	57275	
150 276		**RR**	P	*NO*	NL	52276	57276	
150 277		**RR**	P	*NO*	NL	52277	57277	
150 278	rv	**VW**	P	*AW*	CF	52278	57278	
150 279	v	**VW**	P	*AW*	CF	52279	57279	
150 280	v	**VW**	P	*AW*	CF	52280	57280	University of Glamorgan/ Prifysgol Morgannwg
150 281	v	**VW**	P	*AW*	CF	52281	57281	

150 282	v	**VW**	P	*AW*	CF	52282 57282
150 283		**SR**	P	*AW*	CF	52283 57283
150 284		**SR**	P	*AW*	CF	52284 57284
150 285		**SR**	P	*SR*	HA	52285 57285

CLASS 153   SUPER SPRINTER   LEYLAND BUS

DMSL. Converted by Hunslet-Barclay, Kilmarnock from Class 155 2-car units.

Construction: Steel. Built from Leyland National bus parts on bogied underframes.
Engine: One Cummins NT855R5 of 213 kW (285 h.p.) at 2100 r.p.m.
Bogies: One P3-10 (powered) and one BT38 (non-powered).
Couplers: BSI.
Seating Layout: 2+2 facing/unidirectional.
Dimensions: 23.21 x 2.70 m.

Gangways: Throughout.	**Wheel Arrangement:** 2-B.
Doors: Single-leaf sliding plug.	**Maximum Speed:** 75 m.p.h.

Multiple Working: Within class and with Classes 142, 143, 144, 150, 155, 156, 158, 159, 170.

52301–52335. DMSL. Lot No. 31026 1987–1988. Converted under Lot No.31115 1991–1992. –/75 1T 1W (* –/69 1T 1W). 41.2 t.
57301–57335. DMSL. Lot No. 31027 1987–1988. Converted under Lot No.31115 1991–1992. –/75 1T (* –/69 1T). 41.2 t.

Advertising Livery: 153 314 Norfolk and Norwich Festival (Black and orange).

Notes:

Cars numbered in the 573xx series were renumbered by adding 50 to their original number so that the last two digits correspond with the set number.
Central Trains and Northern (Newton Heath-based) units have been fitted with Chapman seating.
Northern (Neville Hill-based) units have been fitted with Richmond seating.
Most Arriva Trains Wales/Wessex Trains units have been reseated with seats removed from that company's Class 158 units.
One Anglia units have Chapman seating and a bicycle rack.

153 301		**AV**	A	*NO*	NL	52301
153 302	r	**DC**	A	*WX*	EX	52302
153 303	r	**HW**	A	*AW*	CF	52303
153 304		**AV**	A	*NO*	NL	52304
153 305	r	**WX**	A	*WX*	EX	52305
153 306	r*	**PS**	P	*1A*	NC	52306 EDITH CAVELL
153 307		**AV**	A	*NO*	NL	52307
153 308	r	**DC**	A	*WX*	EX	52308
153 309	r*	**AR**	P	*1A*	NC	52309 GERARD FIENNES
153 310	r	**NW**	P	*AW*	CF	52310
153 311	r*	**PS**	P	*AW*	CF	52311
153 312	r	**HW**	A	*AW*	CF	52312
153 313	r	**NW**	P	*AW*	CF	52313
153 314	r*	**AL**	P	*1A*	NC	52314 DELIA SMITH
153 315		**AV**	A	*NO*	NL	52315

153 316		NW	P	NO	NH	52316
153 317		AV	A	NO	NL	52317
153 318	r	WX	A	WX	EX	52318
153 319		AV	A	NO	NL	52319
153 320	r	HW	P	AW	CF	52320
153 321	r	HW	P	AW	CF	52321
153 322	r*	AR	P	1A	NC	52322	BENJAMIN BRITTEN
153 323	r	HW	P	AW	CF	52323
153 324		NW	P	NO	NH	52324
153 325	r	CT	P	CT	TS	52325
153 326	r*	PS	P	AW	CF	52326
153 327	r	HW	P	AW	CF	52327
153 328		AV	A	NO	NL	52328
153 329	r	RR	P	WX	EX	52329
153 330		NW	P	NO	NH	52330
153 331		AV	A	NO	NL	52331
153 332		NW	P	NO	NH	52332
153 333	r	CT	P	CT	TS	52333
153 334	r	CT	P	CT	TS	52334
153 335	r*	AR	P	1A	NC	52335	MICHAEL PALIN
153 351		AV	A	NO	NL	57351
153 352		AV	A	NO	NL	57352
153 353	r	HW	A	AW	CF	57353
153 354	r	CT	P	CT	TS	57354
153 355	r	WX	A	WX	EX	57355
153 356	r	RR	P	CT	TS	57356
153 357		AV	A	NO	NL	57357
153 358		NW	P	NO	NH	57358
153 359		NW	P	NO	NH	57359
153 360		NW	P	NO	NH	57360
153 361	r	NW	P	AW	CF	57361
153 362	r	HW	A	AW	CF	57362	Dylan Thomas 1914–1953
153 363		NW	P	NO	NH	57363
153 364	r	RR	P	CT	TS	57364
153 365	r	CT	P	CT	TS	57365
153 366	r	RR	P	CT	TS	57366
153 367	r	NW	P	AW	CF	57367
153 368	r	WX	A	WX	EX	57368
153 369	r	RR	P	WX	EX	57369
153 370	r	WX	A	WX	EX	57370
153 371	r	CT	P	CT	TS	57371
153 372	r	WX	A	WX	EX	57372
153 373	r	WX	A	WX	EX	57373
153 374	r	DC	A	WX	EX	57374
153 375	r	CT	P	CT	TS	57375
153 376	r	RR	P	CT	TS	57376
153 377	r	DC	A	WX	EX	57377
153 378		AV	A	NO	NL	57378
153 379	r	CT	P	CT	TS	57379
153 380	r	DC	A	WX	EX	57380
153 381	r	CT	P	CT	TS	57381

153 382	r	**DC**	A	*WX*	EX	57382
153 383	r	**CT**	P	*CT*	TS	57383
153 384	r	**CT**	P	*CT*	TS	57384
153 385	r	**CT**	P	*CT*	TS	57385

CLASS 155 SUPER SPRINTER LEYLAND BUS

DMSL–DMS.

Construction: Steel. Built from Leyland National bus parts on bogied underframes.
Engines: One Cummins NT855R5 of 213 kW (285 h.p.) at 2100 r.p.m.
Bogies: One P3-10 (powered) and one BT38 (non-powered).
Couplers: BSI.
Seating Layout: 2+2 facing/unidirectional.
Dimensions: 23.21 x 2.70 m.
Gangways: Throughout.   **Wheel Arrangement:** 2-B – B-2.
Doors: Single-leaf sliding plug.   **Maximum Speed:** 75 m.p.h.
Multiple Working: Within class and with Classes 142, 143, 144, 150, 153, 156, 158, 159, 170.

DMSL. Lot No. 31057 1988. –/80 1TD 1W. 39.4 t.
DMS. Lot No. 31058 1988. –/80. 38.6 t.

Note: These units are owned by West Yorkshire PTE, although managed by Porterbrook Leasing Company.

155 341	**WY**	P	*NO*	NL	52341 57341
155 342	**WY**	P	*NO*	NL	52342 57342
155 343	**WY**	P	*NO*	NL	52343 57343
155 344	**WY**	P	*NO*	NL	52344 57344
155 345	**WY**	P	*NO*	NL	52345 57345
155 346	**WY**	P	*NO*	NL	52346 57346
155 347	**WY**	P	*NO*	NL	52347 57347

CLASS 156 SUPER SPRINTER METRO-CAMMELL

DMSL–DMS.

Construction: Steel.
Engines: One Cummins NT855R5 of 213 kW (285 h.p.) at 2100 r.p.m.
Bogies: One P3-10 (powered) and one BT38 (non-powered).
Couplers: BSI.
Seating Layout: 2+2 facing/unidirectional.
Dimensions: 23.03 x 2.73 m.
Gangways: Throughout.   **Wheel Arrangement:** 2-B – B-2.
Doors: Single-leaf sliding.   **Maximum Speed:** 75 m.p.h.
Multiple Working: Within class and with Classes 142, 143, 144, 150, 153, 155, 158, 159, 170.

DMSL. Lot No. 31028 1988–1989. –/74 (†* –/72, st –/70, u –/68) 1TD 1W. 38.6 t.
DMS. Lot No. 31029 1987–1989. –/76 (q –/78, † –/74, tu –/72) 37.9 t.

Notes: 156 500–156 514 are owned by Strathclyde PTE, although managed by Angel.

Central Trains and Northern (Newton Heath-based) units have been fitted with Chapman seating.

Northern (Neville Hill/Heaton-based) units have been fitted with Richmond seating.

Non standard liveries: 156 426, 156 429, 156 455 and 156 459 All over dark blue with white doors.

156 451 Northern experimental/promotional(1). Two-tone lilac with a white swoosh.

156 425 Northern experimental/promotional(2). White with two-tone lilac swooshs.

156 401	r*	**CT**	P	*CT*	TS	52401	57401
156 402	r*	**P**	P	*1A*	NC	52402	57402
156 403	r*	**CT**	P	*CT*	TS	52403	57403
156 404	r*	**CT**	P	*CT*	TS	52404	57404
156 405	r*	**CT**	P	*CT*	TS	52405	57405
156 406	r*	**CT**	P	*CT*	TS	52406	57406
156 407	r*	**CT**	P	*CT*	TS	52407	57407
156 408	r*	**CT**	P	*CT*	TS	52408	57408
156 409	r*	**RE**	P	*CT*	TS	52409	57409
156 410	r*	**CT**	P	*CT*	TS	52410	57410
156 411	r*	**CT**	P	*CT*	TS	52411	57411
156 412	r*	**CT**	P	*CT*	TS	52412	57412
156 413	r*	**CT**	P	*CT*	TS	52413	57413
156 414	r*	**CT**	P	*CT*	TS	52414	57414
156 415	r*	**CT**	P	*CT*	TS	52415	57415
156 416	r*	**RE**	P	*CT*	TS	52416	57416
156 417	r*	**RE**	P	*CT*	TS	52417	57417
156 418	r*	**CT**	P	*CT*	TS	52418	57418
156 419	r*	**CT**	P	*CT*	TS	52419	57419	
156 420	s	**FS**	P	*NO*	NH	52420	57420	LA' AL RATTY Ravenglass & Eskdale Railway
156 421	s	**FS**	P	*NO*	NH	52421	57421	
156 422	r*	**RE**	P	*CT*	TS	52422	57422
156 423	s	**FS**	P	*NO*	NH	52423	57423
156 424	s	**FS**	P	*NO*	NH	52424	57424
156 425	s	**O**	P	*NO*	NH	52425	57425
156 426	s	**O**	P	*NO*	NH	52426	57426
156 427	s	**FS**	P	*NO*	NH	52427	57427
156 428	s	**FS**	P	*NO*	NH	52428	57428
156 429	s	**O**	P	*NO*	NH	52429	57429
156 430	t	**SC**	A	*SR*	CK	52430	57430
156 431	t	**SC**	A	*SR*	CK	52431	57431
156 432	t	**SC**	A	*SR*	CK	52432	57432
156 433	t	**SC**	A	*SR*	CK	52433	57433	The Kilmarnock Edition
156 434	t	**SC**	A	*SR*	CK	52434	57434
156 435	t	**SC**	A	*SR*	CK	52435	57435
156 436	†	**SC**	A	*SR*	CK	52436	57436
156 437	t	**SC**	A	*SR*	CK	52437	57437

156 438	q	NS	A	NO	NL	52438	57438	
156 439	t	SC	A	SR	CK	52439	57439	
156 440	s	FS	P	NO	NH	52440	57440	
156 441	s	FS	P	NO	NH	52441	57441	
156 442	t	SC	A	SR	CK	52442	57442	
156 443	q	NS	A	NO	HT	52443	57443	
156 444	q	NS	A	NO	HT	52444	57444	
156 445	u	SC	A	SR	CK	52445	57445	
156 446	t	FS	A	SR	CK	52446	57446	
156 447	ru	SR	A	SR	CK	52447	57447	
156 448	q	NS	A	NO	HT	52448	57448	
156 449	ru	SR	A	SR	CK	52449	57449	
156 450	rt	SR	A	SR	CK	52450	57450	
156 451	q	O	A	NO	HT	52451	57451	
156 452	s	FS	P	NO	NH	52452	57452	
156 453	ru	SR	A	SR	CK	52453	57453	
156 454	q	NS	A	NO	HT	52454	57454	
156 455	s	O	P	NO	NH	52455	57455	
156 456	t	SR	A	SR	CK	52456	57456	
156 457	rt	SR	A	SR	CK	52457	57457	
156 458	rt	SR	A	SR	CK	52458	57458	
156 459	s	O	P	NO	NH	52459	57459	
156 460	s	RN	P	NO	NH	52460	57460	
156 461	s	RN	P	NO	NH	52461	57461	
156 462		SR	A	SR	CK	52462	57462	
156 463	q	NS	A	NO	HT	52463	57463	
156 464	s	RN	P	NO	NH	52464	57464	
156 465	ru	SR	A	SR	CK	52465	57465	
156 466	s	FS	P	NO	NH	52466	57466	BUXTON Festival
156 467		SR	A	SR	CK	52467	57467	
156 468	q	NS	A	NO	NL	52468	57468	
156 469	q	NS	A	NO	HT	52469	57469	
156 470	q	NS	A	NO	NL	52470	57470	
156 471	q	NS	A	NO	NL	52471	57471	
156 472	q	NS	A	NO	NL	52472	57472	
156 473	q	NS	A	NO	NL	52473	57473	
156 474	rt	SR	A	SR	CK	52474	57474	
156 475	q	NS	A	NO	NL	52475	57475	
156 476	rt	SR	A	SR	CK	52476	57476	
156 477	t	SR	A	SR	CK	52477	57477	
156 478	rt	SR	A	SR	CK	52478	57478	
156 479	q	NS	A	NO	NL	52479	57479	
156 480	q	NS	A	NO	NL	52480	57480	
156 481	q	NS	A	NO	NL	52481	57481	
156 482	q	NS	A	NO	NL	52482	57482	
156 483	q	NS	A	NO	NL	52483	57483	
156 484	q	NS	A	NO	NL	52484	57484	
156 485	ru	SR	A	SR	CK	52485	57485	
156 486	q	NS	A	NO	NL	52486	57486	
156 487	q	NS	A	NO	NL	52487	57487	
156 488	q	NS	A	NO	NL	52488	57488	

156 489	q	**NS**	A	*NO*	NL	52489	57489
156 490	q	**NS**	A	*NO*	NL	52490	57490
156 491	q	**NS**	A	*NO*	NL	52491	57491
156 492	r†	**SR**	A	*SR*	CK	52492	57492
156 493	rt	**SR**	A	*SR*	CK	52493	57493
156 494	§	**SC**	A	*SR*	CK	52494	57494
156 495	u	**SC**	A	*SR*	CK	52495	57495
156 496	ru	**SR**	A	*SR*	CK	52496	57496
156 497	q	**NS**	A	*NO*	NL	52497	57497
156 498	q	**NS**	A	*NO*	NL	52498	57498
156 499	rt	**SR**	A	*SR*	CK	52499	57499
156 500	u	**SC**	A	*SR*	CK	52500	57500
156 501		**SC**	A	*SR*	CK	52501	57501
156 502		**SC**	A	*SR*	CK	52502	57502
156 503		**SC**	A	*SR*	CK	52503	57503
156 504		**SC**	A	*SR*	CK	52504	57504
156 505		**SC**	A	*SR*	CK	52505	57505
156 506		**SC**	A	*SR*	CK	52506	57506
156 507		**SC**	A	*SR*	CK	52507	57507
156 508		**SC**	A	*SR*	CK	52508	57508
156 509		**SC**	A	*SR*	CK	52509	57509
156 510		**SC**	A	*SR*	CK	52510	57510
156 511		**SC**	A	*SR*	CK	52511	57511
156 512		**SC**	A	*SR*	CK	52512	57512
156 513		**SC**	A	*SR*	CK	52513	57513
156 514		**SC**	A	*SR*	CK	52514	57514

CLASS 158/0   BREL

DMSL(B)–DMSL(A) or DMCL–DMSL or DMCL–MSL–DMSL.

Construction: Welded aluminium.
Engines: 158 701–158 814, 158 961–158 963 & 158 971–158 976 : One Cummins NTA855R of 260 kW (350 h.p.) at 1900 r.p.m.
158 815–158 862: One Perkins 2006-TWH of 260 kW (350 h.p.) at 1900 r.p.m.
158 863–158 872 & 158 964–158 967 One Cummins NTA855R of 300 kW (400 h.p.) at 2100 r.p.m.
Bogies: One BREL P4 (powered) and one BREL T4 (non-powered) per car.
Couplers: BSI.
Seating Layout: 2+2 facing/unidirectional in all standard and first class unless stated. 2+1 facing/unidirectional in 158 747–158 751 first class (declassified in Wessex Trains units).
Dimensions: 22.16 x 2.70 m.
Gangways: Throughout.   **Wheel Arrangement:** 2-B – B-2.
Doors: Twin-leaf swing plug.   **Maximum Speed:** 90 m.p.h.
Multiple Working: Within class and with Classes 142, 143, 144, 150, 153, 155, 156, 159, 170.

DMSL(B). Lot No. 31051 BREL Derby 1989–1992. –/68 1TD 1W. († –/66 1TD 1W, t –/64 1TD 1W). Public telephone and trolley space. 38.5 t.
MSL. Lot No. 31050 BREL Derby 1991. –/70 2T. 38.5 t.
DMSL(A). Lot No. 31052 BREL Derby 1989–1992. –/70 1T († –/68 1T, t –/66 1T). 38.5 t.

The above details refer to the "as built" condition. The following DMSL(B) have now been converted to DMCL as follows:

52701–52744 (First ScotRail/Trans-Pennine Express). 15/51 1TD 1W (* 15/53 1TD 1W).
52747–52751. (Wessex Trains/Trans-Pennine Express). 9/51 1TD 1W.
52760–52779/52781. (Trans-Pennine Express 2-car units). 16/48 1TD 1W.
52798–52814 (Trans-Pennine Express 3-car units). 32/32 1TD 1W.

s – Trans-Pennine and Central Trains units have been refurbished with new shape seat cushions.
Trans-Pennine units are also fitted with table lamps in first class.
t – Arriva Trains Wales "Cambrian Line" units with some seats removed for additional luggage space. Central Trains style seats (code s) retained.
† – Wessex Trains and Arriva Trains Wales units fitted with Chapman seating.

All First ScotRail 158s are "fitted" for RETB. When a unit arrives at Inverness the cab display unit is clipped on and plugged in.

Non-standard livery: 158 750 – As **RE** but with a Trans-Pennine Express blue band along the lower bodyside.

Advertising livery: 158 842 – Western Daily Mail (Silver, white and red with various images).

158 701	*	**SR**	P	*SR*	IS	52701	57701
158 702	*	**SR**	P	*SR*	IS	52702	57702	BBC Scotland – 75 Years
158 703	*	**SR**	P	*SR*	IS	52703	57703
158 704	*	**SR**	P	*SR*	IS	52704	57704
158 705	*	**SR**	P	*SR*	IS	52705	57705
158 706	*	**SR**	P	*SR*	IS	52706	57706
158 707	*	**SR**	P	*SR*	IS	52707	57707	Far North Line 125th ANNIVERSARY
158 708	*	**SR**	P	*SR*	IS	52708	57708
158 709	*	**SR**	P	*SR*	IS	52709	57709
158 710	*	**SR**	P	*SR*	IS	52710	57710
158 711	*	**SR**	P	*SR*	IS	52711	57711
158 712	*	**SR**	P	*SR*	IS	52712	57712
158 713	*	**SR**	P	*SR*	IS	52713	57713
158 714	*	**SR**	P	*SR*	IS	52714	57714
158 715	*	**SR**	P	*SR*	IS	52715	57715	Haymarket
158 716	*	**SR**	P	*SR*	IS	52716	57716
158 717	*	**SR**	P	*SR*	IS	52717	57717
158 718	*	**SR**	P	*SR*	IS	52718	57718
158 719	*	**SR**	P	*SR*	IS	52719	57719
158 720	*	**SR**	P	*SR*	IS	52720	57720
158 721	*	**SR**	P	*SR*	IS	52721	57721
158 722	*	**SR**	P	*SR*	IS	52722	57722
158 723	*	**SR**	P	*SR*	IS	52723	57723
158 724	*	**SR**	P	*SR*	HA	52724	57724
158 725	*	**SR**	P	*SR*	HA	52725	57725
158 726	*	**SR**	P	*SR*	HA	52726	57726
158 727	*	**SR**	P	*SR*	HA	52727	57727
158 728	*	**SR**	P	*SR*	HA	52728	57728

158 729	*	**SR**	P	*SR*	HA	52729	57729
158 730	*	**SR**	P	*SR*	HA	52730	57730
158 731	*	**SR**	P	*SR*	HA	52731	57731
158 732	*	**SR**	P	*SR*	HA	52732	57732
158 733	*	**SR**	P	*SR*	HA	52733	57733
158 734	*	**SR**	P	*SR*	HA	52734	57734
158 735	*	**SR**	P	*SR*	HA	52735	57735
158 736	*	**SR**	P	*SR*	HA	52736	57736
158 738	*	**SR**	P	*SR*	HA	52738	57738
158 739	*	**SR**	P	*SR*	HA	52739	57739
158 740	*	**SR**	P	*SR*	HA	52740	57740
158 741	*	**SR**	P	*SR*	HA	52741	57741
158 742		**TP**	P	*TP*	NL	52742	57742
158 747		**WE**	P	*WX*	EX	52747	57747	Richard Trevithick
158 750		**0**	P	*TP*	NL	52750	57750
158 752		**NW**	P	*NO*	NH	52752	57752
158 753		**NW**	P	*NO*	NH	52753	57753
158 754		**NW**	P	*NO*	NH	52754	57754
158 755		**NW**	P	*NO*	NH	52755	57755
158 756		**NW**	P	*NO*	NH	52756	57756
158 757		**NW**	P	*NO*	NH	52757	57757
158 758		**NW**	P	*NO*	NH	52758	57758
158 759		**NW**	P	*NO*	NH	52759	57759
158 760	s	**TP**	P	*TP*	NL	52760	57760
158 761	s	**TP**	P	*TP*	NL	52761	57761
158 762	s	**TP**	P	*TP*	NL	52762	57762
158 763	s	**TP**	P	*TP*	NL	52763	57763
158 764	s	**TP**	P	*TP*	NL	52764	57764
158 765	s	**TP**	P	*TP*	NL	52765	57765
158 766	s	**TP**	P	*TP*	NL	52766	57766
158 767	s	**TP**	P	*TP*	NL	52767	57767
158 768	s	**TP**	P	*TP*	NL	52768	57768
158 769	s	**TP**	P	*TP*	NL	52769	57769
158 771	s	**TP**	P	*TP*	NL	52771	57771
158 776	s	**TP**	P	*TP*	NL	52776	57776
158 778	s	**TP**	P	*TP*	NL	52778	57778
158 779	s	**TP**	P	*TP*	NL	52779	57779
158 780	s	**CT**	A	*CT*	TS	52780	57780
158 781		**TP**	P	*TP*	NL	52781	57781
158 782	s	**CT**	A	*WX*	EX	52782	57782
158 783	s	**CT**	A	*NO*	HT	52783	57783
158 784	s	**CT**	A	*TP*	NL	52784	57784
158 785	s	**CT**	A	*CT*	TS	52785	57785
158 786	s	**CT**	A	*SW*	SA	52786	57786
158 787	s	**CT**	A	*NO*	HT	52787	57787
158 788	s	**CT**	A	*CT*	TS	52788	57788
158 789	s	**CT**	A	*SW*	SA	52789	57789
158 790	s	**CT**	A	*TP*	NL	52790	57790
158 791	s	**CT**	A	*TP*	NL	52791	57791
158 792	s	**CT**	A	*CT*	TS	52792	57792
158 793	s	**CT**	A	*CT*	TS	52793	57793

158 794	s	**CT**	A	*CT*	TS	52794	57794	
158 795	s	**CT**	A	*CT*	TS	52795	57795	
158 796	s	**CT**	A	*CT*	TS	52796	57796	
158 797	s	**CT**	A	*TP*	NL	52797	57797	
158 798	s	**TP**	P	*TP*	HT	52798	58715	57798
158 799	s	**TP**	P	*TP*	HT	52799	58716	57799
158 800	s	**TP**	P	*TP*	HT	52800	58717	57800
158 801	s	**TP**	P	*TP*	HT	52801	58701	57801
158 802	s	**TP**	P	*TP*	HT	52802	58702	57802
158 803	s	**TP**	P	*TP*	HT	52803	58703	57803
158 804	s	**TP**	P	*TP*	HT	52804	58704	57804
158 805	s	**TP**	P	*TP*	HT	52805	58705	57805
158 806	s	**TP**	P	*TP*	HT	52806	58706	57806
158 807	s	**TP**	P	*TP*	HT	52807	58707	57807
158 808	s	**TP**	P	*TP*	HT	52808	58708	57808
158 809	s	**TP**	P	*TP*	HT	52809	58709	57809
158 810	s	**TP**	P	*TP*	HT	52810	58710	57810
158 811	s	**TP**	P	*TP*	HT	52811	58711	57811
158 812	s	**TP**	P	*TP*	HT	52812	58712	57812
158 813	s	**TP**	P	*TP*	HT	52813	58713	57813
158 814	s	**TP**	P	*TP*	HT	52814	58714	57814
158 818	†	**AV**	A	*AW*	CF	52818	57818	
158 819	†	**GP**	A	*AW*	CF	52819	57819	
158 820	†	**AV**	A	*AW*	CF	52820	57820	
158 821	†	**GP**	A	*AW*	CF	52821	57821	
158 822	†	**WB**	A	*AW*	CF	52822	57822	
158 823	†	**WB**	A	*AW*	CF	52823	57823	
158 824	†	**WB**	A	*AW*	CF	52824	57824	
158 825	†	**GP**	A	*AW*	CF	52825	57825	
158 826	†	**WB**	A	*AW*	CF	52826	57826	
158 827	†	**GP**	A	*AW*	CF	52827	57827	
158 828	†	**AV**	A	*AW*	CF	52828	57828	
158 829	†	**WB**	A	*AW*	CF	52829	57829	
158 830	†	**WB**	A	*AW*	CF	52830	57830	
158 831	†	**WB**	A	*AW*	CF	52831	57831	
158 832	†	**WB**	A	*AW*	CF	52832	57832	
158 833	†	**WB**	A	*AW*	CF	52833	57833	
158 834	†	**WB**	A	*AW*	CF	52834	57834	
158 835	†	**WB**	A	*AW*	CF	52835	57835	
158 836	†	**WB**	A	*AW*	CF	52836	57836	
158 837	†	**AV**	A	*AW*	CF	52837	57837	
158 838	†	**WB**	A	*AW*	CF	52838	57838	
158 839	†	**WB**	A	*AW*	CF	52839	57839	
158 840	†	**AV**	A	*AW*	CF	52840	57840	
158 841	†	**GP**	A	*AW*	CF	52841	57841	
158 842	†	**AL**	A	*AW*	CF	52842	57842	
158 843	†	**WB**	A	*AW*	CF	52843	57843	
158 844	rt	**CT**	A	*AW*	CF	52844	57844	
158 845	rt	**CT**	A	*AW*	CF	52845	57845	
158 846	rt	**CT**	A	*AW*	CF	52846	57846	
158 847	rt	**CT**	A	*AW*	CF	52847	57847	

158 848	rt	**CT**	A	*AW*	CF	52848	57848	
158 849	rt	**CT**	A	*NO*	NL	52849	57849	
158 850	rt	**CT**	A	*NO*	NL	52850	57850	
158 851	rt	**CT**	A	*NO*	NL	52851	57851	
158 852	rt	**CT**	A	*AW*	CF	52852	57852	
158 853	rt	**CT**	A	*AW*	CF	52853	57853	
158 854	rt	**CT**	A	*AW*	CF	52854	57854	
158 855	s	**WE**	A	*WX*	EX	52855	57855	Exmoor Explorer
158 856	s	**CT**	A	*CT*	TS	52856	57856	
158 857	s	**CT**	A	*CT*	TS	52857	57857	
158 858	s	**CT**	A	*CT*	TS	52858	57858	
158 859	s	**CT**	A	*WX*	EX	52859	57859	
158 860	s	**CT**	A	*WX*	EX	52860	57860	
158 861	s	**CT**	A	*WX*	EX	52861	57861	
158 862	s	**CT**	A	*CT*	TS	52862	57862	
158 863	†	**WT**	A	*WX*	EX	52863	57863	
158 867	†	**WT**	A	*WX*	EX	52867	57867	
158 868	†	**WT**	A	*WX*	EX	52868	57868	
158 869	†	**WT**	A	*WX*	EX	52869	57869	
158 870	†	**WT**	A	*WX*	EX	52870	57870	
158 871	†	**WT**	A	*WX*	EX	52871	57871	
158 872	†	**WT**	A	*WX*	EX	52872	57872	
Spare		**WT**	P		ZH	52746		

CLASS 158/9   BREL

DMSL–DMS. Units leased by West Yorkshire PTE. Details as for Class 158/0 except for seating layout and toilets.

DMSL. Lot No. 31051 BREL Derby 1990–1992. –/70 1TD 1W. Public telephone and trolley space. 38.5 t.
DMS. Lot No. 31052 BREL Derby 1990–1992. –/72 and parcels area. 38.5 t.

Note: These units are leased by West Yorkshire PTE and are now managed by HSBC Rail (UK) on behalf of Midland Montague who own the units.

158 901	**YP**	H	*NO*	NL	52901	57901
158 902	**YP**	H	*NO*	NL	52902	57902
158 903	**YP**	H	*NO*	NL	52903	57903
158 904	**YP**	H	*NO*	NL	52904	57904
158 905	**YP**	H	*NO*	NL	52905	57905
158 906	**YP**	H	*NO*	NL	52906	57906
158 907	**YP**	H	*NO*	NL	52907	57907
158 908	**YP**	H	*NO*	NL	52908	57908
158 909	**YP**	H	*NO*	NL	52909	57909
158 910	**YP**	H	*NO*	NL	52910	57910

CLASS 158/0   BREL

Units reformed in 2004/05 for Wessex Trains and Trans-Pennine Express. For vehicle details see above.

Wessex Trains units. 158 960/968–970 to be formed.

Formation: DMSL–DMSL–DMSL

158 960							
158 961	**WT**	P	*WX*	EX	52745	57745	57746
158 962	**WT**	P	*WX*	EX	57751	52751	52749
158 963	**WT**	P	*WX*	EX	52748	57748	57749
158 964 †	**WT**	A	*WX*	EX	57815	52815	57816
158 965 †	**WT**	A	*WX*	EX	57817	52817	57816
158 966 †	**WT**	A	*WX*	EX	52864	57864	57865
158 967 †	**WT**	A	*WX*	EX	52866	57866	52865
158 968							
158 969							
158 970							

First Trans-Pennine Express units.

Formation: DMCL–DMCL*/DMSL–DMSL. *Where 3-car units have a DMCL as the centre vehicle, the first class has been declassified in this vehicle.

158 971	**TP**	P	*TP*	HT	52770	57737	57770
158 972	**TP**	P	*TP*	HT	52772	57737	57772
158 973	**TP**	P	*TP*	HT	52773	57743	57773
158 974	**TP**	P	*TP*	HT	52774	52743	57774
158 975	**TP**	P	*TP*	HT	52775	57744	57775
158 976	**TP**	P	*TP*	HT	52777	52744	57777

CLASS 159   BREL

DMCL–MSL–DMSL. Built as Class 158. Converted before entering passenger service to Class 159 by Rosyth Dockyard.

Construction: Welded aluminium.
Engines: One Cummins NTA855R of 300 kW (400 h.p.) at 2100 r.p.m.
Bogies: One BREL P4 (powered) and one BREL T4 (non-powered) per car.
Couplers: BSI.
Seating Layout: 1: 2+1 facing, 2: 2+2 facing/unidirectional.
Dimensions: 22.16 x 2.70 m.
Gangways: Throughout.   **Wheel Arrangement:** 2-B – B-2 – B-2.
Doors: Twin-leaf swing plug.   **Maximum Speed:** 90 m.p.h.
Multiple Working: Within class and with Classes 142, 143, 144, 150, 153, 155, 156, 158, 170.

DMCL. Lot No. 31051 BREL Derby 1992–1993. 24/28 1TD 1W. 38.5 t.
MSL. Lot No. 31050 BREL Derby 1992–1993. –/72 1T and parcels area 38.5 t.
DMSL. Lot No. 31052 BREL Derby 1992–1993. –/72 1T and parcels area. 38.5 t.

▲ North Western Trains-liveried 142 014 approaches Grindleford with the 10.43 Manchester–Sheffield stopping service on 17/03/03. **George Allsop**

▼ Refurbished 3-car Class 144 in the new West Yorkshire PTE "Metro" livery 144 019 passes Mirfield with a Leeds–Huddersfield service on 29/05/04.
Gavin Morrison

"Visit Bristol" promotional-liveried 143 617 and 143 620 are seen on 10/07/04 leaving Dawlish Warren with the 09.15 Cardiff–Paignton. **Robert Pritchard**

▲ The prototype Class 150 No. 150 001; 21 years old in 2005, passes Cossington, Leicestershire with the 11.41 Lincoln–Shrewsbury on 16/07/03. **Chris Booth**

▼ "Visit Wales" promotional liveried 150 281 and 153 312 are seen at Whitland on 09/08/03 with the 12.16 Pembroke Dock–Swansea service. **Gavin Morrison**

▲ Devon/Cornwall promotional-liveried 153 308 departs Southampton Central on 24/05/04 with a service to Swindon. **Mervyn Turvey**

▼ Old West Yorkshire PTE-liveried 155 346 passes Stourton on 25/02/04 with the 12.04 Leeds–Castleford service. **Jason Rogers**

▲ 156 410 in Central Trains livery passes Longport on 18/05/04 with a Skegness–Crewe service. **Cliff Beeton**

▼ Strathclyde carmine & cream-liveried 156 442 passes Greenhill Lower Junction with the 17.59 Falkirk Grahamston–Glasgow Queen Street on 17/08/04. **Ian Lothian**

ScotRail-liveried 158 728 passes Larbert with the 08.41 Dunblane–Glasgow Queen Street on 05/06/04.　　Ian Lothian

▲ Wessex Trains-liveried 158 869 enters Liskeard with the 10.20 Penzance–Bristol on 15/05/04. **Jonathan Allen**

▼ South West Trains-liveried 159 009 leads a 6-car formation through Lancing with the 07.08 Salisbury–Brighton on 20/09/03. **Alex Dasi-Sutton**

Chiltern Railways-liveried 165 024 leads a 6-car formation near Banbury with a Birmingham–Marylebone service on 02/06/04.

Jason Rogers

▲ Thames Trains-liveried 166 219 (now with First Group brandings as TT are now known as First Great Western Link) arrives at Guildford on 04/09/04 with the 10.34 Reading–Gatwick Airport. **Robert Pritchard**

▼ 168 005 pauses at Banbury on 21/08/04 with the 08.40 Marylebone–Birmingham Snow Hill. **Mark Beal**

▲ 170 202, in the slightly revised "One" livery (the grey is lighter and has a blue tinge) leaves Stowmarket on 28/07/04 with the 15.13 Cambridge–Ipswich.

Gavin Morrison

▼ 170 431 is seen at Inverkeithing on 06/07/04 with the 14.08 Dyce–Edinburgh Waverley.

Steve Taylor

Hull Trains 170 393 is seen at Marholm, north of Peterborough, with a King's Cross–Hull service on 30/07/04. These units are due to transfer to First ScotRail in Spring 2005.

John Rudd

▲ Southern-liveried 171 802 is seen at Derby on 14/06/04, prior to delivery to Selhurst for Southern use.　　**Gavin Morrison**

▼ Although still all in First Group livery, most 175s are now operated by Arriva Trains Wales, with some also used by Trans-Pennine Express. Here 175 108 passes Rhyl Marine Lake with the 09.50 Holyhead–Crewe on 29/07/04.　　**Robert Pritchard**

▲ 180 106 is seen at Goring with the 09.55 Cardiff–Paddington First Great Western service of 25/10/03.   **Rodney Lissenden**

▼ "Hastings" DEMU 1001 was frequently used as cover for Class 205/207 "Thumpers" and new Southern Class 170s on the Ashford–Hastings "Marshlink" line in 2004. On 17/06/04 it leaves Rye with the 11.24 from Ashford.   **Ian Feather**

▲ Virgin Trains-liveried 220 022 "Brighton Voyager" is seen at Beckfoot with the 07.20 Aberdeen–Bournemouth on 18/03/03. **Chris Booth**

▼ 221 103 "Christopher Columbus" passes The Chevin, Derbyshire with the 06.35 Edinburgh–Bristol on 23/10/03. **Paul Robertson**

New Midland Mainline 4-car "Meridian" 222 009 passes Breaston 02/09/04 with a Derby–St. Pancras stopping service.
Jon Barlow

▲ Maroon-liveried Sandite unit 960 010 (977858/55024) is seen at Aylesbury station on 19/08/04. **Paul Shannon**

▼ Test Unit "Iris 2" 901 002 in Network Rail yellow livery is seen at Milton Keynes Central on 08/04/04. **Mark Beal**

Note: Vehicle 58718 is out of service with fire damage.

159 001	SW P	SW	SA	52873	58734	57873	CITY OF EXETER
159 002	SW P	SW	SA	52874	58719	57874	CITY OF SALISBURY
159 003	SW P	SW	SA	52875	58720	57875	TEMPLECOMBE
159 004	SW P	SW	SA	52876	58721	57876	BASINGSTOKE AND DEANE
159 005	SW P	SW	SA	52877	58722	57877	
159 006	SW P	SW	SA	52878	58723	57878	
159 007	SW P	SW	SA	52879	58724	57879	
159 008	SW P	SW	SA	52880	58725	57880	
159 009	SW P	SW	SA	52881	58726	57881	
159 010	SW P	SW	SA	52882	58727	57882	
159 011	SW P	SW	SA	52883	58728	57883	
159 012	SW P	SW	SA	52884	58729	57884	
159 013	SW P	SW	SA	52885	58730	57885	
159 014	SW P	SW	SA	52886	58731	57886	
159 015	SW P	SW	SA	52887	58732	57887	
159 016	SW P	SW	SA	52888	58733	57888	
159 017	SW P		SA	52889		57889	
159 018	SW P	SW	SA	52890	58735	57890	
159 019	SW P	SW	SA	52891	58736	57891	
159 020	SW P	SW	SA	52892	58737	57892	
159 021	SW P	SW	SA	52893	58738	57893	
159 022	SW P	SW	SA	52894	58739	57894	
Spare	SW P		ZC		58718		

CLASS 165/0   NETWORK TURBO   BREL

DMCL-DMS and DMCL-MS-DMS. Chiltern units had their first class seats declassified from January 2003. They are being refurbished and fitted with air-conditioning and DMCLs converted to DMSL.

Construction: Welded aluminium.
Engines: One Perkins 2006-TWH of 260 kW (350 h.p.) at 1900 r.p.m.
Bogies: BREL P3-17 (powered), BREL T3-17 (non-powered).
Couplers: BSI at outer ends, bar within 3-car units.
Seating Layout: 1: 2+2 facing. 2: Unrefurbished units: 3+2 facing/unidirectional. 2: Refurbished units: 2+2/3+2 facing/unidirectional.
Dimensions: 23.50/23.25 x 2.81 m.
Gangways: Within unit only.   **Wheel Arrangement:** 2-B (– B-2) – B-2.
Doors: Twin-leaf swing plug.   **Maximum Speed:** 75 m.p.h.
Multiple Working: Within class and with Classes 166 and 168.

58801–58822 and 58873–58878. DMCL (as built). Lot No. 31087 BREL York 1990. 16/72 1T (* –/89 1T, † –/82 1T). 38.0 t.
58801–58822 and 58873–58878. DMSL (refurbished)*. Lot No. 31087 BREL York 1990. –/89 1T, († –/82 1T). 38.0 t.
58823–58833. DMSL. Lot No. 31089 BREL York 1991–1992. 24/60 1T (* –/89 1T). 37.0 t.
MS. Lot No. 31090 BREL York 1991–1992. –/106. 37.0 t.
DMS. Lot No. 31088 BREL York 1991–1992. –/98 (* –/94). 37.0 t.

Notes:

† Trial refurbished Chiltern Railways unit.
* Fully refurbished Chiltern Railways units.
165 001–165 039 are fitted with tripcocks for working over London Underground tracks between Harrow-on-the-Hill and Amersham.

165 001	*	**CR**	A	*CR*	AL	58801		58834
165 002		**NT**	A	*CR*	AL	58802		58835
165 003		**TT**	A	*CR*	AL	58803		58836
165 004	*	**CR**	A	*CR*	AL	58804		58837
165 005		**TT**	A	*CR*	AL	58805		58838
165 006		**NT**	A	*CR*	AL	58806		58839
165 007		**NT**	A	*CR*	AL	58807		58840
165 008	*	**CR**	A	*CR*	AL	58808		58841
165 009		**NT**	A	*CR*	AL	58809		58842
165 010	*	**CR**	A	*CR*	AL	58810		58843
165 011	*	**CR**	A	*CR*	AL	58811		58844
165 012	*	**CR**	A	*CR*	AL	58812		58845
165 013	†	**CR**	A	*CR*	AL	58813		58846
165 014	*	**CR**	A	*CR*	AL	58814		58847
165 015	*	**CR**	A	*CR*	AL	58815		58848
165 016	*	**CR**	A	*CR*	AL	58816		58849
165 017	*	**CR**	A	*CR*	AL	58817		58850
165 018	*	**CR**	A	*CR*	AL	58818		58851
165 019	*	**CR**	A	*CR*	AL	58819		58852
165 020	*	**CR**	A	*CR*	AL	58820		58853
165 021	*	**CR**	A	*CR*	AL	58821		58854
165 022	*	**CR**	A	*CR*	AL	58822		58855
165 023		**NT**	A	*CR*	AL	58873		58867
165 024	*	**CR**	A	*CR*	AL	58874		58868
165 025	*	**CR**	A	*CR*	AL	58875		58869
165 026	*	**CR**	A	*CR*	AL	58876		58870
165 027		**NT**	A	*CR*	AL	58877		58871
165 028	*	**CR**	A	*CR*	AL	58878		58872
165 029	*	**CR**	A	*CR*	AL	58823	55404	58856
165 030	*	**CR**	A	*CR*	AL	58824	55405	58857
165 031	*	**CR**	A	*CR*	AL	58825	55406	58858
165 032	*	**CR**	A	*CR*	AL	58826	55407	58859
165 033	*	**CR**	A	*CR*	AL	58827	55408	58860
165 034	*	**CR**	A	*CR*	AL	58828	55409	58861
165 035		**NT**	A	*CR*	AL	58829	55410	58862
165 036	*	**CR**	A	*CR*	AL	58830	55411	58863
165 037		**NT**	A	*CR*	AL	58831	55412	58864
165 038	*	**CR**	A	*CR*	AL	58832	55413	58865
165 039	*	**CR**	A	*CR*	AL	58833	55414	58866

CLASS 165/1   NETWORK TURBO   BREL

First Great Western Link units. DMCL–MS–DMS or DMCL–DMS.

Construction: Welded aluminium.
Engines: One Perkins 2006-TWH of 260 kW (350 h.p.) at 1900 r.p.m.
Bogies: BREL P3-17 (powered), BREL T3-17 (non-powered).
Couplers: BSI at outer ends, bar within 3-car units.
Seating Layout: 1: 2+2 facing, 2: 3+2 facing/unidirectional.
Dimensions: 23.50/23.25 x 2.81 m.
Gangways: Within unit only.   **Wheel Arrangement:** 2-B (– B-2) – B-2.
Doors: Twin-leaf swing plug.   **Maximum Speed:** 90 m.p.h.
Multiple Working: Within class and with Classes 166 and 168.

58953–58969. DMCL. Lot No. 31098 BREL York 1992. 16/66 1T. 38.0 t.
58879–58898. DMCL. Lot No. 31096 BREL York 1992. 16/72 1T. 38.0 t.
MS. Lot No. 31099 BREL 1992. –/106. 37.0 t.
DMS. Lot No. 31097 BREL 1992. –/98. 37.0 t.

165 101	TT	A	FK	RG	58953	55415	58916
165 102	TT	A	FK	RG	58954	55416	58917
165 103	TT	A	FK	RG	58955	55417	58918
165 104	TT	A	FK	RG	58956	55418	58919
165 105	TT	A	FK	RG	58957	55419	58920
165 106	TT	A	FK	RG	58958	55420	58921
165 107	TT	A	FK	RG	58959	55421	58922
165 108	TT	A	FK	RG	58960	55422	58923
165 109	TT	A	FK	RG	58961	55423	58924
165 110	TT	A	FK	RG	58962	55424	58925
165 111	TT	A	FK	RG	58963	55425	58926
165 112	TT	A	FK	RG	58964	55426	58927
165 113	TT	A	FK	RG	58965	55427	58928
165 114	TT	A	FK	RG	58966	55428	58929
165 115	TT	A	FK	RG	58968	55430	58931
165 116	TT	A	FK	RG	58969	55431	58932
165 117	TT	A	FK	RG	58879		58933
165 118	TT	A	FK	RG	58880		58934
165 119	TT	A	FK	RG	58881		58935
165 120	TT	A	FK	RG	58882		58936
165 121	TT	A	FK	RG	58883		58937
165 122	TT	A	FK	RG	58884		58938
165 123	TT	A	FK	RG	58885		58939
165 124	TT	A	FK	RG	58886		58940
165 125	TT	A	FK	RG	58887		58941
165 126	TT	A	FK	RG	58888		58942
165 127	TT	A	FK	RG	58889		58943
165 128	TT	A	FK	RG	58890		58944
165 129	TT	A	FK	RG	58891		58945
165 130	TT	A	FK	RG	58892		58946
165 131	TT	A	FK	RG	58893		58947
165 132	TT	A	FK	RG	58894		58948
165 133	TT	A	FK	RG			

165 134	**TT**	A	*FK*	RG	58895	58949
165 135	**TT**	A	*FK*	RG	58896	58950
165 136	**TT**	A	*FK*	RG	58897	58951
165 137	**TT**	A	*FK*	RG	58898	58952

CLASS 166 NETWORK EXPRESS TURBO ABB

DMCL(A)–MS–DMCL(B). First Great Western Link units, built for Paddington–Oxford/Newbury services. Air Conditioned.

Construction: Welded aluminium.
Engines: One Perkins 2006-TWH of 260 kW (350 h.p.) at 1900 r.p.m.
Bogies: BREL P3-17 (powered), BREL T3-17 (non-powered).
Couplers: BSI.
Seating Layout: 1: 2+2 facing, 2: 3+2 facing/unidirectional. 20 standard class seats in 2+2 format in DMCL(B).
Dimensions: 23.50 x 2.81 m.
Gangways: Within unit only. **Wheel Arrangement:** 2-B – B-2 – B-2.
Doors: Twin-leaf swing plug. **Maximum Speed:** 90 m.p.h.
Multiple Working: Within class and with Classes 165 and 168.

DMCL (A). Lot No. 31116 ABB York 1992–1993. 16/75 1T. 39.6 t.
MS. Lot No. 31117 ABB York 1992–1993. –/96. 38.0 t.
DMCL (B). Lot No. 31116 ABB York 1992–1993. 16/72 1T. 39.6 t.

166 201	**TT**	A	*FK*	RG	58101	58601	58122
166 202	**TT**	A	*FK*	RG	58102	58602	58123
166 203	**TT**	A	*FK*	RG	58103	58603	58124
166 204	**TT**	A	*FK*	RG	58104	58604	58125
166 205	**TT**	A	*FK*	RG	58105	58605	58126
166 206	**TT**	A	*FK*	RG	58106	58606	58127
166 207	**TT**	A	*FK*	RG	58107	58607	58128
166 208	**TT**	A	*FK*	RG	58108	58608	58129
166 209	**TT**	A	*FK*	RG	58109	58609	58130
166 210	**TT**	A	*FK*	RG	58110	58610	58131
166 211	**TT**	A	*FK*	RG	58111	58611	58132
166 212	**TT**	A	*FK*	RG	58112	58612	58133
166 213	**TT**	A	*FK*	RG	58113	58613	58134
166 214	**TT**	A	*FK*	RG	58114	58614	58135
166 215	**TT**	A	*FK*	RG	58115	58615	58136
166 216	**TT**	A	*FK*	RG	58116	58616	58137
166 217	**TT**	A	*FK*	RG	58117	58617	58138
166 218	**TT**	A	*FK*	RG	58118	58618	58139
166 219	**TT**	A	*FK*	RG	58119	58619	58140
166 220	**TT**	A	*FK*	RG	58120	58620	58141
166 221	**TT**	A	*FK*	RG	58121	58621	58142

CLASS 168 CLUBMAN ADTRANZ/BOMBARDIER

Various formations. Air conditioned.

Construction: Welded aluminium bodies with bolt-on steel ends.
Engines: One MTU 6R183TD13H of 315 kW (422 h.p.) at 1900 r.p.m.
Transmission: Hydraulic. Voith T211rzze to ZF final drive.
Bogies: One Adtranz P3–23 and one BREL T3–23 per car.
Couplers: BSI at outer ends, bar within unit.
Seating Layout: 2+2 facing/unidirectional.
Dimensions: 24.10/23.61 x 2.70 m.
Gangways: Within unit only.   **Wheel Arrangement:** 2-B (– B-2 – B-2) – B-2.
Doors: Twin-leaf swing plug.   **Maximum Speed:** 100 m.p.h.
Multiple Working: Within class and with Classes 165 and 166.
Fitted with tripcocks for working over London Underground tracks between
Harrow-on-the-Hill and Amersham.

Class 168/0. Original Design. DMSL(A)–MSL–MS–DMSL(B).

58151–58155. DMSL(A). Adtranz Derby 1997–1998. –/60 1TD 1W. 43.7 t.
58651–58655. MSL. Adtranz Derby 1998. –/73 1T. 41.0 t.
58451–58455. MS. Adtranz Derby 1998. –/77. 40.5 t.
58251–58255. DMSL(B). Adtranz Derby 1998. –/68 1T. 43.6 t.

Note: 58451–58455 were formerly numbered 58656–58660 in 168 106–168 110.

168 001	**CR**	P	*CR*	AL	58151	58651	58451	58251
168 002	**CR**	P	*CR*	AL	58152	58652	58452	58252
168 003	**CR**	P	*CR*	AL	58153	58653	58453	58253
168 004	**CR**	P	*CR*	AL	58154	58654	58454	58254
168 005	**CR**	P	*CR*	AL	58155	58655	58455	58255

Class 168/1. These units are effectively Class 170s. DMSL(A)–(MS)–MSL–
DMSL(B).

58156–58163. DMSL(A). Adtranz Derby 2000. –/59 1TD 2W. 45.2 t.
58456–58460. MS. Bombardier Derby 2002. –/76. 41.8 t.
58461–58463. MS. Adtranz Derby 2000. –/76. 42.4 t.
58756–58757. MSL. Bombardier Derby 2002. –/73 1T. 42.9 t.
58256–58263. DMSL(B). Adtranz Derby 2000. –/69 1T. 45.2 t.

Note: 58461–58463 have been renumbered from 58661–58663.

168 106	**CR**	P	*CR*	AL	58156	58456	58756	58256
168 107	**CR**	P	*CR*	AL	58157	58457	58757	58257
168 108	**CR**	P	*CR*	AL	58158	58458		58258
168 109	**CR**	P	*CR*	AL	58159	58459		58259
168 110	**CR**	P	*CR*	AL	58160	58460		58260
168 111	**CR**	H	*CR*	AL	58161	58461		58261
168 112	**CR**	H	*CR*	AL	58162	58462		58262
168 113	**CR**	H	*CR*	AL	58163	58463		58263

Class 168/2. These units are effectively Class 170s. DMSL–(MS)–DMSL.

58164–58169. DMSL(A). Bombardier Derby 2003–2004. –/59 1TD 2W. 45.4 t.

58464/58468/58469. MS. Bombardier Derby 2003–2004. –/76. 44.0 t.
58264–58269. DMSL(B). Bombardier Derby 2003–2004. –/69 1T. 45.5 t.

168 214	**CR**	P	*CR*	AL	58164	58464	58264
168 215	**CR**	P	*CR*	AL	58165		58265
168 216	**CR**	P	*CR*	AL	58166		58266
168 217	**CR**	P	*CR*	AL	58167		58267
168 218	**CR**	P	*CR*	AL	58168	58468	58268
168 219	**CR**	P	*CR*	AL	58169	58469	58269

CLASS 170 TURBOSTAR ADTRANZ/BOMBARDIER

Various formations. Air conditioned.

Construction: Welded aluminium bodies with bolt-on steel ends.
Engines: One MTU 6R183TD13H of 315 kW (422 h.p.) at 1900 r.p.m.
Transmission: Hydraulic. Voith T211rzze to ZF final drive.
Bogies: One Adtranz P3–23 and one BREL T3–23 per car.
Couplers: BSI at outer ends, bar within later build units.
Seating Layout: 1: 2+1 facing/unidirectional (2+2 in first class in Class 170/1 end cars). 2: 2+2 facing/unidirectional.
Dimensions: 24.10 x 2.70 m unless stated.
Gangways: Within unit only.   **Wheel Arrangement:** 2-B (– B-2) – B-2.
Doors: Twin-leaf swing plug.   **Maximum Speed:** 100 m.p.h.
Multiple Working: Within class and with Classes 150, 153, 155, 156, 158 and 159.

Class 170/1. Central Trains units. Former Midland Mainline units, these now have their first class declassified. DMCL–MCRMB–DMCL or DMCL–DMCL.

DMCL (A). Adtranz Derby 1998–1999. 12/45 1TD 2W. 45.0 t.
MCRMB. Adtranz Derby 2001. 21/22 and bar. 43.0 t.
DMCL (B). Adtranz Derby 1998–1999. 12/52 1T. Catering point. 44.8 t

Note: The DMCL(A) and DMCL(B) in the 3-car units have had their former first class end sections declassified.

170 101	**CM**	P	*CT*	TS	50101	55101	79101
170 102	**CM**	P	*CT*	TS	50102	55102	79102
170 103	**MM**	P	*CT*	TS	50103	55103	79103
170 104	**MM**	P	*CT*	TS	50104	55104	79104
170 105	**CM**	P	*CT*	TS	50105	55105	79105
170 106	**CM**	P	*CT*	TS	50106	55106	79106
170 107	**CM**	P	*CT*	TS	50107	55107	79107
170 108	**CM**	P	*CT*	TS	50108	55108	79108
170 109	**CM**	P	*CT*	TS	50109	55109	79109
170 110	**CM**	P	*CT*	TS	50110	55110	79110
170 111	**MM**	P	*CT*	TS	50111		79111
170 112	**MM**	P	*CT*	TS	50112		79112
170 113	**MM**	P	*CT*	TS	50113		79113
170 114	**MM**	P	*CT*	TS	50114		79114
170 115	**MM**	P	*CT*	TS	50115		79115
170 116	**MM**	P	*CT*	TS	50116		79116
170 117	**MM**	P	*CT*	TS	50117		79117

Class 170/2. One Anglia 3-car units. DMCL–MSLRB–DMSL.

DMCL. Adtranz Derby 1999. 29/3 1TD 2W. 45.0 t.
MSLRB. Adtranz Derby 1999. –/58 1T. Buffet and guard's office 45.3 t.
DMSL. Adtranz Derby 1999. –/66 1T. 43.4 t.

170 201	**1**	P	*1A*	NC	50201	56201	79201
170 202	**1**	P	*1A*	NC	50202	56202	79202
170 203	**1**	P	*1A*	NC	50203	56203	79203
170 204	**1**	P	*1A*	NC	50204	56204	79204
170 205	**1**	P	*1A*	NC	50205	56205	79205
170 206	**1**	P	*1A*	NC	50206	56206	79206
170 207	**1**	P	*1A*	NC	50207	56207	79207
170 208	**1**	P	*1A*	NC	50208	56208	79208

Class 170/2. One Anglia 2-car units. DMSL–DMCL.

DMSL. Bombardier Derby 2002. –/57 1TD 2W. 45.7 t.
DMCL. Bombardier Derby 2002. 9/53 1T. 45.7 t.

170 270	**1**	P	*1A*	NC	50270	79270
170 271	**AN**	P	*1A*	NC	50271	79271
170 272	**AN**	P	*1A*	NC	50272	79272
170 273	**AN**	P	*1A*	NC	50273	79273

Class 170/3. South West Trains units. DMCL–DMCL or DMCL–DMSL.

50301–50308. DMCL(A). Adtranz Derby 2000. 9/43 1TD 2W. 45.8 t.
50392. DMCL(A). Bombardier Derby 2003. 9/43 1TD 2W. 46.6 t.
79301–79308. DMCL(B). Adtranz Derby 2000. 9/53 1T. 45.8 t.
79392. DMCL(B). Bombardier Derby 2003. 9/53 1T. 46.5 t.

Note: 170 392 was initially numbered 170 727 in error and painted into Southern livery before being repainted into South West Trains livery.

170 301	**SW**	P	*SW*	SA	50301	79301
170 302	**SW**	P	*SW*	SA	50302	79302
170 303	**SW**	P	*SW*	SA	50303	79303
170 304	**SW**	P	*SW*	SA	50304	79304
170 305	**SW**	P	*SW*	SA	50305	79305
170 306	**SW**	P	*SW*	SA	50306	79306
170 307	**SW**	P	*SW*	SA	50307	79307
170 308	**SW**	P	*SW*	SA	50308	79308
170 392	**SW**	P	*SW*	SA	50392	79392

Class 170/3. Hull Trains units. Due to transfer to First ScotRail in Spring 2005.
DMCL–MSLRB–DMSL.
Dimensions: 23.62/23.61 × 2.75 m.

DMCL. Bombardier Derby 2004. 29/5 1TD 2W. 46.5 t.
MSLRB. Bombardier Derby 2004. –/60 1T. Buffet and guard's office 44.7 t.
DMSL. Bombardier Derby 2004. –/71 1T. 46.3 t.

170 393	**HT**	P	*HT*	IL	50393	56393	79393
170 394	**HT**	P	*HT*	IL	50394	56394	79394
170 395	**HT**	P	*HT*	IL	50395	56395	79395
170 396	**HT**	P	*HT*	IL	50396	56396	79396

Class 170/3. Porterbrook spot hire units. DMCL–MC–DMCL.

DMCL(A). Bombardier Derby 2002. 9/43 1TD 1W. 45.4 t.
MC. Bombardier Derby 2002. 22/36. 43.0 t.
DMCL(B). Bombardier Derby 2002. 9/53 1T. 45.8 t.

170 397	**P**	P	*CT*	TS	50397	56397	79397
170 398	**P**	P	*CT*	TS	50398	56398	79398

Class 170/3. Porterbrook spot hire unit. DMCL–DMCL.

DMCL(A). Bombardier Derby 2001. 9/43 1TD 2W. 45.8 t.
DMCL(B). Bombardier Derby 2001. 9/53 1T. 45.8 t.

Advertising Livery: 170 399 Derwent Valley Mills World Heritage Site (green, grey and blue with various images).

170 399	**AL**	P	*CT*	TS	50399	79399

Class 170/4. First ScotRail "express" units. DMCL–MS–DMCL.
Dimensions: 23.62/23.61 x 2.75 m unless stated.

DMCL(A). Adtranz Derby 1999–2001. 9/43 1TD 2W. 45.2 t.
MS. Adtranz Derby 1999–2001. –/76. 42.5 t.
DMCL(B). Adtranz Derby 1999–2001. 9/53 1T. 45.2 t.

170 401	**FS**	P	*SR*	HA	50401	56401	79401
170 402	**SR**	P	*SR*	HA	50402	56402	79402
170 403	**SR**	P	*SR*	HA	50403	56403	79403
170 404	**SR**	P	*SR*	HA	50404	56404	79404
170 405	**FS**	P	*SR*	HA	50405	56405	79405
170 406	**SR**	P	*SR*	HA	50406	56406	79406
170 407	**SR**	P	*SR*	HA	50407	56407	79407
170 408	**SR**	P	*SR*	HA	50408	56408	79408
170 409	**SR**	P	*SR*	HA	50409	56409	79409
170 410	**SR**	P	*SR*	HA	50410	56410	79410
170 411	**SR**	P	*SR*	HA	50411	56411	79411
170 412	**SR**	P	*SR*	HA	50412	56412	79412
170 413	**SR**	P	*SR*	HA	50413	56413	79413
170 414	**SR**	P	*SR*	HA	50414	56414	79414
170 415	**SR**	P	*SR*	HA	50415	56415	79415
170 416	**SR**	H	*SR*	HA	50416	56416	79416
170 417	**SR**	H	*SR*	HA	50417	56417	79417
170 418	**SR**	H	*SR*	HA	50418	56418	79418
170 419	**SR**	H	*SR*	HA	50419	56419	79419
170 420	**SR**	H	*SR*	HA	50420	56420	79420
170 421	**SR**	H	*SR*	HA	50421	56421	79421
170 422	**SR**	H	*SR*	HA	50422	56422	79422
170 423	**SR**	H	*SR*	HA	50423	56423	79423
170 424	**SR**	H	*SR*	HA	50424	56424	79424

Class 170/4. First ScotRail "express" units. DMCL–MS–DMSL or DMCL–MS–DMSL (see notes below).
Dimensions: 23.62/23.61 x 2.75 m.

DMCL. Bombardier Derby 2003–2005. 9/43 1TD 2W. 46.8 t.
MS. Bombardier Derby 2003–2005. –/76. 43.7 t.
DMSL. Bombardier Derby 2003–2005. –/67 1T. 46.8 t.

IMPORTANT NOTE: 170 425–170 432 delivered DMCL–MS–DMSL, to become DMCL–MS–DMCL.

The DMSL/DMCLs of units 170 425–170 432 and 170 450–170 457 are to be swapped.

170 425	**SR**	P	*SR*	HA	50425	56425	79450
170 426	**SR**	P	*SR*	HA	50426	56426	79451
170 427	**SR**	P	*SR*	HA	50427	56427	79452
170 428	**SR**	P	*SR*	HA	50428	56428	79453
170 429	**SR**	P	*SR*	HA	50429	56429	79454
170 430	**SR**	P	*SR*	HA	50430	56430	79455
170 431	**SR**	P	*SR*	HA	50431	56431	79456
170 432	**SR**	P	*SR*	HA	50432	56432	79457
170 433		P			50433	56433	79433
170 434		P			50434	56434	79434

Class 170/4. First ScotRail "suburban" units. DMSL–MS–DMCL or DMSL–MS–DMSL (see notes below).
Dimensions: 23.62/23.61 x 2.75 m.

DMSL. Bombardier Derby 2004–2005. –/55 1TD 2W. 46.3 t.
MS. Bombardier Derby 2004–2005. –/76. 43.4 t.
DMCL. Bombardier Derby 2004–2005. 9/53 1T. 46.5 t.

IMPORTANT NOTE: 170 450–170 457 delivered DMSL–MS–DMCL, to become DMSL–MS–DMSL.

The DMCL/DMSLs of units 170 450–170 457 and 170 425–170 432 are to be swapped.

Non-standard livery: 170 456 & 170 457 – All over dark blue with white doors and front-end cab sections.

170 450	**P**	P	*SR*	HA	50450	56450	79425
170 451	**P**	P	*SR*	HA	50451	56451	79426
170 452	**P**	P	*SR*	HA	50452	56452	79427
170 453	**P**	P	*SR*	HA	50453	56453	79428
170 454	**P**	P	*SR*	HA	50454	56454	79429
170 455	**P**	P	*SR*	HA	50455	56455	79430
170 456	**0**	P	*SR*	HA	50456	56456	79431
170 457	**0**	P	*SR*	HA	50457	56457	79432
170 458	**P**	P	*SR*	HA	50458	56458	79458
170 459	**P**	P	*SR*	HA	50459	56459	79459
170 460	**P**	P	*SR*	HA	50460	56460	79460
170 461	**P**	P	*SR*	HA	50461	56461	79461

Class 170/4. First ScotRail units. Standard class only Strathclyde PTE units. DMSL–MS–DMSL.

50470–50471. DMSL(A). Adtranz Derby 2001. –/55 1TD 2W. 45.1 t.
50472–50478. DMSL(A). Bombardier Derby 2004–2005. –/57 1TD 2W. 46.3 t.
56470–56471. MS. Adtranz Derby 2001. –/76. 42.4 t.
56472–56478. MS. Bombardier Derby 2004–2005. –/76. 43.4 t.
79470–79471. DMSL(B). Adtranz Derby 2001. –/67 1T. 45.1 t.
79472–79478. DMSL(B). Bombardier Derby 2004–2005. –/67 1T. 46.4 t.

170 470	**SC**	P	*SR*	HA	50470	56470	79470
170 471	**SC**	P	*SR*	HA	50471	56471	79471
170 472	**SP**	P	*SR*	HA	50472	56472	79472
170 473	**SP**	P	*SR*	HA	50473	56473	79473
170 474	**SP**	P	*SR*	HA	50474	56474	79474
170 475	**SP**	P	*SR*	HA	50475	56475	79475
170 476	**SP**	P	*SR*	HA	50476	56476	79476
170 477	**SP**	P	*SR*	HA	50477	56477	79477
170 478	**SP**	P			50478	56478	79478

Class 170/5. Central Trains 2-car units. DMSL–DMSL.

DMSL(A). Adtranz Derby 1999–2000. –/55 1TD 2W. 45.8 t.
DMSL(B). Adtranz Derby 1999–2000. –/67 1T. 45.9 t.

Advertising liveries:

170 505 Bullring shopping centre, Birmingham – black and brown with various images.
170 513 Robin Hood Line promotional livery – Lime green, green and red with various images.

170 501	r	**CT**	P	*CT*	TS	50501	79501
170 502	r	**CT**	P	*CT*	TS	50502	79502
170 503	r	**CT**	P	*CT*	TS	50503	79503
170 504	r	**CT**	P	*CT*	TS	50504	79504
170 505	r	**AL**	P	*CT*	TS	50505	79505
170 506	r	**CT**	P	*CT*	TS	50506	79506
170 507	r	**CT**	P	*CT*	TS	50507	79507
170 508	r	**CT**	P	*CT*	TS	50508	79508
170 509	r	**CT**	P	*CT*	TS	50509	79509
170 510	r	**CT**	P	*CT*	TS	50510	79510
170 511	r	**CT**	P	*CT*	TS	50511	79511
170 512	r	**CT**	P	*CT*	TS	50512	79512
170 513	r	**AL**	P	*CT*	TS	50513	79513
170 514	r	**CT**	P	*CT*	TS	50514	79514
170 515	r	**CT**	P	*CT*	TS	50515	79515
170 516	r	**CT**	P	*CT*	TS	50516	79516
170 517	r	**CT**	P	*CT*	TS	50517	79517
170 518	r	**CT**	P	*CT*	TS	50518	79518
170 519	r	**CT**	P	*CT*	TS	50519	79519
170 520	r	**CT**	P	*CT*	TS	50520	79520
170 521	r	**CT**	P	*CT*	TS	50521	79521
170 522	r	**CT**	P	*CT*	TS	50522	79522
170 523	r	**CT**	P	*CT*	TS	50523	79523

Class 170/6. Central Trains 3-car units. DMSL–MS–DMSL.

DMSL(A). Adtranz Derby 2000. –/55 1TD 2W. 45.8 t.
MS. Adtranz Derby 2000. –/74. 42.4 t.
DMSL(B). Adtranz Derby 2000. –/67 1T. 45.9 t.

170 630	r	**CT**	P	*CT*	TS	50630	56630	79630
170 631	r	**CT**	P	*CT*	TS	50631	56631	79631
170 632	r	**CT**	P	*CT*	TS	50632	56632	79632
170 633	r	**CT**	P	*CT*	TS	50633	56633	79633
170 634	r	**CT**	P	*CT*	TS	50634	56634	79634
170 635	r	**CT**	P	*CT*	TS	50635	56635	79635
170 636	r	**CT**	P	*CT*	TS	50636	56636	79636
170 637	r	**CT**	P	*CT*	TS	50637	56637	79637
170 638	r	**CT**	P	*CT*	TS	50638	56638	79638
170 639	r	**CT**	P	*CT*	TS	50639	56639	79639

CLASS 171   TURBOSTAR   BOMBARDIER

DMCL–DMSL or DMCL–MS–MS–DMCL. Southern units. Air conditioned.

Construction: Welded aluminium bodies with bolt-on steel ends.
Engines: One MTU 6R183TD13H of 315 kW (422 h.p.) at 1900 r.p.m.
Transmission: Hydraulic. Voith T211rzze to ZF final drive.
Bogies: One Adtranz P3–23 and one BREL T3–23 per car.
Couplers: Dellner 12 at outer ends, bar within unit (Class 171/8s).
Seating Layout: 1: 2+1 facing/unidirectional. 2: 2+2 facing/unidirectional.
Gangways: Within unit only.   **Wheel Arrangement:** 2-B (– B-2) – B-2.
Doors: Twin-leaf swing plug.   **Maximum Speed:** 100 m.p.h.
Multiple Working: Within class and with EMU Classes 375 and 377 only.

Class 171/7. Southern 2-car units. DMCL–DMSL.
Dimensions: 24.10 x 2.70 m.

Notes: 171 721–171 726 were built as Class 170s, but renumbered as 171s on fitting with Dellner 12 couplers.
171 727–171 729 on order.

50721–50726. DMCL. Bombardier Derby 2003. 9/43 1TD 2W. 47.6 t.
50727–50729. DMCL. Bombardier Derby 2005. 9/43 1TD 2W. 46.3 t.
79721–79726. DMSL. Bombardier Derby 2003. –/64 1T. 47.8 t.
79727–79729. DMSL. Bombardier Derby 2005. –/64 1T. 46.2 t.

171 721	**SN**	P	*SN*	SU	50721	79721
171 722	**SN**	P	*SN*	SU	50722	79722
171 723	**SN**	P	*SN*	SU	50723	79723
171 724	**SN**	P	*SN*	SU	50724	79724
171 725	**SN**	P	*SN*	SU	50725	79725
171 726	**SN**	P	*SN*	SU	50726	79726
171 727	**SN**	P			50727	79727
171 728	**SN**	P			50728	79728
171 729	**SN**	P			50729	79729

Class 171/8. Southern 4-car units. DMCL(A)–MS–MS–DMCL(B).
Dimensions: 23.70/23.61 x 2.75 m.

DMCL(A). Bombardier Derby 2004. 9/43 1TD 2W. 46.5 t.
MS. Bombardier Derby 2004. –/74. 43.7 t.
DMCL(B). Bombardier Derby 2004. 9/50 1T. 46.5 t.

171 801	**SN**	P	*SN*	SU	50801	54801	56801	79801
171 802	**SN**	P	*SN*	SU	50802	54802	56802	79802
171 803	**SN**	P	*SN*	SU	50803	54803	56803	79803
171 804	**SN**	P	*SN*	SU	50804	54804	56804	79804
171 805	**SN**	P	*SN*	SU	50805	54805	56805	79805
171 806	**SN**	P	*SN*	SU	50806	54806	56806	79806

CLASS 175   CORADIA 1000   ALSTOM

Air Conditioned.

Construction: Steel.
Engines: One Cummins N14 of 335 kW (450 h.p.).
Transmission: Hydraulic. Voith T211rzze to ZF final drive.
Bogies:
Couplers: Scharfenberg outer ends and bar within unit (Class 175/1).
Seating Layout: 2+2 facing/unidirectional.
Dimensions: 23.06/23.93 x 2.80 m.
Gangways: Within unit only.   **Wheel Arrangement:** 2-B (– B-2) – B-2.
Doors: Single-leaf swing plug.   **Maximum Speed:** 100 m.p.h.
Multiple Working: Within class and with Class 180.

Note: Although operated by Arriva Trains Wales several Class 175s are hired back to Trans-Pennine Express and Northern for use on Manchester Airport to Blackpool/Barrow & Millom/Windermere services.

Class 175/0. DMSL–DMSL. 2-car units.

DMSL(A). Alstom Birmingham 1999–2000. –/54 1TD 2W. 50.7 t.
DMSL(B). Alstom Birmingham 1999–2000. –/64 1T. 50.7 t.

175 001	**FS**	A	*AW*	CH	50701	79701
175 002	**FS**	A	*AW*	CH	50702	79702
175 003	**FS**	A	*AW*	CH	50703	79703
175 004	**FS**	A	*AW*	CH	50704	79704
175 005	**FS**	A	*AW*	CH	50705	79705
175 006	**FS**	A	*AW*	CH	50706	79706
175 007	**FS**	A	*AW*	CH	50707	79707
175 008	**FS**	A	*AW*	CH	50708	79708
175 009	**FS**	A	*AW*	CH	50709	79709
175 010	**FS**	A	*AW*	CH	50710	79710
175 011	**FS**	A	*AW*	CH	50711	79711

Names (carried on one side of each DMSL):

175 004	MENCAP National Colleges Pengwern College
175 006	Brondyffryn Trust
175 008	Valhalla Blackpool Pleasure Beach

Class 175/1. DMSL–MSL–DMSL. 3-car units.

DMSL(A). Alstom Birmingham 1999–2001. –/54 1TD 2W. 50.7 t.
MSL. Alstom Birmingham 1999–2001. –/68 1T. 47.5 t.
DMSL(B). Alstom Birmingham 1999–2001. –/64 1T. 50.7 t.

175 101	**FS**	A	*AW*	CH	50751	56751	79751
175 102	**FS**	A	*AW*	CH	50752	56752	79752
175 103	**FS**	A	*AW*	CH	50753	56753	79753
175 104	**FS**	A	*AW*	CH	50754	56754	79754
175 105	**FS**	A	*AW*	CH	50755	56755	79755
175 106	**FS**	A	*AW*	CH	50756	56756	79756
175 107	**FS**	A	*AW*	CH	50757	56757	79757
175 108	**FS**	A	*AW*	CH	50758	56758	79758
175 109	**FS**	A	*AW*	CH	50759	56759	79759
175 110	**FS**	A	*AW*	CH	50760	56760	79760
175 111	**FS**	A	*AW*	CH	50761	56761	79761
175 112	**FS**	A	*AW*	CH	50762	56762	79762
175 113	**FS**	A	*AW*	CH	50763	56763	79763
175 114	**FS**	A	*AW*	CH	50764	56764	79764
175 115	**FS**	A	*AW*	CH	50765	56765	79765
175 116	**FS**	A	*AW*	CH	50766	56766	79766

Names (carried on one side of each DMSL):

175 103	Mum
175 107	CORONATION ST. ROVERS RETURN
175 111	Brief Encounter
175 112	South Lakes Wild Animal Park SUMATRAN TIGER
175 114	Commonwealth Cruiser
175 116	PETER VL JONES Community Rail Officer – Conwy Valley Line

CLASS 180   ADELANTE   ALSTOM

Air Conditioned.

Construction: Steel.
Engines: One Cummins QSK19 of 560 kW (750 h.p.) at 2100 r.p.m.
Transmission: Hydraulic. Voith T312br to Voith final drive.
Bogies: Alstom MB2.
Couplers: Scharfenberg.
Seating Layout: 1: 2+1 facing/unidirectional, 2: 2+2 facing/unidirectional.
Dimensions: 23.71/23.03 x 2.80 m.
Gangways: Within unit only.
Wheel Arrangement: 2-B – B-2 – B-2 – B-2 – B-2.
Doors: Single-leaf swing plug.   **Maximum Speed:** 125 m.p.h.
Multiple Working: Within class and with Class 175.

DMSL(A). Alstom Birmingham 2000–2001. –/46 2W 1TD. 51.7 t.
MFL. Alstom Birmingham 2000–2001. 42/– 1T 1W + catering point. 49.6 t.
MSL. Alstom Birmingham 2000–2001. –/68 1T. 49.5 t.
MSLRB. Alstom Birmingham 2000–2001. –/56 1T. 50.3 t.
DMSL(B). Alstom Birmingham 2000–2001. –/56 1T. 51.4 t.

180 101	FG	A	GW	OO	50901	54901	55901	56901	59901
180 102	FG	A	GW	OO	50902	54902	55902	56902	59902
180 103	FG	A	GW	OO	50903	54903	55903	56903	59903
180 104	FG	A	GW	OO	50904	54904	55904	56904	59904
180 105	FG	A	GW	OO	50905	54905	55905	56905	59905
180 106	FG	A	GW	OO	50906	54906	55906	56906	59906
180 107	FG	A	GW	OO	50907	54907	55907	56907	59907
180 108	FG	A	GW	OO	50908	54908	55908	56908	59908
180 109	FG	A	GW	OO	50909	54909	55909	56909	59909
180 110	FG	A	GW	OO	50910	54910	55910	56910	59910
180 111	FG	A	GW	OO	50911	54911	55911	56911	59911
180 112	FG	A	GW	OO	50912	54912	55912	56912	59912
180 113	FG	A	GW	OO	50913	54913	55913	56913	59913
180 114	FG	A	GW	OO	50914	54914	55914	56914	59914

CLASS 185   DESIRO UK   SIEMENS

Air Conditioned. New units on order for Trans-Pennine Express.

Construction: Steel.
Engines: One Cummins engine of 560 kW (750 h.p.) at 2100 r.p.m.
Transmission: Voith.
Bogies: Siemens.
Couplers: Dellner 12.
Seating Layout: 1: 2+1 facing/unidirectional, 2: 2+2 facing/unidirectional.
Dimensions:
Gangways: Within unit only.
Wheel Arrangement: 2-B – 2-B – B-2.
Doors: Double-leaf sliding plug.   **Maximum Speed:** 100 m.p.h.
Multiple Working: Within class.

DMCL. Siemens Uerdingen 2004–2006. 15/26 2W 1TD.   . t.
MSL. Siemens Uerdingen 2004–2006. –/72 1T.   . t.
DMS. Siemens Uerdingen 2004–2006. –/68.   . t.

185 101	FG	A	51101	53101	54101
185 102	FG	A	51102	53102	54102
185 103	FG	A	51103	53103	54103
185 104	FG	A	51104	53104	54104
185 105	FG	A	51105	53105	54105
185 106	FG	A	51106	53106	54106
185 107	FG	A	51107	53107	54107
185 108	FG	A	51108	53108	54108
185 109	FG	A	51109	53109	54109
185 110	FG	A	51110	53110	54110
185 111	FG	A	51111	53111	54111
185 112	FG	A	51112	53112	54112
185 113	FG	A	51113	53113	54113
185 114	FG	A	51114	53114	54114
185 115	FG	A	51115	53115	54115
185 116	FG	A	51116	53116	54116

185 117	**FG**	A	51117	53117	54117
185 118	**FG**	A	51118	53118	54118
185 119	**FG**	A	51119	53119	54119
185 120	**FG**	A	51120	53120	54120
185 121	**FG**	A	51121	53121	54121
185 122	**FG**	A	51122	53122	54122
185 123	**FG**	A	51123	53123	54123
185 124	**FG**	A	51124	53124	54124
185 125	**FG**	A	51125	53125	54125
185 126	**FG**	A	51126	53126	54126
185 127	**FG**	A	51127	53127	54127
185 128	**FG**	A	51128	53128	54128
185 129	**FG**	A	51129	53129	54129
185 130	**FG**	A	51130	53130	54130
185 131	**FG**	A	51131	53131	54131
185 132	**FG**	A	51132	53132	54132
185 133	**FG**	A	51133	53133	54133
185 134	**FG**	A	51134	53134	54134
185 135	**FG**	A	51135	53135	54135
185 136	**FG**	A	51136	53136	54136
185 137	**FG**	A	51137	53137	54137
185 138	**FG**	A	51138	53138	54138
185 139	**FG**	A	51139	53139	54139
185 140	**FG**	A	51140	53140	54140
185 141	**FG**	A	51141	53141	54141
185 142	**FG**	A	51142	53142	54142
185 143	**FG**	A	51143	53143	54143
185 144	**FG**	A	51144	53144	54144
185 145	**FG**	A	51145	53145	54145
185 146	**FG**	A	51146	53146	54146
185 147	**FG**	A	51147	53147	54147
185 148	**FG**	A	51148	53148	54148
185 149	**FG**	A	51149	53149	54149
185 150	**FG**	A	51150	53150	54150
185 151	**FG**	A	51151	53151	54151

3.2. DIESEL ELECTRIC UNITS

The following features are standard to ex-BR Southern Region diesel-electric multiple unit power cars (Classes 201–207):

Construction: Steel.
Engine: One English Electric 4SRKT Mk. 2 of 450 kW (600 h.p.) at 850 r.p.m.
Main Generator: English Electric EE824.
Traction Motors: Two English Electric EE507 mounted on the inner bogie.

Bogies: SR Mk. 4. (Former EMU TSL vehicles have Commonwealth bogies).
Couplers: Drophead buckeye.
Doors: Manually operated slam.
Brakes: Electro-pneumatic and automatic air.
Maximum Speed: 75 m.p.h.
Multiple Working: Other ex-BR Southern Region DEMU vehicles.

CLASS 201/202 PRESERVED "HASTINGS" UNIT BR

DMBS–2TSL–TSRB–TSL–DMBS.

Preserved unit made up from two Class 201 short-frame cars and three Class 202 long-frame cars. The "Hastings" units were made with narrow body-profiles for use on the section between Tonbridge and Battle which had tunnels of restricted loading gauge. These tunnels were converted to single track operation in the 1980s thus allowing standard loading gauge stock to be used. The set also contains a Class 411 EMU trailer (not Hastings line gauge) and a Class 422 EMU buffet car.

Gangways: Within unit only.
Seating Layout: 2+2 facing.
Dimensions: 18.40 x 2.70 m (60000), 20.35 x 2.50 m (60116/60118/60529), 18.36 x 2.74 m (60501), 20.35 x 2.82 m (69337), 20.30 x 2.82 m (70262).

60000. DMBS. Lot No. 30329 Eastleigh 1957. –/22. 55.0 t.
60116. DMBS (Spare). Lot No. 30395 Eastleigh 1957. –/31. 56.0 t.
60118. DMBS. Lot No. 30395 Eastleigh 1957. –/30. 56.0 t.
60501. TSL. Lot No. 30331 Eastleigh 1957. –/52 2T. 29.5 t.
60529. TSL. Lot No. 30397 Eastleigh 1957. –/60 2T. 30.5 t.
69337. TSRB (ex Class 422 EMU). Lot No. 30805 York 1970. –/40. 35.0 t.
70262. TSL (ex Class 411/5 EMU). Lot No. 30455 Eastleigh 1958–1959. –/64 2T. 31.5 t.

| 201 001 | **G** | HD *HD* | SE | 60000 60529 70262 69337 60501 60118 |
| Spare | **G** | HD *HD* | SE | 60116 |

Names:

60000 Hastings
60116 Mountfield
60118 Tunbridge Wells

CLASS 205/0 (3H)   BR "HAMPSHIRE"

Southern unit retained as cover for new Class 171s. DMBS–TS–DTCsoL.

Gangways: Non-gangwayed.
Seating Layout: 3+2 facing or compartments.
Dimensions: 20.33 x 2.82 m (DMBS), 20.28 x 2.82 m (TS), 20.36 x 2.82 m (DTCsoL).

60117. DMBS. Lot No. 30332 Eastleigh 1957. –/52. 56 t.
60674. TS. Lot No. 30672 Eastleigh 1960–1962. –/104. 30 t.
60828. DTCsoL. Lot No. 30673 Eastleigh 1960–1962. 13/62 2T. 32 t.

205 018	**CX**	P	*SN*	SU	60117	60674	60828

CLASS 220   VOYAGER   BOMBARDIER

DMS–MSRMB–MS–DMF.

Construction: Steel.
Engine: Cummins of 750 h.p. (560 kW) at 1800 r.p.m.
Transmission: Two Alstom Onix 800 three-phase traction motors of 275 kW.
Braking: Rheostatic and electro-pneumatic.
Bogies: Bombardier B5005.
Couplers: Dellner.
Seating Layout: 1: 2+1 facing/unidirectional, 2: 2+2 mainly unidirectional.
Dimensions: 23.67/23.00 x 2.73 m.
Gangways: Within unit only.
Wheel Arrangement: 1A-A1 – 1A-A1 – 1A-A1 – 1A-A1.
Doors: Single-leaf swing plug.
Maximum Speed: 125 m.p.h.
Multiple Working: Within class and with Classes 221 and 222. Also with Dellner coupler-fitted Class 57 locomotives.

DMS. Bombardier Brugge/Wakefield 2000–2001. –/42 1TD 1W. 48.0 t.
MSRMB. Bombardier Brugge/Wakefield 2000–2001. –/58. 45.0 t.
MS. Bombardier Brugge/Wakefield 2000–2001. –/60 1TD 1W. 44.5 t.
DMF. Bombardier Brugge/Wakefield 2000–2001. 26/– 1TD 1W. 48.1 t.

220 001	**VT**	HX	*VX*	CZ	60301	60701	60201	60401
220 002	**VT**	HX	*VX*	CZ	60302	60702	60202	60402
220 003	**VT**	HX	*VX*	CZ	60303	60703	60203	60403
220 004	**VT**	HX	*VX*	CZ	60304	60704	60204	60404
220 005	**VT**	HX	*VX*	CZ	60305	60705	60205	60405
220 006	**VT**	HX	*VX*	CZ	60306	60706	60206	60406
220 007	**VT**	HX	*VX*	CZ	60307	60707	60207	60407
220 008	**VT**	HX	*VX*	CZ	60308	60708	60208	60408
220 009	**VT**	HX	*VX*	CZ	60309	60709	60209	60409
220 010	**VT**	HX	*VX*	CZ	60310	60710	60210	60410
220 011	**VT**	HX	*VX*	CZ	60311	60711	60211	60411
220 012	**VT**	HX	*VX*	CZ	60312	60712	60212	60412
220 013	**VT**	HX	*VX*	CZ	60313	60713	60213	60413

220 014	**VT**	HX	*VX*	CZ	60314	60714	60214	60414
220 015	**VT**	HX	*VX*	CZ	60315	60715	60215	60415
220 016	**VT**	HX	*VX*	CZ	60316	60716	60216	60416
220 017	**VT**	HX	*VX*	CZ	60317	60717	60217	60417
220 018	**VT**	HX	*VX*	CZ	60318	60718	60218	60418
220 019	**VT**	HX	*VX*	CZ	60319	60719	60219	60419
220 020	**VT**	HX	*VX*	CZ	60320	60720	60220	60420
220 021	**VT**	HX	*VX*	CZ	60321	60721	60221	60421
220 022	**VT**	HX	*VX*	CZ	60322	60722	60222	60422
220 023	**VT**	HX	*VX*	CZ	60323	60723	60223	60423
220 024	**VT**	HX	*VX*	CZ	60324	60724	60224	60424
220 025	**VT**	HX	*VX*	CZ	60325	60725	60225	60425
220 026	**VT**	HX	*VX*	CZ	60326	60726	60226	60426
220 027	**VT**	HX	*VX*	CZ	60327	60727	60227	60427
220 028	**VT**	HX	*VX*	CZ	60328	60728	60228	60428
220 029	**VT**	HX	*VX*	CZ	60329	60729	60229	60429
220 030	**VT**	HX	*VX*	CZ	60330	60730	60230	60430
220 031	**VT**	HX	*VX*	CZ	60331	60731	60231	60431
220 032	**VT**	HX	*VX*	CZ	60332	60732	60232	60432
220 033	**VT**	HX	*VX*	CZ	60333	60733	60233	60433
220 034	**VT**	HX	*VX*	CZ	60334	60734	60234	60434

Names (carried on MS):

220 001	Somerset Voyager
220 002	Forth Voyager
220 003	Solent Voyager
220 004	Cumbrian Voyager
220 005	Guildford Voyager
220 006	Clyde Voyager
220 007	Thames Voyager
220 008	Draig Gymreig/Welsh Dragon
220 009	Gatwick Voyager
220 010	Ribble Voyager
220 011	Tyne Voyager
220 012	Lanarkshire Voyager
220 013	Gwibiwr De Cymru/South Wales Voyager
220 014	South Yorkshire Voyager
220 015	Solway Voyager
220 016	Midland Voyager
220 017	BOMBARDIER Voyager
220 018	Dorset Voyager
220 019	Mersey Voyager
220 020	Wessex Voyager
220 021	Staffordshire Voyager
220 022	Brighton Voyager
220 023	Mancunian Voyager
220 024	Sheffield Voyager
220 025	Severn Voyager
220 026	Stagecoach Voyager
220 027	Avon Voyager
220 028	Black Country Voyager
220 029	Vyajer Kernewek/Cornish Voyager
220 030	Devon Voyager
220 031	Tay Voyager
220 032	Grampian Voyager
220 033	Fife Voyager
220 034	Yorkshire Voyager

CLASS 221   SUPER VOYAGER   BOMBARDIER

DMS–MSRMB–MS(–MS)–DMF. Tilting units.

Construction: Steel.
Engine: Cummins of 750 h.p. (560 kW) at 1800 r.p.m.
Transmission: Two Alstom Onix 800 three-phase traction motors of 275 kW.
Braking: Rheostatic and electro-pneumatic.
Bogies: Bombardier HVP.
Couplers: Dellner.
Seating Layout: 1: 2+1 facing/unidirectional, 2: 2+2 mainly unidirectional.
Dimensions: 23.67 x 2.73 m.
Gangways: Within unit only.
Wheel Arrangement: 1A-A1 – 1A-A1 – 1A-A1 (– 1A-A1) – 1A-A1.
Doors: Single-leaf swing plug.
Maximum Speed: 125 m.p.h.
Multiple Working: Within class and with Classes 220 and 222. Also with Dellner coupler-fitted Class 57 locomotives.

DMS. Bombardier Brugge/Wakefield 2001–2002. –/42 1TD 1W. 56.6 t.
MSRMB. Bombardier Brugge/Wakefield 2001–2002. –/58. 53.1 t.
60951–60994. MS. Bombardier Brugge/Wakefield 2001–2002. –/60 1TD 1W. 56.6 t.
60851–60890. MS. Bombardier Brugge/Wakefield 2001–2002. –/60 1TD 1W. 53.1 t.
DMF. Bombardier Brugge/Wakefield 2001–2002. 26/– 1TD 1W. 56.6 t.

221 101	**VT**	HX	*VX*	CZ	60351	60751	60951	60851	60451
221 102	**VT**	HX	*VX*	CZ	60352	60752	60952	60852	60452
221 103	**VT**	HX	*VX*	CZ	60353	60753	60953	60853	60453
221 104	**VT**	HX	*VX*	CZ	60354	60754	60954	60854	60454
221 105	**VT**	HX	*VX*	CZ	60355	60755	60955	60855	60455
221 106	**VT**	HX	*VX*	CZ	60356	60756	60956	60856	60456
221 107	**VT**	HX	*VX*	CZ	60357	60757	60957	60857	60457
221 108	**VT**	HX	*VX*	CZ	60358	60758	60958	60858	60458
221 109	**VT**	HX	*VX*	CZ	60359	60759	60959	60859	60459
221 110	**VT**	HX	*VX*	CZ	60360	60760	60960	60860	60460
221 111	**VT**	HX	*VX*	CZ	60361	60761	60961	60861	60461
221 112	**VT**	HX	*VX*	CZ	60362	60762	60962	60862	60462
221 113	**VT**	HX	*VX*	CZ	60363	60763	60963	60863	60463
221 114	**VT**	HX	*VX*	CZ	60364	60764	60964	60864	60464
221 115	**VT**	HX	*VX*	CZ	60365	60765	60965	60865	60465
221 116	**VT**	HX	*VX*	CZ	60366	60766	60966	60866	60466
221 117	**VT**	HX	*VX*	CZ	60367	60767	60967	60867	60467
221 118	**VT**	HX	*VX*	CZ	60368	60768	60968	60868	60468
221 119	**VT**	HX	*VX*	CZ	60369	60769	60969	60869	60469
221 120	**VT**	HX	*VX*	CZ	60370	60770	60970	60870	60470
221 121	**VT**	HX	*VX*	CZ	60371	60771	60971	60871	60471
221 122	**VT**	HX	*VX*	CZ	60372	60772	60972	60872	60472
221 123	**VT**	HX	*VX*	CZ	60373	60773	60973	60873	60473
221 124	**VT**	HX	*VX*	CZ	60374	60774	60974	60874	60474
221 125	**VT**	HX	*VX*	CZ	60375	60775	60975	60875	60475
221 126	**VT**	HX	*VX*	CZ	60376	60776	60976	60876	60476

221 127	**VT**	HX	*VX*	CZ	60377	60777	60977	60877	60477
221 128	**VT**	HX	*VX*	CZ	60378	60778	60978	60878	60478
221 129	**VT**	HX	*VX*	CZ	60379	60779	60979	60879	60479
221 130	**VT**	HX	*VX*	CZ	60380	60780	60980	60880	60480
221 131	**VT**	HX	*VX*	CZ	60381	60781	60981	60881	60481
221 132	**VT**	HX	*VX*	CZ	60382	60782	60982	60882	60482
221 133	**VT**	HX	*VX*	CZ	60383	60783	60983	60883	60483
221 134	**VT**	HX	*VX*	CZ	60384	60784	60984	60884	60484
221 135	**VT**	HX	*VX*	CZ	60385	60785	60985	60885	60485
221 136	**VT**	HX	*VX*	CZ	60386	60786	60986	60886	60486
221 137	**VT**	HX	*VX*	CZ	60387	60787	60987	60887	60487
221 138	**VT**	HX	*VX*	CZ	60388	60788	60988	60888	60488
221 139	**VT**	HX	*VX*	CZ	60389	60789	60989	60889	60489
221 140	**VT**	HX	*VX*	CZ	60390	60790	60990	60890	60490
221 141	**VT**	HX	*VX*	CZ	60391	60791	60991		60491
221 142	**VT**	HX	*VX*	CZ	60392	60792	60992		60492
221 143	**VT**	HX	*VX*	CZ	60393	60793	60993		60493
221 144	**VT**	HX	*VX*	CZ	60394	60794	60994		60494

Names (carried on MS No. 609xx):

221 101	Louis Bleriot	221 123	Henry Hudson
221 102	John Cabot	221 124	Charles Lindbergh
221 103	Christopher Columbus	221 125	Henry the Navigator
221 104	Sir John Franklin	221 126	Captain Robert Scott
221 105	William Baffin	221 127	Wright Brothers
221 106	Willem Barents	221 128	Captain John Smith
221 107	Sir Martin Frobisher	221 129	George Vancouver
221 108	Sir Ernest Shackleton	221 130	Michael Palin
221 109	Marco Polo	221 131	Edgar Evans
221 110	James Cook	221 132	William Speirs Bruce
221 111	Roald Amundsen	221 133	Alexander Selkirk
221 112	Ferdinand Magellan	221 134	Mary Kingsley
221 113	Sir Walter Raleigh	221 135	Donald Campbell
221 114	Sir Francis Drake	221 136	Yuri Gagarin
221 115	Sir Francis Chichester	221 137	Mayflower Pilgrims
221 116	David Livingstone	221 138	Thor Heyerdahl
221 117	Sir Henry Morton Stanley	221 139	Leif Erikson
221 118	Mungo Park	221 140	Vasco da Gama
221 119	Amelia Earhart	221 141	Amerigo Vespucci
221 120	Amy Johnson	221 142	Matthew Flinders
221 121	Charles Darwin	221 143	Auguste Picard
221 122	Doctor Who	221 144	Prince Madoc

CLASS 222   MERIDIAN   BOMBARDIER

Construction: Steel.
Engine: Cummins of 750 h.p. (560 kW) at 1800 r.p.m.
Transmission: Two Alstom Onix 800 three-phase traction motors of 275 kW.
Braking: Rheostatic and electro-pneumatic.
Bogies: Bombardier B5005.
Couplers: Dellner at outer ends, bar within unit.
Seating Layout: 1: 2+1, 2: 2+2 facing/unidirectional.
Dimensions: 23.85/23.00 x 2.73 m.
Gangways: Within unit only.
Wheel Arrangement: All cars 1A-A1.
Doors: Single-leaf swing plug.
Maximum Speed: 125 m.p.h.
Multiple Working: Within class and with Classes 220 and 221.

222 001–222 007. DMRFO–MFO–MFO–MSORMB–MSO–MSO–MSO–MSO–
DMSO. 9-car units. Ordered for Midland Mainline but after testing these units
are being stored as they are not currently required. Ultimate operator at present
unknown!

DMRFO. Bombardier Brugge 2004–2005. 22/– 1TD 1W. 52.8 t.
MFO. Bombardier Brugge 2004–2005. 42/– 1T. 48.2 t.
MSO. Bombardier Brugge 2004–2005. –/70 1T. 48.6 t.
MSORMB. Bombardier Brugge 2004–2005. –/62. 49.6 t.
DMSO. Bombardier Brugge 2004–2005. –/40 1TD 1W. 51.0 t.

222 001	**MN**	H		60241	60441	60341	60621	60561
				60551	60541	60531	60161	
222 002	**MN**	H		60242	60442	60342	60622	60562
				60552	60542	60532	60162	
222 003	**MN**	H		60243	60443	60343	60623	60563
				60553	60543	60533	60163	
222 004	**MN**	H		60244	60444	60344	60624	60564
				60554	60544	60534	60164	
222 005	**MN**	H		60245	60445	60345	60625	60565
				60555	60545	60535	60165	
222 006	**MN**	H		60246	60446	60346	60626	60566
				60556	60546	60536	60166	
222 007	**MN**	H		60247	60447	60347	60627	60567
				60557	60547	60537	60167	

222 008–222 023. DMRFO–MCO–MSORMB–DMSO. Midland Mainline 4-car units.

DMRFO. Bombardier Brugge 2003–2004. 22/– 1TD 1W. 52.8 t.
MCO. Bombardier Brugge 2003–2004. 28/22 1T. 48.6 t.
MSORMB. Bombardier Brugge 2003–2004. –/62. 49.6 t.
DMSO. Bombardier Brugge 2003–2004. –/40 1TD 1W. 51.0 t.

222 008	**MN**	H	*MM*	CZ	60248	60918	60628	60168
222 009	**MN**	H	*MM*	CZ	60249	60919	60629	60169
222 010	**MN**	H	*MM*	CZ	60250	60920	60630	60170
222 011	**MN**	H	*MM*	CZ	60251	60921	60631	60171

222 012	**MN**	H	*MM*	CZ	60252	60922	60632	60172
222 013	**MN**	H	*MM*	CZ	60253	60923	60633	60173
222 014	**MN**	H	*MM*	CZ	60254	60924	60634	60174
222 015	**MN**	H	*MM*	CZ	60255	60925	60635	60175
222 016	**MN**	H	*MM*	CZ	60256	60926	60636	60176
222 017	**MN**	H	*MM*	CZ	60257	60927	60637	60177
222 018	**MN**	H	*MM*	CZ	60258	60928	60638	60178
222 019	**MN**	H	*MM*	CZ	60259	60929	60639	60179
222 020	**MN**	H	*MM*	CZ	60260	60930	60640	60180
222 021	**MN**	H	*MM*	CZ	60261	60931	60641	60181
222 022	**MN**	H	*MM*	CZ	60262	60932	60642	60182
222 023	**MN**	H	*MM*	CZ	60263	60933	60643	60183

222 101–222 104. DMRFO–MSORMB–MSO–DMSO. 4-car units for Hull Trains.

DMRFO. Bombardier Brugge 2005. 22/– 1TD 1W. 52.8 t.
MSO. Bombardier Brugge 2005. –/70 1T. 48.6 t.
MSORMB. Bombardier Brugge 2005. –/62. 49.6 t.
DMSO. Bombardier Brugge 2005. –/40 1TD 1W. 51.0 t.

222 101	**HP**	H		60271	60571	60681	60191
222 102	**HP**	H		60272	60572	60682	60192
222 103	**HP**	H		60273	60573	60683	60193
222 104	**HP**	H		60274	60574	60684	60194

3.3. SERVICE DMUS

This section lists vehicles not used for passenger-carrying purposes. Some vehicles are numbered in the special service stock number series.

CLASS 901   ULTRASONIC TEST UNIT

DM–DM. Converted 1986 from Class 101. Gangwayed within unit. Often operates with either Overhead Line Equipment Test Coach 975091 (see Page 347) or 999602 (see below) as a centre car.

Construction: Aluminium alloy body on steel underframe.
Engines: Two Leyland 680/1 of 112 kW (150 h.p.) at 1800 r.p.m. per power car.
Transmission: Mechanical. Cardan shaft and freewheel to a four-speed epicyclic gearbox with a further cardan shaft to the final drive, each engine driving the inner axle of one bogie.

Brakes: Air.	**Bogies:** DD15 (motor) and DT11 (trailer).
Couplers: Screw couplings.	**Maximum Speed:** 70 m.p.h.
Brakes: Air.	**Dimensions:** 18.50 x 2.82 m.

Multiple Working: "Blue Square" coupling code. First generation vehicles may be coupled together to work in multiple up to a maximum of 6 motor cars or 12 cars in total in a formation. First generation vehicles may not be coupled in multiple with second generation vehicles.

977391. DM. Lot No. 30500 Metro-Cammell. 1959. 32.5 t.
977392. DM. Lot No. 30254 Metro-Cammell. 1956. 32.5 t.

901 001	**Y**	NR *SO*	ZA	977391	(51433)	977392	(53167)

CLASS 901 ULTRASONIC TEST UNIT (ADDITIONAL VEHICLE)

T. Converted 1986 from Class 432 EMU. Gangwayed. Operates with 977391/977392 (see above).

Construction: Steel.	**Maximum Speed:** 70 m.p.h.
Bogies: SR Mk. 6.	**Couplings:** Screw.
Brakes: Twin pipe vacuum.	**Multiple Working:** Blue Square.
Doors: Manually operated slam.	**Dimensions:** 20.35 x 2.82 m.

999602. T. Lot No. 30862 York 1974. 55.5 t.

-	**Y**	NR *SO*	ZA	999602	(62483)

CLASS 901   TEST UNIT (Iris 2)

DM–DM. Converted 1991 from Class 101. Gangwayed within unit.

For details see above.

977693. DM. Lot No. 30261 Metro-Cammell. 1957. 32.5 t.
977694. DM. Lot No. 30276 Metro-Cammell. 1958. 32.5 t.

901 002	**Y**	NR *SO*	DF	977693	(53222)	977694	(53338)

CLASS 930   SANDITE/DE-ICING UNIT

DMB–T–DMB. Converted 1993 from Class 205. Gangwayed within unit. Sandite Trailer 977870 is replaced by De-icing trailer 977364 (see below) as required.

Construction: Steel.
Engine: One English Electric 4SRKT Mk. 2 of 450 kW (600 h.p.) at 850 r.p.m.
Transmission: Electric. Two English Electric EE507 traction motors mounted on the bogie at the non-driving end of each power car.
Maximum Speed: 75 m.p.h.   **Bogies:** SR Mk. 4.
Brakes: Electro-pneumatic and automatic air.
Doors: Manually operated slam.   **Couplings:** Drophead buckeye.
Multiple Working: Classes 201–207.
Dimensions: 20.33 x 2.82 x 3.87 m. (DMB); 20.28 x 2.82 m.

977939–977940. DMB. Lot No. 30671 Eastleigh 1962. 56.0 t.
977870. T. Lot No. 30542 Eastleigh 1959. 30.5 t.

930 301	RO	NR	*SN*	SU	977939	(60145)	977870	(60660)
					977940	(60149)		

UNCLASSIFIED   DE-ICING UNIT

T. Converted 1960 from 4-Sub EMU vehicle. Non gangwayed. Operates with 977939/977940 (see above) in place of Sandite Trailer 977870.

Construction: Steel.
Maximum Speed: 70 m.p.h.   **Couplings:** Drophead buckeye.
Bogies: Central 43 inch.   **Multiple Working:** SR system.
Brakes: Electro-pneumatic and automatic air.
Doors: Manually operated slam.   **Dimensions:** 19.99 x 2.74 m.

977364. T. Southern Railway Eastleigh 1946. 29.0 t.

-	RO	NR	*SN*	SU	977364	(10400)

CLASS 950   TRACK ASSESSMENT UNIT

DM–DM. Purpose built service unit. Gangwayed within unit.

Construction: Steel.
Engine: One Cummins NT-855-RT5 of 213 kW (285 h.p.) at 2100 r.p.m. per power car.
Transmission: Hydraulic. Voith T211r with cardan shafts to Gmeinder GM190 final drive.
Maximum Speed: 75 m.p.h.   **Couplers:** BSI automatic.
Bogies: BP38 (powered), BT38 (non-powered).
Brakes: Electro-pneumatic.   **Dimensions:** 20.06 x 2.82 m.
Doors: Manually operated slam & power operated sliding.
Multiple Working: Classes 142, 143, 144, 150, 153, 155, 156, 158, 159, 170.

999600. DM. Lot No. 4060 BREL York 1987. 35.0 t.
999601. DM. Lot No. 4061 BREL York 1987. 35.0 t.

950 001	RK	NR	*SO*	ZA	999600	999601

CLASS 960 — SANDITE & SERVICE UNITS

DMB. Converted 1991/1993 from Class 121. Non gangwayed.

For details see Page 173.

960 011 is a Video Survey Unit.
960 012 is undergoing a further conversion for South West Trains, for use as a Route Learning Unit.
960 014 is now a Route Learning Unit.

977723. DMB. Lot No. 30518 Pressed Steel 1960. 38.0 t.
977858–60/66/73. DMB. Lot No. 30518 Pressed Steel 1960. 38.0 t.

960 010	M	NR	*CR*	AL	977858	(55024)
960 011	RK	NR	*BB*	AP	977859	(55025)
960 012	SD	SW		CP	977860	(55028)
960 013	N	NR		AL	977866	(55030)
960 014	BG	CR	*CR*	AL	977873	(55022)
960 021	RO	NR	*CR*	AL	977723	(55021)

CLASS 960 — SANDITE UNIT

DMB. Converted 1991 from Class 122. Non gangwayed.

Construction: Steel.
Engines: Two Leyland 1595 of 112 kW (150 h.p.) at 1800 r.p.m.
Transmission: Mechanical. Cardan shaft and freewheel to a four-speed epicyclic gearbox with a further cardan shaft to the final drive, each engine driving the inner axle of one bogie.
Maximum Speed: 70 m.p.h.

Bogies: DD10.	**Couplings:** Screw.
Brakes: Twin pipe vacuum.	**Multiple Working:** Blue Square.
Doors: Manually operated slam.	**Dimensions:** 20.45 x 2.82 m.

975042. DMB. Lot No. 30419 Gloucester 1958. 36.5 t.

960 015	Y	NR	*CR*	AL	975042	(55019)

CLASS 960 — 3-CAR WATER-JETTING UNIT

DMB–IMV–DMB. Converted 2003/04 from Class 117. Non gangwayed.

Construction. Steel.
Engines: Two Leyland 1595 of 112 kW (150 h.p.) at 1800 r.p.m.
Transmission: Mechanical. Cardan shaft and freewheel to a four-speed epicyclic gearbox with a further cardan shaft to the final drive, each engine driving the inner axle of one bogie.
Maximum Speed: 70 m.p.h.

Bogies: DD10.	**Couplings:** Screw.
Brakes: Twin pipe vacuum.	**Multiple Working:** Blue Square.
Doors: Manually operated slam.	**Dimensions:** 20.45 x 2.84 m.

977987/977988. DMB. Lot No. 30419 Gloucester 1960. 35.9 t.
977992. IMV (Intermedite Motor Vehicle). Lot No. 30419 Gloucester 1959.
34.5 t.

```
960 301    G    CR  CR    AL    977987  (51371)   977992 (51375)
                                977988  (51413)
```

CLASS 960   EMERGENCY TRAIN UNITS

Converted from Class 121. Severn Tunnel Emergency Train units.

For details see Page 173.

DMB. Lot No. 30518 Pressed Steel 1960. 38.5 t.

```
960 302    Y    NR  E     SJ    977975  (55027)
960 303    Y    NR  E     SJ    977976  (55031)
```

CLASS 960   DRIVER TRAINING UNIT

Converted from Class 121.

For details see Page 173.

977968. DMB.

```
-          ES   CA  CA    RU    977968  (55029)
```

CLASS 960 TRACK ASSESSMENT/RECORDING UNIT

DM–DM. Universal track recording unit for video inspections, for measuring
rail profiles etc. Plasser type UFM 160-1. Full details awaited.

Construction:	**Engine:**
Transmission:	
Maximum Speed: 100 m.p.h.	**Weight:** 68.0 t.
Brakes:	**Dimensions:** 23.86 x 2.57 m.

999700. DM. Austria 2002.
999701. DM. Austria 2002.

```
-          ES   ES  CA    RU    999700  999701
```

CLASS 960 TRACK ASSESSMENT/RECORDING UNIT

DM. Full details awaited. Plasser & Theurer EM-SA+ RT100 Survey Cars.

Construction:	**Engine:**
Transmission:	
Maximum Speed: 55 m.p.h.	**Weight:** 57 t.
Brakes:	**Dimensions:** 17.70 x 2.75 m.

999800/1. DM. Austria 2004.

```
-          ES   NR  CA    RU    999800
-          ES   NR  CA    RU    999801
```

UNCLASSIFIED   NR INSPECTION SALOON

T. Converted from Class 202 TRB 60755 at Stewarts Lane in 1969/1970 for use as a BR Southern Region General Manager's Saloon. Overhauled by Fragonset/FM Rail in 2004/05 for use as a Network Rail New Trains Project Saloon. Can be used in push-pull mode with suitably equipped locomotives.

Construction: Steel.
Maximum Speed: 90 m.p.h. *restricted when in propelling mode.
Couplers: Drophead buckeye.   **Bogies:** SR Mk. 4.
Brakes: **Dimensions:** 20.45 x 2.74 m
Doors: Manually operated slam.

975025. DM. BR Eastleigh. 1958. 34.5 t.

| 975025 | G | NR | FM | LU | CAROLINE |

4. DMUS AWAITING DISPOSAL

The list below comprises vehicles awaiting disposal which are stored on the Network Rail network.

IMPORTANT NOTE: DMUs already at scrapyards are not included in this list.

Class 101

Spare	**RR**	A	PY	51189	51496	51506	54056	54061
				54393				
Spare	**S**	A	PY	51231	51435	51500	53268	
Spare	**BG**	X	NL	54342				

Class 117

Spare	**N**	A	PY	51350	51366	51383	51408
Spare	**RR**	CR	AL	51411			

Class 122

-	**LH**	X	TE	977941 (55012)

Class 165

Spare	**NT**	A	ZC	58930

Class 205

205 009	**CX**	P	Tonbridge West Yard	60108	60658	60808
205 012	**CX**	P	SU	60111		60811
Spare	**N**	AM	ZG	60650		

Class 951

Spare	**N**	AM	ZG	977696 (60522)

4. ELECTRIC MULTIPLE UNITS

INTRODUCTION

EMU CLASSES

Principal details and dimensions are quoted for each class in metric and/or imperial units as considered appropriate bearing in mind common UK usage.

All dimensions and weights are quoted for vehicles in an "as new" condition with all necessary supplies on board. Dimensions are quoted in the order length x overall width. All lengths quoted are over buffers or couplers as appropriate. Where two lengths are quoted, the first refers to outer vehicles in a set and the second to inner vehicles.

Bogie Types are quoted in the format motored/non-motored (e.g BP20/BT13 denotes BP20 motored bogies and BT non-motored bogies).

Unless noted to the contrary, all vehicles listed have bar couplings at non-driving ends.

Vehicles ordered under the auspices of BR were allocated a Lot (batch) number when ordered and these are quoted in class headings and sub-headings. Vehicles ordered since 1995 have no Lot Numbers, but the manufacturer and location that they were built is given.

NUMERICAL LISTINGS

25 kV AC 50 Hz overhead Electric Multiple Units (EMUs) and dual voltage EMUs are listed in numerical order of set numbers. Individual "loose" vehicles are listed in numerical order after vehicles formed into fixed formations. Where numbers carried are different to those officially allocated, these are noted in class headings where appropriate.

750 V DC third rail EMUs are listed in numerical order of class number, then in numerical order of set number. Some of these use the former Southern Region four-digit set numbers. These are derived from theoretical six digit set numbers which are the four-digit set number prefixed by the first two numbers of the class.

Where sets or vehicles have been renumbered in recent years, former numbering detail is shown alongside current detail. Each entry is laid out as in the following example:

Set No.	Detail	Livery	Owner	Operator	Allocation	Formation			
377 137	s	**SN**	P	SN	Bl	78537	77137	78937	78737

Detail Differences. Only detail differences which currently affect the areas and types of train which vehicles may work are shown. All other detail differences are specifically excluded. Where such differences occur within a class or part class, these are shown alongside the individual set or vehicle number. Meaning of abbreviations are detailed in individual class headings.

Set Formations. Set formations shown are those normally maintained. Readers should note some set formations might be temporarily varied from time to time to suit maintenance and/or operational requirements. Vehicles shown as "Spare" are not formed in any regular set formation.

Codes. Codes are used to denote the livery, owner, operator and depot of each unit. Details of these will be found in section 7 of this book. Where a unit or spare car is off-lease, the operator column will be left blank.

Names. Only names carried with official sanction are listed. As far as possible names are shown in UPPER/lower case characters as actually shown on the name carried on the vehicle(s). Unless otherwise shown, complete units are regarded as named rather than just the individual car(s) which carry the name.

GENERAL INFORMATION

CLASSIFICATION AND NUMBERING

25 kV AC 50 Hz overhead and "Versatile" EMUs are classified in the series 300–399.

750 V DC third rail EMUs are classified in the series 400–599.
Service units are classified in the series 900–949.

EMU individual cars are numbered in the series 61000–78999, except for vehicles used on the Isle of Wight – which are numbered in a separate series.

Prior to privatisation, Service Stock individual cars were numbered in the series 975000–975999 and 977000–977999, although this series was not used exclusively for EMU vehicles. Since privatisation, use of these series has been sporadic, vehicles often now retaining their former numbers.

Any vehicle constructed or converted to replace another vehicle following accident damage and carrying the same number as the original vehicle is denoted by the suffix[II] in this publication.

OPERATING CODES

These codes are used by train operating company staff to describe the various different types of vehicles and normally appear on data panels on the inner (i.e. non driving) ends of vehicles.

A "B" prefix indicates a battery vehicle.
A "P" prefix indicates a trailer vehicle on which is mounted the pantograph, instead of the default case where the pantograph is mounted on a motor vehicle.

The first part of the code describes whether or not the car has a motor or a driving cab as follows:

DM Driving motor.
M   Motor

DT Driving trailer
T   Trailer

The next letter is a "B" for cars with a brake compartment.
This is followed by the saloon details:

F   First
S   Standard
C   Composite

The next letter denotes the style of accommodation as follows:

O   Open
K   Side compartment with lavatory
so Semi-open (part compartments, part open). All other vehicles are assumed
    to consist solely of open saloons.

Finally vehicles with a buffet are suffixed RB or RMB for a miniture buffet.

Where two vehicles of the same type are formed within the same unit, the
above codes may be suffixed by (A) and (B) to differentiate between the vehicles.

A composite is a vehicle containing both first and standard class
accommodation, whilst a brake vehicle is a vehicle containing separate specific
accommodation for the conductor.

Special Note: Where vehicles have been declassified, the correct operating
code which describes the actual vehicle layout is quoted in this publication.

The following codes are used to denote special types of vehicle:

DMLF   Driving Motor Lounge First
DMLV   Driving Motor Luggage Van
MBRBS Motor buffet standard with luggage space and guard's compartment.
TFH   Trailer First with Handbrake

BUILD DETAILS

Lot Numbers
Vehicles ordered under the auspices of BR were allocated a lot (batch) number
when ordered and these are quoted in class headings and sub-headings.

Builders
These are shown in class headings. Abbreviations used are found in section 7.8.

Information on sub-contracting works which built parts of vehicles e.g. the
underframes etc. is not shown.

ACCOMMODATION

The information given in class headings and sub-headings is in the form F/S
nT (or TD) nW. For example 12/54 1T 1W denotes 12 first class and 54 standard
class seats, 1 toilet and 1 wheelchair space. The seating layout of open saloons
is shown as 2+1, 2+2 or 3+2 as the case may be. Where units have first class
accommodation as well as standard and the layout is different for each class
then these are shown separately prefixed by '1:' and '2:'. Compartments are
three seats a side in first class and mostly four a side in standard class in EMUs.

4.1. 25 kV AC 50 Hz OVERHEAD & DUAL VOLTAGE UNITS.

Note: Except where otherwise stated, all units in this section operate on 25 kV AC 50 Hz overhead only.

CLASS 306   METRO-CAMMELL/BRCW

Museum unit which is currently stored out of use, but may be used on main line work in the future (with One Great Eastern). Originally built as 1500 V DC, but converted to AC in 1960/61.

Formation: DMSO–TBSO–DTSO.
Construction: Steel.   **Doors:** Power-operated sliding.
Traction Motors: Four Crompton-Parkinson 155 kW.
Gangways: None.   **Bogies:** LNER ED6/ET6.
Couplers: Screw.   **Maximum Speed:** 70 m.p.h.
Seating Layout: 2+2 facing.
Dimensions: 19.16/17.40/17.63 x 2.95 m.
Braking: Tread brakes.   **Multiple Working:** Within class.

DMSO. Lot No. 363 Metro-Cammell 1949. –/62. 52.0 t.
TBSO. Lot No. 365 BRCW 1949. –/46. 27.0 t.
DTSO. Lot No. 364 Metro-Cammell 1949. –/60. 28.0 t.

306 017	**G**	H	IL	65217	65417	65617

CLASS 313   BREL YORK

WAGN/Silverlink inner suburban units.

Formation: DMSO–PTSO–BDMSO.
Systems: 25 kV AC overhead/750 V DC third rail.
Construction: Steel underframe, aluminium alloy body and roof.
Traction Motors: Four GEC G310AZ of 82.125 kW.
Doors: Sliding.   **Control System:** Camshaft.
Gangways: Within unit + end doors.   **Bogies:** BX1.
Couplers: Tightlock.   **Maximum Speed:** 75 m.p.h.
Seating Layout: 3+2 facing.   **Dimensions:** 20.33/20.18 x 2.82 m.
Braking: Disc and rheostatic.
Multiple Working: Within class.

DMSO. Lot No. 30879 1976–1977. –/74. 36.0 t.
PTSO. Lot No. 30880 1976–1977. –/84 (313/0), –/80 (313/1). 31.0 t.
BDMSO. Lot No. 30885 1976–1977. –/74. 37.5 t.

Advertising Liveries: 313 027, 313 043, 313 050, 313 057, 313 064 WAGN Family Travelcard ("Go to town with WAGN") – White.
313 060, WAGN "Intalink" livery – White with a yellow and green bodyside stripe.

Class 313/0. Standard Design. All now refurbished with high back seats.

313 018	**WP**	H	*WN*	HE	62546	71230	62610
313 024	**WP**	H	*WN*	HE	62552	71236	62616
313 025	**WP**	H	*WN*	HE	62553	71237	62617
313 026	**WP**	H	*WN*	HE	62554	71238	62618
313 027	**AL**	H	*WN*	HE	62555	71239	62619
313 028	**WP**	H	*WN*	HE	62556	71240	62620
313 029	**U**	H	*WN*	HE	62557	71241	62621
313 030	**WP**	H	*WN*	HE	62558	71242	62622
313 031	**WP**	H	*WN*	HE	62559	71243	62623
313 032	**U**	H	*WN*	HE	62560	71244	62643
313 033	**U**	H	*WN*	HE	62561	71245	62625
313 035	**U**	H	*WN*	HE	62563	71247	62627
313 036	**U**	H	*WN*	HE	62564	71248	62628
313 037	**U**	H	*WN*	HE	62565	71249	62629
313 038	**U**	H	*WN*	HE	62566	71250	62630
313 039	**U**	H	*WN*	HE	62567	71251	62631
313 040	**U**	H	*WN*	HE	62568	71252	62632
313 041	**U**	H	*WN*	HE	62569	71253	62633
313 042	**WP**	H	*WN*	HE	62570	71254	62634
313 043	**AL**	H	*WN*	HE	62571	71255	62635
313 044	**U**	H	*WN*	HE	62572	71256	62636
313 045	**U**	H	*WN*	HE	62573	71257	62637
313 046	**U**	H	*WN*	HE	62574	71258	62638
313 047	**U**	H	*WN*	HE	62575	71259	62639
313 048	**N**	H	*WN*	HE	62576	71260	62640
313 049	**U**	H	*WN*	HE	62577	71261	62641
313 050	**AL**	H	*WN*	HE	62578	71262	62649
313 051	**U**	H	*WN*	HE	62579	71263	62624
313 052	**WP**	H	*WN*	HE	62580	71264	62644
313 053	**WP**	H	*WN*	HE	62581	71265	62645
313 054	**WP**	H	*WN*	HE	62582	71266	62646
313 055	**WP**	H	*WN*	HE	62583	71267	62647
313 056	**WP**	H	*WN*	HE	62584	71268	62648
313 057	**AL**	H	*WN*	HE	62585	71269	62642
313 058	**N**	H	*WN*	HE	62586	71270	62650
313 059	**WP**	H	*WN*	HE	62587	71271	62651
313 060	**AL**	H	*WN*	HE	62588	71272	62652
313 061	**N**	H	*WN*	HE	62589	71273	62653
313 062	**WP**	H	*WN*	HE	62590	71274	62654
313 063	**WP**	H	*WN*	HE	62591	71275	62655
313 064	**AL**	H	*WN*	HE	62592	71276	62656

Class 313/1. Extra shoegear for Silverlink services.

313 101	**SL**	H	*SL*	BY	62529	71213	62593
313 102	**SL**	H	*SL*	BY	62530	71214	62594
313 103	**SL**	H	*SL*	BY	62531	71215	62595
313 104	**SL**	H	*SL*	BY	62532	71216	62596
313 105	**SL**	H	*SL*	BY	62533	71217	62597
313 106	**SL**	H	*SL*	BY	62534	71218	62598

313 107	**SL**	H	*SL*	BY	62535	71219	62599
313 108	**SL**	H	*SL*	BY	62536	71220	62600
313 109	**SL**	H	*SL*	BY	62537	71221	62601
313 110	**SL**	H	*SL*	BY	62538	71222	62602
313 111	**SL**	H	*SL*	BY	62539	71223	62603
313 112	**SL**	H	*SL*	BY	62540	71224	62604
313 113	**SL**	H	*SL*	BY	62541	71225	62605
313 114	**SL**	H	*SL*	BY	62542	71226	62606
313 115	**SL**	H	*SL*	BY	62543	71227	62607
313 116	**SL**	H	*SL*	BY	62544	71228	62608
313 117	**SL**	H	*SL*	BY	62545	71229	62609
313 119	**SL**	H	*SL*	BY	62547	71231	62611
313 120	**SL**	H	*SL*	BY	62548	71232	62612
313 121	**SL**	H	*SL*	BY	62549	71233	62613
313 122	**SL**	H	*SL*	BY	62550	71234	62614
313 123	**SL**	H	*SL*	BY	62551	71235	62615
313 134	**SL**	H	*SL*	BY	62562	71246	62626

Names (carried on PTSO):

| 313 109 | Arnold Leah | | 313 116 | Nikola Tesla |
| 313 120 | PARLIAMENT HILL | | | |

CLASS 314   BREL YORK

First ScotRail inner suburban units.

Formation: DMSO–PTSO–DMSO.
Construction: Steel underframe, aluminium alloy body and roof.
Traction Motors: Four GEC G310AZ (* Brush TM61-53) of 82.125 kW.
Doors: Sliding.   **Control System:** Thyristor.
Gangways: Within unit + end doors.   **Bogies:** BX1.
Couplers: Tightlock   **Maximum Speed:** 75 m.p.h.
Seating Layout: 3+2 facing.   **Dimensions:** 20.33/20.18 × 2.82 m.
Braking: Disc and rheostatic.
Multiple Working: Within class and with Class 315.

64583–64614. DMSO. Lot No. 30912 1979. –/68. 34.5 t.
64588ᴵᴵ. DMSO. Lot No. 30908 1978–1980. Rebuilt Railcare Glasgow 1996 from
Class 507 No. 64426. The original 64588 has been scrapped.
This vehicle has an experimental seating layout. –/74. 35.63 t.
PTSO. Lot No. 30913 1979. –/76. 33.0 t.

314 201	*	**S**	A	*SR*	GW	64583	71450	64584
314 202	*	**S**	A	*SR*	GW	64585	71451	64586
314 203	*	**SC**	A	*SR*	GW	64587	71452	64588ᴵᴵ
314 204	*	**SC**	A	*SR*	GW	64589	71453	64590
314 205	*	**SC**	A	*SR*	GW	64591	71454	64592
314 206	*	**SC**	A	*SR*	GW	64593	71455	64594
314 207		**SC**	A	*SR*	GW	64595	71456	64596
314 208		**SC**	A	*SR*	GW	64597	71457	64598
314 209		**SC**	A	*SR*	GW	64599	71458	64600

314 210	**SC**	A	*SR*	GW	64601	71459	64602
314 211	**SC**	A	*SR*	GW	64603	71460	64604
314 212	**SC**	A	*SR*	GW	64605	71461	64606
314 213	**SC**	A	*SR*	GW	64607	71462	64608
314 214	**SC**	A	*SR*	GW	64609	71463	64610
314 215	**SC**	A	*SR*	GW	64611	71464	64612
314 216	**SC**	A	*SR*	GW	64613	71465	64614

Name (carried on PTSO):

314 203   European Union

CLASS 315   BREL YORK

One Great Eastern and WAGN inner suburban units.

Formation: DMSO–TSO–PTSO–DMSO.
Construction: Steel underframe, aluminium alloy body and roof.
Traction Motors: Four Brush TM61-53 (* GEC G310AZ) of 82.125 kW.
Doors: Sliding.   **Control System:** Thyristor.
Gangways: Within unit + end doors.   **Bogies:** BX1.
Couplers: Tightlock   **Maximum Speed:** 75 m.p.h.
Seating Layout: 3+2 facing.   **Dimensions:** 20.33/20.18 x 2.82 m.
Braking: Disc and rheostatic.
Multiple Working: Within class and with Class 314.

64461–64582. DMSO. Lot No. 30902 1980–1981. –/74. 35.0 t.
71281–71341. TSO. Lot No. 30904 1980–1981. –/86. 25.5 t.
71389–71449. PTSO. Lot No. 30903 1980–1981. –/84. 32.0 t.

Non-Standard/Advertising liveries:

315 804, 315 806, 315 809 and 315 812 All-over First Group blue.
315 844 and 315 858 Crime Prevention – White and red with various images.
315 845 WAGN Family Travelcard ("Go to town with WAGN") – White.
315 857 WAGN "Intalink" livery – White with a yellow and green bodyside stripe.

315 801	**GE**	H	*IE*	IL	64461	71281	71389	64462
315 802	**GE**	H	*IE*	IL	64463	71282	71390	64464
315 803	**GE**	H	*IE*	IL	64465	71283	71391	64466
315 804	**O**	H	*IE*	IL	64467	71284	71392	64468
315 805	**GE**	H	*IE*	IL	64469	71285	71393	64470
315 806	**O**	H	*IE*	IL	64471	71286	71394	64472
315 807	**GE**	H	*IE*	IL	64473	71287	71395	64474
315 808	**GE**	H	*IE*	IL	64475	71288	71396	64476
315 809	**O**	H	*IE*	IL	64477	71289	71397	64478
315 810	**GE**	H	*IE*	IL	64479	71290	71398	64480
315 811	**GE**	H	*IE*	IL	64481	71291	71399	64482
315 812	**O**	H	*IE*	IL	64483	71292	71400	64484
315 813	**GE**	H	*IE*	IL	64485	71293	71401	64486
315 814	**GE**	H	*IE*	IL	64487	71294	71402	64488
315 815	**GE**	H	*IE*	IL	64489	71295	71403	64490
315 816	**GE**	H	*IE*	IL	64491	71296	71404	64492

315 817		**GE**	H	*IE*	IL	64493	71297	71405	64494
315 818		**GE**	H	*IE*	IL	64495	71298	71406	64496
315 819		**GE**	H	*IE*	IL	64497	71299	71407	64498
315 820		**GE**	H	*IE*	IL	64499	71300	71408	64500
315 821		**GE**	H	*IE*	IL	64501	71301	71409	64502
315 822		**GE**	H	*IE*	IL	64503	71302	71410	64504
315 823		**GE**	H	*IE*	IL	64505	71303	71411	64506
315 824		**GE**	H	*IE*	IL	64507	71304	71412	64508
315 825		**GE**	H	*IE*	IL	64509	71305	71413	64510
315 826		**GE**	H	*IE*	IL	64511	71306	71414	64512
315 827		**GE**	H	*IE*	IL	64513	71307	71415	64514
315 828		**GE**	H	*IE*	IL	64515	71308	71416	64516
315 829		**GE**	H	*IE*	IL	64517	71309	71417	64518
315 830		**GE**	H	*IE*	IL	64519	71310	71418	64520
315 831		**GE**	H	*IE*	IL	64521	71311	71419	64522
315 832		**GE**	H	*IE*	IL	64523	71312	71420	64524
315 833		**GE**	H	*IE*	IL	64525	71313	71421	64526
315 834		**GE**	H	*IE*	IL	64527	71314	71422	64528
315 835		**GE**	H	*IE*	IL	64529	71315	71423	64530
315 836		**GE**	H	*IE*	IL	64531	71316	71424	64532
315 837		**GE**	H	*IE*	IL	64533	71317	71425	64534
315 838		**GE**	H	*IE*	IL	64535	71318	71426	64536
315 839		**GE**	H	*IE*	IL	64537	71319	71427	64538
315 840		**GE**	H	*IE*	IL	64539	71320	71428	64540
315 841		**GE**	H	*IE*	IL	64541	71321	71429	64542
315 842	*	**GE**	H	*IE*	IL	64543	71322	71430	64544
315 843	*	**GE**	H	*IE*	IL	64545	71323	71431	64546
315 844	*	**AL**	H	*1W*	HE	64547	71324	71432	64548
315 845	*	**AL**	H	*1W*	HE	64549	71325	71433	64550
315 846	*	**U**	H	*1W*	HE	64551	71326	71434	64552
315 847	*	**U**	H	*1W*	HE	64553	71327	71435	64554
315 848	*	**U**	H	*1W*	HE	64555	71328	71436	64556
315 849	*	**U**	H	*1W*	HE	64557	71329	71437	64558
315 850	*	**U**	H	*1W*	HE	64559	71330	71438	64560
315 851	*	**U**	H	*1W*	HE	64561	71331	71439	64562
315 852	*	**U**	H	*1W*	HE	64563	71332	71440	64564
315 853	*	**U**	H	*1W*	HE	64565	71333	71441	64566
315 854	*	**U**	H	*1W*	HE	64567	71334	71442	64568
315 855	*	**U**	H	*1W*	HE	64569	71335	71443	64570
315 856	*	**U**	H	*1W*	HE	64571	71336	71444	64572
315 857	*	**AL**	H	*1W*	HE	64573	71337	71445	64574
315 858	*	**AL**	H	*1W*	HE	64579	71338	71446	64580
315 859	*	**WP**	H	*1W*	HE	64577	71339	71447	64578
315 860	*	**WP**	H	*1W*	HE	64575	71340	71448	64576
315 861	*	**WP**	H	*1W*	HE	64581	71341	71449	64582

CLASS 317   BREL

One West Anglia, WAGN and Thameslink outer suburban units.

Formation: Various.
Construction: Steel.
Traction Motors: Four GEC G315BZ of 247.5 kW.
Doors: Sliding.   **Control System:** Thyristor.
Gangways: Throughout   **Bogies:** BP20 (MSO), BT13 (others).
Couplers: Tightlock.   **Maximum Speed:** 100 m.p.h.
Seating Layout: Various.   **Dimensions:** 20.13/20.18 x 2.82 m.
Braking: Disc.
Multiple Working: Within class and with Classes 318, 319, 320, 321, 322 and 323.

Class 317/1. Pressure ventilated.

Formation: DTSO–MSO–TCO–DTSO.
Seating Layout: 1: 2+2 facing, 2: 3+2 facing.

DTSO(A) Lot No. 30955 York 1981–1982. –/74. 29.5 t.
MSO. Lot No. 30958 York 1981–1982. –/79. 49.0 t.
TCO. Lot No. 30957 Derby 1981–1982. 22/46 2T. 29.0 t. Retention toilets (decommissioned).
DTSO(B) Lot No. 30956 York 1981–1982. –/70. (* –/71). 29.5 t.

Notes: 317 301–317 307/311/312/313/315/316 are on hire to Thameslink for the duration of the Thameslink tunnel blockade.

Non-standard livery: 317 301–317 306 are in the former LTS Rail livery (white & blue with grey & green bands).

317 301	0	A	TR	HE	77024	62661	71577	77048
317 302	0	A	TR	HE	77001	62662	71578	77049
317 303	0	A	TR	HE	77002	62663	71579	77050
317 304	0	A	TR	HE	77003	62664	71580	77051
317 305	0	A	TR	HE	77004	62665	71581	77052
317 306	0	A	TR	HE	77005	62666	71582	77053
317 307	WP	A	TR	HE	77006	62667	71583	77054
317 311	WP	A	TR	HE	77010	62697	71587	77058
317 312	WP	A	TR	HE	77011	62672	71588	77059
317 313	WP	A	TR	HE	77012	62673	71589	77060
317 315	WP	A	TR	HE	77014	62675	71591	77062
317 316	WP	A	TR	HE	77015	62676	71592	77063
317 317	WP	A	1W	HE	77016	62677	71593	77064
317 318	WP	A	1W	HE	77017	62678	71594	77065
317 320	WP	A	1W	HE	77019	62680	71596	77067
317 321	WP	A	1W	HE	77020	62681	71597	77068
317 324	WP	A	1W	HE	77023	62684	71600	77071
317 325	WP	A	1W	HE	77000	62685	71601	77072
317 326	WP	A	1W	HE	77025	62686	71602	77073
317 327	WP	A	1W	HE	77026	62687	71603	77074
317 328	WP	A	1W	HE	77027	62688	71604	77075
317 330	WP	A	1W	HE	77043	62704	71606	77077

317 331		**WP**	A	*1W*	HE	77030	62691	71607	77078
317 333		**WP**	A	*1W*	HE	77032	62693	71609	77080
317 334		**WP**	A	*1W*	HE	77033	62694	71610	77081
317 335		**WP**	A	*1W*	HE	77034	62695	71611	77082
317 336		**WP**	A	*1W*	HE	77035	62696	71612	77083
317 337	*	**WP**	A	*WN*	HE	77036	62671	71613	77084
317 338	*	**WP**	A	*WN*	HE	77037	62698	71614	77085
317 339	*	**WP**	A	*WN*	HE	77038	62699	71615	77086
317 340	*	**WP**	A	*WN*	HE	77039	62700	71616	77087
317 341	*	**WP**	A	*WN*	HE	77040	62701	71617	77088
317 342	*	**WP**	A	*WN*	HE	77041	62702	71618	77089
317 343	*	**WP**	A	*WN*	HE	77042	62703	71619	77090
317 344	*	**WP**	A	*WN*	HE	77029	62690	71620	77091
317 345	*	**WP**	A	*WN*	HE	77044	62705	71621	77092
317 346	*	**WP**	A	*WN*	HE	77045	62706	71622	77093
317 347	*	**WP**	A	*WN*	HE	77046	62707	71623	77094
317 348	*	**WP**	A	*WN*	HE	77047	62708	71624	77095

Name (carried on TCO):

317 348   Richard A Jenner

Class 317/6. Convection heating. Units converted from Class 317/2 by Railcare Wolverton 1998–99 with new seating layouts.

Formation: DTSO–MSO–TSO–DTCO.
Seating Layout: 2+2 facing.

77200–77219. DTSO. Lot No. 30994 York 1985–1986. –/64. 29.2 t.
77280–77283. DTSO. Lot No. 31007 York 1987. –/64. 29.5 t.
62846–62865. MSO. Lot No. 30996 York 1985–1986. –/70. 49.0 t.
62886–62889. MSO. Lot No. 31009 York 1987. –/70. 49.0 t.
71734–71753. TSO. Lot No. 30997 York 1985–1986. –/62 2T. 29.0 t.
71762–71765. TSO. Lot No. 31010 York 1987. –/62 2T. 29.0 t.
77220–77239. DTCO. Lot No. 30995 York 1985–1986. 24/48. 29.5 t.
77284–77287. DTCO. Lot No. 31008 York 1987. 24/48. 29.5 t.

317 649	(317 349)	**WN**	A	*1W*	HE	77200	62846	71734	77220
317 650	(317 350)	**WN**	A	*1W*	HE	77201	62847	71735	77221
317 651	(317 351)	**WN**	A	*1W*	HE	77202	62848	71736	77222
317 652	(317 352)	**1**	A	*1W*	HE	77203	62849	71739	77223
317 653	(317 353)	**1**	A	*1W*	HE	77204	62850	71738	77224
317 654	(317 354)	**1**	A	*1W*	HE	77205	62851	71737	77225
317 655	(317 355)	**1**	A	*1W*	HE	77206	62852	71740	77226
317 656	(317 356)	**WN**	A	*1W*	HE	77207	62853	71742	77227
317 657	(317 357)	**WN**	A	*1W*	HE	77208	62854	71741	77228
317 658	(317 358)	**WN**	A	*1W*	HE	77209	62855	71743	77229
317 659	(317 359)	**WN**	A	*1W*	HE	77210	62856	71744	77230
317 660	(317 360)	**1**	A	*1W*	HE	77211	62857	71745	77231
317 661	(317 361)	**WN**	A	*1W*	HE	77212	62858	71746	77232
317 662	(317 362)	**WN**	A	*1W*	HE	77213	62859	71747	77233
317 663	(317 363)	**WN**	A	*1W*	HE	77214	62860	71748	77234
317 664	(317 364)	**WN**	A	*1W*	HE	77215	62861	71749	77235

317 665	(317 365)	**WN**	A	*1W*	HE	77216	62862	71750	77236
317 666	(317 366)	**WN**	A	*1W*	HE	77217	62863	71752	77237
317 667	(317 367)	**WN**	A	*1W*	HE	77218	62864	71751	77238
317 668	(317 368)	**WN**	A	*1W*	HE	77219	62865	71753	77239
317 669	(317 369)	**WN**	A	*1W*	HE	77280	62886	71762	77284
317 670	(317 370)	**WN**	A	*1W*	HE	77281	62887	71763	77285
317 671	(317 371)	**WN**	A	*1W*	HE	77282	62888	71764	77286
317 672	(317 372)	**1**	A	*1W*	HE	77283	62889	71765	77287

Name (carried on TCO):

317 654   RICHARD WELLS

Class 317/7. Units converted from Class 317/1 by Railcare Wolverton 2000 for Stansted Express service between London Liverpool Street and Stansted. Air conditioning. Fitted with luggage stacks.

Formation: DTSO–MSO–TSO–DTCO.
Seating Layout: 1: 2+1 facing, 2: 2+2 facing.

DTSO Lot No. 30955 York 1981–1982. –/52 + catering point. 31.4 t.
MSO. Lot No. 30958 York 1981–1982. –/62. 51.3 t.
TSO. Lot No. 30957 Derby 1981–1982. –/42 1W 1T 1TD. 30.2 t. Retention toilets (decommissioned).
DTCO Lot No. 30956 York 1981–1982. 22/16 + catering point. 31.6 t.

Advertising livery: Vehicles 77055 of 317 708, 77066 of 317 719, 77069 of 317 722, 77070 of 317 723 and 77079 of 317 732 – Finspreads (white, blue and orange with various images).

317 708	(317 308)	**SX**	A	*1S*	HE	77007	62668	71584	77055
317 709	(317 309)	**SX**	A	*1S*	HE	77008	62669	71585	77056
317 710	(317 310)	**SX**	A	*1S*	HE	77009	62670	71586	77057
317 714	(317 314)	**SX**	A	*1S*	HE	77013	62674	71590	77061
317 719	(317 319)	**SX**	A	*1S*	HE	77018	62679	71595	77066
317 722	(317 392)	**SX**	A	*1S*	HE	77021	62682	71598	77069
317 723	(317 393)	**SX**	A	*1S*	HE	77022	62683	71599	77070
317 729	(317 329)	**1S**	A	*1S*	HE	77028	62689	71605	77076
317 732	(317 332)	**SX**	A	*1S*	HE	77031	62692	71608	77079

Names (carried on DTCO):

317 709   Len Camp
317 723   The Tottenham Flyer

CLASS 318 BREL YORK

First ScotRail outer suburban units.

Formation: DTSO–MSO–DTSO.
Construction: Steel.
Traction Motors: Four Brush TM 2141 of 268 kW.
Doors: Sliding. **Control System:** Thyristor.
Gangways: Throughout. **Bogies:** BP20 (MSO), BT13 (others).
Couplers: Tightlock **Maximum Speed:** 90 m.p.h.
Seating Layout: 3+2 facing. **Dimensions:** 20.86 x 2.82 m.
Braking: Disc.
Multiple Working: Within class and with Classes 317, 319, 320, 321, 322 and 323.

77240–77259. DTSO. Lot No. 30999 1985–1986. –/66 1T. 30.0 t.
77288. DTSO. Lot No. 31020 1987. –/66 1T. 30.0 t.
62866–62885. MSO. Lot No. 30998 1985–1986. –/79. 50.9 t.
62890. MSO. Lot No. 31019 1987. –/79. 50.9 t.
77260–77279. DTSO. Lot No. 31000 1985–1986. –/71. 29.6 t.
77289. DTSO. Lot No. 31021 1987. –/71. 29.6 t.

318 250	**SC**	H	*SR*	GW	77240	62866	77260
318 251	**SC**	H	*SR*	GW	77241	62867	77261
318 252	**SC**	H	*SR*	GW	77242	62868	77262
318 253	**SC**	H	*SR*	GW	77243	62869	77263
318 254	**SC**	H	*SR*	GW	77244	62870	77264
318 255	**SC**	H	*SR*	GW	77245	62871	77265
318 256	**SC**	H	*SR*	GW	77246	62872	77266
318 257	**SC**	H	*SR*	GW	77247	62873	77267
318 258	**SC**	H	*SR*	GW	77248	62874	77268
318 259	**SC**	H	*SR*	GW	77249	62875	77269
318 260	**SC**	H	*SR*	GW	77250	62876	77270
318 261	**SC**	H	*SR*	GW	77251	62877	77271
318 262	**SC**	H	*SR*	GW	77252	62878	77272
318 263	**SC**	H	*SR*	GW	77253	62879	77273
318 264	**SC**	H	*SR*	GW	77254	62880	77274
318 265	**SC**	H	*SR*	GW	77255	62881	77275
318 266	**SC**	H	*SR*	GW	77256	62882	77276
318 267	**SC**	H	*SR*	GW	77257	62883	77277
318 268	**SC**	H	*SR*	GW	77258	62884	77278
318 269	**SC**	H	*SR*	GW	77259	62885	77279
318 270	**SC**	H	*SR*	GW	77288	62890	77289

Names (carried on MSO):

318 259	Citizens' Network		318 266	STRATHCLYDER

CLASS 319   BREL YORK

Thameslink express and outer suburban units.

System: 25 kV AC overhead/750 V DC third rail.
Formation: Various.
Construction: Steel.
Traction Motors: Four GEC G315BZ of 268 kW.
Doors: Sliding.   **Control System:** GTO chopper.
Gangways: Within unit + end doors.   **Bogies:** P7-4 (MSO), T3-7 (others).
Couplers: Tightlock   **Maximum Speed:** 100 m.p.h.
Seating Layout: Various.   **Dimensions:** 20.17/20.16 x 2.82 m.
Braking: Disc.
Multiple Working: Within class and with Classes 317, 318, 320, 321, 322 and 323.

Class 319/0. DTSO–MSO–TSO–DTSO.

Seating Layout: 3+2 facing.

DTSO(A). Lot No. 31022 (odd nos.) 1987–1988. –/82. 28.2 t.
MSO. Lot No. 31023 1987–1988. –/82. 49.2 t.
TSO. Lot No. 31024 1987–1988. –/77 2T. 31.0 t.
DTSO(B). Lot No. 31025 (even nos.) 1987–1988. –/78. 28.1 t.

319 001	**CX**	P	*TR*	SU	77291	62891	71772	77290
319 002	**CX**	P	*TR*	SU	77293	62892	71773	77292
319 003	**CX**	P	*TR*	SU	77295	62893	71774	77294
319 004	**CX**	P	*TR*	SU	77297	62894	71775	77296
319 005	**CX**	P	*TR*	SU	77299	62895	71776	77298
319 006	**CX**	P	*TR*	SU	77301	62896	71777	77300
319 007	**CX**	P	*TR*	SU	77303	62897	71778	77302
319 008	**CX**	P	*TR*	SU	77305	62898	71779	77304
319 009	**CX**	P	*TR*	SU	77307	62899	71780	77306
319 010	**CX**	P	*TR*	SU	77309	62900	71781	77308
319 011	**CX**	P	*TR*	SU	77311	62901	71782	77310
319 012	**CX**	P	*TR*	SU	77313	62902	71783	77312
319 013	**CX**	P	*TR*	SU	77315	62903	71784	77314

Names (carried on TSO):

319 008	Cheriton	319 011	John Ruskin College
319 009	Coquelles	319 013	The Surrey Hills

Class 319/2. DTSO–MSO–TSO–DTCO. Units converted from Class 319/0 for express services from London to Brighton. Pantographs refitted for use with Thameslink.

Seating Layout: 1: 2+1 facing, 2: 2+2 facing.
DTSO. Lot No. 31022 (odd nos.) 1987–1988. –/64. 28.2 t.
MSO. Lot No. 31023 1987–1988. –/60 2T. (including 12 seats in a "snug" under the pantograph area). External sliding doors sealed adjacent to this area. 49.2 t.
TSO. Lot No. 31024 1987–1988. –/52 1T 1TD. 31.0 t.
DTCO. Lot No. 31025 (even nos.) 1987–1988. 18/36. 28.1 t.

Advertising liveries: 319 214 Continental Airlines (mid blue with gold and yellow script).
319 215, 319 218, 319 220 Connex Days out/"Family Zone" (Yellow, green and red with various images).

319 214	**AL**	P	*TR*	SU	77317	62904	71785	77316
319 215	**AL**	P	*TR*	SU	77319	62905	71786	77318
319 216	**CX**	P	*TR*	SU	77321	62906	71787	77320
319 217	**CX**	P	*TR*	SU	77323	62907	71788	77322
319 218	**AL**	P	*TR*	SU	77325	62908	71789	77324
319 219	**CX**	P	*TR*	SU	77327	62909	71790	77326
319 220	**AL**	P	*TR*	SU	77329	62910	71791	77328

Names (carried on TSO):

319 215	London	319 218	Croydon
319 217	Brighton		

Class 319/3. DTSO–MSO–TSO–DTSO. Converted from Class 319/1 by replacing first class seats with standard class seats. Used mainly on the Luton–Sutton/ Wimbledon routes.
Seating Layout: 3+2 facing.

DTSO(A). Lot No. 31063 1990. –/70. 29.0 t.
MSO. Lot No. 31064 1990. –/78. 50.6 t.
TSO. Lot No. 31065 1990. –/74 2T. 31.0 t.
DTSO(B). Lot No. 31066 1990. –/78. 29.7 t.

319 361	**TR**	P	*TR*	SU	77459	63043	71929	77458
319 362	**TR**	P	*TR*	SU	77461	63044	71930	77460
319 363	**TR**	P	*TR*	SU	77463	63045	71931	77462
319 364	**TR**	P	*TR*	SU	77465	63046	71932	77464
319 365	**TR**	P	*TR*	SU	77467	63047	71933	77466
319 366	**TR**	P	*TR*	SU	77469	63048	71934	77468
319 367	**TR**	P	*TR*	SU	77471	63049	71935	77470
319 368	**TR**	P	*TR*	SU	77473	63050	71936	77472
319 369	**TR**	P	*TR*	SU	77475	63051	71937	77474
319 370	**TR**	P	*TR*	SU	77477	63052	71938	77476
319 371	**TR**	P	*TR*	SU	77479	63053	71939	77478
319 372	**TR**	P	*TR*	SU	77481	63054	71940	77480
319 373	**TR**	P	*TR*	SU	77483	63055	71941	77482
319 374	**TR**	P	*TR*	SU	77485	63056	71942	77484
319 375	**TR**	P	*TR*	SU	77487	63057	71943	77486
319 376	**TR**	P	*TR*	SU	77489	63058	71944	77488
319 377	**TR**	P	*TR*	SU	77491	63059	71945	77490
319 378	**TR**	P	*TR*	SU	77493	63060	71946	77492
319 379	**TR**	P	*TR*	SU	77495	63061	71947	77494
319 380	**TR**	P	*TR*	SU	77497	63062	71948	77496
319 381	**TR**	P	*TR*	SU	77973	63093	71979	77974
319 382	**TR**	P	*TR*	SU	77975	63094	71980	77976
319 383	**TR**	P	*TR*	SU	77977	63095	71981	77978
319 384	**TR**	P	*TR*	SU	77979	63096	71982	77980
319 385	**TR**	P	*TR*	SU	77981	63097	71983	77982
319 386	**TR**	P	*TR*	SU	77983	63098	71984	77984

Class 319/4. DTCO–MSO–TSO–DTSO. Converted from Class 319/0. Refurbished with carpets. DTSO(A) converted to composite. Used mainly on the Bedford–Gatwick–Brighton route.
Seating Layout: 1: 2+1 facing 2: 2+2/3+2 facing.

77331–77381. DTCO. Lot No. 31022 (odd nos.) 1987–1988. 12/54. 28.2 t.
77431–77457. DTCO. Lot No. 31038 (odd nos.) 1988. 12/54. 28.2 t.
62911–62936. MSO. Lot No. 31023 1987–1988. –/77. 49.2 t.
62961–62974. MSO. Lot No. 31039 1988. –/77. 49.2 t.
71792–71817. TSO. Lot No. 31024 1987–1988. –/72 2T. 31.0 t.
71866–71879. TSO. Lot No. 31040 1988. –/72 2T. 31.0 t.
77330–77380. DTSO. Lot No. 31025 (even nos.) 1987–1988. –/74. 28.1 t.
77430–77456. DTSO. Lot No. 31041 (even nos.) 1988. –/74. 28.1 t.

Advertising liveries: 319 422 "Back the bid" (London's Oympic bid 2012) – blue with various images.
319 431, 319 456 Continental Airlines (mid blue with gold and yellow script).

319 421	**TR**	P	*TR*	SU	77331	62911	71792	77330
319 422	**AL**	P	*TR*	SU	77333	62912	71793	77332
319 423	**TR**	P	*TR*	SU	77335	62913	71794	77334
319 424	**TR**	P	*TR*	SU	77337	62914	71795	77336
319 425	**TR**	P	*TR*	SU	77339	62915	71796	77338
319 426	**TR**	P	*TR*	SU	77341	62916	71797	77340
319 427	**TR**	P	*TR*	SU	77343	62917	71798	77342
319 428	**TR**	P	*TR*	SU	77345	62918	71799	77344
319 429	**TR**	P	*TR*	SU	77347	62919	71800	77346
319 430	**TR**	P	*TR*	SU	77349	62920	71801	77348
319 431	**AL**	P	*TR*	SU	77351	62921	71802	77350
319 432	**TR**	P	*TR*	SU	77353	62922	71803	77352
319 433	**TR**	P	*TR*	SU	77355	62923	71804	77354
319 434	**TR**	P	*TR*	SU	77357	62924	71805	77356
319 435	**TR**	P	*TR*	SU	77359	62925	71806	77358
319 436	**TR**	P	*TR*	SU	77361	62926	71807	77360
319 437	**TR**	P	*TR*	SU	77363	62927	71808	77362
319 438	**TR**	P	*TR*	SU	77365	62928	71809	77364
319 439	**TR**	P	*TR*	SU	77367	62929	71810	77366
319 440	**TR**	P	*TR*	SU	77369	62930	71811	77368
319 441	**TR**	P	*TR*	SU	77371	62931	71812	77370
319 442	**TR**	P	*TR*	SU	77373	62932	71813	77372
319 443	**TR**	P	*TR*	SU	77375	62933	71814	77374
319 444	**TR**	P	*TR*	SU	77377	62934	71815	77376
319 445	**TR**	P	*TR*	SU	77379	62935	71816	77378
319 446	**TR**	P	*TR*	SU	77381	62936	71817	77380
319 447	**TR**	P	*TR*	SU	77431	62961	71866	77430
319 448	**TR**	P	*TR*	SU	77433	62962	71867	77432
319 449	**TR**	P	*TR*	SU	77435	62963	71868	77434
319 450	**TR**	P	*TR*	SU	77437	62964	71869	77436
319 451	**TR**	P	*TR*	SU	77439	62965	71870	77438
319 452	**TR**	P	*TR*	SU	77441	62966	71871	77440
319 453	**TR**	P	*TR*	SU	77443	62967	71872	77442
319 454	**TR**	P	*TR*	SU	77445	62968	71873	77444

319 455	**TR**	P	*TR*	SU	77447	62969	71874	77446
319 456	**AL**	P	*TR*	SU	77449	62970	71875	77448
319 457	**TR**	P	*TR*	SU	77451	62971	71876	77450
319 458	**TR**	P	*TR*	SU	77453	62972	71877	77452
319 459	**TR**	P	*TR*	SU	77455	62973	71878	77454
319 460	**TR**	P	*TR*	SU	77457	62974	71879	77456

CLASS 320   BREL YORK

First ScotRail suburban units.

Formation: DTSO–MSO–DTSO.
Construction: Steel
Traction Motors: Four Brush TM2141B of 268 kW.
Doors: Sliding.   **Control System:** Thyristor.
Gangways: Within unit.   **Bogies:** P7-4 (MSO), T3-7 (others).
Couplers: Tightlock   **Maximum Speed:** 75 m.p.h.
Seating Layout: 3+2 facing.   **Dimensions:** 19.33 x 2.82 m.
Braking: Disc.
Multiple Working: Within class and with Classes 317, 318, 319, 321, 322 and 323.

DTSO (A). Lot No. 31060 1990. –/76 1W. 30.7 t.
MSO. Lot No. 31062 1990. –/76 1W. 52.1 t.
DTSO (B). Lot No. 31061 1990. –/75. 31.7 t.

320 301	**SC**	H	*SR*	GW	77899	63021	77921
320 302	**SC**	H	*SR*	GW	77900	63022	77922
320 303	**SC**	H	*SR*	GW	77901	63023	77923
320 304	**SC**	H	*SR*	GW	77902	63024	77924
320 305	**SC**	H	*SR*	GW	77903	63025	77925
320 306	**SC**	H	*SR*	GW	77904	63026	77926
320 307	**SC**	H	*SR*	GW	77905	63027	77927
320 308	**SC**	H	*SR*	GW	77906	63028	77928
320 309	**SC**	H	*SR*	GW	77907	63029	77929
320 310	**SC**	H	*SR*	GW	77908	63030	77930
320 311	**SC**	H	*SR*	GW	77909	63031	77931
320 312	**SC**	H	*SR*	GW	77910	63032	77932
320 313	**SC**	H	*SR*	GW	77911	63033	77933
320 314	**SC**	H	*SR*	GW	77912	63034	77934
320 315	**SC**	H	*SR*	GW	77913	63035	77935
320 316	**SC**	H	*SR*	GW	77914	63036	77936
320 317	**SC**	H	*SR*	GW	77915	63037	77937
320 318	**SC**	H	*SR*	GW	77916	63038	77938
320 319	**SC**	H	*SR*	GW	77917	63039	77939
320 320	**SC**	H	*SR*	GW	77918	63040	77940
320 321	**SC**	H	*SR*	GW	77919	63041	77941
320 322	**SC**	H	*SR*	GW	77920	63042	77942

Names (carried on MSO):

320 305	GLASGOW SCHOOL OF ART 1844–150–1994
320 306	Model Rail Scotland
320 308	High Road 20th Anniversary 2000

320 309	Radio Clyde 25th Anniversary
320 311	Royal College of Physicians and Surgeons of Glasgow
320 312	Sir William A Smith Founder of the Boys' Brigade
320 321	The Rt. Hon. John Smith, QC, MP
320 322	Festive Glasgow Orchid

CLASS 321   BREL YORK

Formation: DTCO (DTSO on Class 321/9)–MSO–TSO–DTSO.
Construction: Steel.
Traction Motors: Four Brush TM2141C (268 kW).
Doors: Sliding.   **Control System:** Thyristor.
Gangways: Within unit.   **Bogies:** P7-4 (MSO), T3-7 (others).
Couplers: Tightlock.   **Maximum Speed:** 100 m.p.h.
Seating Layout: 1: 2+2 facing, 2: 3+2 facing.
Dimensions: 19.95/19.92 x 2.82 m.
Braking: Disc.
Multiple Working: Within class and with Classes 317, 318, 319, 320, 322 and 323.

Class 321/3. One Great Eastern units. (321 334–338 on hire to Silverlink).

DTCO. Lot No. 31053 1988–1990. 16/57. 29.7 t.
MSO. Lot No. 31054 1988–1990. –/82. 51.5 t.
TSO. Lot No. 31055 1988–1990. –/75 2T. 29.1 t.
DTSO. Lot No. 31056 1988–1990. –/78. 29.7 t.

321 301	**GE**	H	*IE*	IL	78049	62975	71880	77853
321 302	**GE**	H	*IE*	IL	78050	62976	71881	77854
321 303	**GE**	H	*IE*	IL	78051	62977	71882	77855
321 304	**GE**	H	*IE*	IL	78052	62978	71883	77856
321 305	**GE**	H	*IE*	IL	78053	62979	71884	77857
321 306	**GE**	H	*IE*	IL	78054	62980	71885	77858
321 307	**GE**	H	*IE*	IL	78055	62981	71886	77859
321 308	**GE**	H	*IE*	IL	78056	62982	71887	77860
321 309	**GE**	H	*IE*	IL	78057	62983	71888	77861
321 310	**GE**	H	*IE*	IL	78058	62984	71889	77862
321 311	**GE**	H	*IE*	IL	78059	62985	71890	77863
321 312	**GE**	H	*IE*	IL	78060	62986	71891	77864
321 313	**GE**	H	*IE*	IL	78061	62987	71892	77865
321 314	**GE**	H	*IE*	IL	78062	62988	71893	77866
321 315	**GE**	H	*IE*	IL	78063	62989	71894	77867
321 316	**GE**	H	*IE*	IL	78064	62990	71895	77868
321 317	**GE**	H	*IE*	IL	78065	62991	71896	77869
321 318	**GE**	H	*IE*	IL	78066	62992	71897	77870
321 319	**GE**	H	*IE*	IL	78067	62993	71898	77871
321 320	**GE**	H	*IE*	IL	78068	62994	71899	77872
321 321	**GE**	H	*IE*	IL	78069	62995	71900	77873
321 322	**GE**	H	*IE*	IL	78070	62996	71901	77874
321 323	**GE**	H	*IE*	IL	78071	62997	71902	77875
321 324	**GE**	H	*IE*	IL	78072	62998	71903	77876
321 325	**GE**	H	*IE*	IL	78073	62999	71904	77877

321 326	**GE**	H	*IE*	IL	78074	63000	71905	77878
321 327	**GE**	H	*IE*	IL	78075	63001	71906	77879
321 328	**GE**	H	*IE*	IL	78076	63002	71907	77880
321 329	**GE**	H	*IE*	IL	78077	63003	71908	77881
321 330	**GE**	H	*IE*	IL	78078	63004	71909	77882
321 331	**GE**	H	*IE*	IL	78079	63005	71910	77883
321 332	**GE**	H	*IE*	IL	78080	63006	71911	77884
321 333	**GE**	H	*IE*	IL	78081	63007	71912	77885
321 334	**GE**	H	*SL*	BY	78082	63008	71913	77886
321 335	**GE**	H	*SL*	BY	78083	63009	71914	77887
321 336	**GE**	H	*SL*	BY	78084	63010	71915	77888
321 337	**GE**	H	*SL*	BY	78085	63011	71916	77889
321 338	**GE**	H	*SL*	BY	78086	63012	71917	77890
321 339	**GE**	H	*IE*	IL	78087	63013	71918	77891
321 340	**GE**	H	*IE*	IL	78088	63014	71919	77892
321 341	**GE**	H	*IE*	IL	78089	63015	71920	77893
321 342	**GE**	H	*IE*	IL	78090	63016	71921	77894
321 343	**GE**	H	*IE*	IL	78091	63017	71922	77895
321 344	**GE**	H	*IE*	IL	78092	63018	71923	77896
321 345	**GE**	H	*IE*	IL	78093	63019	71924	77897
321 346	**GE**	H	*IE*	IL	78094	63020	71925	77898
321 347	**GE**	H	*IE*	IL	78131	63105	71991	78280
321 348	**GE**	H	*IE*	IL	78132	63106	71992	78281
321 349	**GE**	H	*IE*	IL	78133	63107	71993	78282
321 350	**GE**	H	*IE*	IL	78134	63108	71994	78283
321 351	**GE**	H	*IE*	IL	78135	63109	71995	78284
321 352	**GE**	H	*IE*	IL	78136	63110	71996	78285
321 353	**GE**	H	*IE*	IL	78137	63111	71997	78286
321 354	**GE**	H	*IE*	IL	78138	63112	71998	78287
321 355	**GE**	H	*IE*	IL	78139	63113	71999	78288
321 356	**GE**	H	*IE*	IL	78140	63114	72000	78289
321 357	**GE**	H	*IE*	IL	78141	63115	72001	78290
321 358	**GE**	H	*IE*	IL	78142	63116	72002	78291
321 359	**GE**	H	*IE*	IL	78143	63117	72003	78292
321 360	**GE**	H	*IE*	IL	78144	63118	72004	78293
321 361	**GE**	H	*IE*	IL	78145	63119	72005	78294
321 362	**GE**	H	*IE*	IL	78146	63120	72006	78295
321 363	**GE**	H	*IE*	IL	78147	63121	72007	78296
321 364	**GE**	H	*IE*	IL	78148	63122	72008	78297
321 365	**GE**	H	*IE*	IL	78149	63123	72009	78298
321 366	**GE**	H	*IE*	IL	78150	63124	72010	78299

Names (carried on TSO):

321 312	Southend-on-Sea
321 321	NSPCC ESSEX FULL STOP
321 334	GEOFFREY FREEMAN ALLEN
321 336	Amsterdam
321 343	RSA–RAILWAY STUDY ASSOCIATION
321 351	GURKHA

Class 321/4. Silverlink/One Great Eastern units.

DTCO. Lot No. 31067 1989–1990. 28/40. 29.8 t.
MSO. Lot No. 31068 1989–1990. –/79. 51.6 t.
TSO. Lot No. 31069 1989–1990. –/74 2T. 29.2 t.
DTSO. Lot No. 31070 1989–1990. –/78. 29.8 t.

Note: The DTCOs of One Great Eastern units have had 12 first class seats declassified.

321 401	**SL**	H	*SL*	BY	78095	63063	71949	77943
321 402	**SL**	H	*SL*	BY	78096	63064	71950	77944
321 403	**SL**	H	*SL*	BY	78097	63065	71951	77945
321 404	**SL**	H	*SL*	BY	78098	63066	71952	77946
321 405	**SL**	H	*SL*	BY	78099	63067	71953	77947
321 406	**SL**	H	*SL*	BY	78100	63068	71954	77948
321 407	**SL**	H	*SL*	BY	78101	63069	71955	77949
321 408	**SL**	H	*SL*	BY	78102	63070	71956	77950
321 409	**SL**	H	*SL*	BY	78103	63071	71957	77951
321 410	**SL**	H	*SL*	BY	78104	63072	71958	77952
321 411	**SL**	H	*SL*	BY	78105	63073	71959	77953
321 412	**SL**	H	*SL*	BY	78106	63074	71960	77954
321 413	**SL**	H	*SL*	BY	78107	63075	71961	77955
321 414	**SL**	H	*SL*	BY	78108	63076	71962	77956
321 415	**SL**	H	*SL*	BY	78109	63077	71963	77957
321 416	**SL**	H	*SL*	BY	78110	63078	71964	77958
321 417	**SL**	H	*SL*	BY	78111	63079	71965	77959
321 418	**SL**	H	*SL*	BY	78112	63080	71968	77962
321 419	**SL**	H	*SL*	BY	78113	63081	71967	77961
321 420	**SL**	H	*SL*	BY	78114	63082	71966	77960
321 421	**SL**	H	*SL*	BY	78115	63083	71969	77963
321 422	**SL**	H	*SL*	BY	78116	63084	71970	77964
321 423	**SL**	H	*SL*	BY	78117	63085	71971	77965
321 424	**SL**	H	*SL*	BY	78118	63086	71972	77966
321 425	**SL**	H	*SL*	BY	78119	63087	71973	77967
321 426	**SL**	H	*SL*	BY	78120	63088	71974	77968
321 427	**SL**	H	*SL*	BY	78121	63089	71975	77969
321 428	**SL**	H	*SL*	BY	78122	63090	71976	77970
321 429	**SL**	H	*SL*	BY	78123	63091	71977	77971
321 430	**SL**	H	*SL*	BY	78124	63092	71978	77972
321 431	**SL**	H	*SL*	BY	78151	63125	72011	78300
321 432	**SL**	H	*SL*	BY	78152	63126	72012	78301
321 433	**SL**	H	*SL*	BY	78153	63127	72013	78302
321 434	**SL**	H	*SL*	BY	78154	63128	72014	78303
321 435	**SL**	H	*SL*	BY	78155	63129	72015	78304
321 436	**SL**	H	*SL*	BY	78156	63130	72016	78305
321 437	**SL**	H	*SL*	BY	78157	63131	72017	78306
321 438	**GE**	H	*IE*	IL	78158	63132	72018	78307
321 439	**GE**	H	*IE*	IL	78159	63133	72019	78308
321 440	**GE**	H	*IE*	IL	78160	63134	72020	78309
321 441	**GE**	H	*IE*	IL	78161	63135	72021	78310
321 442	**GE**	H	*IE*	IL	78162	63136	72022	78311

321 443	GE	H	*IE*	IL	78125	63099	71985	78274
321 444	GE	H	*IE*	IL	78126	63100	71986	78275
321 445	GE	H	*IE*	IL	78127	63101	71987	78276
321 446	1	H	*IE*	IL	78128	63102	71988	78277
321 447	GE	H	*IE*	IL	78129	63103	71989	78278
321 448	GE	H	*IE*	IL	78130	63104	71990	78279

Names (carried on TSO):

321 407	HERTFORDSHIRE WRVS
321 413	Bill Green
321 427	Major Tim Warr
321 444	Essex Lifeboats

Class 321/9. DTSO(A)–MSO–TSO–DTSO(B). Units leased by West Yorkshire PTE from International Bank of Scotland. Managed by Porterbrook Leasing Company.
Dimensions: 19.33 x 2.82 m.

DTSO(A). Lot No. 31108 1991. –/77. 29.0 t.
MSO. Lot No. 31109 1991. –/79. 51.0 t.
TSO. Lot No. 31110 1991. –/74 2T. 29.0 t.
DTSO(B). Dia. EE277. Lot No. 31111 1991. –/77. 29.0 t.

321 901	WY	P	*NO*	NL	77990	63153	72128	77993
321 902	WY	P	*NO*	NL	77991	63154	72129	77994
321 903	WY	P	*NO*	NL	77992	63155	72130	77995

CLASS 322   BREL YORK

Units built for use on Stansted Airport services. Now working with One Great Eastern.

Formation: DTCO (declassified)–TSO–MSO–DTSO.
Construction: Steel.
Traction Motors: Four Brush TM2141C (268 kW).
Doors: Sliding.
Gangways: Within unit.
Couplers: Tightlock.
Control System: Thyristor.
Bogies: P7-4 (MSO), T3-7 (others).
Maximum Speed: 100 m.p.h.
Seating Layout: 1: 2+1 facing, 2: 2+2 facing.
Dimensions: 19.95/19.92 x 2.82 m.
Braking: Disc.
Multiple Working: Within class and with Classes 317, 318, 319, 320, 321 and 323.

DTCO. Lot No. 31094 1990. 35/22. 29.3 t.
TSO. Lot No. 31093 1990. –/60 2T. 28.8 t.
MSO. Lot No. 31092 1990. –/70. 51.5 t.
DTSO. Lot No. 31091 1990. –/65. 29.1 t.

Non-Standard livery: Stansted Skytrain livery (light grey with a yellow stripe).

322 481	0	H	*1E*	IL	78163	72023	63137	77985
322 482	0	H	*1E*	IL	78164	72024	63138	77986
322 483	0	H	*1E*	IL	78165	72025	63139	77987
322 484	NW	H	*1E*	IL	78166	72026	63140	77988
322 485	0	H	*1E*	IL	78167	72027	63141	77989

CLASS 323 HUNSLET TRANSPORTATION PROJECTS

Birmingham and Greater Manchester area suburban units.

Formation: DMSO–PTSO–DMSO.
Construction: Welded aluminium alloy.
Doors: Sliding plug.
Traction Motors: Four Holec DMKT 52/24 asynchronous of 146 kW.
Gangways: Within unit.
Bogies: SRP BP62 (DMSO), BT52 (PTSO).
Couplers: Tightlock   **Maximum Speed:** 100 m.p.h.
Seating Layout: 3+2 facing/unidirectional.
Dimensions: 23.37/23.44 x 2.80 m.
Braking: Disc.
Multiple Working: Within class and with Classes 317, 318, 319, 320, 321 and 322.

DMSO(A). Lot No. 31112 Hunslet 1992–1993. –/98 (* –/82). 39.1 t.
TSO. Lot No. 31113 Hunslet 1992–1993. –/88 1T. (* –/80 1T). 36.5 t.
DMSO(B). Lot No. 31114 Hunslet 1992–1993. –/98 (* –/82). 39.1 t.

Note: Most Centro units have now been fitted with on-train Television screens.

323 201	**CO**	P	*CT*	SI	64001	72201	65001
323 202	**CO**	P	*CT*	SI	64002	72202	65002
323 203	**CO**	P	*CT*	SI	64003	72203	65003
323 204	**CO**	P	*CT*	SI	64004	72204	65004
323 205	**CO**	P	*CT*	SI	64005	72205	65005
323 206	**CO**	P	*CT*	SI	64006	72206	65006
323 207	**CO**	P	*CT*	SI	64007	72207	65007
323 208	**CO**	P	*CT*	SI	64008	72208	65008
323 209	**CO**	P	*CT*	SI	64009	72209	65009
323 210	**CO**	P	*CT*	SI	64010	72210	65010
323 211	**CO**	P	*CT*	SI	64011	72211	65011
323 212	**CO**	P	*CT*	SI	64012	72212	65012
323 213	**CO**	P	*CT*	SI	64013	72213	65013
323 214	**CO**	P	*CT*	SI	64014	72214	65014
323 215	**CO**	P	*CT*	SI	64015	72215	65015
323 216	**CO**	P	*CT*	SI	64016	72216	65016
323 217	**CO**	P	*CT*	SI	64017	72217	65017
323 218	**CO**	P	*CT*	SI	64018	72218	65018
323 219	**CO**	P	*CT*	SI	64019	72219	65019
323 220	**CO**	P	*CT*	SI	64020	72220	65020
323 221	**CO**	P	*CT*	SI	64021	72221	65021
323 222	**CO**	P	*CT*	SI	64022	72222	65022
323 223	* **FS**	P	*NO*	LG	64023	72223	65023
323 224	* **FS**	P	*NO*	LG	64024	72224	65024
323 225	* **FS**	P	*NO*	LG	64025	72225	65025
323 226	**FS**	P	*NO*	LG	64026	72226	65026
323 227	**FS**	P	*NO*	LG	64027	72227	65027
323 228	**FS**	P	*NO*	LG	64028	72228	65028
323 229	**FS**	P	*NO*	LG	64029	72229	65029
323 230	**FS**	P	*NO*	LG	64030	72230	65030

323 231	**FS**	P	*NO*	LG	64031	72231	65031
323 232	**FS**	P	*NO*	LG	64032	72232	65032
323 233	**FS**	P	*NO*	LG	64033	72233	65033
323 234	**FS**	P	*NO*	LG	64034	72234	65034
323 235	**FS**	P	*NO*	LG	64035	72235	65035
323 236	**FS**	P	*NO*	LG	64036	72236	65036
323 237	**FS**	P	*NO*	LG	64037	72237	65037
323 238	**FS**	P	*NO*	LG	64038	72238	65038
323 239	**FS**	P	*NO*	LG	64039	72239	65039
323 240	**CO**	P	*CT*	SI	64040	72340	65040
323 241	**CO**	P	*CT*	SI	64041	72341	65041
323 242	**CO**	P	*CT*	SI	64042	72342	65042
323 243	**CO**	P	*CT*	SI	64043	72343	65043

CLASS 325   ABB DERBY

Postal units based on Class 319. Compatible with diesel/electric locomotive haulage.

Formation: DTPMV–MPMV–TPMV–DTPMV.
System: 25 kV AC overhead/750 V DC third rail.
Construction: Steel.
Traction Motors: Four GEC G315BZ of 268 kW.
Doors: Roller shutter.   **Control System:** GTO chopper.
Gangways: None.   **Bogies:** P7-4 (MSO), T3-7 (others).
Couplers: Drop-head buckeye.   **Maximum Speed:** 100 m.p.h.
Braking: Disc.   **Dimensions:** 19.33 x 2.82 m.
Multiple Working: Within class.

DTPMV. Lot No. 31144 1995. 29.1 t.
MPMV. Lot No. 31145 1995. 49.5 t.
TPMV. Lot No. 31146 1995. 30.7 t.

325 001	**RM**	RM *GB*	WN	68300	68340	68360	68301
325 002	**RM**	RM *GB*	WN	68302	68341	68361	68303
325 003	**RM**	RM *GB*	WN	68304	68342	68362	68305
325 004	**RM**	RM *GB*	WN	68306	68343	68363	68307
325 005	**RM**	RM *GB*	WN	68308	68344	68364	68309
325 006	**RM**	RM *GB*	WN	68310	68345	68365	68311
325 007	**RM**	RM *GB*	WN	68312	68346	68366	68313
325 008	**RM**	RM *GB*	WN	68314	68347	68367	68315
325 009	**RM**	RM *GB*	WN	68316	68348	68368	68317
325 010	**RM**	RM *GB*	WN	68318	68349	68369	68319
325 011	**RM**	RM *GB*	WN	68320	68350	68370	68321
325 012	**RM**	RM *GB*	WN	68322	68351	68371	68323
325 013	**RM**	RM *GB*	WN	68324	68352	68372	68325
325 014	**RM**	RM *GB*	WN	68326	68353	68373	68327
325 015	**RM**	RM *GB*	WN	68328	68354	68374	68329
325 016	**RM**	RM *GB*	WN	68330	68355	68375	68331

Names (carried on one side of each DTPMV):

325 002	Royal Mail North Wales & North West
325 006	John Grierson
325 008	Peter Howarth C.B.E.

CLASS 332   HEATHROW EXPRESS   SIEMENS

Dedicated Heathrow Express units. Five units were increased from 4-car to 5-car in 2002. Usually operate in coupled pairs.

Formations: Various.
Construction: Steel.   **Doors:** Sliding plug.
Traction Motors: Two Siemens monomotors asynchronous of 350 kW.
Gangways: Within unit.   **Bogies:** CAF.
Couplers: Scharfenberg   **Maximum Speed:** 100 m.p.h.
Seating Layout: 1: 2+1 facing, 2: 2+2 mainly unidirectional.
Dimensions: 23.63/23.35 x 2.75 m.   **Braking:** Disc.
Multiple Working: Within class and with Class 333.
Heating & ventilation: Air conditioning.

332 001–332 007. DMFO–TSO–PTSO–(TSO)–DMSO.

DMFO. CAF 1997–1998. 26/–. 48.8 t.
72400–72413. TSO. CAF 1997–1998. –/56 35.8 t.
72414–72418. TSO. CAF 2002. –/56 35.8 t.
PTSO. CAF 1997–1998. –/44 1TD 1W. 45.6 t.
DMSO. CAF 1997–1998. –/48. 48.8 t.
DMLFO. CAF 1997–1998. 14/– 1W. 48.8 t.

Advertising livery: Vehicles 78401, 78402, 78405, 78406, 78408, 78410, 78412 carry Royal Bank of Scotland advertising livery (deep blue).

332 001	**HE**	HE *HE*	OH	78400	72412	63400		78401
332 002	**HE**	HE *HE*	OH	78402	72409	63401		78403
332 003	**HE**	HE *HE*	OH	78404	72407	63402		78405
332 004	**HE**	HE *HE*	OH	78406	72405	63403		78407
332 005	**HE**	HE *HE*	OH	78408	72411	63404	72417	78409
332 006	**HE**	HE *HE*	OH	78410	72410	63405	72415	78411
332 007	**HE**	HE *HE*	OH	78412	72401	63406	72414	78413

332 008–332 014. DMSO–TSO–PTSO–(TSO)–DMLFO.

Advertising livery: Vehicles 78414, 78416, 78419, 78421, 78423, 78425, 78427 carry Royal Bank of Scotland advertising livery (deep blue).

332 008	**HE**	HE *HE*	OH	78414	72413	63407	72418	78415
332 009	**HE**	HE *HE*	OH	78416	72400	63408	72416	78417
332 010	**HE**	HE *HE*	OH	78418	72402	63409		78419
332 011	**HE**	HE *HE*	OH	78420	72403	63410		78421
332 012	**HE**	HE *HE*	OH	78422	72404	63411		78423
332 013	**HE**	HE *HE*	OH	78424	72408	63412		78425
332 014	**HE**	HE *HE*	OH	78426	72406	63413		78427

CLASS 333   SIEMENS

West Yorkshire area suburban units.

Formation: DMSO–PTSO–TSO–DMSO.
Construction: Steel.   **Doors:** Sliding plug.
Traction Motors: Two Siemens monomotors asynchronous of 350 kW.
Gangways: Within unit.   **Bogies:** CAF.
Couplers: Scharfenberg   **Maximum Speed:** 100 m.p.h.
Seating Layout: 3+2 facing/unidirectional.
Dimensions: 22.95/22.90/23.35 x 2.57 m.
Braking: Disc.
Multiple Working: Within class and with Class 332.
Heating & ventilation: Air conditioning.

DMSO(A). (Odd Nos.) CAF 2001. –/90. 50.6 t.
PTSO. CAF 2001. –/73 1TD 2W. 46.7 t.
TSO. CAF 2002–2003. –/100. 38.5 t.
DMSO(B). (Even Nos.) CAF 2001. –/90. 50.6 t.

Notes: 333 001–333 008 were made up to 4-car units from 3-car units in 2002.
333 009–333 016 were made up to 4-car units from 3-car units in 2003.

333 001	**YN**	A	*NO*	NL	78451	74461	74477	78452
333 002	**YN**	A	*NO*	NL	78453	74462	74478	78454
333 003	**YN**	A	*NO*	NL	78455	74463	74479	78456
333 004	**YN**	A	*NO*	NL	78457	74464	74480	78458
333 005	**YN**	A	*NO*	NL	78459	74465	74481	78460
333 006	**YN**	A	*NO*	NL	78461	74466	74482	78462
333 007	**YN**	A	*NO*	NL	78463	74467	74483	78464
333 008	**YN**	A	*NO*	NL	78465	74468	74484	78466
333 009	**YN**	A	*NO*	NL	78467	74469	74485	78468
333 010	**YN**	A	*NO*	NL	78469	74470	74486	78470
333 011	**YN**	A	*NO*	NL	78471	74471	74487	78472
333 012	**YN**	A	*NO*	NL	78473	74472	74488	78474
333 013	**YN**	A	*NO*	NL	78475	74473	74489	78476
333 014	**YN**	A	*NO*	NL	78477	74474	74490	78478
333 015	**YN**	A	*NO*	NL	78479	74475	74491	78480
333 016	**YN**	A	*NO*	NL	78481	74476	74492	78482

CLASS 334 JUNIPER ALSTOM BIRMINGHAM

First ScotRail outer suburban units.

Formation: DMSO–PTSO–DMSO.
Construction: Steel.   **Doors:** Sliding plug.
Traction Motors: Two Alstom ONIX 800 asynchronous of 270 kW.
Gangways: Within unit.   **Bogies:** Alstom LTB3/TBP3.
Couplers: Tightlock.   **Maximum Speed:** 100 m.p.h.
Seating Layout: 2+2 facing/unidirectional (3+2 in PTSO).
Dimensions: 21.01/19.94 x 2.80 m.   **Braking:** Disc.

Multiple Working: Within class.
Heating & ventilation: Pressure heating and ventilation.

64101–64140. DMSO. Alstom Birmingham 1999–2001. –/64. 42.6 t.
PTSO. Alstom Birmingham 1999–2001. –/55 1TD 1W. 39.4 t.
65101–65140. DMSO. Alstom Birmingham 1999–2001. –/64. 42.6 t.

334 001	**SP**	H	*SR*	GW	64101	74301	65101
334 002	**SP**	H	*SR*	GW	64102	74302	65102
334 003	**SP**	H	*SR*	GW	64103	74303	65103
334 004	**SP**	H	*SR*	GW	64104	74304	65104
334 005	**SP**	H	*SR*	GW	64105	74305	65105
334 006	**SP**	H	*SR*	GW	64106	74306	65106
334 007	**SP**	H	*SR*	GW	64107	74307	65107
334 008	**SP**	H	*SR*	GW	64108	74308	65108
334 009	**SP**	H	*SR*	GW	64109	74309	65109
334 010	**SP**	H	*SR*	GW	64110	74310	65110
334 011	**SP**	H	*SR*	GW	64111	74311	65111
334 012	**SP**	H	*SR*	GW	64112	74312	65112
334 013	**SP**	H	*SR*	GW	64113	74313	65113
334 014	**SP**	H	*SR*	GW	64114	74314	65114
334 015	**SP**	H	*SR*	GW	64115	74315	65115
334 016	**SP**	H	*SR*	GW	64116	74316	65116
334 017	**SP**	H	*SR*	GW	64117	74317	65117
334 018	**SP**	H	*SR*	GW	64118	74318	65118
334 019	**SP**	H	*SR*	GW	64119	74319	65119
334 020	**SP**	H	*SR*	GW	64120	74320	65120
334 021	**SP**	H	*SR*	GW	64121	74321	65121
334 022	**SP**	H	*SR*	GW	64122	74322	65122
334 023	**SP**	H	*SR*	GW	64123	74323	65123
334 024	**SP**	H	*SR*	GW	64124	74324	65124
334 025	**SP**	H	*SR*	GW	64125	74325	65125
334 026	**SP**	H	*SR*	GW	64126	74326	65126
334 027	**SP**	H	*SR*	GW	64127	74327	65127
334 028	**SP**	H	*SR*	GW	64128	74328	65128
334 029	**SP**	H	*SR*	GW	64129	74329	65129
334 030	**SP**	H	*SR*	GW	64130	74330	65130
334 031	**SP**	H	*SR*	GW	64131	74331	65131
334 032	**SP**	H	*SR*	GW	64132	74332	65132
334 033	**SP**	H	*SR*	GW	64133	74333	65133
334 034	**SP**	H	*SR*	GW	64134	74334	65134
334 035	**SP**	H	*SR*	GW	64135	74335	65135
334 036	**SP**	H	*SR*	GW	64136	74336	65136
334 037	**SP**	H	*SR*	GW	64137	74337	65137
334 038	**SP**	H	*SR*	GW	64138	74338	65138
334 039	**SP**	H	*SR*	GW	64139	74339	65139
334 040	**SP**	H	*SR*	GW	64140	74340	65140

Name (carried on PTSO):

334 001   Donald Dewar

CLASS 350   DESIRO UK   SIEMENS

New "West Coast" units. For use by Silverlink, Central and Virgin. Formerly to form part of the now aborted South West Trains 5-car Class 450/2 order.

Formation: DMCO–PTSO–TSO–DMCO.
Systems: 25 kV AC overhead.
Construction: Welded aluminium.   **Doors:** Sliding plug.
Traction Motors: 4 Siemens 1TB2016-0GB02 asynchronous of 250 kW.
Gangways: Throughout.   **Bogies:** SGP SF5000.
Couplers: Dellner 12.   **Maximum Speed:** 100 m.p.h.
Seating Layout: 1: 2+1 facing, 2: 2+2 facing/unidirectional.
Dimensions: 20.34 x 2.80 m.   **Multiple Working:** Within class.
Braking: Disc & regenerative.
Heating & ventilation: Air conditioning.

DMCO(A). Siemens Uerdingen 2004. –/60. 48.7 t.
PTSO. Siemens Wien 2004. 24/34 1T. 36.2 t.
TSO. Siemens Wien 2004. –/59 1TD 2W. 45.2 t.
DMCO(B). Siemens Uerdingen 2004. –/60. 49.2 t.

350 101	**WD**	A	63761	66811	66861	63711
350 102	**WD**	A	63762	66812	66862	63712
350 103	**WD**	A	63763	66813	66863	63713
350 104	**WD**	A	63764	66814	66864	63714
350 105	**WD**	A	63765	66815	66865	63715
350 106	**WD**	A	63766	66816	66866	63716
350 107	**WD**	A	63767	66817	66867	63717
350 108	**WD**	A	63768	66818	66868	63718
350 109	**WD**	A	63769	66819	66869	63719
350 110	**WD**	A	63770	66820	66870	63720
350 111	**WD**	A	63771	66821	66871	63721
350 112	**WD**	A	63772	66822	66872	63722
350 113	**WD**	A	63773	66823	66873	63723
350 114	**WD**	A	63774	66824	66874	63724
350 115	**WD**	A	63775	66825	66875	63725
350 116	**WD**	A	63776	66826	66876	63726
350 117	**WD**	A	63777	66827	66877	63727
350 118	**WD**	A	63778	66828	66878	63728
350 119	**WD**	A	63779	66829	66879	63729
350 120	**WD**	A	63780	66830	66880	63730
350 121	**WD**	A	63781	66831	66881	63731
350 122	**WD**	A	63782	66832	66882	63732
350 123	**WD**	A	63783	66833	66883	63733
350 124	**WD**	A	63784	66834	66884	63734
350 125	**WD**	A	63785	66835	66885	63735
350 126	**WD**	A	63786	66836	66886	63736
350 127	**WD**	A	63787	66837	66887	63737
350 128	**WD**	A	63788	66838	66888	63738
350 129	**WD**	A	63789	66839	66889	63739
350 130	**WD**	A	63790	66840	66890	63740

CLASS 357 ELECTROSTAR
ADTRANZ/BOMBARDIER DERBY

c2c units. Provision for 750 V DC supply if required.

Formation: DMSO–MSO–PTSO–DMSO.
Construction: Welded aluminium alloy underframe, sides and roof with steel ends. All sections bolted together.
Traction Motors: Two Adtranz asynchronous of 250 kW.
Doors: Sliding plug.
Gangways: Within unit.   **Bogies:** Adtranz P3-25/T3-25.
Couplers: Tightlock.   **Maximum Speed:** 100 m.p.h.
Seating Layout: 3+2 facing/unidirectional.
Dimensions: 20.40/19.99 x 2.80 m.
Braking: Disc & regenerative.   **Multiple Working:** Within class.
Heating & ventilation: Air conditioning.

Class 357/0. Owned by Porterbrook Leasing.

DMSO(A). Adtranz Derby 1999–2001. –/71. 40.7 t.
MSO. Adtranz Derby 1999–2001. –/78. 39.5 t.
PTSO. Adtranz Derby 1999–2001. –/62 1TD 2W. 36.7 t.
DMSO(B). Adtranz Derby 1999–2001. –/71. 40.7 t.

357 001	**C2**	P	*C2*	EM	67651	74151	74051	67751
357 002	**C2**	P	*C2*	EM	67652	74152	74052	67752
357 003	**C2**	P	*C2*	EM	67653	74153	74053	67753
357 004	**C2**	P	*C2*	EM	67654	74154	74054	67754
357 005	**C2**	P	*C2*	EM	67655	74155	74055	67755
357 006	**C2**	P	*C2*	EM	67656	74156	74056	67756
357 007	**C2**	P	*C2*	EM	67657	74157	74057	67757
357 008	**C2**	P	*C2*	EM	67658	74158	74058	67758
357 009	**C2**	P	*C2*	EM	67659	74159	74059	67759
357 010	**C2**	P	*C2*	EM	67660	74160	74060	67760
357 011	**C2**	P	*C2*	EM	67661	74161	74061	67761
357 012	**C2**	P	*C2*	EM	67662	74162	74062	67762
357 013	**C2**	P	*C2*	EM	67663	74163	74063	67763
357 014	**C2**	P	*C2*	EM	67664	74164	74064	67764
357 015	**C2**	P	*C2*	EM	67665	74165	74065	67765
357 016	**C2**	P	*C2*	EM	67666	74166	74066	67766
357 017	**C2**	P	*C2*	EM	67667	74167	74067	67767
357 018	**C2**	P	*C2*	EM	67668	74168	74068	67768
357 019	**C2**	P	*C2*	EM	67669	74169	74069	67769
357 020	**C2**	P	*C2*	EM	67670	74170	74070	67770
357 021	**C2**	P	*C2*	EM	67671	74171	74071	67771
357 022	**C2**	P	*C2*	EM	67672	74172	74072	67772
357 023	**C2**	P	*C2*	EM	67673	74173	74073	67773
357 024	**C2**	P	*C2*	EM	67674	74174	74074	67774
357 025	**C2**	P	*C2*	EM	67675	74175	74075	67775
357 026	**C2**	P	*C2*	EM	67676	74176	74076	67776
357 027	**C2**	P	*C2*	EM	67677	74177	74077	67777

357 028	C2	P	C2	EM	67678	74178	74078	67778
357 029	C2	P	C2	EM	67679	74179	74079	67779
357 030	C2	P	C2	EM	67680	74180	74080	67780
357 031	C2	P	C2	EM	67681	74181	74081	67781
357 032	C2	P	C2	EM	67682	74182	74082	67782
357 033	C2	P	C2	EM	67683	74183	74083	67783
357 034	C2	P	C2	EM	67684	74184	74084	67784
357 035	C2	P	C2	EM	67685	74185	74085	67785
357 036	C2	P	C2	EM	67686	74186	74086	67786
357 037	C2	P	C2	EM	67687	74187	74087	67787
357 038	C2	P	C2	EM	67688	74188	74088	67788
357 039	C2	P	C2	EM	67689	74189	74089	67789
357 040	C2	P	C2	EM	67690	74190	74090	67790
357 041	C2	P	C2	EM	67691	74191	74091	67791
357 042	C2	P	C2	EM	67692	74192	74092	67792
357 043	C2	P	C2	EM	67693	74193	74093	67793
357 044	C2	P	C2	EM	67694	74194	74094	67794
357 045	C2	P	C2	EM	67695	74195	74095	67795
357 046	C2	P	C2	EM	67696	74196	74096	67796

Names (carried on DMSO(A) and DMSO(B) (one plate on each)):

357 001 BARRY FLAXMAN
357 003 JASON LEONARD
357 011 JOHN LOWING
357 028 London, Tilbury & Southend Railway 1854–2004

Class 357/2. Owned by Angel Trains.

Note: Five unspecified Class 357/2s are on hire to One Great Eastern on a rolling basis for use on certain London Liverpool Street–Southend Victoria services.

DMSO(A). Bombardier Derby 2001–2002. –/71. 41.0 t.
MSO. Bombardier Derby 2001–2002. –/78. 39.5 t.
PTSO. Bombardier Derby 2001–2002. –/62 1TD 2W. 36.7 t.
DMSO(B). Bombardier Derby 2001–2002. –/71. 41.0 t.

357 201	C2	A	C2	EM	68601	74701	74601	68701
357 202	C2	A	C2	EM	68602	74702	74602	68702
357 203	C2	A	C2	EM	68603	74703	74603	68703
357 204	C2	A	C2	EM	68604	74704	74604	68704
357 205	C2	A	C2	EM	68605	74705	74605	68705
357 206	C2	A	C2	EM	68606	74706	74606	68706
357 207	C2	A	C2	EM	68607	74707	74607	68707
357 208	C2	A	C2	EM	68608	74708	74608	68708
357 209	C2	A	C2	EM	68609	74709	74609	68709
357 210	C2	A	C2	EM	68610	74710	74610	68710
357 211	C2	A	C2	EM	68611	74711	74611	68711
357 212	C2	A	C2	EM	68612	74712	74612	68712
357 213	C2	A	C2	EM	68613	74713	74613	68713
357 214	C2	A	C2	EM	68614	74714	74614	68714
357 215	C2	A	C2	EM	68615	74715	74615	68715
357 216	C2	A	C2	EM	68616	74716	74616	68716
357 217	C2	A	C2	EM	68617	74717	74617	68717

357 218	**C2**	A	*C2*	EM	68618	74718	74618	68718
357 219	**C2**	A	*C2*	EM	68619	74719	74619	68719
357 220	**C2**	A	*C2*	EM	68620	74720	74620	68720
357 221	**C2**	A	*C2*	EM	68621	74721	74621	68721
357 222	**C2**	A	*C2*	EM	68622	74722	74622	68722
357 223	**C2**	A	*C2*	EM	68623	74723	74623	68723
357 224	**C2**	A	*C2*	EM	68624	74724	74624	68724
357 225	**C2**	A	*C2*	EM	68625	74725	74625	68725
357 226	**C2**	A	*C2*	EM	68626	74726	74626	68726
357 227	**C2**	A	*C2*	EM	68627	74727	74627	68727
357 228	**C2**	A	*C2*	EM	68628	74728	74628	68728

Names (carried on DMSO(A) and DMSO(B) (one plate on each)):

357 201 KEN BIRD
357 202 KENNY MITCHELL
357 203 HENRY POMFRETT
357 204 DEREK FLOWERS

CLASS 360/1   DESIRO UK   SIEMENS

One Great Eastern units.

Formation: DMCO–PTSO–TSO–DMCO.
Systems: 25 kV AC overhead.
Construction: Welded aluminium.   **Doors:** Sliding plug.
Traction Motors: 4 Siemens 1TB2016-0GB02 asynchronous of 250 kW.
Gangways: Within unit.   **Bogies:** SGP SF5000.
Couplers: Dellner 12.   **Maximum Speed:** 100 m.p.h.
Seating Layout: 1: 2+2 facing, 2: 3+2 facing/unidirectional.
Dimensions: 20.34 x 2.80 m.   **Multiple Working:** Within class.
Braking: Disc & regenerative.
Heating & ventilation: Air conditioning.

DMCO(A). Siemens Uerdingen 2002–2003. 8/59. 45.0 t.
PTSO. Siemens Wien 2002–2003. –/69 1TD 2W. 43.0 t.
TSO. Siemens Wien 2002–2003. –/78. 35.0 t.
DMCO(B). Siemens Uerdingen 2002–2003. 8/59. 45.0 t.

360 101	**FS**	A	*IE*	IL	65551	72551	74551	68551
360 102	**FS**	A	*IE*	IL	65552	72552	74552	68552
360 103	**FS**	A	*IE*	IL	65553	72553	74553	68553
360 104	**FS**	A	*IE*	IL	65554	72554	74554	68554
360 105	**FS**	A	*IE*	IL	65555	72555	74555	68555
360 106	**FS**	A	*IE*	IL	65556	72556	74556	68556
360 107	**FS**	A	*IE*	IL	65557	72557	74557	68557
360 108	**FS**	A	*IE*	IL	65558	72558	74558	68558
360 109	**FS**	A	*IE*	IL	65559	72559	74559	68559
360 110	**FS**	A	*IE*	IL	65560	72560	74560	68560
360 111	**FS**	A	*IE*	IL	65561	72561	74561	68561
360 112	**FS**	A	*IE*	IL	65562	72562	74562	68562
360 113	**FS**	A	*IE*	IL	65563	72563	74563	68563
360 114	**FS**	A	*IE*	IL	65564	72564	74564	68564

360 115	**FS**	A	*IE*	IL	65565	72565	74565	68565
360 116	**FS**	A	*IE*	IL	65566	72566	74566	68566
360 117	**FS**	A	*IE*	IL	65567	72567	74567	68567
360 118	**FS**	A	*IE*	IL	65568	72568	74568	68568
360 119	**FS**	A	*IE*	IL	65569	72569	74569	68569
360 120	**FS**	A	*IE*	IL	65570	72570	74570	68570
360 121	**FS**	A	*IE*	IL	65571	72571	74571	68571

CLASS 360/2   DESIRO UK   SIEMENS

Original 4-car Class 350 testbed units rebuilt for use by Heathrow Express on Paddington–Heathrow stopping services from Spring 2005 – "Heathrow Connect" (the service will be jointly run with First Great Western Link). All units will eventually be strengthened to 5-cars and a fifth unit (360 205) is due for delivery in 2006.

Formations: DMSO–PTSO–TSO–DMSO.
Systems: 25 kV AC overhead.
Construction: Welded aluminium.   **Doors:** Sliding plug.
Traction Motors: 4 Siemens 1TB2016-0GB02 asynchronous of 250 kW.
Gangways: Within unit.   **Bogies:** SGP SF5000.
Couplers: Dellner 12.   **Maximum Speed:** 100 m.p.h.
Seating Layout: 3+2 facing/unidirectional.
Dimensions: 20.34 x 2.80 m.   **Multiple Working:** Within class.
Braking: Disc & regenerative.
Heating & ventilation: Air conditioning.

DMSO(A). Siemens Uerdingen 2002–2005. –/63. 44.8 t.
PTSO. Siemens Uerdingen 2002–2005. –/66 1TD 2W. 44.2 t.
TSO. Siemens Uerdingen 2002–2005. –/74. 34.8 t.
DMSO(B). Siemens Uerdingen 2002–2005. –/63. 44.4 t.

360 201	**HC**	HE	OH	78431	63421	72421	78441
360 202	**HC**	HE	OH	78432	63422	72422	78442
360 203	**HC**	HE	OH	78433	63423	72423	78443
360 204	**HC**	HE	OH	78434	63424	72424	78444

CLASS 365 NETWORKER EXPRESS ABB YORK

WAGN outer suburban units.

Formations: DMCO–TSO–PTSO–DMCO.
Systems: 25 kV AC overhead. All units have now had their third rail shoegear removed.
Construction: Welded aluminium alloy.
Traction Motors: Four GEC-Alsthom G354CX asynchronous of 157 kW.
Doors: Sliding plug.
Gangways: Within unit.   **Bogies:** ABB P3-16/T3-16.
Couplers: Tightlock.   **Maximum Speed:** 100 m.p.h.
Seating Layout: 1: 2+2 facing, 2: 3+2 facing.
Dimensions: 20.89 x 2.81 m.

Braking: Disc, rheostatic & regenerative.
Multiple Working: Within class and with Classes 465 and 466.

DMCO(A). Lot No. 31133 1994–1995. 12/56. 41.7 t.
TSO. Lot No. 31134 1994–1995. –/59 1TD. 32.9 t.
PTSO. Lot No. 31135 1994–1995. –/68 1T. 34.6 t.
DMCO(B). Lot No. 31136 1994–1995. 12/56. 41.7 t.

365 501	**NT**	H	*WN*	HE	65894	72241	72240	65935
365 502	**NT**	H	*WN*	HE	65895	72243	72242	65936
365 503	**NT**	H	*WN*	HE	65896	72245	72244	65937
365 504	**NT**	H	*WN*	HE	65897	72247	72246	65938
365 505	**NT**	H	*WN*	HE	65898	72249	72248	65939
365 506	**NT**	H	*WN*	HE	65899	72251	72250	65940
365 507	**NT**	H	*WN*	HE	65900	72253	72252	65941
365 508	**NT**	H	*WN*	HE	65901	72255	72254	65942
365 509	**NT**	H	*WN*	HE	65902	72257	72256	65943
365 510	**NT**	H	*WN*	HE	65903	72259	72258	65944
365 511	**NT**	H	*WN*	HE	65904	72261	72260	65945
365 512	**NT**	H	*WN*	HE	65905	72263	72262	65946
365 513	**NT**	H	*WN*	HE	65906	72265	72264	65947
365 514	**NT**	H	*WN*	HE	65907	72267	72266	65948
365 515	**NT**	H	*WN*	HE	65908	72269	72268	65949
365 516	**NT**	H	*WN*	HE	65909	72271	72270	65950
365 517	**NT**	H	*WN*	HE	65910	72273	72272	65951
365 518	**NT**	H	*WN*	HE	65911	72275	72274	65952
365 519	**NT**	H	*WN*	HE	65912	72277	72276	65953
365 520	**NT**	H	*WN*	HE	65913	72279	72278	65954
365 521	**NT**	H	*WN*	HE	65914	72281	72280	65955
365 522	**NT**	H	*WN*	HE	65915	72283	72282	65956
365 523	**NT**	H	*WN*	HE	65916	72285	72284	65957
365 524	**NT**	H	*WN*	HE	65917	72287	72286	65958
365 525	**NT**	H	*WN*	HE	65918	72289	72288	65959
365 526	**NT**	H		ZC	65919	72291	72290	65960
365 527	**NT**	H	*WN*	HE	65920	72293	72292	65961
365 528	**NT**	H	*WN*	HE	65921	72295	72294	65962
365 529	**NT**	H	*WN*	HE	65922	72297	72296	65963
365 530	**NT**	H	*WN*	HE	65923	72299	72298	65964
365 531	**NT**	H	*WN*	HE	65924	72301	72300	65965
365 532	**NT**	H	*WN*	HE	65925	72303	72302	65966
365 533	**NT**	H	*WN*	HE	65926	72305	72304	65967
365 534	**NT**	H	*WN*	HE	65927	72307	72306	65968
365 535	**NT**	H	*WN*	HE	65928	72309	72308	65969
365 536	**NT**	H	*WN*	HE	65929	72311	72310	65970
365 537	**NT**	H	*WN*	HE	65930	72313	72312	65971
365 538	**NT**	H	*WN*	HE	65931	72315	72314	65972
365 539	**NT**	H	*WN*	HE	65932	72317	72316	65973
365 540	**NT**	H	*WN*	HE	65933	72319	72318	65974
365 541	**NT**	H	*WN*	HE	65934	72321	72320	65975

CLASS 375 ELECTROSTAR
ADTRANZ/BOMBARDIER DERBY

South Eastern Trains express and outer suburban units.

Systems: 25 kV AC overhead/750 V DC third rail (some third rail only with provision for retro-fitting of AC equipment).
Formations: Various.
Construction: Welded aluminium alloy underframe, sides and roof with steel ends. All sections bolted together.
Traction Motors: Two Adtranz asynchronous of 250 kW.
Doors: Sliding plug.   **Bogies:** Adtranz P3-25/T3-25.
Gangways: Throughout.   **Maximum Speed:** 100 m.p.h.
Couplers: Dellner 12.   **Heating & ventilation:** Air conditioning.
Seating Layout: 1: 2+2 facing/unidirectional (seats behind drivers cab in each DMCO). 2: 2+2 facing/unidirectional (375/3, 375/6, 375/7 and 375/8), 3+2 facing/unidirectional (375/9).
Dimensions: 20.40/19.99 x 2.80 m.   **Braking:** Disc & regenerative.
Multiple Working: Within class and with Classes 376 and 377.

Class 375/3. Express units. 750 V DC only. DMCO–TSO–DMCO.

DMCO(A). Bombardier Derby 2001–2002. 12/48. 43.8 t.
TSO. Bombardier Derby 2001–2002. –/56 1TD 2W. 35.5 t.
DMCO(B). Bombardier Derby 2001–2002. 12/48. 43.8 t.

375 301	**CN**	H	*SE*	RM	67921	74351	67931
375 302	**CN**	H	*SE*	RM	67922	74352	67932
375 303	**CN**	H	*SE*	RM	67923	74353	67933
375 304	**CN**	H	*SE*	RM	67924	74354	67934
375 305	**CN**	H	*SE*	RM	67925	74355	67935
375 306	**CN**	H	*SE*	RM	67926	74356	67936
375 307	**CN**	H	*SE*	RM	67927	74357	67937
375 308	**CN**	H	*SE*	RM	67928	74358	67938
375 309	**CN**	H	*SE*	RM	67929	74359	67939
375 310	**CN**	H	*SE*	RM	67930	74360	67940

Class 375/6. Express units. 25 kV AC/750 V DC. DMCO–MSO–PTSO–DMCO.

DMCO(A). Adtranz Derby 1999–2001. 12/48. 46.2 t.
MSO. Adtranz Derby 1999–2001. –/66 1T. 40.5 t.
PTSO. Adtranz Derby 1999–2001. –/56 1TD 2W. 40.7 t.
DMCO(B). Adtranz Derby 1999–2001. 12/48. 46.2 t.

Non-Standard livery: 375 610 is as **CN** but with blue doors instead of yellow and a gold band instead of a grey band on the lower bodyside (a special "Golden Jubilee" livery).

375 601	**CN**	H	*SE*	RM	67801	74251	74201	67851
375 602	**CN**	H	*SE*	RM	67802	74252	74202	67852
375 603	**CN**	H	*SE*	RM	67803	74253	74203	67853
375 604	**CN**	H	*SE*	RM	67804	74254	74204	67854
375 605	**CN**	H	*SE*	RM	67805	74255	74205	67855

375 606	**CN**	H	*SE*	RM	67806	74256	74206	67856
375 607	**CN**	H	*SE*	RM	67807	74257	74207	67857
375 608	**CN**	H	*SE*	RM	67808	74258	74208	67858
375 609	**CN**	H	*SE*	RM	67809	74259	74209	67859
375 610	**O**	H	*SE*	RM	67810	74260	74210	67860
375 611	**CN**	H	*SE*	RM	67811	74261	74211	67861
375 612	**CN**	H	*SE*	RM	67812	74262	74212	67862
375 613	**CN**	H	*SE*	RM	67813	74263	74213	67863
375 614	**CN**	H	*SE*	RM	67814	74264	74214	67864
375 615	**CN**	H	*SE*	RM	67815	74265	74215	67865
375 616	**CN**	H	*SE*	RM	67816	74266	74216	67866
375 617	**CN**	H	*SE*	RM	67817	74267	74217	67867
375 618	**CN**	H	*SE*	RM	67818	74268	74218	67868
375 619	**CN**	H	*SE*	RM	67819	74269	74219	67869
375 620	**CN**	H	*SE*	RM	67820	74270	74220	67870
375 621	**CN**	H	*SE*	RM	67821	74271	74221	67871
375 622	**CN**	H	*SE*	RM	67822	74272	74222	67872
375 623	**CN**	H	*SE*	RM	67823	74273	74223	67873
375 624	**CN**	H	*SE*	RM	67824	74274	74224	67874
375 625	**CN**	H	*SE*	RM	67825	74275	74225	67875
375 626	**CN**	H	*SE*	RM	67826	74276	74226	67876
375 627	**CN**	H	*SE*	RM	67827	74277	74227	67877
375 628	**CN**	H	*SE*	RM	67828	74278	74228	67878
375 629	**CN**	H	*SE*	RM	67829	74279	74229	67879
375 630	**CN**	H	*SE*	RM	67830	74280	74230	67880

Names (carried on one side of each MSO or TSO):

375 608	Bromley Travelwise	375 610	Royal Tunbridge Wells
375 611	Dr. William Harvey	375 619	Driver John Neve
375 623	Hospice in the Weald	375 624	White Cliffs Country

Class 375/7. Express units. 750 V DC only. DMCO–MSO–TSO–DMCO.

DMCO(A). Bombardier Derby 2001–2002. 12/48. 43.8 t.
MSO. Bombardier Derby 2001–2002. –/66 1T. 36.4 t.
TSO. Bombardier Derby 2001–2002. –/56 1TD 2W. 34.1 t.
DMCO(B). Bombardier Derby 2001–2002. 12/48. 43.8 t.

375 701	**CN**	H	*SE*	RM	67831	74281	74231	67881
375 702	**CN**	H	*SE*	RM	67832	74282	74232	67882
375 703	**CN**	H	*SE*	RM	67833	74283	74233	67883
375 704	**CN**	H	*SE*	RM	67834	74284	74234	67884
375 705	**CN**	H	*SE*	RM	67835	74285	74235	67885
375 706	**CN**	H	*SE*	RM	67836	74286	74236	67886
375 707	**CN**	H	*SE*	RM	67837	74287	74237	67887
375 708	**CN**	H	*SE*	RM	67838	74288	74238	67888
375 709	**CN**	H	*SE*	RM	67839	74289	74239	67889
375 710	**CN**	H	*SE*	RM	67840	74290	74240	67890
375 711	**CN**	H	*SE*	RM	67841	74291	74241	67891
375 712	**CN**	H	*SE*	RM	67842	74292	74242	67892
375 713	**CN**	H	*SE*	RM	67843	74293	74243	67893
375 714	**CN**	H	*SE*	RM	67844	74294	74244	67894
375 715	**CN**	H	*SE*	RM	67845	74295	74245	67895

Names (carried on one side of each MSO or TSO):

375 701   Kent Air Ambulance Explorer
375 703   Dickens Traveller

Class 375/8. Express units. 750 V DC only. DMCO–MSO–TSO–DMCO.

DMCO(A). Bombardier Derby 2004. 12/48. 43.3 t.
MSO. Bombardier Derby 2004. –/66 1T. 39.8 t.
TSO. Bombardier Derby 2004. –/52 1TD 2W. 35.9 t.
DMCO(B). Bombardier Derby 2004. 12/52. 43.3 t.

375 801	**CN**	H	*SE*	RM	73301	79001	78201	73701
375 802	**CN**	H	*SE*	RM	73302	79002	78202	73702
375 803	**CN**	H	*SE*	RM	73303	79003	78203	73703
375 804	**CN**	H	*SE*	RM	73304	79004	78204	73704
375 805	**CN**	H	*SE*	RM	73305	79005	78205	73705
375 806	**CN**	H	*SE*	RM	73306	79006	78206	73706
375 807	**CN**	H	*SE*	RM	73307	79007	78207	73707
375 808	**CN**	H	*SE*	RM	73308	79008	78208	73708
375 809	**CN**	H	*SE*	RM	73309	79009	78209	73709
375 810	**CN**	H	*SE*	RM	73310	79010	78210	73710
375 811	**CN**	H	*SE*	RM	73311	79011	78211	73711
375 812	**CN**	H	*SE*	RM	73312	79012	78212	73712
375 813	**CN**	H	*SE*	RM	73313	79013	78213	73713
375 814	**CN**	H	*SE*	RM	73314	79014	78214	73714
375 815	**CN**	H	*SE*	RM	73315	79015	78215	73715
375 816	**CN**	H	*SE*	RM	73316	79016	78216	73716
375 817	**CN**	H	*SE*	RM	73317	79017	78217	73717
375 818	**CN**	H	*SE*	RM	73318	79018	78218	73718
375 819	**CN**	H	*SE*	RM	73319	79019	78219	73719
375 820	**CN**	H	*SE*	RM	73320	79020	78220	73720
375 821	**CN**	H	*SE*	RM	73321	79021	78221	73721
375 822	**CN**	H	*SE*	RM	73322	79022	78222	73722
375 823	**CN**	H	*SE*	RM	73323	79023	78223	73723
375 824	**CN**	H	*SE*	RM	73324	79024	78224	73724
375 825	**CN**	H	*SE*	RM	73325	79025	78225	73725
375 826	**CN**	H	*SE*	RM	73326	79026	78226	73726
375 827	**CN**	H	*SE*	RM	73327	79027	78227	73727
375 828	**CN**	H	*SE*	RM	73328	79028	78228	73728
375 829	**CN**	H	*SE*	RM	73329	79029	78229	73729
375 830	**CN**	H	*SE*	RM	73330	79030	78230	73730

Name (carried on one side of each MSO or TSO):

375 830   City of London

Class 375/9. Outer suburban units. 750 V DC only. DMCO–MSO–TSO–DMCO.

DMCO(A). Bombardier Derby 2003–2004. 12/59. 43.4 t.
MSO. Bombardier Derby 2003–2004. –/73 1T. 39.3 t.
TSO. Bombardier Derby 2003–2004. –/59 1TD 2W. 35.6 t.
DMCO(B). Bombardier Derby 2003–2004. 12/59. 43.4 t.

375 901	**CN**	H	*SE*	RM	73331	79031	79061	73731
375 902	**CN**	H	*SE*	RM	73332	79032	79062	73732
375 903	**CN**	H	*SE*	RM	73333	79033	79063	73733
375 904	**CN**	H	*SE*	RM	73334	79034	79064	73734
375 905	**CN**	H	*SE*	RM	73335	79035	79065	73735
375 906	**CN**	H	*SE*	RM	73336	79036	79066	73736
375 907	**CN**	H	*SE*	RM	73337	79037	79067	73737
375 908	**CN**	H	*SE*	RM	73338	79038	79068	73738
375 909	**CN**	H	*SE*	RM	73339	79039	79069	73739
375 910	**CN**	H	*SE*	RM	73340	79040	79070	73740
375 911	**CN**	H	*SE*	RM	73341	79041	79071	73741
375 912	**CN**	H	*SE*	RM	73342	79042	79072	73742
375 913	**CN**	H	*SE*	RM	73343	79043	79073	73743
375 914	**CN**	H	*SE*	RM	73344	79044	79074	73744
375 915	**CN**	H	*SE*	RM	73345	79045	79075	73745
375 916	**CN**	H	*SE*	RM	73346	79046	79076	73746
375 917	**CN**	H	*SE*	RM	73347	79047	79077	73747
375 918	**CN**	H	*SE*	RM	73348	79048	79078	73748
375 919	**CN**	H	*SE*	RM	73349	79049	79079	73749
375 920	**CN**	H	*SE*	RM	73350	79050	79080	73750
375 921	**CN**	H	*SE*	RM	73351	79051	79081	73751
375 922	**CN**	H	*SE*	RM	73352	79052	79082	73752
375 923	**CN**	H	*SE*	RM	73353	79053	79083	73753
375 924	**CN**	H	*SE*	RM	73354	79054	79084	73754
375 925	**CN**	H	*SE*	RM	73355	79055	79085	73755
375 926	**CN**	H	*SE*	RM	73356	79056	79086	73756
375 927	**CN**	H	*SE*	RM	73357	79057	79087	73757

CLASS 376   ELECTROSTAR   BOMBARDIER DERBY

South Eastern Trains inner suburban units.

Systems: 750 V DC third rail.
Formation: DMSO–MSO–TSO–MSO–DMSO.
Construction: Welded aluminium alloy underframe, sides and roof with steel ends. All sections bolted together.   **Doors:** Sliding.
Traction Motors: Two Bombardier asynchronous of 250 kW.
Gangways: Within unit.   **Bogies:** Bombardier P3-25/T3-25.
Couplers: Dellner 12.   **Maximum Speed:** 75 m.p.h.
Seating Layout: 2+2 low density facing (with more standee room and greater use of "perch" seats).
Dimensions: 20.40/19.99 x 2.80 m.   **Braking:** Disc & regenerative.
Heating & ventilation: Pressure heating and ventilation.
Multiple Working: Within class and with Classes 375 and 377.

DMSO(A). Bombardier Derby 2004–2005. –/42 1W. 42.1 t.
MSO. Bombardier Derby 2004–2005. –/48. 36.2 t.
TSO. Bombardier Derby 2004–2005. –/48. 36.3 t.
DMSO(B). Bombardier Derby 2004–2005. –/42 1W. 42.1 t.

| 376 001 | **CN** | H | | | 61101 | 63301 | 64301 | 63501 | 61601 |
| 376 002 | **CN** | H | *SE* | SG | 61102 | 63302 | 64302 | 63502 | 61602 |

376 003	**CN**	H	*SE*	SG	61103	63303	64303	63503	61603
376 004	**CN**	H	*SE*	SG	61104	63304	64304	63504	61604
376 005	**CN**	H	*SE*	SG	61105	63305	64305	63505	61605
376 006	**CN**	H	*SE*	SG	61106	63306	64306	63506	61606
376 007	**CN**	H	*SE*	SG	61107	63307	64307	63507	61607
376 008	**CN**	H	*SE*	SG	61108	63308	64308	63508	61608
376 009	**CN**	H	*SE*	SG	61109	63309	64309	63509	61609
376 010	**CN**	H	*SE*	SG	61110	63310	64310	63510	61610
376 011	**CN**	H	*SE*	SG	61111	63311	64311	63511	61611
376 012	**CN**	H	*SE*	SG	61112	63312	64312	63512	61612
376 013	**CN**	H	*SE*	SG	61113	63313	64313	63513	61613
376 014	**CN**	H	*SE*	SG	61114	63314	64314	63514	61614
376 015	**CN**	H	*SE*	SG	61115	63315	64315	63515	61615
376 016	**CN**	H	*SE*	SG	61116	63316	64316	63516	61616
376 017	**CN**	H	*SE*	SG	61117	63317	64317	63517	61617
376 018	**CN**	H	*SE*	SG	61118	63318	64318	63518	61618
376 019	**CN**	H	*SE*	SG	61119	63319	64319	63519	61619
376 020	**CN**	H	*SE*	SG	61120	63320	64320	63520	61620
376 021	**CN**	H	*SE*	SG	61121	63321	64321	63521	61621
376 022	**CN**	H	*SE*	SG	61122	63322	64322	63522	61622
376 023	**CN**	H	*SE*	SG	61123	63323	64323	63523	61623
376 024	**CN**	H	*SE*	SG	61124	63324	64324	63524	61624
376 025	**CN**	H	*SE*	SG	61125	63325	64325	63525	61625
376 026	**CN**	H	*SE*	SG	61126	63326	64326	63526	61626
376 027	**CN**	H	*SE*	SG	61127	63327	64327	63527	61627
376 028	**CN**	H	*SE*	SG	61128	63328	64328	63528	61628
376 029	**CN**	H	*SE*	SG	61129	63329	64329	63529	61629
376 030	**CN**	H			61130	63330	64330	63530	61630
376 031	**CN**	H			61131	63331	64331	63531	61631
376 032	**CN**	H			61132	63332	64332	63532	61632
376 033	**CN**	H			61133	63333	64333	63533	61633
376 034	**CN**	H			61134	63334	64334	63534	61634
376 035	**CN**	H			61135	63335	64335	63535	61635
376 036	**CN**	H			61136	63336	64336	63536	61636

CLASS 377   ELECTROSTAR   BOMBARDIER DERBY

Southern express and outer suburban units.

Systems: 25 kV AC overhead/750 V DC third rail or third rail only with provision for retro-fitting of AC equipment.
Formations: Various.
Construction: Welded aluminium alloy underframe, sides and roof with steel ends. All sections bolted together.   **Doors**: Sliding plug.
Traction Motors: Two Bombardier asynchronous of 250 kW.
Gangways: Throughout.   **Bogies**: Bombardier P3-25/T3-25.
Couplers: Dellner 12.   **Maximum Speed**: 100 m.p.h.
Seating Layout: Various.   **Dimensions**: 20.40/19.99 x 2.80 m.
Braking: Disc & regenerative.
Heating & ventilation: Air conditioning.
Multiple Working: Within class and with Classes 375 and 376.

Class 377/1. 750 V DC only. DMCO–MSO–TSO–DMCO.
Seating layout: 1: 2+2 facing/unidirectional, 2: 2+2 facing/unidirectional
(377 101–377 119), 3+2 and 2+2 facing/unidirectional (377 120–377 164).

DMCO(A). Bombardier Derby 2002–2003. 12/48 (s 12/56, t 12/48). 43.4 t.
MSO. Bombardier Derby 2002–2003. –/66 (s –/70, t –/70). 1T. 39.0 t.
TSO. Bombardier Derby 2002–2003. –/56 (s –/60, t –/54). 1TD 2W. 35.4 t.
DMCO(B). Bombardier Derby 2002–2003. 12/48 (s 12/56, t 12/58). 43.4 t.

377 101		**SN**	P	*SN*	BI	78501	77101	78901	78701
377 102		**SN**	P	*SN*	BI	78502	77102	78902	78702
377 103		**SN**	P	*SN*	BI	78503	77103	78903	78703
377 104		**SN**	P	*SN*	BI	78504	77104	78904	78704
377 105		**SN**	P	*SN*	BI	78505	77105	78905	78705
377 106		**SN**	P	*SN*	BI	78506	77106	78906	78706
377 107		**SN**	P	*SN*	BI	78507	77107	78907	78707
377 108		**SN**	P	*SN*	BI	78508	77108	78908	78708
377 109		**SN**	P	*SN*	BI	78509	77109	78909	78709
377 110		**SN**	P	*SN*	BI	78510	77110	78910	78710
377 111		**SN**	P	*SN*	BI	78511	77111	78911	78711
377 112		**SN**	P	*SN*	BI	78512	77112	78912	78712
377 113		**SN**	P	*SN*	BI	78513	77113	78913	78713
377 114		**SN**	P	*SN*	BI	78514	77114	78914	78714
377 115		**SN**	P	*SN*	BI	78515	77115	78915	78715
377 116		**SN**	P	*SN*	BI	78516	77116	78916	78716
377 117		**SN**	P	*SN*	BI	78517	77117	78917	78717
377 118		**SN**	P	*SN*	BI	78518	77118	78918	78718
377 119		**SN**	P	*SN*	BI	78519	77119	78919	78719
377 120	s	**SN**	P	*SN*	BI	78520	77120	78920	78720
377 121	s	**SN**	P	*SN*	BI	78521	77121	78921	78721
377 122	s	**SN**	P	*SN*	BI	78522	77122	78922	78722
377 123	s	**SN**	P	*SN*	BI	78523	77123	78923	78723
377 124	s	**SN**	P	*SN*	BI	78524	77124	78924	78724
377 125	s	**SN**	P	*SN*	BI	78525	77125	78925	78725
377 126	s	**SN**	P	*SN*	BI	78526	77126	78926	78726
377 127	s	**SN**	P	*SN*	BI	78527	77127	78927	78727
377 128	s	**SN**	P	*SN*	BI	78528	77128	78928	78728
377 129	s	**SN**	P	*SN*	BI	78529	77129	78929	78729
377 130	s	**SN**	P	*SN*	BI	78530	77130	78930	78730
377 131	s	**SN**	P	*SN*	BI	78531	77131	78931	78731
377 132	s	**SN**	P	*SN*	BI	78532	77132	78932	78732
377 133	s	**SN**	P	*SN*	BI	78533	77133	78933	78733
377 134	s	**SN**	P	*SN*	BI	78534	77134	78934	78734
377 135	s	**SN**	P	*SN*	BI	78535	77135	78935	78735
377 136	s	**SN**	P	*SN*	BI	78536	77136	78936	78736
377 137	s	**SN**	P	*SN*	BI	78537	77137	78937	78737
377 138	s	**SN**	P	*SN*	BI	78538	77138	78938	78738
377 139	s	**SN**	P	*SN*	BI	78539	77139	78939	78739
377 140	t	**SN**	P		MW	78540	77140	78940	78740
377 141	t	**SN**	P	*SN*	BI	78541	77141	78941	78741
377 142	t	**SN**	P		MW	78542	77142	78942	78742
377 143	t	**SN**	P		MW	78543	77143	78943	78743

377 144	t	**SN**	P		MW	78544	77144	78944	78744
377 145	t	**SN**	P	_SN_	BI	78545	77145	78945	78745
377 146	t	**SN**	P	_SN_	BI	78546	77146	78946	78746
377 147	t	**SN**	P	_SN_	BI	78547	77147	78947	78747
377 148	t	**SN**	P		MW	78548	77148	78948	78748
377 149	t	**SN**	P	_SN_	BI	78549	77149	78949	78749
377 150	t	**SN**	P	_SN_	BI	78550	77150	78950	78750
377 151	t	**SN**	P	_SN_	BI	78551	77151	78951	78751
377 152	t	**SN**	P	_SN_	BI	78552	77152	78952	78752
377 153	t	**SN**	P	_SN_	BI	78553	77153	78953	78753
377 154	t	**SN**	P	_SN_	BI	78554	77154	78954	78754
377 155	t	**SN**	P	_SN_	BI	78555	77155	78955	78755
377 156	t	**SN**	P	_SN_	BI	78556	77156	78956	78756
377 157	t	**SN**	P		MW	78557	77157	78957	78757
377 158	t	**SN**	P	_SN_	BI	78558	77158	78958	78758
377 159	t	**SN**	P	_SN_	BI	78559	77159	78959	78759
377 160	t	**SN**	P	_SN_	BI	78560	77160	78960	78760
377 161	t	**SN**	P	_SN_	BI	78561	77161	78961	78761
377 162	t	**SN**	P	_SN_	BI	78562	77162	78962	78762
377 163	t	**SN**	P	_SN_	BI	78563	77163	78963	78763
377 164	t	**SN**	P	_SN_	BI	78564	77164	78964	78764

Class 377/2. 25 kV AC/750 V DC. DMCO–MSO–PTSO–DMCO. These dual-voltage units can be used on the Watford Junction–Gatwick Airport/Brighton services.
Seating layout: 1: 2+2 facing/unidirectional, 2: 2+2/3+2 facing/unidirectional (3+2 seating in middle cars).

DMCO(A). Bombardier Derby 2003–2004. 12/48. 44.2 t.
MSO. Bombardier Derby 2003–2004. –/69 1T. 39.8 t.
PTSO. Bombardier Derby 2003–2004. –/57 1TD 2W. 40.1 t.
DMCO(B). Bombardier Derby 2003–2004. 12/48. 44.2 t.

377 201	**SN**	P	_SN_	SU	78571	77171	78971	78771
377 202	**SN**	P	_SN_	SU	78572	77172	78972	78772
377 203	**SN**	P	_SN_	SU	78573	77173	78973	78773
377 204	**SN**	P	_SN_	SU	78574	77174	78974	78774
377 205	**SN**	P	_SN_	SU	78575	77175	78975	78775
377 206	**SN**	P	_SN_	SU	78576	77176	78976	78776
377 207	**SN**	P	_SN_	SU	78577	77177	78977	78777
377 208	**SN**	P	_SN_	SU	78578	77178	78978	78778
377 209	**SN**	P	_SN_	SU	78579	77179	78979	78779
377 210	**SN**	P	_SN_	SU	78580	77180	78980	78780
377 211	**SN**	P	_SN_	SU	78581	77181	78981	78781
377 212	**SN**	P	_SN_	SU	78582	77182	78982	78782
377 213	**SN**	P	_SN_	SU	78583	77183	78983	78783
377 214	**SN**	P	_SN_	SU	78584	77184	78984	78784
377 215	**SN**	P	_SN_	SU	78585	77185	78985	78785

Class 377/3. 750 V DC only. DMCO–TSO–DMCO.
Note: Units built as Class 375, but renumbered in the Class 377/3 range when fitted with Dellner 12 couplers.
Seating Layout: 1: 2+2 facing/unidirectional, 2: 2+2 facing/unidirectional.

DMCO(A). Bombardier Derby 2001–2002. 12/48. 43.5 t.
TSO. Bombardier Derby 2001–2002. –/56 1TD 2W. 35.4 t.
DMCO(B). Bombardier Derby 2001–2002. 12/48. 43.5 t.

377 301	(375 311)	**SN**	P	*SN*	BI	68201	74801	68401
377 302	(375 312)	**SN**	P	*SN*	BI	68202	74802	68402
377 303	(375 313)	**SN**	P	*SN*	BI	68203	74803	68403
377 304	(375 314)	**SN**	P	*SN*	BI	68204	74804	68404
377 305	(375 315)	**SN**	P	*SN*	BI	68205	74805	68405
377 306	(375 316)	**SN**	P	*SN*	BI	68206	74806	68406
377 307	(375 317)	**SN**	P	*SN*	BI	68207	74807	68407
377 308	(375 318)	**SN**	P	*SN*	BI	68208	74808	68408
377 309	(375 319)	**SN**	P	*SN*	BI	68209	74809	68409
377 310	(375 320)	**SN**	P	*SN*	BI	68210	74810	68410
377 311	(375 321)	**SN**	P	*SN*	BI	68211	74811	68411
377 312	(375 322)	**SN**	P	*SN*	BI	68212	74812	68412
377 313	(375 323)	**SN**	P	*SN*	BI	68213	74813	68413
377 314	(375 324)	**SN**	P	*SN*	BI	68214	74814	68414
377 315	(375 325)	**SN**	P	*SN*	BI	68215	74815	68415
377 316	(375 326)	**SN**	P	*SN*	BI	68216	74816	68416
377 317	(375 327)	**SN**	P	*SN*	BI	68217	74817	68417
377 318	(375 328)	**SN**	P	*SN*	BI	68218	74818	68418
377 319	(375 329)	**SN**	P	*SN*	BI	68219	74819	68419
377 320	(375 330)	**SN**	P	*SN*	BI	68220	74820	68420
377 321	(375 331)	**SN**	P	*SN*	BI	68221	74821	68421
377 322	(375 332)	**SN**	P	*SN*	BI	68222	74822	68422
377 323	(375 333)	**SN**	P	*SN*	BI	68223	74823	68423
377 324	(375 334)	**SN**	P	*SN*	BI	68224	74824	68424
377 325	(375 335)	**SN**	P	*SN*	BI	68225	74825	68425
377 326	(375 336)	**SN**	P	*SN*	BI	68226	74826	68426
377 327	(375 337)	**SN**	P	*SN*	BI	68227	74827	68427
377 328	(375 338)	**SN**	P	*SN*	BI	68228	74828	68428

Class 377/4. DMCO–MSO–TSO–DMCO. Units currently on delivery.
Seating Layout: 1: 2+2 facing/unidirectional, 2: 2+2/3+2 facing/unidirectional (3+2 seating in middle cars).

DMCO(A). Bombardier Derby 2004–2005. 10/48. 43.1 t.
MSO. Bombardier Derby 2004–2005. –/69 1T. 39.3 t.
TSO. Bombardier Derby 2004–2005. –/56 1TD 2W. 35.3 t.
DMCO(B). Bombardier Derby 2004–2005. 10/48. 43.1 t.

377 401	**SN**	P	*SN*	BI	73401	78801	78601	73801
377 402	**SN**	P	*SN*	BI	73402	78802	78602	73802
377 403	**SN**	P	*SN*	BI	73403	78803	78603	73803
377 404	**SN**	P	*SN*	BI	73404	78804	78604	73804
377 405	**SN**	P	*SN*	BI	73405	78805	78605	73805
377 406	**SN**	P	*SN*	BI	73406	78806	78606	73806
377 407	**SN**	P	*SN*	BI	73407	78807	78607	73807
377 408	**SN**	P	*SN*	BI	73408	78808	78608	73808
377 409	**SN**	P	*SN*	BI	73409	78809	78609	73809
377 410	**SN**	P	*SN*	BI	73410	78810	78610	73810
377 411	**SN**	P	*SN*	BI	73411	78811	78611	73811

377 412	**SN**	P	*SN*	Bl	73412	78812	78612	73812
377 413	**SN**	P	*SN*	Bl	73413	78813	78613	73813
377 414	**SN**	P	*SN*	Bl	73414	78814	78614	73814
377 415	**SN**	P	*SN*	Bl	73415	78815	78615	73815
377 416	**SN**	P	*SN*	Bl	73416	78816	78616	73816
377 417	**SN**	P	*SN*	Bl	73417	78817	78617	73817
377 418	**SN**	P	*SN*	Bl	73418	78818	78618	73818
377 419	**SN**	P	*SN*	Bl	73419	78819	78619	73819
377 420	**SN**	P	*SN*	Bl	73420	78820	78620	73820
377 421	**SN**	P	*SN*	Bl	73421	78821	78621	73821
377 422	**SN**	P	*SN*	Bl	73422	78822	78622	73822
377 423	**SN**	P	*SN*	Bl	73423	78823	78623	73823
377 424	**SN**	P	*SN*	Bl	73424	78824	78624	73824
377 425	**SN**	P	*SN*	Bl	73425	78825	78625	73825
377 426	**SN**	P	*SN*	Bl	73426	78826	78626	73826
377 427	**SN**	P	*SN*	Bl	73427	78827	78627	73827
377 428	**SN**	P	*SN*	Bl	73428	78828	78628	73828
377 429	**SN**	P	*SN*	Bl	73429	78829	78629	73829
377 430	**SN**	P	*SN*	Bl	73430	78830	78630	73830
377 431	**SN**	P	*SN*	Bl	73431	78831	78631	73831
377 432	**SN**	P	*SN*	Bl	73432	78832	78632	73832
377 433	**SN**	P	*SN*	Bl	73433	78833	78633	73833
377 434	**SN**	P	*SN*	Bl	73434	78834	78634	73834
377 435	**SN**	P	*SN*	Bl	73435	78835	78635	73835
377 436	**SN**	P	*SN*	Bl	73436	78836	78636	73836
377 437	**SN**	P	*SN*	Bl	73437	78837	78637	73837
377 438	**SN**	P	*SN*	Bl	73438	78838	78638	73838
377 439	**SN**	P	*SN*	Bl	73439	78839	78639	73839
377 440	**SN**	P	*SN*	Bl	73440	78840	78640	73840
377 441	**SN**	P	*SN*	Bl	73441	78841	78641	73841
377 442	**SN**	P	*SN*	Bl	73442	78842	78642	73842
377 443	**SN**	P	*SN*	Bl	73443	78843	78643	73843
377 444	**SN**	P	*SN*	Bl	73444	78844	78644	73844
377 445	**SN**	P	*SN*	Bl	73445	78845	78645	73845
377 446	**SN**	P	*SN*	Bl	73446	78846	78646	73846
377 447	**SN**	P	*SN*	Bl	73447	78847	78647	73847
377 448	**SN**	P	*SN*	Bl	73448	78848	78648	73848
377 449	**SN**	P			73449	78849	78649	73849
377 450	**SN**	P			73450	78850	78650	73850
377 451	**SN**	P			73451	78851	78651	73851
377 452	**SN**	P			73452	78852	78652	73852
377 453	**SN**	P			73453	78853	78653	73853
377 454	**SN**	P			73454	78854	78654	73854
377 455	**SN**	P			73455	78855	78655	73855
377 456	**SN**	P			73456	78856	78656	73856
377 457	**SN**	P			73457	78857	78657	73857
377 458	**SN**	P			73458	78858	78658	73858
377 459	**SN**	P			73459	78859	78659	73859
377 460	**SN**	P			73460	78860	78660	73860
377 461	**SN**	P			73461	78861	78661	73861
377 462	**SN**	P			73462	78862	78662	73862

377 463	**SN**	P	73463	78863	78663	73863
377 464	**SN**	P	73464	78864	78664	73864
377 465	**SN**	P	73465	78865	78665	73865
377 466	**SN**	P	73466	78866	78666	73866
377 467	**SN**	P	73467	78867	78667	73867
377 468	**SN**	P	73468	78868	78668	73868
377 469	**SN**	P	73469	78869	78669	73869
377 470	**SN**	P	73470	78870	78670	73870
377 471	**SN**	P	73471	78871	78671	73871
377 472	**SN**	P	73472	78872	78672	73872
377 473	**SN**	P	73473	78873	78673	73873
377 474	**SN**	P	73474	78874	78674	73874
377 475	**SN**	P	73475	78875	78675	73875

CLASS 390 PENDOLINO ALSTOM BIRMINGHAM

Tilting Virgin West Coast units.

Formation: DMRFO–MFO–PTFO–MFO–TSO–MSO–PTSRMB–MSO–DMSO.
Construction: Welded aluminium alloy.
Traction Motors: Two Alstom ONIX 800 of 425 kW.
Doors: Sliding plug.   **Bogies:** Fiat-SIG.
Gangways: Within unit.   **Couplers:** Dellner 12.
Design Speed: 140 m.p.h.   **Maximum Speed:** 125 m.p.h.
Seating Layout: 1: 2+1 facing, 2: 2+2 facing/unidirectional.
Dimensions: 24.80/23.90 x 2.73 m.
Braking: Disc, rheostatic & regenerative.
Heating & ventilation: Air conditioning.
Multiple Working: Within class and with Dellner coupler-fitted Class 57
locomotives.

DMRFO: Alstom Birmingham 2001–2005. 18/–. 55.6 t.
MFO(A): Alstom Birmingham 2001–2005. 39/– 1TD 1W. 52.0 t.
PTFO: Alstom Birmingham 2001–2005. 44/– 1T. 50.1 t.
MFO(B): Alstom Birmingham 2001–2005. 46/– 1T. 51.8 t.
TSO: Alstom Birmingham 2001–2005. –/76 1T. 45.5 t.
MSO(A): Alstom Birmingham 2001–2005. –/66 1TD 1W. 50.0 t.
PTSRMB: Alstom Birmingham 2001–2005. –/48. 52.0 t.
MSO(B): Alstom Birmingham 2001–2005. –/64 1TD 1W. 51.7 t.
DMSO: Alstom Birmingham 2001–2005. –/46 1T. 51.0 t.

Note: Units up to 390 034 were delivered as 8-car sets, without the TSO (688xx).
During 2004 and early 2005 these units had their 9th cars added.

390 001	**VT**	A	*VW*	MA	69101	69401	69501	69601	68801
					69701	69801	69901	69201	
390 002	**VT**	A	*VW*	MA	69102	69402	69502	69602	68802
					69702	69802	69902	69202	
390 003	**VT**	A	*VW*	MA	69103	69403	69503	69603	68803
					69703	69803	69903	69203	
390 004	**VT**	A	*VW*	MA	69104	69404	69504	69604	68804
					69704	69804	69904	69204	

390 005	**VT**	A	*VW*	MA	69105	69405	69505	69605	68805
					69705	69805	69905	69205	
390 006	**VT**	A	*VW*	MA	69106	69406	69506	69606	68806
					69706	69806	69906	69206	
390 007	**VT**	A	*VW*	MA	69107	69407	69507	69607	68807
					69707	69807	69907	69207	
390 008	**VT**	A	*VW*	MA	69108	69408	69508	69608	68808
					69708	69808	69908	69208	
390 009	**VT**	A	*VW*	MA	69109	69409	69509	69609	68809
					69709	69809	69909	69209	
390 010	**VT**	A	*VW*	MA	69110	69410	69510	69610	68810
					69710	69810	69910	69210	
390 011	**VT**	A	*VW*	MA	69111	69411	69511	69611	68811
					69711	69811	69911	69211	
390 012	**VT**	A	*VW*	MA	69112	69412	69512	69612	68812
					69712	69812	69912	69212	
390 013	**VT**	A	*VW*	MA	69113	69413	69513	69613	68813
					69713	69813	69913	69213	
390 014	**VT**	A	*VW*	MA	69114	69414	69514	69614	68814
					69714	69814	69914	69214	
390 015	**VT**	A	*VW*	MA	69115	69415	69515	69615	68815
					69715	69815	69915	69215	
390 016	**VT**	A	*VW*	MA	69116	69416	69516	69616	68816
					69716	69816	69916	69216	
390 017	**VT**	A	*VW*	MA	69117	69417	69517	69617	68817
					69717	69817	69917	69217	
390 018	**VT**	A	*VW*	MA	69118	69418	69518	69618	68818
					69718	69818	69918	69218	
390 019	**VT**	A	*VW*	MA	69119	69419	69519	69619	68819
					69719	69819	69919	69219	
390 020	**VT**	A	*VW*	MA	69120	69420	69520	69620	68820
					69720	69820	69920	69220	
390 021	**VT**	A	*VW*	MA	69121	69421	69521	69621	68821
					69721	69821	69921	69221	
390 022	**VT**	A	*VW*	MA	69122	69422	69522	69622	68822
					69722	69822	69922	69222	
390 023	**VT**	A	*VW*	MA	69123	69423	69523	69623	68823
					69723	69823	69923	69223	
390 024	**VT**	A	*VW*	MA	69124	69424	69524	69624	68824
					69724	69824	69924	69224	
390 025	**VT**	A	*VW*	MA	69125	69425	69525	69625	68825
					69725	69825	69925	69225	
390 026	**VT**	A	*VW*	MA	69126	69426	69526	69626	68826
					69726	69826	69926	69226	
390 027	**VT**	A	*VW*	MA	69127	69427	69527	69627	68827
					69727	69827	69927	69227	
390 028	**VT**	A	*VW*	MA	69128	69428	69528	69628	68828
					69728	69828	69928	69228	
390 029	**VT**	A	*VW*	MA	69129	69429	69529	69629	68829
					69729	69829	69929	69229	

390 030	**VT**	A	*VW*	MA	69130	69430	69530	69630	68830
					69730	69830	69930	69230	
390 031	**VT**	A	*VW*	MA	69131	69431	69531	69631	68831
					69731	69831	69931	69231	
390 032	**VT**	A	*VW*	MA	69132	69432	69532	69632	68832
					69732	69832	69932	69232	
390 033	**VT**	A	*VW*	MA	69133	69433	69533	69633	68833
					69733	69833	69933	69233	
390 034	**VT**	A	*VW*	MA	69134	69434	69534	69634	68834
					69734	69834	69934	69234	
390 035	**VT**	A	*VW*	MA	69135	69435	69535	69635	68835
					69735	69835	69935	69235	
390 036	**VT**	A	*VW*	MA	69136	69436	69536	69636	68836
					69736	69836	69936	69236	
390 037	**VT**	A	*VW*	MA	69137	69437	69537	69637	68837
					69737	69837	69937	69237	
390 038	**VT**	A	*VW*	MA	69138	69438	69538	69638	68838
					69738	69838	69938	69238	
390 039	**VT**	A	*VW*	MA	69139	69439	69539	69639	68839
					69739	69839	69939	69239	
390 040	**VT**	A	*VW*	MA	69140	69440	69540	69640	68840
					69740	69840	69940	69240	
390 041	**VT**	A	*VW*	MA	69141	69441	69541	69641	68841
					69741	69841	69941	69241	
390 042	**VT**	A	*VW*	MA	69142	69442	69542	69642	68842
					69742	69842	69942	69242	
390 043	**VT**	A	*VW*	MA	69143	69443	69543	69643	68843
					69743	69843	69943	69243	
390 044	**VT**	A	*VW*	MA	69144	69444	69544	69644	68844
					69744	69844	69944	69244	
390 045	**VT**	A	*VW*	MA	69145	69445	69545	69645	68845
					69745	69845	69945	69245	
390 046	**VT**	A	*VW*	MA	69146	69446	69546	69646	68846
					69746	69846	69946	69246	
390 047	**VT**	A	*VW*	MA	69147	69447	69547	69647	68847
					69747	69847	69947	69247	
390 048	**VT**	A	*VW*	MA	69148	69448	69548	69648	68848
					69748	69848	69948	69248	
390 049	**VT**	A	*VW*	MA	69149	69449	69549	69649	68849
					69749	69849	69949	69249	
390 050	**VT**	A	*VW*	MA	69150	69450	69550	69650	68850
					69750	69850	69950	69250	
390 051	**VT**	A	*VW*	MA	69151	69451	69551	69651	68851
					69751	69851	69951	69251	
390 052	**VT**	A	*VW*	MA	69152	69452	69552	69652	68852
					69752	69852	69952	69252	
390 053	**VT**	A	*VW*	MA	69153	69453	69553	69653	68853
					69753	69853	69953	69253	

Names (carried on MFO No. 696xx):

390 001	Virgin Pioneer	390 028	City of Preston
390 002	Virgin Angel	390 029	City of Stoke-on-Trent
390 003	Virgin Hero	390 030	City of Edinburgh
390 004	Virgin Scot	390 031	City of Liverpool
390 005	City of Wolverhampton	390 032	City of Birmingham
390 006	Virgin Sun	390 033	City of Glasgow
390 007	Virgin Lady	390 034	City of Carlisle
390 008	Virgin King	390 035	City of Lancaster
390 009	Virgin Queen	390 036	City of Coventry
390 010	Chris Green	390 037	Virgin Difference
390 011	City of Lichfield	390 038	City of London
390 012	Virgin Star	390 039	Virgin Quest
390 013	Virgin Spirit	390 040	Virgin Pathfinder
390 014	City of Manchester	390 041	City of Chester
390 015	Virgin Crusader	390 042	City of Bangor/Dinas Bangor
390 016	Virgin Champion	390 043	Virgin Explorer
390 017	Virgin Prince	390 044	Virgin Lionheart
390 018	Virgin Princess	390 045	Virgin Valiant
390 019	Virgin Warrior	390 046	Virgin Soldiers
390 020	Virgin Cavalier	390 047	Virgin Atlantic
390 021	Virgin Dream	390 048	Virgin Harrier
390 022	Virgin Hope	390 049	Virgin Express
390 023	Virgin Glory	390 050	Virgin Invader
390 024	Virgin Venturer	390 051	Virgin Ambassador
390 025	Virgin Stagecoach	390 052	Virgin Knight
390 026	Virgin Enterprise	390 053	Mission Accomplished
390 027	Virgin Buccaneer		

4.2. 750 V DC THIRD RAIL EMUs

These classes use the third rail system at 750–850 V DC. In addition to the class number, the old SR designations e.g. 4 Vep are quoted. Outer couplings are buckeyes on units built before 1982 with bar couplings within the units. Newer units have Tightlock or Dellner outer couplers. All units of Classes 411, 421 and 423 are scheduled for withdrawal by November 2005, apart from two units to be retained for use on the Lymington line.

CLASS 411/412 BR EASTLEIGH

Units built for the Kent Coast Electrification. Refurbished and fitted with hopper ventilators, "Inter-City 70" seats and fluorescent lighting.

SR designation: 4 Cep.
Formation: DMSO–TBCK–TSO–DMSO.
Construction: Steel. **Doors:** Slam.
Gangways: Throughout. **Electrical Equipment:** 1966-type.
Traction Motors: Two EE507 of 185 kW. **Couplers:** Buckeye.
Bogies: One Mk. 4 († Mark 6) motor bogie (DMSO). Commonwealth († B5 (SR)) trailer bogies.
Maximum Speed: 90 m.p.h. **Dimensions:** 20.18 x 2.82 m.
Seating Layout: 1: Compartments, 2: 2+2 facing (one compartment in TBCK).
Braking: Tread brakes.
Multiple Working: Within class and with Classes 421 and 423.

DMSO (A). –/64. 44.2 t.
TBCK. 24/6 2T. 36.2 t.
TSOL. –/64 2T. 33.8 t.
DMSO (B). –/64. 43.5 t.

Lot numbers and build dates are as follows, all cars being built at Eastleigh:

61355/61372/61373/61384. 30454 1958–1959.
61712/61713/61798/61799/61804/61805. 30619 1960–1961.
70229. 30450 1958.
70294/70300. 30455 1958–1959.
70337/70343/70354. 30456 1958–1959.
70512/70539. 30620 1960–1961.
70561/70607. 30621 1960–1961.

Class 411/5. Standard units.

1697	† **ST**	P	*SE*	RM	61373	70337	70294	61372
1698	† **ST**	P	*SE*	RM	61355	70343	70300	61384
1699	† **ST**	P	*SE*	RM	61712	70561	70512	61713

Class 412/1. "Greyhound" 4 Cep units. Former "Beps" that have had their buffet cars replaced with a TSO.

2311	**ST**	P	*SW*	FR	61804	70607	70539	61805
2315	**ST**	P	*SW*	FR	61798	70354	70229	61799

CLASS 421   BR YORK

Units built for Portsmouth and Brighton lines. Facelifted with new trim and fluorescent lighting in saloons.

SR designation: 3 Cig or 4 Cig.
Formation: DTCso–MBSO–DTCso or DTCso–MBSO–TSO–DTCso.
Construction: Steel.   **Doors:** Slam.
Gangways: Throughout.   **Electrical Equipment:** 1966-type.
Traction Motors: Four EE507 of 185 kW.   **Couplers:** Buckeye.
Bogies: Mark 6 motor bogies (MBSO). B5 (SR) bogies (trailer cars).
Maximum Speed: 90 m.p.h.   **Dimensions:** 20.18 x 2.82 m.
Seating Layout: 1: Compartments, 2: 2+2 facing (plus one four-a-side compartment per DTC).
Braking: Tread brakes.
Multiple Working: Within class and with Classes 411 and 423.

Phase 1 vehicles (only remaining in Class 421/7 units).

70713/70720/70722. TSO. Lot No. 30730 1964–1965. –/72. 31.5 t.

Phase 2 sets.

76562. DTCso(A). Lot No. 30802 1970. 18/36 2T (–/54 2T†, –/60 2T§). 35.5 t.
76581–76608. DTCso(A). Lot No. 30806 1970. 18/36 2T (–/54 2T†, –/60 2T§). 35.5 t.
76721–76782. DTCso(A). Lot No. 30814 1970–1972. 18/36 2T (–/54 2T†, –/60 2T§). 35.5 t.
62278/62286. MBSO. Lot No. 30804 1970. –/56. 49 t.
62287–62314. MBSO. Lot No. 30808 1970. –/56. 49 t.
62359–62420. MBSO. Lot No. 30816 1970. –/56. 49 t.
70969–70992. TSO. Lot No. 30809 1970–1971. –/72. 31.5t.
71039–71100. TSO. Lot No. 30817 1970. –/72. 31.5t.
71928. TSO. Lot No. 30805 1970. –/72. 31.5t.
76572. DTCso(B). Lot No. 30802 1970. 24/28 2T. 35 t.
76613–76636. DTCso(B). Lot No. 30807 1970. 24/28 2T. 35 t.
76792–76853. DTCso(B). Lot No. 30815 1970–1972. 24/28 2T. 35 t.

Notes: DTCso(A) were built with three first class compartments and one standard class compartment. On units marked † the three first class compartments have been declassified, whilst on units marked § all they have been converted to standard.

Class 421/5. Phase 2 units. These sets are known as "Greyhound" units and are fitted with an additional stage of field weakening to improve the maximum attainable speed. This term is traditional on the lines of the former London & South Western railway, as it was formerly applied to their Class T9 4–4–0 express steam locomotives.

1302	**ST**	P	*SW*	FR	76584	62290	70970	76614
1304	**ST**	H	*SW*	FR	76583	62289	70969	76613
1309	**ST**	H	*SW*	FR	76594	62300	70980	76624
1312	**ST**	H	*SW*	FR	76562	62278	71928	76572
1316	**ST**	H	*SW*	FR	76585	62291	70971	76615

Former number of converted buffet car:

71928 (69331)

Class 421/8. "Greyhound" units formed of former Class 422 units with the TRSB replaced by a Class 411/5 TSO.

1392	**ST**	P	*SW*	FR	76811	62378	70273	76740
1393	**ST**	P	*SW*	FR	76746	62384	70527	76817
1395	**ST**	P	*SW*	FR	76850	62417	70662	76779
1396	**ST**	P	*SW*	FR	76803	62370	70531	76732
1397	**ST**	P	*SW*	FR	76749	62387	70515	76820
1398	**ST**	P	*SW*	FR	76819	62386	70292	76748
1399	**ST**	P	*SW*	FR	76747	62385	70508	76818

Class 421/7. Phase 2 units rebuilt at Wessex Traincare/Alstom Eastleigh 1997–1998 for Brighton–Portsmouth "Coastway" line. Compartments opened out, first class seating replaced by standard with a TSO removed. Units still in service had TSOs refitted in 2003, these are Phase 1 vehicles.
SR designation: 4 Cop.
Formation: DTSso–MBSO–TSO–DTSso.
Diagram Numbers: EE245 + ED264 + EE245.
Accommodation: –/60 1T + –/56 1W + –/72 + –/60 1T.

Note: TSOs of units below are owned by Angel.

1404	§	**CX**	P	*SN*	BI	76602	62308	70713	76632
1410	§	**CX**	P	*SN*	BI	76734	62372	70720	76805
1411	§	**CX**	P	*SN*	BI	76570	62286	70722	76580

Class 421/7. South West Trains unit with TSO removed (DTCso–MBSO–DTCso). Generally dedicated to Brockenhurst–Lymington Harbour shuttles.
SR designation: 3 Cig.

1499	**ST**	P	*SW*	BM	76726	62364	76797

Class 421/4. Phase 2 units.

1805	†	**CX**	A	*SN*	BI	76782	62420	71100	76853
1831	†	**CX**	A	*SN*	BI	76598	62304	70984	76628
1851	†	**U**	A	*SN*	BI	76721	62359	71039	76792
1853	†	**U**	A	*SN*	BI	76606	62312	70992	76636
1854	†	**GA**	A	*SN*	BI	76738	62376	71056	76809
1856	†	**GA**	A	*SN*	BI	76739	62377	71057	76810
1858	§	**GA**	A	*SN*	BI	76604	62310	70990	76634
1859	§	**GA**	A	*SN*	BI	76727	62365	71045	76798
1860	§	**GA**	A	*SN*	BI	76752	62390	71070	76823
1861	§	**GA**	A	*SN*	BI	76735	62373	71053	76806
1862	†	**GA**	A	*SN*	BI	76736	62374	71054	76807
1863	†	**CX**	A	*SN*	BI	76742	62380	71060	76813
1864	†	**CX**	A	*SN*	BI	76741	62379	71059	76812
1865	†	**CX**	A	*SN*	BI	76745	62383	71063	76639
1866	†	**CX**	A	*SN*	BI	76743	62381	71061	76814
1867	†	**CX**	A	*SN*	BI	76744	62382	71062	76815
1868	†	**CX**	A	*SN*	BI	76751	62389	71069	76822
1869	†	**CX**	A	*SN*	BI	76753	62391	71071	76804

1881	**ST**	H	*SW*	FR	76762	62400	71080	76833
1882	**ST**	H	*SW*	FR	76765	62403	71083	76836
1883	**ST**	H	*SW*	FR	76764	62402	71082	76835
1884	**ST**	H	*SW*	FR	76767	62405	71085	76838
1888	**ST**	H	*SW*	FR	76773	62411	71091	76844
1890	**ST**	H	*SW*	FR	76775	62413	71093	76846

CLASS 423   BR DERBY/YORK

Outer suburban units. Facelifted with fluorescent lighting.

SR designation: 4 Vep.
Formation: DTCso–MBSO–TSO–DTCso.
Construction: Steel.   **Doors:** Slam.
Gangways: Throughout.   **Electrical Equipment:** 1966-type.
Traction Motors: Four EE507 of 185 kW.   **Couplers:** Buckeye.
Bogies: Two Mk. 4 motor bogies (MBSO). B5 (SR) bogies (trailer cars).
Maximum Speed: 90 m.p.h.   **Dimensions:** 20.18 x 2.82 m.
Seating Layout: 1: Compartments, 2: 3+2 facing or compartments.
Braking: Tread brakes.
Multiple Working: Within class and with Classes 411 and 421.

62121–62139. MBSO. Lot No. 30760 Derby 1967. –/76. 49 t.
62185–62216. MBSO. Lot No. 30773 York 1967–1968. –/76. 49 t.
62217–62266. MBSO. Lot No. 30794 York 1968–1969. –/76. 49 t.
62267–62276. MBSO. Lot No. 30800 York 1970. –/76. 49 t.
62317–62352. MBSO. Lot No. 30813 York 1970–1973. –/76. 49 t.
62435–62475. MBSO. Lot No. 30851 York 1973–1974. –/76. 49 t.
70781–70798. TSO. Lot No. 30759 Derby 1967. –/98. 31.5 t.
70873–70906. TSO. Lot No. 30772 York 1967–1968. –/98. 31.5 t.
70907–70954. TSO. Lot No. 30793 York 1968–1969. –/98. 31.5 t.
70960–70963. TSO. Lot No. 30801 York 1970. –/98. 31.5 t.
70998–71032. TSO. Lot No. 30812 York 1970–1973. –/98. 31.5 t.
71115–71155. TSO. Lot No. 30852 York 1973–1974. –/98. 31.5 t.
76230–76263. DTCso Lot No. 30758 York 1967. 18/46 1T. 35 t.
76335–76402. DTCso. Lot No. 30771 York 1967–1968. 18/46 1T. 35 t.
76441–76536. DTCso. Lot No. 30792 York 1968–1969. 18/46 1T. 35 t.
76547–76554. DTCso. Lot No. 30799 York 1970. 18/46 1T. 35 t.
76643–76712. DTCso. Lot No. 30811 York 1970–1973. 18/46 1T. 35 t.
76861–76942. DTCso. Lot No. 30853 York 1973–1974. 18/46 1T. 35 t.

Class 423/1. Standard units.

3401	**ST**	H	*SW*	WD	76871	62276	70781	76872
3402	**ST**	H	*SW*	WD	76233	62123	70782	76232
3403	**CX**	H	*SN*	BI	76234	62254	70783	76235
3405	**ST**	H	*SW*	WD	76239	62271	70785	76238
3407	**ST**	H	*SW*	WD	76243	62348	70787	76242
3408	**ST**	H	*SW*	WD	76244	62435	70788	76245
3411	**ST**	H	*SW*	WD	76250	62342	70791	76251
3412	**CX**	A	*SE*	RM	76252	62340	70792	76253
3415	**N**	H	*SW*	WD	76258	62462	70795	76259
3416	**CX**	A	*SE*	RM	76261	62451	70796	76260

3417	B	H	SW	WD	76262	62236	70797	76263
3424	CX	A	SE	RM	76354	62185	70882	76353
3434	ST	H	SW	WD	76462	62218	70917	76461
3445	CX	A	SE	RM	76450	62242	70911	76449
3446	CX	A	SE	RM	76532	62243	70952	76531
3447	CX	A	SE	RM	76380	62199	70895	76379
3448	CX	A	SE	RM	76376	62221	70886	76375
3449	CX	A	SE	RM	76336	62205	70873	76335
3450	CX	A	SE	RM	76460	62203	70916	76459
3453	CX	A	SE	RM	76382	62226	70896	76381
3454	CX	A	SE	RM	76390	62200	70798	76389
3456	ST	H	SW	WD	76455	62210	70914	76230
3458	ST	H	SW	WD	76394	62209	70902	76393
3459	ST	H	SW	WD	76396	62224	70903	76395
3466	ST	H	SW	WD	76464	62214	70918	76463
3467	ST	H	SW	WD	76446	62217	70909	76445
3468	ST	H	SW	WD	76448	62267	70910	76447
3470	ST	H	SW	WD	76496	62220	70934	76495
3471	CX	A	SE	RM	76498	62269	70935	76497
3472	CX	A	SE	RM	76500	62244	70936	76499
3474	CX	A	SE	RM	76504	62246	70938	76503
3475	CX	A	SE	RM	76552	62270	70962	76551
3479	CX	H	SN	BI	76655	62272	71004	76656
3481	ST	H	SW	WD	76647	62324	70900	76648
3482	CX	H	SN	BI	76657	62320	71005	76658
3483	CX	H	SN	BI	76661	62233	71007	76662
3484	CX	H	SN	BI	76476	62325	70924	76475
3485	CX	H	SN	BI	76508	62327	70940	76507
3486	CX	H	SN	BI	76478	62234	70925	76477
3487	CX	A	SE	RM	76645	62250	70941	76509
3488	CX	H	SN	BI	76663	62235	71008	76664
3489	CX	H	SN	BI	76665	62251	71009	76666
3490	CX	H	SN	BI	76695	62328	71024	76696
3491	CX	A	SE	RM	76337	62436	70927	76481
3492	CX	A	SE	RM	76667	62344	71010	76668
3494	CX	A	SE	RM	76675	62330	71014	76676
3495	CX	A	SE	RM	76699	62331	71026	76700
3496	CX	A	SE	RM	76673	62334	71013	76674
3497	CX	A	SE	RM	76671	62346	71012	76672
3498	CX	A	SE	RM	76701	62333	71027	76702
3499	CX	A	SE	RM	76901	62347	71135	76902
3500	CX	A	SE	RM	76924	62455	70921	76469
3505	CX	P	SN	BI	76472	62352	70922	76471
3508	ST	H	SW	WD	76643	62273	70998	76644
3511	CX	A	SE	RM	76893	62135	70999	76646
3514	GA	P	SN	BI	76683	62136	71018	76684
3516	ST	H	SW	WD	76693	62268	71023	76694
3520	ST	H	SW	WD	76697	62131	71024	76698
3521	CX	A	SE	RM	76484	62345	70928	76483
3523	CX	H	SN	BI	76651	62139	71002	76652
3524	CX	H	SN	BI	76466	62322	70919	76370

3530	CX	H	SN	BI	76468	62256	70920	76467
3531	CX	H	SN	BI	76649	62230	71001	76650
3535	CX	P	SN	BI	76677	62335	71015	76678
3536	ST	H	SW	WD	76384	62207	70897	76383
3539	ST	H	SW	WD	76862	62122	71115	76861
3540	ST	H	SW	WD	76863	62128	71116	76864
3542	ST	H	SW	WD	76480	62127	70926	76479
3544	CX	A	SE	RM	76892	62454	71124	76894
3545	CX	A	SE	RM	76875	62121	71122	76876
3547	CX	A	SE	RM	76895	62126	71132	76896
3548	CX	A	SE	RM	76903	62452	71136	76904
3553	CX	A	SE	RM	76913	62241	71141	76914
3560	CX	A	SE	RM	76897	62191	71133	76898
3562	CX	A	SE	RM	76907	62129	71138	76908
3564	CX	A	SE	RM	76883	62458	71126	76884
3565	CX	A	SE	RM	76877	62134	71123	76878
3568	CX	A	SE	RM	76887	62440	71128	76888
3569	ST	H	SW	WD	76344	62448	70877	76343
3572	CX	A	SE	RM	76879	62468	71124	76880
3573	CX	A	SE	RM	76919	62444	71145	76920
3574	CX	A	SE	RM	76929	62464	71149	76930
3576	ST	H	SW	WD	76362	62196	70890	76361
3577	CX	A	SE	RM	76933	62459	71151	76934
3579	CX	A	SE	RM	76935	62471	71152	76936
3581	ST	H	SW	WD	76366	62198	70888	76365
3583	CX	A	SE	RM	76937	62450	71153	76938
3584	CX	A	SE	RM	76881	62473	71125	76882
3585	CX	A	SE	RM	76939	62445	71154	76940
3586	CX	A	SE	RM	76921	62474	71122	76922
3587	CX	A	SE	RM	76925	62465	71147	76926
3589	CX	A	SE	RM	76911	62466	71140	76912
3590	CX	A	SE	RM	76941	62460	71155	76942
3591	CX	A	SE	RM	76917	62475	71143	76918
3809	N	P	SW	WD	76516	62253	70944	76515
3810	N	P	SW	WD	76709	62252	71031	76710
3811	N	P	SW	WD	76514	62249	70943	76513
3812	ST	P	SW	WD	76703	62238	71028	76704

Name (carried on MBSO):

3417   Gordon Pettitt

Class 423/8. Reformed Southern units (converted from 4 Vops and 4 Veps).

SR designation: 4 Vip.
Formation: DTCso–MBSO–TSO–DTSso.
DTSso seat –/70 1T.

3821	CX	P	SN	BI	76711	62262	70951	76530
3822	CX	P	SN	BI	76529	62351	71032	76712
3842	CX	P	SN	BI	76519	62343	70887	76363
3843	CX	P	SN	BI	76681	62350	70931	76489
3844	CX	P	SN	BI	76490	62231	71017	76682

Class 423/9. Units converted for "South London Metro" service.

SR designation: 4 Vop.
Formation: DTSso–MBSO–TSO–DTSso.
DTSso seat –/70 1T.

3901	**CX**	P	*SN*	BI	76402	62227	70906	76401
3902	**CX**	P	*SN*	BI	76364	62260	70949	76525
3903	**CX**	P	*SN*	BI	76536	62213	70954	76535
3904	**CX**	P	*SN*	BI	76691	62336	71022	76692
3905	**CX**	P	*SN*	BI	76398	62266	70904	76397
3907	**CX**	P	*SN*	BI	76506	62259	70939	76505
3908	**CX**	P	*SN*	BI	76442	62265	70907	76441
3911	**CX**	P	*SN*	BI	76548	62247	70960	76547
3912	**CX**	P	*SN*	BI	76492	62216	70932	76491
3916	**CX**	P	*SN*	BI	76518	62258	70945	76517
3918	**CX**	P	*SN*	BI	76528	62321	70950	76527
3919	**CX**	P	*SN*	BI	76554	62317	70963	76553

CLASS 442   WESSEX EXPRESS BREL DERBY

Stock built for Waterloo–Bournemouth–Weymouth service. Now also used on certain Portsmouth Harbour services. Can be hauled and heated by any ETH-fitted locomotive.

SR designation: 5 Wes.
Formation: DTFso–TSO–MBRSM–TSO–DTSO.
Construction: Steel.   **Doors:** Sliding plug.
Gangways: Throughout.   **Electrical Equipment:** 1986-type.
Traction Motors: Four EE546 of 300 kW recovered from class 432.
Bogies: Two BREL P7 motor bogies (MBSO). T4 bogies (trailer cars).
Maximum Speed: 100 m.p.h.   **Couplers:** Buckeye.
Seating Layout: 1: 2+2 facing/compartments, 2: 2+2 facing/unidirectional.
Dimensions: 22.15 x 2.74 m.   **Braking:** Tread brakes.
Heating & Ventilation: Air conditioning.
Multiple Working: Within class and with Classes 411, 423 and locos of Classes 33/1 and 73 in emergency.

DTFso. Lot No. 31030 Derby 1988–1989. 50/– 1T. (36 in six compartments and 14 in one saloon). Public Telephone. 34.0 t.
TSO (A). Lot No. 31032 Derby 1988–1989. –/82 2T. 34.0 t.
MBRSM. Lot No. 31034 Derby 1988–1989. Modified Adtranz Crewe 1998. –/52 1W. 55.4 t.
TSO (B). Lot No. 31033 Derby 1988–1989. –/78 2T 1W. 34.0 t.
DTSO. Lot No. 31031 Derby 1988–1989. –/78 1T. 34.0 t.

2401	**SW**	A	*SW*	BM	77382	71818	62937	71842	77406
2402	**SW**	A	*SW*	BM	77383	71819	62938	71843	77407
2403	**SW**	A	*SW*	BM	77384	71820	62941	71844	77408
2404	**SW**	A	*SW*	BM	77385	71821	62939	71845	77409
2405	**SW**	A	*SW*	BM	77386	71822	62944	71846	77410
2406	**SW**	A	*SW*	BM	77389	71823	62942	71847	77411

2407	**SW**	A *SW*	BM	77388	71824	62943	71848	77412
2408	**SW**	A *SW*	BM	77387	71825	62945	71849	77413
2409	**SW**	A *SW*	BM	77390	71826	62946	71850	77414
2410	**SW**	A *SW*	BM	77391	71827	62948	71851	77415
2411	**SW**	A *SW*	BM	77392	71828	62940	71858	77422
2412	**SW**	A *SW*	BM	77393	71829	62947	71853	77417
2413	**SW**	A *SW*	BM	77394	71830	62949	71854	77418
2414	**SW**	A *SW*	BM	77395	71831	62950	71855	77419
2415	**SW**	A *SW*	BM	77396	71832	62951	71856	77420
2416	**SW**	A *SW*	BM	77397	71833	62952	71857	77421
2417	**SW**	A *SW*	BM	77398	71834	62953	71852	77416
2418	**SW**	A *SW*	BM	77399	71835	62954	71859	77423
2419	**SW**	A *SW*	BM	77400	71836	62955	71860	77424
2420	**SW**	A *SW*	BM	77401	71837	62956	71861	77425
2421	**SW**	A *SW*	BM	77402	71838	62957	71862	77426
2422	**SW**	A *SW*	BM	77403	71839	62958	71863	77427
2423	**SW**	A *SW*	BM	77404	71840	62959	71864	77428
2424	**SW**	A *SW*	BM	77405	71841	62960	71865	77429

Names (carried on MBRSM):

2401	BEAULIEU
2402	COUNTY OF HAMPSHIRE
2403	THE NEW FOREST
2404	BOROUGH OF WOKING
2405	CITY OF PORTSMOUTH
2406	VICTORY
2407	THOMAS HARDY
2408	COUNTY OF DORSET
2409	BOURNEMOUTH ORCHESTRAS
2410	MERIDIAN TONIGHT
2411	THE RAILWAY CHILDREN
2412	SPECIAL OLYMPICS
2415	MARY ROSE
2416	MUM IN A MILLION 1997, DOREEN SCANLON
2417	WOKING HOMES
2418	WESSEX CANCER TRUST
2419	BBC SOUTH TODAY
2420	CITY OF SOUTHAMPTON
2422	OPERATION OVERLORD
2423	COUNTY OF SURREY
2424	GERRY NEWSON

CLASS 444   DESIRO UK   SIEMENS

New 5-car South West Trains express units.

Formation: DMCO–TSO–TSO–TSORMB–DMSO.
Construction: Aluminium.   **Doors:** Single-leaf sliding plug.
Traction Motors: 4 Siemens 1TB2016-0GB02 asynchronous of 250 kW.
Gangways: Throughout.   **Bogies:** SGP SF5000.
Couplers: Dellner 12.   **Maximum Speed:** 100 m.p.h.
Seating Layout: 1: 2+1 facing/unidirectional, 2: 2+2 facing/unidirectional.
Dimensions: 23.57 m x 2.80 m.
Braking: Disc and rheostatic.
Heating & Ventilation: Air conditioning.
Multiple Working: Within class and with Class 450.

DMSO. Siemens Wien/Uerdingen 2003–2004. –/76. 52.0 t.
TSO. Siemens Wien/Uerdingen 2003–2004. –/76 1T. 41.0 t.
TSORMB. Siemens Wien/Uerdingen 2003–2004. –/47 1T 1TD 2W. 42.0 t.
DMCO. Siemens Wien/Uerdingen 2003–2004. 35/24. 52.0 t.

444 001	**SW**	A			63801	67101	67151	67201	63851
444 002	**SW**	A			63802	67102	67152	67202	63852
444 003	**SW**	A			63803	67103	67153	67203	63853
444 004	**SW**	A	*SW*	NT	63804	67104	67154	67204	63854
444 005	**SW**	A	*SW*	NT	63805	67105	67155	67205	63855
444 006	**SW**	A			63806	67106	67156	67206	63856
444 007	**SW**	A	*SW*	NT	63807	67107	67157	67207	63857
444 008	**SW**	A	*SW*	NT	63808	67108	67158	67208	63858
444 009	**SW**	A	*SW*	NT	63809	67109	67159	67209	63859
444 010	**SW**	A	*SW*	NT	63810	67110	67160	67210	63860
444 011	**SW**	A	*SW*	NT	63811	67111	67161	67211	63861
444 012	**SW**	A	*SW*	NT	63812	67112	67162	67212	63862
444 013	**SW**	A	*SW*	NT	63813	67113	67163	67213	63863
444 014	**SW**	A	*SW*	NT	63814	67114	67164	67214	63864
444 015	**SW**	A	*SW*	NT	63815	67115	67165	67215	63865
444 016	**SW**	A	*SW*	NT	63816	67116	67166	67216	63866
444 017	**SW**	A	*SW*	NT	63817	67117	67167	67217	63867
444 018	**SW**	A	*SW*	NT	63818	67118	67168	67218	63868
444 019	**SW**	A	*SW*	NT	63819	67119	67169	67219	63869
444 020	**SW**	A	*SW*	NT	63820	67120	67170	67220	63870
444 021	**SW**	A	*SW*	NT	63821	67121	67171	67221	63871
444 022	**SW**	A	*SW*	NT	63822	67122	67172	67222	63872
444 023	**SW**	A	*SW*	NT	63823	67123	67173	67223	63873
444 024	**SW**	A	*SW*	NT	63824	67124	67174	67224	63874
444 025	**SW**	A	*SW*	NT	63825	67125	67175	67225	63875
444 026	**SW**	A	*SW*	NT	63826	67126	67176	67226	63876
444 027	**SW**	A	*SW*	NT	63827	67127	67177	67227	63877
444 028	**SW**	A	*SW*	NT	63828	67128	67178	67228	63878
444 029	**SW**	A	*SW*	NT	63829	67129	67179	67229	63879
444 030	**SW**	A	*SW*	NT	63830	67130	67180	67230	63880
444 031	**SW**	A	*SW*	NT	63831	67131	67181	67231	63881

444 032	SW	A			63832	67132	67182	67232	63882
444 032	SW	A			63832	67132	67182	67232	63882
444 033	SW	A	SW	NT	63833	67133	67183	67233	63883
444 034	SW	A			63834	67134	67184	67234	63884
444 035	SW	A			63835	67135	67185	67235	63885
444 036	SW	A	SW	NT	63836	67136	67186	67236	63886
444 037	SW	A	SW	NT	63837	67137	67187	67237	63887
444 038	SW	A			63838	67138	67188	67238	63888
444 039	SW	A	SW	NT	63839	67139	67189	67239	63889
444 040	SW	A	SW	NT	63840	67140	67190	67240	63890
444 041	SW	A			63841	67141	67191	67241	63891
444 042	SW	A			63842	67142	67192	67242	63892
444 043	SW	A			63843	67143	67193	67243	63893
444 044	SW	A			63844	67144	67194	67244	63894
444 045	SW	A			63845	67145	67195	67245	63895

Names (carried on TSORMB):

444 018 THE FAB 444

CLASS 450   DESIRO UK   SIEMENS

New 4-car South West Trains outer suburban units.

Formation: DMSO–TCO–TSO–DMSO.
Construction: Aluminium.   **Doors:** Sliding plug.
Traction Motors: 4 Siemens 1TB2016-0GB02 asynchronous of 250 kW.
Gangways: Throughout.   **Bogies:** SGP SF5000.
Couplers: Dellner 12.   **Maximum Speed:** 100 m.p.h.
Seating Layout: 1: 2+2 facing/unidirectional, 2: 3+2 facing/unidirectional.
Dimensions: 20.34 x 2.80 m.
Braking: Disc and rheostatic.
Heating & Ventilation: Air conditioning.
Multiple Working: Within class and with Class 444.

DMSO(A). Siemens Uerdingen/Wien 2002–2004. –/70. 46.0 t.
TCO. Siemens Uerdingen/Wien 2002–2004. 24/36 1T. 35.0 t.
TSO. Siemens Uerdingen/Wien 2002–2004. –/70 1TD 2W. 35.0 t.
DMSO(B). Siemens Uerdingen/Wien 2002–2004. –/70. 46.0 t.

450 001	SD	A			63201	64201	68101	63601
450 002	SD	A	SW	NT	63202	64202	68102	63602
450 003	SD	A	SW	NT	63203	64203	68103	63603
450 004	SD	A	SW	NT	63204	64204	68104	63604
450 005	SD	A	SW	NT	63205	64205	68105	63605
450 006	SD	A	SW	NT	63206	64206	68106	63606
450 007	SD	A	SW	NT	63207	64207	68107	63607
450 008	SD	A	SW	NT	63208	64208	68108	63608
450 009	SD	A	SW	NT	63209	64209	68109	63609
450 010	SD	A	SW	NT	63210	64210	68110	63610
450 011	SD	A	SW	NT	63211	64211	68111	63611
450 012	SD	A	SW	NT	63212	64212	68112	63612
450 013	SD	A	SW	NT	63213	64213	68113	63613
450 014	SD	A	SW	NT	63214	64214	68114	63614

450 015	**SD**	A	*SW*	NT	63215	64215	68115	63615
450 016	**SD**	A	*SW*	NT	63216	64216	68116	63616
450 017	**SD**	A	*SW*	NT	63217	64217	68117	63617
450 018	**SD**	A	*SW*	NT	63218	64218	68118	63618
450 019	**SD**	A	*SW*	NT	63219	64219	68119	63619
450 020	**SD**	A	*SW*	NT	63220	64220	68120	63620
450 021	**SD**	A	*SW*	NT	63221	64221	68121	63621
450 022	**SD**	A	*SW*	NT	63222	64222	68122	63622
450 023	**SD**	A	*SW*	NT	63223	64223	68123	63623
450 024	**SD**	A	*SW*	NT	63224	64224	68124	63624
450 025	**SD**	A	*SW*	NT	63225	64225	68125	63625
450 026	**SD**	A	*SW*	NT	63226	64226	68126	63626
450 027	**SD**	A	*SW*	NT	63227	64227	68127	63627
450 028	**SD**	A	*SW*	NT	63228	64228	68128	63628
450 029	**SD**	A	*SW*	NT	63229	64229	68129	63629
450 030	**SD**	A	*SW*	NT	63230	64230	68130	63630
450 031	**SD**	A	*SW*	NT	63231	64231	68131	63631
450 032	**SD**	A	*SW*	NT	63232	64232	68132	63632
450 033	**SD**	A	*SW*	NT	63233	64233	68133	63633
450 034	**SD**	A	*SW*	NT	63234	64234	68134	63634
450 035	**SD**	A	*SW*	NT	63235	64235	68135	63635
450 036	**SD**	A	*SW*	NT	63236	64236	68136	63636
450 037	**SD**	A	*SW*	NT	63237	64237	68137	63637
450 038	**SD**	A	*SW*	NT	63238	64238	68138	63638
450 039	**SD**	A	*SW*	NT	63239	64239	68139	63639
450 040	**SD**	A	*SW*	NT	63240	64240	68140	63640
450 041	**SD**	A	*SW*	NT	63241	64241	68141	63641
450 042	**SD**	A	*SW*	NT	63242	64242	68142	63642
450 043	**SD**	A	*SW*	NT	63243	64243	68143	63643
450 044	**SD**	A	*SW*	NT	63244	64244	68144	63644
450 045	**SD**	A	*SW*	NT	63245	64245	68145	63645
450 046	**SD**	A	*SW*	NT	63246	64246	68146	63646
450 047	**SD**	A	*SW*	NT	63247	64247	68147	63647
450 048	**SD**	A	*SW*	NT	63248	64248	68148	63648
450 049	**SD**	A	*SW*	NT	63249	64249	68149	63649
450 050	**SD**	A	*SW*	NT	63250	64250	68150	63650
450 051	**SD**	A	*SW*	NT	63251	64251	68151	63651
450 052	**SD**	A	*SW*	NT	63252	64252	68152	63652
450 053	**SD**	A	*SW*	NT	63253	64253	68153	63653
450 054	**SD**	A	*SW*	NT	63254	64254	68154	63654
450 055	**SD**	A	*SW*	NT	63255	64255	68155	63655
450 056	**SD**	A	*SW*	NT	63256	64256	68156	63656
450 057	**SD**	A	*SW*	NT	63257	64257	68157	63657
450 058	**SD**	A	*SW*	NT	63258	64258	68158	63658
450 059	**SD**	A	*SW*	NT	63259	64259	68159	63659
450 060	**SD**	A	*SW*	NT	63260	64260	68160	63660
450 061	**SD**	A	*SW*	NT	63261	64261	68161	63661
450 062	**SD**	A	*SW*	NT	63262	64262	68162	63662
450 063	**SD**	A	*SW*	NT	63263	64263	68163	63663
450 064	**SD**	A	*SW*	NT	63264	64264	68164	63664
450 065	**SD**	A	*SW*	NT	63265	64265	68165	63665

450 066	**SD**	A	*SW*	NT	63266	64266	68166	63666
450 067	**SD**	A	*SW*	NT	63267	64267	68167	63667
450 068	**SD**	A	*SW*	NT	63268	64268	68168	63668
450 069	**SD**	A	*SW*	NT	63269	64269	68169	63669
450 070	**SD**	A	*SW*	NT	63270	64270	68170	63670
450 071	**SD**	A	*SW*	NT	63271	64271	68171	63671
450 072	**SD**	A	*SW*	NT	63272	64272	68172	63672
450 073	**SD**	A	*SW*	NT	63273	64273	68173	63673
450 074	**SD**	A	*SW*	NT	63274	64274	68174	63674
450 075	**SD**	A	*SW*	NT	63275	64275	68175	63675
450 076	**SD**	A	*SW*	NT	63276	64276	68176	63676
450 077	**SD**	A	*SW*	NT	63277	64277	68177	63677
450 078	**SD**	A	*SW*	NT	63278	64278	68178	63678
450 079	**SD**	A	*SW*	NT	63279	64279	68179	63679
450 080	**SD**	A	*SW*	NT	63280	64280	68180	63680
450 081	**SD**	A	*SW*	NT	63281	64281	68181	63681
450 082	**SD**	A	*SW*	NT	63282	64282	68182	63682
450 083	**SD**	A	*SW*	NT	63283	64283	68183	63683
450 084	**SD**	A	*SW*	NT	63284	64284	68184	63684
450 085	**SD**	A	*SW*	NT	63285	64285	68185	63685
450 086	**SD**	A	*SW*	NT	63286	64286	68186	63686
450 087	**SD**	A	*SW*	NT	63287	64287	68187	63687
450 088	**SD**	A	*SW*	NT	63288	64288	68188	63688
450 089	**SD**	A	*SW*	NT	63289	64289	68189	63689
450 090	**SD**	A	*SW*	NT	63290	64290	68190	63690
450 091	**SD**	A			63291	64291	68191	63691
450 092	**SD**	A	*SW*	NT	63292	64292	68192	63692
450 093	**SD**	A	*SW*	NT	63293	64293	68193	63693
450 094	**SD**	A	*SW*	NT	63294	64294	68194	63694
450 095	**SD**	A	*SW*	NT	63295	64295	68195	63695
450 096	**SD**	A	*SW*	NT	63296	64296	68196	63696
450 097	**SD**	A	*SW*	NT	63297	64297	68197	63697
450 098	**SD**	A	*SW*	NT	63298	64298	68198	63698
450 099	**SD**	A	*SW*	NT	63299	64299	68199	63699
450 100	**SD**	A	*SW*	NT	63300	64300	68200	63700
450 101	**SD**	A			63701	66851	66801	63751
450 102	**SD**	A	*SW*	NT	63702	66852	66802	63752
450 103	**SD**	A	*SW*	NT	63703	66853	66803	63753
450 104	**SD**	A	*SW*	NT	63704	66854	66804	63754
450 105	**SD**	A			63705	66855	66805	63755
450 106	**SD**	A			63706	66856	66806	63756
450 107	**SD**	A	*SW*	NT	63707	66857	66807	63757
450 108	**SD**	A			63708	66858	66808	63758
450 109	**SD**	A			63709	66859	66809	63759
450 110	**SD**	A			63710	66860	66810	63760

Names (carried on DMSO(B)):

450 015   DESIRO
450 042   TRELOAR COLLEGE

CLASS 455   BR YORK

South West Trains/Southern inner suburban units.

Formation: DTSO–MSO–TSO–DTSO.
Construction: Steel. Class 455/7 TSO have a steel underframe and an aluminium alloy body & roof.
Doors: Sliding.
Gangways: Within unit + end doors.   **Electrical Equipment:** 1966-type.
Traction Motors: Four GEC507-20J of 185 kW some recovered from Class 405.
Bogies: P7 (motor) and T3 (455/8 & 455/9) BX1 (455/7) trailer.
Couplers: Tightlock.   **Braking:** Disc brakes.
Maximum Speed: 75 m.p.h.
Seating Layout: 3+2 facing unless shown.
Dimensions: 20.28/20.18 x 2.82 m.
Heating & Ventilation: Various.
Multiple Working: Within class and with Class 456.

Notes: Southern refurbished units (shown as "t") have been fitted with in-cab air conditioning systems meaning that the end door has been sealed up. Seating layout of Southern refurbished units remains 3+2 facing, but with high-back seats. Wheelchair spaces have been put in.

South West Trains refurbished units (shown as "s") have 2+2 facing/unidirectional seating layout, including tip-up and "perch" seating.

Class 455/7. Second series with TSOs originally in Class 508. Pressure heating and ventilation.

DTSO. Lot No. 30976 1984–1985. –/74 (s –/54 1W). 29.5 t.
MSO. Lot No. 30975 1984–1985. –/84 (s –/68). 45.5 t.
TSO. Lot No. 30944 1977–1980. –/86 (s –/68). 25.5 t.

5701		**ST**	P	*SW*	WD	77727	62783	71545	77728
5702		**ST**	P	*SW*	WD	77729	62784	71547	77730
5703		**ST**	P	*SW*	WD	77731	62785	71540	77732
5704		**ST**	P	*SW*	WD	77733	62786	71548	77734
5705	s	**SS**	P	*SW*	WD	77735	62787	71565	77736
5706		**ST**	P	*SW*	WD	77737	62788	71534	77738
5707	s	**SS**	P	*SW*	WD	77739	62789	71536	77740
5708		**ST**	P	*SW*	WD	77741	62790	71560	77742
5709		**N**	P	*SW*	WD	77743	62791	71532	77744
5710		**ST**	P	*SW*	WD	77745	62792	71566	77746
5711	s	**SS**	P	*SW*	WD	77747	62793	71542	77748
5712		**ST**	P	*SW*	WD	77749	62794	71546	77750
5713		**N**	P	*SW*	WD	77751	62795	71567	77752
5714		**ST**	P	*SW*	WD	77753	62796	71539	77754
5715		**ST**	P	*SW*	WD	77755	62797	71535	77756
5716		**ST**	P	*SW*	WD	77757	62798	71564	77758
5717		**ST**	P	*SW*	WD	77759	62799	71528	77760
5718		**ST**	P	*SW*	WD	77761	62800	71557	77762
5719		**ST**	P	*SW*	WD	77763	62801	71558	77764
5720		**ST**	P	*SW*	WD	77765	62802	71568	77766

5721	**ST**	P	*SW*	WD	77767	62803	71553	77768
5722	**ST**	P	*SW*	WD	77769	62804	71533	77770
5723	**ST**	P	*SW*	WD	77771	62805	71526	77772
5724	**ST**	P	*SW*	WD	77773	62806	71561	77774
5725	**ST**	P	*SW*	WD	77775	62807	71541	77776
5726	**ST**	P	*SW*	WD	77777	62808	71556	77778
5727	**ST**	P	*SW*	WD	77779	62809	71562	77780
5728	**ST**	P	*SW*	WD	77781	62810	71527	77782
5729	**ST**	P	*SW*	WD	77783	62811	71550	77784
5730	**ST**	P	*SW*	WD	77785	62812	71551	77786
5731	**ST**	P	*SW*	WD	77787	62813	71555	77788
5732	**ST**	P	*SW*	WD	77789	62814	71552	77790
5733	s **SS**	P	*SW*	WD	77791	62815	71549	77792
5734	**ST**	P	*SW*	WD	77793	62816	71531	77794
5735	**ST**	P	*SW*	WD	77795	62817	71563	77796
5736	**ST**	P	*SW*	WD	77797	62818	71554	77798
5737	**ST**	P	*SW*	WD	77799	62819	71544	77800
5738	**ST**	P	*SW*	WD	77801	62820	71529	77802
5739	**ST**	P	*SW*	WD	77803	62821	71537	77804
5740	**ST**	P	*SW*	WD	77805	62822	71530	77806
5741	**ST**	P	*SW*	WD	77807	62823	71559	77808
5742	**ST**	P	*SW*	WD	77809	62824	71543	77810
5750	**ST**	P	*SW*	WD	77811	62825	71538	77812

Names (carried on TSO):

5731	VARIETY CLUB
5735	The Royal Borough of Kingston
5750	Wimbledon Train Care

Class 455/8. First series. Pressure heating and ventilation.

DTSO. Lot No. 30972 York 1982–1984. –/74 (s –/54 1W). 29.5 t.
MSO. Lot No. 30973 York 1982–1984. –/84 (s –/68, t –/78 2W). 50.0 t.
TSO. Lot No. 30974 York 1982–1984. –/84. (s –/68). 28.0 t.

Advertising Liveries: 5853 Cotes du Rhone wine (All over deep red with various images).
5856 Legoland Windsor (Yellow, blue and red with various images).
5868 Golden Jubilee/Hampton Court Palace (Gold with various images).
5869 Royal British Legion poppy appeal (white with poppy images).

455 801	**CX**	H	*SN*	SU	77579	62709	71637	77580
5802	**CX**	H	*SN*	SU	77581	62710	71664	77582
5803	**CX**	H	*SN*	SU	77583	62711	71639	77584
5804	**CX**	H	*SN*	SU	77585	62712	71640	77586
5805	**CX**	H	*SN*	SU	77587	62713	71641	77588
5806	**CX**	H	*SN*	SU	77589	62714	71642	77590
5807	**CX**	H	*SN*	SU	77591	62715	71643	77592
455 808	**SN**	H	*SN*	SU	77593	62716	71644	77594
455 809	**SN**	H	*SN*	SU	77595	62717	71645	77596
5810	**CX**	H	*SN*	SU	77597	62718	71646	77598
5811	**CX**	H	*SN*	SU	77599	62719	71647	77600
455 812	**SN**	H	*SN*	SU	77601	62720	71648	77602

455 813	SN		H	*SN*	SU	77603	62721	71649	77604
5814	CX		H	*SN*	SU	77605	62722	71650	77606
5815	CX		H	*SN*	SU	77607	62723	71651	77608
455 816	t	SN	H	*SN*	SU	77609	62724	71652	77633
455 817	t	SN	H	*SN*	SU	77611	62725	71653	77612
5818	CX		H	*SN*	SU	77613	62726	71654	77614
455 819	SN		H	*SN*	SU	77615	62727	71655	77616
455 820	t	SN	H	*SN*	SU	77617	62728	71656	77618
5821	CX		H	*SN*	SU	77619	62729	71657	77620
5822	CX		H	*SN*	SU	77621	62730	71658	77622
455 823	SN		H	*SN*	SU	77623	62731	71659	77624
455 824	SN		H	*SN*	SU	77637	62732	71660	77626
455 825	SN		H	*SN*	SU	77627	62733	71661	77628
455 826	t	SN	H	*SN*	SU	77629	62734	71662	77630
5827	CX		H	*SN*	SU	77610	62735	71663	77632
455 828	t	SN	H	*SN*	SU	77631	62736	71638	77634
455 829	t	SN	H	*SN*	SU	77635	62737	71665	77636
455 830	t	SN	H	*SN*	SU	77625	62743	71666	77638
455 831	t	SN	H	*SN*	SU	77639	62739	71667	77640
5832	U		H	*SN*	SU	77641	62740	71668	77642
455 833	t	SN	H	*SN*	SU	77643	62741	71669	77644
455 834	t	SN	H	*SN*	SU	77645	62742	71670	77646
455 835	SN		H	*SN*	SU	77647	62738	71671	77648
455 836	t	SN	H	*SN*	SU	77649	62744	71672	77650
455 837	t	SN	H	*SN*	SU	77651	62745	71673	77652
455 838	SN		H	*SN*	SU	77653	62746	71674	77654
5839	N		H	*SN*	SU	77655	62747	71675	77656
455 840	t	SN	H	*SN*	SU	77657	62748	71676	77658
455 841	SN		H	*SN*	SU	77659	62749	71677	77660
5842	N		H	*SN*	SU	77661	62750	71678	77662
5843	N		H	*SN*	SU	77663	62751	71679	77664
5844	N		H	*SN*	SU	77665	62752	71680	77666
455 845	t	SN	H	*SN*	SU	77667	62753	71681	77668
5846	N		H	*SN*	SU	77669	62754	71682	77670
5847	ST		P	*SW*	WD	77671	62755	71683	77672
5848	ST		P	*SW*	WD	77673	62756	71684	77674
5849	ST		P	*SW*	WD	77675	62757	71685	77676
5850	ST		P	*SW*	WD	77677	62758	71686	77678
5851	ST		P	*SW*	WD	77679	62759	71687	77680
5852	ST		P	*SW*	WD	77681	62760	71688	77682
5853	AL		P	*SW*	WD	77683	62761	71689	77684
5854	ST		P	*SW*	WD	77685	62762	71690	77686
5855	ST		P	*SW*	WD	77687	62763	71691	77688
5856	AL		P	*SW*	WD	77689	62764	71692	77690
5857	ST		P	*SW*	WD	77691	62765	71693	77692
5858	ST		P	*SW*	WD	77693	62766	71694	77694
5859	ST		P	*SW*	WD	77695	62767	71695	77696
5860	ST		P	*SW*	WD	77697	62768	71696	77698
5861	ST		P	*SW*	WD	77699	62769	71697	77700
5862	ST		P	*SW*	WD	77701	62770	71698	77702
5863	ST		P	*SW*	WD	77703	62771	71699	77704

5864	**ST**	P	*SW*	WD	77705	62772	71700	77706
5865	**ST**	P	*SW*	WD	77707	62773	71701	77708
5866	**ST**	P	*SW*	WD	77709	62774	71702	77710
5867	**ST**	P	*SW*	WD	77711	62775	71703	77712
5868	**AL**	P	*SW*	WD	77713	62776	71704	77714
5869	**AL**	P	*SW*	WD	77715	62777	71705	77716
5870	**ST**	P	*SW*	WD	77717	62778	71706	77718
5871	**ST**	P	*SW*	WD	77719	62779	71707	77720
5872	**ST**	P	*SW*	WD	77721	62780	71708	77722
5873	**ST**	P	*SW*	WD	77723	62781	71709	77724
5874	**ST**	P	*SW*	WD	77725	62782	71710	77726

Class 455/9. Third series. Convection heating.

DTSO. Lot No. 30991 York 1985. –/74 (s –/54 1W). 29.0 t.
MSO. Lot No. 30992 York 1985. –/84 (s –/68). 45.5 t.
TSO. Lot No. 30993 York 1985. –/84 (s –/68). 27.1 t.
TSO†. Lot No. 30932 Derby 1981. –/84. 26.5 t.

Note: † Prototype vehicle 67400 converted from a Class 210 DEMU.

5901		**ST**	P	*SW*	WD	77813	62826	71714	77814
5902		**ST**	P	*SW*	WD	77815	62827	71715	77816
5903		**ST**	P	*SW*	WD	77817	62828	71716	77818
5904	s	**SS**	P	*SW*	WD	77819	62829	71717	77820
5905		**ST**	P	*SW*	WD	77821	62830	71725	77822
5906		**ST**	P	*SW*	WD	77823	62831	71719	77824
5907		**ST**	P	*SW*	WD	77825	62832	71720	77826
5908		**ST**	P	*SW*	WD	77827	62833	71721	77828
5909		**ST**	P	*SW*	WD	77829	62834	71722	77830
5910		**ST**	P	*SW*	WD	77831	62835	71723	77832
5911		**ST**	P	*SW*	WD	77833	62836	71724	77834
5912	†	**ST**	P	*SW*	WD	77835	62837	67400	77836
5913		**ST**	P	*SW*	WD	77837	62838	71726	77838
5914		**ST**	P	*SW*	WD	77839	62839	71727	77840
5915		**ST**	P	*SW*	WD	77841	62840	71728	77842
5916		**ST**	P	*SW*	WD	77843	62841	71729	77844
5917		**ST**	P	*SW*	WD	77845	62842	71730	77846
5918		**ST**	P	*SW*	WD	77847	62843	71732	77848
5919		**ST**	P	*SW*	WD	77849	62844	71718	77850
5920		**ST**	P	*SW*	WD	77851	62845	71733	77852

CLASS 456   BREL YORK

Southern inner suburban units.

Formation: DMSO–DTSO.
Construction: Steel underframe, aluminium alloy body & roof.
Doors: Sliding.
Gangways: Within unit.   **Electrical Equipment:** 1966-type.
Traction Motors: Two GEC507-20J of 185 kW some recovered from Class 405.
Bogies: P7 (motor) and T3 (trailer).   **Couplers:** Tightlock.
Maximum Speed: 75 m.p.h.   **Seating Layout:** 3+2 facing.

Dimensions: 20.61 x 2.82 m.   **Braking:** Disc brakes.
Heating & Ventilation: Convection heating.
Multiple class Working: Within class and with Class 455.

DMSO. Lot No. 31073 1990–1991. –/79. 41.1 t.
DTSO. Lot No. 31074 1990–1991. –/73 1T. 31.4 t.

456 001	**N**	P	*SN*	SU	64735	78250
456 002	**N**	P	*SN*	SU	64736	78251
456 003	**N**	P	*SN*	SU	64737	78252
456 004	**N**	P	*SN*	SU	64738	78253
456 005	**N**	P	*SN*	SU	64739	78254
456 006	**N**	P	*SN*	SU	64740	78255
456 007	**N**	P	*SN*	SU	64741	78256
456 008	**N**	P	*SN*	SU	64742	78257
456 009	**N**	P	*SN*	SU	64743	78258
456 010	**N**	P	*SN*	SU	64744	78259
456 011	**N**	P	*SN*	SU	64745	78260
456 012	**N**	P	*SN*	SU	64746	78261
456 013	**N**	P	*SN*	SU	64747	78262
456 014	**N**	P	*SN*	SU	64748	78263
456 015	**N**	P	*SN*	SU	64749	78264
456 016	**N**	P	*SN*	SU	64750	78265
456 017	**N**	P	*SN*	SU	64751	78266
456 018	**N**	P	*SN*	SU	64752	78267
456 019	**N**	P	*SN*	SU	64753	78268
456 020	**N**	P	*SN*	SU	64754	78269
456 021	**N**	P	*SN*	SU	64755	78270
456 022	**N**	P	*SN*	SU	64756	78271
456 023	**N**	P	*SN*	SU	64757	78272
456 024	**CX**	P	*SN*	SU	64758	78273

Name (carried on DTSO): 456 024 Sir Cosmo Bonsor.

CLASS 458   JUNIPER   ALSTOM BIRMINGHAM

South West Trains outer suburban units.

Formation: DMCO–PTSO–MSO–DMCO.
SR designation: 4 Jop.
Construction: Steel.   **Doors:** Sliding plug.
Gangways: Throughout.   **Electrical Equipment:** IGBT control.
Traction Motors: Two Alstom ONIX 800 asynchronous of 270 kW.
Couplers: Scharfenberg.   **Bogies:** ACR.
Maximum Speed: 100 m.p.h.   **Dimensions:** 21.16/19.94 x 2.80 m.
Seating Layout: 1: 2+2 facing, 2: 3+2 facing/unidirectional.
Braking: Disc and regenerative brakes.**Multiple Working:** Within class.
Heating & Ventilation: Air conditioning.

DMCO(A). Alstom 1998–2000. 12/63. 45.2 t.
PTSO. Alstom 1998–2000. –/49 1TD 2W. 33.3 t.
MSO. Alstom 1998–2000. –/75 1T. 40.6 t.
DMCO(B). Alstom 1998–2000. 12/63. 45.2 t.

8001	**SW**	P	*SW*	WD	67601	74001	74101	67701
8002	**SW**	P	*SW*	WD	67602	74002	74102	67702
8003	**SW**	P	*SW*	WD	67603	74003	74103	67703
8004	**SW**	P	*SW*	WD	67604	74004	74104	67704
8005	**SW**	P	*SW*	WD	67605	74005	74105	67705
8006	**SW**	P	*SW*	WD	67606	74006	74106	67706
8007	**SW**	P	*SW*	WD	67607	74007	74107	67707
8008	**SW**	P	*SW*	WD	67608	74008	74108	67708
8009	**SW**	P	*SW*	WD	67609	74009	74109	67709
8010	**SW**	P	*SW*	WD	67610	74010	74110	67710
8011	**SW**	P	*SW*	WD	67611	74011	74111	67711
8012	**SW**	P	*SW*	WD	67612	74012	74112	67712
8013	**SW**	P	*SW*	WD	67613	74013	74113	67713
8014	**SW**	P	*SW*	WD	67614	74014	74114	67714
8015	**SW**	P	*SW*	WD	67615	74015	74115	67715
8016	**SW**	P	*SW*	WD	67616	74016	74116	67716
8017	**SW**	P	*SW*	WD	67617	74017	74117	67717
8018	**SW**	P	*SW*	WD	67618	74018	74118	67718
8019	**SW**	P	*SW*	WD	67619	74019	74119	67719
8020	**SW**	P	*SW*	WD	67620	74020	74120	67720
8021	**SW**	P	*SW*	WD	67621	74021	74121	67721
8022	**SW**	P	*SW*	WD	67622	74022	74122	67722
8023	**SW**	P	*SW*	WD	67623	74023	74123	67723
8024	**SW**	P	*SW*	WD	67624	74024	74124	67724
8025	**SW**	P	*SW*	WD	67625	74025	74125	67725
8026	**SW**	P	*SW*	WD	67626	74026	74126	67726
8027	**SW**	P	*SW*	WD	67627	74027	74127	67727
8028	**SW**	P	*SW*	WD	67628	74028	74128	67728
8029	**SW**	P	*SW*	WD	67629	74029	74129	67729
8030	**SW**	P	*SW*	WD	67630	74030	74130	67730

CLASS 460   GEC-ALSTHOM JUNIPER

Gatwick Express units. Only the last two digits of the unit number are carried on the front ends of these units.

Formation: DMLFO–TFO–TCO–2MSO–TSO–MSO–DMSO.
SR designation: 8 Gat.
Construction: Steel.   **Doors:** Sliding plug.
Gangways: Within unit.   **Electrical Equipment:** IGBT control.
Traction Motors: Two Alstom ONIX 800 asynchronous of 270 kW.
Couplers: Scharfenberg.
Maximum Speed: 100 m.p.h.   **Bogies:** ACR.
Seating Layout: 1: 2+1 facing, 2: 2+2 facing/unidirectional.
Dimensions: 21.01/19.94 x 2.80 m. **Braking:** Disc and regenerative brakes.
Heating & Ventilation: Air conditioning.   **Multiple Working:** Within class.

DMLFO. Alstom 1998–1999. 10/– 42.6 t.
TFO. Alstom 1998–1999. 28/– 1TD 1W. 33.5 t.
TCO. Alstom 1998–1999. 9/42 1T. 34.9 t.
MSO(A). Alstom 1998–1999. –/60. 42.5 t.
MSO(B). Alstom 1998–1999. –/60. 42.5 t.

TSO. Alstom 1998–1999. –/38 1TD 1W. 35.2 t.
MSO(C). Alstom 1998–1999. –/60. 40.5 t.
DMSO. Alstom 1998–1999. –/56. 45.3 t.

Advertising livery: 460 003 and 460 005 Continental Airlines (mid blue with gold and yellow script).

460 001	**GV**	P	*GX*	SL	67901	74401	74411	74421
					74431	74441	74451	67911
460 002	**GV**	P	*GX*	SL	67902	74402	74412	74422
					74432	74442	74452	67912
460 003	**AL**	P	*GX*	SL	67903	74403	74413	74423
					74433	74443	74453	67913
460 004	**GV**	P	*GX*	SL	67904	74404	74414	74424
					74434	74444	74454	67914
460 005	**AL**	P	*GX*	SL	67905	74405	74415	74425
					74435	74445	74455	67915
460 006	**GV**	P	*GX*	SL	67906	74406	74416	74426
					74436	74446	74456	67916
460 007	**GV**	P	*GX*	SL	67907	74407	74417	74427
					74437	74447	74457	67917
460 008	**GV**	P	*GX*	SL	67908	74408	74418	74428
					74438	74448	74458	67918

CLASS 465   NETWORKER

South Eastern Trains suburban units.

Formation: DMSO–TSO–TSO–DMSO.
Construction: Welded aluminium alloy.
Doors: Sliding plug.
Gangways: Within unit.   **Electrical Equipment**: GTO inverters.
Traction Motors: Four Brush TIM970 (Classes 465/0 and 465/1) or GEC-Alsthom G352AY (Class 465/2) asynchronous of 280 kW.
Couplers: Tightlock.
Bogies: BREL P3/T3 (Classes 465/0 and 465/1) SRP BP62/BT52 (Class 465/2).
Maximum Speed: 75 m.p.h.   **Dimensions**: 20.89/20.06 x 2.81 m.
Seating Layout: 3+2 (* 2+2) facing/unidirectional.
Braking: Disc, rheostatic and regenerative.
Multiple Working: Within class and with Classes 365 and 466.

64759–64808. DMSO(A). Lot No. 31100 BREL York 1991–1993. –/86 (* –/74). 39.2 t.
64809–64858. DMSO(B). Lot No. 31100 BREL York 1991–1993. –/86 (* –/74). 39.2 t.
65700–65749. DMSO(A). Lot No. 31103 Metro-Cammell 1991–1993. –/86. 39.2 t.
65750–65799. DMSO(B). Lot No. 31103 Metro-Cammell 1991–1993. –/86. 39.2 t.
65800–65846. DMSO(A). Lot No. 31130 ABB York 1993–1994. –/86. 39.2 t.
65847–65893. DMSO(B). Lot No. 31130 ABB York 1993–1994. –/86. 39.2 t.
72028–72126 (even nos.) TSO. Lot No. 31102 BREL York 1991–1993. –/90 (* –/80). 27.2 t.
72029–72127 (odd nos.) TSO. Lot No. 31101 BREL York 1991–1993. –/86 1T (* –/76 1T). 28.0 t.
72719–72817 (odd nos.) TSO. Lot No. 31104 Metro-Cammell 1991–1992. –/86 1T. 28.0 t.

72720–72818 (even nos.) TSO. Lot No. 31105 Metro-Cammell 1991–1992. –/90. 27.2 t.
72900–72992 (even nos.) TSO. Lot No. 31102 ABB York 1993–1994. –/90. 27.2 t.
72901–72993 (odd nos.) TSO. Lot No. 31101 ABB York 1993–1994. –/86 1T. 28.0 t.

Class 465/0. Built by BREL/ABB.

465 001	**CB**	H	*SE*	SG	64759	72028	72029	64809
465 002	**CB**	H	*SE*	SG	64760	72030	72031	64810
465 003	**CB**	H	*SE*	SG	64761	72032	72033	64811
465 004	**NT**	H	*SE*	SG	64762	72034	72035	64812
465 005	**NT**	H	*SE*	SG	64763	72036	72037	64813
465 006	**CB**	H	*SE*	SG	64764	72038	72039	64814
465 007	**CB**	H	*SE*	SG	64765	72040	72041	64815
465 008	**CB**	H	*SE*	SG	64766	72042	72043	64816
465 009	**CB**	H	*SE*	SG	64767	72044	72045	64817
465 010	**CB**	H	*SE*	SG	64768	72046	72047	64818
465 011	**CB**	H	*SE*	SG	64769	72048	72049	64819
465 012	**CB**	H	*SE*	SG	64770	72050	72051	64820
465 013	**CB**	H	*SE*	SG	64771	72052	72053	64821
465 014	* **CB**	H	*SE*	SG	64772	72054	72055	64822
465 015	**CB**	H	*SE*	SG	64773	72056	72057	64823
465 016	**CB**	H	*SE*	SG	64774	72058	72059	64824
465 017	**CB**	H	*SE*	SG	64775	72060	72061	64825
465 018	**CB**	H	*SE*	SG	64776	72062	72063	64826
465 019	**CB**	H	*SE*	SG	64777	72064	72065	64827
465 020	**CB**	H	*SE*	SG	64778	72066	72067	64828
465 021	**NT**	H	*SE*	SG	64779	72068	72069	64829
465 022	**NT**	H	*SE*	SG	64780	72070	72071	64830
465 023	**NT**	H	*SE*	SG	64781	72072	72073	64831
465 024	**NT**	H	*SE*	SG	64782	72074	72075	64832
465 025	**NT**	H	*SE*	SG	64783	72076	72077	64833
465 026	**NT**	H	*SE*	SG	64784	72078	72079	64834
465 027	**NT**	H	*SE*	SG	64785	72080	72081	64835
465 028	**NT**	H	*SE*	SG	64786	72082	72083	64836
465 029	**NT**	H	*SE*	SG	64787	72084	72085	64837
465 030	**NT**	H	*SE*	SG	64788	72086	72087	64838
465 031	**NT**	H	*SE*	SG	64789	72088	72089	64839
465 032	**NT**	H	*SE*	SG	64790	72090	72091	64840
465 033	**NT**	H	*SE*	SG	64791	72092	72093	64841
465 034	**NT**	H	*SE*	SG	64792	72094	72095	64842
465 035	**NT**	H	*SE*	SG	64793	72096	72097	64843
465 036	**NT**	H	*SE*	SG	64794	72098	72099	64844
465 037	**NT**	H	*SE*	SG	64795	72100	72101	64845
465 038	**NT**	H	*SE*	SG	64796	72102	72103	64846
465 039	**NT**	H	*SE*	SG	64797	72104	72105	64847
465 040	**NT**	H	*SE*	SG	64798	72106	72107	64848
465 041	**NT**	H	*SE*	SG	64799	72108	72109	64849
465 042	**NT**	H	*SE*	SG	64800	72110	72111	64850
465 043	**NT**	H	*SE*	SG	64801	72112	72113	64851
465 044	**NT**	H	*SE*	SG	64802	72114	72115	64852
465 045	**NT**	H	*SE*	SG	64803	72116	72117	64853

465 046	**NT**	H	*SE*	SG	64804	72118	72119	64854
465 047	**NT**	H	*SE*	SG	64805	72120	72121	64855
465 048	**NT**	H	*SE*	SG	64806	72122	72123	64856
465 049	**NT**	H	*SE*	SG	64807	72124	72125	64857
465 050	**NT**	H	*SE*	SG	64808	72126	72127	64858

Class 465/1. Built by BREL/ABB. Similar to Class 465/0 but with detail differences.

465 151	**NT**	H	*SE*	SG	65800	72900	72901	65847
465 152	**NT**	H	*SE*	SG	65801	72902	72903	65848
465 153	**NT**	H	*SE*	SG	65802	72904	72905	65849
465 154	**NT**	H	*SE*	SG	65803	72906	72907	65850
465 155	**NT**	H	*SE*	SG	65804	72908	72909	65851
465 156	**NT**	H	*SE*	SG	65805	72910	72911	65852
465 157	**NT**	H	*SE*	SG	65806	72912	72913	65853
465 158	**NT**	H	*SE*	SG	65807	72914	72915	65854
465 159	**NT**	H	*SE*	SG	65808	72916	72917	65855
465 160	**NT**	H	*SE*	SG	65809	72918	72919	65856
465 161	**NT**	H	*SE*	SG	65810	72920	72921	65857
465 162	**NT**	H	*SE*	SG	65811	72922	72923	65858
465 163	**NT**	H	*SE*	SG	65812	72924	72925	65859
465 164	**NT**	H	*SE*	SG	65813	72926	72927	65860
465 165	**NT**	H	*SE*	SG	65814	72928	72929	65861
465 166	**NT**	H	*SE*	SG	65815	72930	72931	65862
465 167	**NT**	H	*SE*	SG	65816	72932	72933	65863
465 168	**NT**	H	*SE*	SG	65817	72934	72935	65864
465 169	**NT**	H	*SE*	SG	65818	72936	72937	65865
465 170	**NT**	H	*SE*	SG	65819	72938	72939	65866
465 171	**NT**	H	*SE*	SG	65820	72940	72941	65867
465 172	**NT**	H	*SE*	SG	65821	72942	72943	65868
465 173	**NT**	H	*SE*	SG	65822	72944	72945	65869
465 174	**NT**	H	*SE*	SG	65823	72946	72947	65870
465 175	**NT**	H	*SE*	SG	65824	72948	72949	65871
465 176	**NT**	H	*SE*	SG	65825	72950	72951	65872
465 177	**NT**	H	*SE*	SG	65826	72952	72953	65873
465 178	**NT**	H	*SE*	SG	65827	72954	72955	65874
465 179	**NT**	H	*SE*	SG	65828	72956	72957	65875
465 180	**NT**	H	*SE*	SG	65829	72958	72959	65876
465 181	**NT**	H	*SE*	SG	65830	72960	72961	65877
465 182	**NT**	H	*SE*	SG	65831	72962	72963	65878
465 183	**NT**	H	*SE*	SG	65832	72964	72965	65879
465 184	**NT**	H	*SE*	SG	65833	72966	72967	65880
465 185	**NT**	H	*SE*	SG	65834	72968	72969	65881
465 186	**NT**	H	*SE*	SG	65835	72970	72971	65882
465 187	**NT**	H	*SE*	SG	65836	72972	72973	65883
465 188	**NT**	H	*SE*	SG	65837	72974	72975	65884
465 189	**NT**	H	*SE*	SG	65838	72976	72977	65885
465 190	**NT**	H	*SE*	SG	65839	72978	72979	65886
465 191	**NT**	H	*SE*	SG	65840	72980	72981	65887
465 192	**NT**	H	*SE*	SG	65841	72982	72983	65888
465 193	**NT**	H	*SE*	SG	65842	72984	72985	65889

465 194	**NT**	H	*SE*	SG	65843	72986	72987	65890
465 195	**NT**	H	*SE*	SG	65844	72988	72989	65891
465 196	**NT**	H	*SE*	SG	65845	72990	72991	65892
465 197	**NT**	H	*SE*	SG	65846	72992	72993	65893

Class 465/2. Built by Metro-Cammell.

Advertising livery: 465 214 Continental Airlines (mid blue with gold and yellow script).

465 201	**CN**	A	*SE*	SG	65700	72719	72720	65750
465 202	**CN**	A	*SE*	SG	65701	72721	72722	65751
465 203	**CN**	A	*SE*	SG	65702	72723	72724	65752
465 204	**CN**	A	*SE*	SG	65703	72725	72726	65753
465 205	**CN**	A	*SE*	SG	65704	72727	72728	65754
465 206	**CN**	A	*SE*	SG	65705	72729	72730	65755
465 207	**CN**	A	*SE*	SG	65706	72731	72732	65756
465 208	**CN**	A	*SE*	SG	65707	72733	72734	65757
465 209	**CN**	A	*SE*	SG	65708	72735	72736	65758
465 210	**CN**	A	*SE*	SG	65709	72737	72738	65759
465 211	**CN**	A	*SE*	SG	65710	72739	72740	65760
465 212	**CN**	A	*SE*	SG	65711	72741	72742	65761
465 213	**CN**	A	*SE*	SG	65712	72743	72744	65762
465 214	**AL**	A	*SE*	SG	65713	72745	72746	65763
465 215	**CN**	A	*SE*	SG	65714	72747	72748	65764
465 216	**CN**	A	*SE*	SG	65715	72749	72750	65765
465 217	**CN**	A	*SE*	SG	65716	72751	72752	65766
465 218	**CN**	A	*SE*	SG	65717	72753	72754	65767
465 219	**CN**	A	*SE*	SG	65718	72755	72756	65768
465 220	**CN**	A	*SE*	SG	65719	72757	72758	65769
465 221	**CN**	A	*SE*	SG	65720	72759	72760	65770
465 222	**CN**	A	*SE*	SG	65721	72761	72762	65771
465 223	**CN**	A	*SE*	SG	65722	72763	72764	65772
465 224	**CN**	A	*SE*	SG	65723	72765	72766	65773
465 225	**CN**	A	*SE*	SG	65724	72767	72768	65774
465 226	**CN**	A	*SE*	SG	65725	72769	72770	65775
465 227	**CN**	A	*SE*	SG	65726	72771	72772	65776
465 228	**NT**	A	*SE*	SG	65727	72773	72774	65777
465 229	**CN**	A	*SE*	SG	65728	72775	72776	65778
465 230	**CN**	A	*SE*	SG	65729	72777	72778	65779
465 231	**NT**	A	*SE*	SG	65730	72779	72780	65780
465 232	**CN**	A	*SE*	SG	65731	72781	72782	65781
465 233	**CN**	A	*SE*	SG	65732	72783	72784	65782
465 234	**CN**	A	*SE*	SG	65733	72785	72786	65783
465 235	**CN**	A	*SE*	SG	65734	72787	72788	65784
465 236	**NT**	A	*SE*	SG	65735	72789	72790	65785
465 237	**CN**	A	*SE*	SG	65736	72791	72792	65786
465 238	**NT**	A	*SE*	SG	65737	72793	72794	65787
465 239	**CN**	A	*SE*	SG	65738	72795	72796	65788
465 240	**CN**	A	*SE*	SG	65739	72797	72798	65789
465 241	**CN**	A	*SE*	SG	65740	72799	72800	65790
465 242	**CN**	A	*SE*	SG	65741	72801	72802	65791

465 243	CN	A	*SE*	SG	65742	72803	72804	65792
465 244	CN	A	*SE*	SG	65743	72805	72806	65793
465 245	CN	A	*SE*	SG	65744	72807	72808	65794
465 246	CN	A	*SE*	SG	65745	72809	72810	65795
465 247	CN	A	*SE*	SG	65746	72811	72812	65796
465 248	CN	A	*SE*	SG	65747	72813	72814	65797
465 249	CN	A	*SE*	SG	65748	72815	72816	65798
465 250	NT	A	*SE*	SG	65749	72817	72818	65799

CLASS 466   NETWORKER   GEC-ALSTHOM

South Eastern Trains suburban units.

Formation: DMSO–DTSO.
Construction: Welded aluminium alloy.
Doors: Sliding plug.
Gangways: Within unit.   **Electrical Equipment:** GTO inverters.
Traction Motors: Four GEC-Alsthom G352AY asynchronous of 280 kW.
Couplers: Tightlock.   **Bogies:** SRP BP62/BT52.
Maximum Speed: 75 m.p.h.   **Dimensions:** 20.80 x 2.80 m.
Seating Layout: 3+2 (* 2+2) facing/unidirectional.
Braking: Disc, rheostatic and regenerative.
Multiple Working: Within class and Classes 365 and 465.

DMSO. Lot No. 31128 Birmingham 1993–1994. –/86 (* –/72). 40.6 t.
DTSO. Lot No. 31129 Birmingham 1993–1994. –/82 1T (* –/68 1T). 31.4 t.

466 001		NT	A	*SE*	SG	64860	78312
466 002		CN	A	*SE*	SG	64861	78313
466 003		CN	A	*SE*	SG	64862	78314
466 004		CN	A	*SE*	SG	64863	78315
466 005		CN	A	*SE*	SG	64864	78316
466 006		CN	A	*SE*	SG	64865	78317
466 007		CN	A	*SE*	SG	64866	78318
466 008		NT	A	*SE*	SG	64867	78319
466 009		NT	A	*SE*	SG	64868	78320
466 010		NT	A	*SE*	SG	64869	78321
466 011		NT	A	*SE*	SG	64870	78322
466 012		NT	A	*SE*	SG	64871	78323
466 013		NT	A	*SE*	SG	64872	78324
466 014		NT	A	*SE*	SG	64873	78325
466 015		NT	A	*SE*	SG	64874	78326
466 016		CN	A	*SE*	SG	64875	78327
466 017	*	NT	A	*SE*	SG	64876	78328
466 018		CN	A	*SE*	SG	64877	78329
466 019		NT	A	*SE*	SG	64878	78330
466 020		CN	A	*SE*	SG	64879	78331
466 021		CN	A	*SE*	SG	64880	78332
466 022		CN	A	*SE*	SG	64881	78333
466 023		CN	A	*SE*	SG	64882	78334
466 024		CN	A	*SE*	SG	64883	78335

466 025	**CN**	A	*SE*	SG	64884	78336
466 026	**CN**	A	*SE*	SG	64885	78337
466 027	**CN**	A	*SE*	SG	64886	78338
466 028	**CN**	A	*SE*	SG	64887	78339
466 029	**CN**	A	*SE*	SG	64888	78340
466 030	**CN**	A	*SE*	SG	64889	78341
466 031	**CN**	A	*SE*	SG	64890	78342
466 032	**CN**	A	*SE*	SG	64891	78343
466 033	**CN**	A	*SE*	SG	64892	78344
466 034	**CN**	A	*SE*	SG	64893	78345
466 035	**CN**	A	*SE*	SG	64894	78346
466 036	**NT**	A	*SE*	SG	64895	78347
466 037	**CN**	A	*SE*	SG	64896	78348
466 038	**NT**	A	*SE*	SG	64897	78349
466 039	**CN**	A	*SE*	SG	64898	78350
466 040	**NT**	A	*SE*	SG	64899	78351
466 041	**NT**	A	*SE*	SG	64900	78352
466 042	**NT**	A	*SE*	SG	64901	78353
466 043	**NT**	A	*SE*	SG	64902	78354

CLASS 483   METRO-CAMMELL

Built 1938 onwards for LTE. Converted 1989–1990 for Isle of Wight Line.

Formation: DMSO–DMSO.
System: 660 V DC third rail.
Construction: Steel.   **Doors:** Sliding.
Gangways: None. End doors.   **Electrical Equipment:** IGBT control.
Traction Motors: Two Crompton Parkinson/GEC/BTH LT100 of 125 kW.
Couplers: Wedglock.   **Bogies:** LT design.
Maximum Speed: 45 m.p.h.   **Multiple Working:** Within class.
Seating Layout: Longitudinal or 2+2 facing/unidirectional.
Dimensions: 16.15 x 2.69 m.   **Braking:** Tread brakes.

Notes: The last three numbers of the unit number only are carried.
Former London Underground numbers are shown in parentheses.

DMSO (A). Lot No. 31071. –/40. 27.4 t.
DMSO (B). Lot No. 31072. –/42. 27.4 t.

Non-standard livery: 483 007 and 483 009 Original London Transport Maroon
and cream.

483 002	**IL**	H	*IL*	RY	122	(10221)	225	(11142)
483 003	**N**	H		RY	123	(10116)	221	(11184)
483 004	**IL**	H	*IL*	RY	124	(10205)	224	(11205)
483 006	**IL**	H	*IL*	RY	126	(10297)	226	(11297)
483 007	**0**	H	*IL*	RY	127	(10291)	227	(11291)
483 008	**IL**	H	*IL*	RY	128	(10255)	228	(11255)
483 009	**0**	H	*IL*	RY	129	(10289)	229	(11229)

CLASS 488   BR DERBY

Converted 1983–1984 from Mk. 2F FOs and TSOs for Victoria–Gatwick services. The seating layout was modified with and the removal of one toilet to provide additional luggage space.

Formation: TFOH–TSO (Class 488/3 only)–TSOH.
Construction: Steel.   **Doors:** Slam.
Gangways: Throughout.   **Couplers:** Buckeye.
Bogies: B4.   **Maximum Speed:** 90 m.p.h.
Seating Layout: 1: 2+1 facing 2: 2+2 facing.
Dimensions: 20.60 x 2.84 m.   **Braking:** Tread brakes.
Heating & Ventilation: Air conditioning.
Multiple Working: SR.

72501–72509. TFOH. Lot No. 30859 Derby 1973–1974. 41/– 1T. 35.0 t.
72603–72614/72617/72620–72643. TSOH. Lot No. 30860 Derby 1973–1974. –/48 1T. 33.5 t.
72615/72645. TSOH. Lot No. 30846 Derby 1973. –/48 1T. 33.5 t.
72702–72714. TSO. Lot No. 30860 Derby 1973–1974. –/48 1T. 33.5 t.

Advertising Livery: As **GX** but with a deep blue instead of a white lower bodyside, advertising Continental Airlines.

Class 488/2. TFOH–TSOH. **Note:** TFOH fitted with public telephone.

8202	**GX**	P	*GX*	SL	72501 (3382)	72617 (6086)
8206	**GX**	P	*GX*	SL	72505 (3415)	72629 (6048)
8208	**AL**	GB		PB	72507 (3412)	72643 (6040)
Spare	**AL**	NR		DY	72640 (6097)	
Spare	**AL**	NR		DY	72641 (6079)	

Class 488/3. TSOH–TSO–TSOH.

8303	**GX**	NR		DY	72603 (6093)	72702 (6099)	72608 (6077)
8308	**GX**	NR		DY	72614 (6090)	72707 (6127)	72615 (5938)
8311	**GX**	P	*GX*	SL	72620 (6140)	72710 (6003)	72621 (6108)
8312	**GX**	GB		PY	72622 (6004)	72711 (6109)	72623 (6118)
8315	**GX**	GB		PY	72636 (6071)	72714 (6092)	72645 (5942)

CLASS 489   BR EASTLEIGH

Converted 1983–1984 from Class 414/3 (2 Hap) DMBSOs to work with Class 488.

Formation: DMLV.
Construction: Steel.   **Doors:** Slam.
Gangways: Gangwayed at inner end only.   **Electrical Equipment:** 1966-type.
Traction Motors: Two EE507 of 185 kW.   **Couplers:** Buckeye.
Bogies: Mark 4.   **Maximum Speed:** 90 m.p.h.
Dimensions: 20.00 x 2.82 m.   **Braking:** Tread brakes.
Multiple Working: SR.

▲ Silverlink-liveried 313 103 passes Headstone Lane with a Watford Junction–Euston service on 02/03/04. **Hugh Ballantyne**

▼ 315 859 passes Bethnal Green with a Liverpool Street–Hertford service on 5 August. Although in WAGN purple livery, this unit is now operated by One West Anglia. **Darren Ford**

▲ One Stansted Express-liveried 317 729 passes Bethnal Green with a Stansted Airport service on 5 August. **Darren Ford**

▼ Strathclyde PTE-liveried 318 265 stands at Partick on 11/04/03 with a Bellgrove service. **Mark Beal**

▲ Thameslink-liveried 319 459 is seen at Salfords with the 12.57 Bedford–Brighton on 30/03/04. **Rodney Lissenden**

▼ 320 301 at Dalmuir with the 14.11 to Bellgrove via Yoker service on 30/07/04. **Murdoch Currie**

▲ "One"-liveried 321 446 is seen at Brantham with an Ipswich–Liverpool Street service on 20/04/04. **Jason Rogers**

▼ First Group (suburban)-liveried 323 239 is seen near Longport with the 17.57 Stoke–Manchester Piccadilly of 02/06/04. **Cliff Beeton**

▲ With the leading vehicle in an advertising livery for the Royal Bank of Scotland Heathrow Express units 332 005 and 332 001 near Southall with the 09.25 Heathrow Terminal 4–Paddington. **Alex Dasi-Sutton**

▼ West Yorkshire PTE-liveried 333 006 is seen at Bingley on 06/07/04 with the 09.42 Bradford Forster Square–Skipton service. **Gavin Morrison**

▲ 334 028 is seen at Troon on 04/06/04 with the 18.43 Ayr–Glasgow Central.
Alex Dasi-Sutton

▼ One of the new Siemens Class 350/1 "West Coast" Desiro units is seen on test at Velim test circuit in the Czech Republic on 07/08/04. **Quintus Vosman**

▲ c2c-liveried 357 031 passes Chalkwell on 24/03/04 with the 12.50 Shoeburyness–Fenchurch Street service. **Anthony Kay**

▼ 360 108 passes Terling near Witham, Essex with the 12.30 Ipswich–Liverpool Street service on 26/04/04. **Anthony Kay**

▲ All Class 365s are now operated by WAGN and are in Network South-East livery. On 06/10/03 365 531 in seen in charge of the 09.15 King's Cross–Cambridge service near Royston. **Anthony Kay**

▼ South Eastern Trains suburban Electrostar 375 915 leads an 8-car formation near Paddock Wood on 15/05/04 with the 09.56 Cannon Street–Ramsgate. This service started from Cannon Street because of planned engineering works at Charing Cross. **Alex Dasi-Sutton**

▲ New South Eastern Trains inner-suburban Class 376s made their debut in passenger service in Summer 2004. On 19/08/04 376 002 pauses at Sundridge Park with the 14.39 London Bridge–Bromley North additional. **Rodney Lissenden**

▼ Southern Electrostar 377 138 is seen near Fratton with the 12.12 Portsmouth Harbour–Brighton "Coastway" service on 23/04/04. **Chris Wilson**

▲ Pendolino 390 003 "Virgin Hero" passes Cartland, South Lanarkshire with a Polmadie–Edinburgh driver training run on 28/01/04. **Ian Lothian**

▼ 2005 should be the last year for "Slam-door" Mark 1 EMU operations on the Southern Region. Connex-liveried, but Southern-operated Class 421 "Cig" 1901 with Class 423 "Vep" 3483 arrives at South Croydon with the 16.23 Victoria–East Grinstead "Route 66" working on 16/04/04. **Shaun Bamford**

▲ South West Trains have repainted Class 423 No. 3417 into original blue livery for its final months in service. On 14/08/04 it arrives at Vauxhall with the 15.45 Waterloo–Southampton Central service (with 3812). **Mark Beal**

▼ South West Trains-liveried Class 442 2416 is seen at Basingstoke on 07/11/03 with the 11.00 Southampton–Waterloo. **Anthony Kay**

▲ 444 018 and 444 019 are seen near Fratton with the 12.17 Portsmouth Harbour–Waterloo on 23/04/04. The Class 444s will be dedicated to this route.
Chris Wilson

▼ South West Trains suburban-liveried 450 055 is seen at St. Denys with the 16.33 Portsmouth Harbour–Southampton on 30/07/04. **Anthony Kay**

▲ Stagecoach-liveried Class 455 No. 5708 leads an 8-car formation near Shepperton with a service from Waterloo on 14/06/04. This livery will be superceded by a new SWT inner suburban red livery for 455s, as they are refurbished at Ashford Chart Leacon over the next few years. **Kim Fullbrook**

▼ Class 458 No. 8009 is seen near Chertsey with the 11.27 Waterloo–Weybridge on 09/12/03. **Rodney Lissenden**

▲ Gatwick Express unit 460 005, in an advertising livery for Continental Airlines, passes Salfords with a Victoria–Gatwick service on 30/03/04. **Rodney Lissenden**

▼ The Connex South Eastern white/yellow livery had been perpetuated by the current operator South Eastern Trains. On 07/09/04 recently repainted 465 208 and 465 232 arrive at London Bridge with the 17.03 Higham–Cannon Street.
Robert Pritchard

▲ Stagecoach Island Line "Dinosaur"-liveried 483 006 arrives at Ryde St. Johns Road with the 08.53 Shanklin–Ryde Pier Head on 06/07/04.　　**Martyn Hilbert**

▼ Eurostar set 3214/13 is seen near Bromley South with the 12.39 Waterloo International–Brussels Midi on 04/02/04.　　**Robert Pritchard**

▲ New Merseyrail-liveried 507 010 is seen at Birkdale with a Hunts Cross–Southport service on 19/05/04. **Martyn Hilbert**

▼ Connex-liveried 508 212 passes Lee with an e.c.s. working on 13/05/04.
Rodney Lissenden

DMLV. Lot No. 30452 1959. 42.0 t.

9102	**GX**	NR		TH	68501	(61281)
9104	**GX**	P	*GX*	SL	68503	(61277)
9105	**GX**	GB		PB	68504	(61286)
9106	**GX**	GB		PB	68505	(61299)
9109	**GX**	NR		TH	68508	(61272)
9110	**GX**	P	*GX*	SL	68509	(61280)

CLASS 507   BREL YORK

Merseyrail suburban units.

Formation: BDMSO–TSO–DMSO.
System: 750 V DC third rail.
Traction Motors: Four GEC G310AZ of 82.125 kW.
Construction: Steel underframe, aluminium alloy body and roof.
Doors: Sliding.
Gangways: Within unit + end doors.   **Bogies:** BX1.
Couplers: Tightlock.   **Maximum Speed:** 75 m.p.h.
Seating Layout: 3+2 facing unless shown.
Braking: Disc and rheostatic.   **Dimensions:** 20.33/20.18 x 2.82 m.
Multiple Working: Within class and with Class 508.

BDMSO. Lot No. 30906 1978–1980. –/68 1W (* –/59 1W). 37.0 t.
TSO. Lot No. 30907 1978–1980. –/86 (* –/74). 25.5 t.
DMSO. Lot No. 30908 1978–1980. –/68 1W (* –/59 1W). 35.5 t.

Note: Refurbished Merseyrail units (shown as *) have 2+2 high-back seating.

507 001	*	**ME**	A	*ME*	BD	64367	71342	64405
507 002	*	**ME**	A	*ME*	BD	64368	71343	64406
507 003	*	**ME**	A	*ME*	BD	64369	71344	64407
507 004	*	**ME**	A	*ME*	BD	64388	71345	64408
507 005	*	**ME**	A	*ME*	BD	64371	71346	64409
507 006	*	**ME**	A	*ME*	BD	64372	71347	64410
507 007	*	**ME**	A	*ME*	BD	64373	71348	64411
507 008		**MY**	A	*ME*	BD	64374	71349	64412
507 009		**MY**	A	*ME*	BD	64375	71350	64413
507 010	*	**ME**	A	*ME*	BD	64376	71351	64414
507 011	*	**ME**	A	*ME*	BD	64377	71352	64415
507 012		**MY**	A	*ME*	BD	64378	71353	64416
507 013		**MY**	A	*ME*	BD	64379	71354	64417
507 014		**MT**	A	*ME*	BD	64380	71355	64418
507 015		**MT**	A	*ME*	BD	64381	71356	64419
507 016	*	**ME**	A	*ME*	BD	64382	71357	64420
507 017	*	**ME**	A	*ME*	BD	64383	71358	64421
507 018	*	**ME**	A	*ME*	BD	64384	71359	64422
507 019	*	**ME**	A	*ME*	BD	64385	71360	64423
507 020	*	**ME**	A	*ME*	BD	64386	71361	64424
507 021	*	**ME**	A	*ME*	BD	64387	71362	64425
507 023	*	**ME**	A	*ME*	BD	64389	71364	64427
507 024		**MY**	A	*ME*	BD	64390	71365	64428

507 025	MY		A	ME	BD	64391	71366	64429
507 026	MY		A	ME	BD	64392	71367	64430
507 027	ME	*	A	ME	BD	64393	71368	64431
507 028	MT		A	ME	BD	64394	71369	64432
507 029	MT		A	ME	BD	64395	71370	64433
507 030	ME	*	A	ME	BD	64396	71371	64434
507 031	MT		A	ME	BD	64397	71372	64435
507 032	MY		A	ME	BD	64398	71373	64436
507 033	MT		A	ME	BD	64399	71374	64437

CLASS 508   BREL YORK

Merseyrail/South Eastern Trains/Silverlink suburban units.

Formation: DMSO–TSO–BDMSO.
System: 750 V DC third rail.
Traction Motors: Four GEC G310AZ of 82.125 kW.
Construction: Steel underframe, aluminium alloy body and roof.
Doors: Sliding.
Gangways: Within unit + end doors.   **Bogies:** BX1.
Couplers: Tightlock.   **Maximum Speed:** 75 m.p.h.
Seating Layout: 3+2 facing unless shown.
Braking: Disc and rheostatic.   **Dimensions:** 20.18 x 2.82 m.
Multiple Working: Within class and with Class 507.

DMSO. Lot No. 30979 1979–1980. –/68 1W (* –/59 1W). 36.0 t.
TSO. Lot No. 30980 1979–1980. –/86 (* –/74). 26.5 t.
BDMSO. Lot No. 30981 1979–1980. –/68 1W (* –/59 1W). 36.5 t.

Class **508/1**. Standard design.

Notes: Units currently shown as stored out of use at Alstom, Eastleigh (ZG) are to be refurbished for Merseyrail.
Vehicle 64671 of 508 123 carries Arriva blue livery, applied as a trial.
Refurbished Merseyrail units (shown as *) have 2+2 high-back seating.

508 103	ME	*	A	ME	BD	64651	71485	64694
508 104	ME	*	A	ME	BD	64652	71486	64695
508 108	ME	*	A	ME	BD	64656	71490	64699
508 110	ME	*	A	ME	BD	64658	71492	64701
508 111	ME	*	A	ME	BD	64659	71493	64702
508 112	ME	*	A	ME	BD	64660	71494	64703
508 114	ME	*	A	ME	BD	64662	71496	64705
508 115	ME	*	A	ME	BD	64663	71497	64706
508 117	ME	*	A	ME	BD	64665	71499	64708
508 120	ME	*	A	ME	BD	64668	71502	64711
508 122	MT		A		ZG	64670	71504	64713
508 123	MT		A		ZG	64671	71505	64714
508 124	ME	*	A	ME	BD	64672	71506	64715
508 125	ME	*	A	ME	BD	64673	71507	64716
508 126	ME	*	A	ME	BD	64674	71508	64717
508 127	ME	*	A	ME	BD	64675	71509	64718
508 128	ME	*	A	ME	BD	64676	71510	64719

508 130	*	**ME**	A	*ME*	BD	64678	71512	64721
508 131	*	**ME**	A	*ME*	BD	64679	71513	64722
508 134	*	**ME**	A	*ME*	BD	64682	71516	64725
508 136	*	**ME**	A	*ME*	BD	64684	71518	64727
508 137	*	**ME**	A	*ME*	BD	64685	71519	64728
508 138	*	**ME**	A	*ME*	BD	64686	71520	64729
508 139	*	**ME**	A	*ME*	BD	64687	71521	64730
508 140	*	**ME**	A	*ME*	BD	64688	71522	64731
508 141	*	**ME**	A	*ME*	BD	64689	71523	64732
508 143	*	**ME**	A	*ME*	BD	64691	71525	64734

Class 508/2. Facelifted South Eastern Trains units. Refurbished 1998–1999 by Wessex Traincare/Alstom, Eastleigh.

DMSO. Lot No. 30979 1979–1980. –/66. 36.0 t.
TSO. Lot No. 30980 1979–1980. –/79 1W. 26.5 t.
BDMSO. Lot No. 30981 1979–1980. –/74. 36.5 t.

508 201	(508 101)	**CX**	A	*SE*	GI	64649	71483	64692
508 202	(508 105)	**CX**	A	*SE*	GI	64653	71487	64696
508 203	(508 106)	**CX**	A	*SE*	GI	64654	71488	64697
508 204	(508 107)	**CX**	A	*SE*	GI	64655	71489	64698
508 205	(508 109)	**CX**	A	*SE*	GI	64657	71491	64700
508 206	(508 113)	**CX**	A	*SE*	GI	64661	71495	64704
508 207	(508 116)	**CX**	A	*SE*	GI	64664	71498	64707
508 208	(508 119)	**CX**	A	*SE*	GI	64667	71501	64710
508 209	(508 121)	**CX**	A	*SE*	GI	64669	71503	64712
508 210	(508 129)	**CX**	A	*SE*	GI	64677	71511	64720
508 211	(508 132)	**CX**	A	*SE*	GI	64680	71514	64723
508 212	(508 133)	**CX**	A	*SE*	GI	64681	71515	64724

Class 508/3. Facelifted units for Silverlink for use on Euston–Watford Junction services. Refurbished 2002–2003 by Alstom, Eastleigh. Details as Class 508/1.

508 301	(508 102)	**SL**	A	*SL*	WN	64650	71484	64693
508 302	(508 135)	**SL**	A	*SL*	WN	64683	71517	64726
508 303	(508 142)	**SL**	A	*SL*	WN	64690	71524	64733

4.3. EUROSTAR UNITS (CLASS 373)

Eurostar units were built for and are normally used on services between Britain and Continental Europe via the Channel Tunnel. Apart from such workings units may be used as follows:

- SNCF-owned units 3203/04, 3225/26 and 3227/28 have been removed from the Eurostar pool, and only operate SNCF-internal services between Paris and Lille.
- Three 8-car sets are used daily by GNER for its "White Rose" services.

Each train consists of two Eurostar units coupled, with a motor car at each driving end. Services starting from/terminating at London Waterloo International are formed of two 10-car units coupled, whilst GNER services are formed of two 8-car units coupled. All units are articulated with an extra motor bogie on the coach adjacent to the motor car.

Sets marked "r" have been refurbished as part of a programme to run from September 2004 to October 2005.

DM–MSO–4TSO–RB–2TFO–TBFO or DM–MSO–3TSO–RB–TFO–TBFO.
Gangwayed within pair of units. Air conditioned.
Construction: Steel.
Supply Systems: 25 kV AC 50 Hz overhead or 3000 V DC overhead or 750 V DC third rail (* also equipped for 1500 V DC overhead operation).
Wheel Arrangement: Bo–Bo + Bo–2–2–2–2–2–2–2–2.
Length: 22.15 m (DM), 21.85 m (MS & TBF), 21.97 (TBFO), 18.70 m (other cars).
Maximum Speed: 186 m.p.h. (300 km/h).
Built: 1992–1993 by GEC-Alsthom/Brush/ANF/De Dietrich/BN Construction/ACEC.
Note: DM vehicles carry the set numbers indicated below.

10-Car Sets. Built for services starting from/terminating at London Waterloo. Individual vehicles in each set are allocated numbers 373xxx0 + 373xxx1 + 373xxx2 + 373xxx3 + 373xxx4 + 373xxx5 + 373xxx6 + 373xxx7 + 373xxx8 + 373xxx9, where 3xxx denotes the set number.

Non-standard livery: 0 – grey with silver ends, TGV symbol and green or blue doors.

373xxx0 series. DM. Lot No. 31118 1992–1995. 68.5 t.
373xxx1 series. MSO. Lot No. 31119 1992–1995. –/48 2T. 44.6 t.
373xxx2 series. TSO. Lot No. 31120 1992–1995. –/58 1T (r –/56 1T). 28.1 t.
373xxx3 series. TSO. Lot No. 31121 1992–1995. –/58 2T (r –/56 2T). 29.7 t.
373xxx4 series. TSO. Lot No. 31122 1992–1995. –/58 1T (r –/56 1T). 28.3 t.
373xxx5 series. TSO. Lot No. 31123 1992–1995. –/58 2T (r –/56 2T). 29.2 t.
373xxx6 series. RB. Lot No.31124 1992–1995. 31.1 t.
373xxx7 series. TFO. Lot No. 31125 1992–1995. 39/– 1T. 29.6 t.
373xxx8 series.TFO. Lot No. 31126 1992–1995. 39/– 1T. 32.2 t.
373xxx9 series.TBFO. Lot No. 31127 1992–1995. 25/– 1TD. 39.4 t.

3001	**EU**	EU	*EU*	NP	3006	**EU**	EU	*EU*	NP
3002	**EU**	EU	*EU*	NP	3007	**EU**	EU	*EU*	NP
3003 r	**EU**	EU	*EU*	NP	3008	**EU**	EU	*EU*	NP
3004 r	**EU**	EU	*EU*	NP	3009 r	**EU**	EU	*EU*	NP
3005	**EU**	EU	*EU*	NP	3010 r	**EU**	EU	*EU*	NP

3011	**EU**	EU	*EU*	NP		3207	*	**EU**	SF	*EU*	LY MICHEL HOLLARD
3012	**EU**	EU	*EU*	NP		3208	*	**EU**	SF	*EU*	LY MICHEL HOLLARD
3013	**EU**	EU	*EU*	NP		3209	*	**EU**	SF	*EU*	LY
3014	**EU**	EU	*EU*	NP		3210	*	**EU**	SF	*EU*	LY
3015	**EU**	EU	*EU*	NP		3211		**EU**	SF	*EU*	LY
3016	**EU**	EU	*EU*	NP		3212		**EU**	SF	*EU*	LY
3017	**EU**	EU	*EU*	NP		3213		**EU**	SF	*EU*	LY
3018	**EU**	EU	*EU*	NP		3214		**EU**	SF	*EU*	LY
3019	**EU**	EU	*EU*	NP		3215	*	**EU**	SF	*EU*	LY
3020	**EU**	EU	*EU*	NP		3216	*	**EU**	SF	*EU*	LY
3021	**EU**	EU	*EU*	NP		3217		**EU**	SF	*EU*	LY
3022	**EU**	EU	*EU*	NP		3218		**EU**	SF	*EU*	LY
3101	**EU**	SB		FF		3219	r	**EU**	SF	*EU*	LY
3102	**EU**	SB		FF		3220	r	**EU**	SF	*EU*	LY
3103	**EU**	SB	*EU*	FF		3221		**EU**	SF	*EU*	LY
3104	**EU**	SB	*EU*	FF		3222		**EU**	SF	*EU*	LY
3105	**EU**	SB	*EU*	FF		3223	*	**EU**	SF	*EU*	LY
3106	**EU**	SB	*EU*	FF		3224	*	**EU**	SF	*EU*	LY
3107	**EU**	SB	*EU*	FF		3225	*	**0**	SF	*SF*	LY
3108	**EU**	SB	*EU*	FF		3226	*	**0**	SF	*SF*	LY
3201	* **EU**	SF	*EU*	LY		3227	*	**0**	SF	*SF*	LY
3202	* **EU**	SF	*EU*	LY		3228	*	**0**	SF	*SF*	LY
3203	* **0**	SF	*SF*	LY		3229	*	**EU**	SF	*EU*	LY
3204	* **0**	SF	*SF*	LY		3230	*	**EU**	SF	*EU*	LY
3205	**EU**	SF	*EU*	LY		3231		**EU**	SF	*EU*	LY
3206	**EU**	SF	*EU*	LY		3232		**EU**	SF	*EU*	LY

8-Car Sets. Built for Regional Eurostar services. Individual vehicles in each set are allocated numbers 373xxx0 + 373xxx1 + 373xxx2 + 373xxx3 + 373xxx5 + 373xxx6 + 373xxx7 + 373xxx9, where 3xxx denotes the set number.
Set 3313/14 is used by Eurostar for special workings.

3733xx0 series. DM. 68.5 t.
3733xx1 series. MSO. –/48 1T. 44.6 t.
3733xx2 series. TSO. –/58 2T. 28.1 t.
3733xx3 series. TSO. –/58 1T. 29.7 t.
3733xx5 series. TSO. –/58 1T. 29.2 t.
3733xx6 series. RB. 31.1 t.
3733xx7 series. TFO. 39/– 1T. 29.6 t.
3733xx9 series. TBFO. 18/– 1TD. 39.4 t.

3301	**GN**	EU	*GN*	NP		3308	**EU**	EU		NP
3302	**GN**	EU	*GN*	NP		3309	**EU**	EU	*GN*	NP
3303	**GN**	EU	*GN*	NP The White Rose		3310	**EU**	EU	*GN*	NP
3304	**GN**	EU	*GN*	NP The White Rose		3311	**EU**	EU	*GN*	NP
3305	**GN**	EU	*GN*	NP Yorkshire Forward		3312	**EU**	EU	*GN*	NP
3306	**GN**	EU	*GN*	NP Golden Jubilee		3313	**EU**	EU	*EU*	NP
3307	**EU**	EU		NP		3314	**EU**	EU	*EU*	NP

Spare DM:

3999	**EU**	EU	*EU*	NP

Other names: 3313 and 3314; ENTENTE CORDIALE

4.4 SERVICE EMUS

CLASS 910/0   BRAKE FORCE RUNNER SETS

Converted from Class 488/3 ex-Gatwick Express hauled stock (formerly Mark 2 coaches). Used as part of Network Rail's Radio Survey locomotive-hauled trains. Radio Survey Train 1 usually operates with 910 001, Radio Equipment Survey Coach 977868 (see Page 348) and Overhead Line Equipment Test Coach 975091 (see Page 347). Radio Survey Train 2 usually operates with 910 002, Radio Survey Coach 977869 (see Page 348) and Track Recording Coach 999508 (see Page 348). Vehicles 72630 and 72631 are used in the Locomotive-hauled Network Rail Ultrasonic Test Train with 62482 (see below) and Ultrasonic Test Coach 99666 (see Page 344).

Formation: TSOH–TSO–TSOH.
Construction: Steel.
Gangways: Throughout.
Couplers: Buckeye (ends). Bar-coupled within sets
Maximum Speed: 90 m.p.h.
Braking: Tread brakes.
Multiple Working: SR type.

Doors: Slam.
Bogies: B4.

Dimensions: 20.18 x 2.82 m.

72612–72616/72630/72631/72639. TFOH. Lot No. 30860 Derby 1973–1974. 33.5 t.
72706/72708. TSO. Lot No. 30860 Derby 1973–1974. 33.5 t.

910 001	**RK**	NR	*SO*	ZA	72616 (6007)	72708 (6095)	72639 (6070)
910 002	**RK**	NR	*SO*	ZA	72612 (6156)	72706 (6143)	72613 (6126)
-	**RK**	NR	*SO*	ZA	72630 (6094)		72631 (6096)

ULTRASONIC TEST TRAIN (ADDITIONAL VEHICLE)

T. Converted 2003 from Class 432 EMU. Gangwayed. Operates with 72630, 72631 and 99666 as part of the Locomotive-hauled Ultrasonic Test Train (see above).

Construction: Steel.
Bogies: SR Mk. 6.
Brakes: Twin pipe vacuum.
Doors: Manually operated slam.

Maximum Speed: 75 m.p.h.
Couplings: Buckeye.
Multiple Working: Blue Square.
Dimensions: 19.66 x 2.82 m.

62482. T. Lot No. 30862 York 1974. 50.7 t.

-	**RK**	NR	*SO*	ZA	62482

ULTRASONIC TEST VEHICLE

Undergoing conversion for Network Rail, from Class 421 MBSO 62356. Details awaited.

999506. MBSO. Lot No. 30816 York 1970.   . t.

999506	**Y**	NR		LH

CLASS 930/0   TRAINING UNIT

Converted from Class 411/4 (No. 1505). Currently used as a Static Training Unit.

Formation: DM–TB–DM.
Supply System: 750 V DC third rail.
Traction Motors: Two English Electric 507 of 185 kW.

Construction: Steel.	**Doors:** Slam.
Gangways: Within unit.	**Bogies:** Mk. 4/Commonwealth.
Couplers: Buckeye.	**Maximum Speed:** 90 m.p.h.
Braking: Tread brakes.	**Dimensions:** 20.34 x 2.82 m.
Multiple Working: SR type.	

977861. DM. Lot No. 30111 Eastleigh 1956. 44.2 t.
977862. TB. Lot No. 30110 Eastleigh 1956. 36.2 t.
977863. DM. Lot No. 30108 Eastleigh 1956. 43.5 t.

930 082	**CX**	SN	*SN*	SU	977861	(61044)	977862	(70039)
					977863	(61038)		

CLASS 930/2 SANDITE/DE-ICING/TRACTOR UNITS

Converted from Class 416/2.

Formation: DMB–DMB.
Supply System: 750 V DC third rail.
Traction Motors: Two English Electric 507 of 185 kW.

Construction: Steel.	**Doors:** Slam.
Gangways: Within unit.	**Bogies:** Mk. 3B.
Couplers: Buckeye.	**Maximum Speed:** 75 m.p.h.
Braking: Tread brakes.	**Dimensions:** 20.44 x 2.82 m.
Multiple Working: SR type.	

977566/977567. DMB. Lot No. 30116 Eastleigh 1954–1955. 40.5 t.
977804/977864. DMB. Lot No. 30119 Eastleigh 1954. 40.5 t.
977805/977865/977871. DMB. Lot No. 30167 Eastleigh 1955. 40.5 t.
977872/977924/977925. DMB. Lot. No. 30314. Eastleigh 1956–1958. 40.5 t.
977874/977875. DMB. Lot No. 30114 Eastleigh 1954. 40.5 t.

930 204	**RK**	SN	*SN*	SU	977874	(65302)	977875	(65304)
930 206	**RK**	SN	*SN*	SU	977924	(65382)	977925	(65379)

CLASS 960/2   HITACHI "V" TRAIN

Hitachi Traction System Verification Train ("V" Train).
Converted 2003 from vehicles from Class 310 units 310 109 and 310 113 and
Class 423 MBSO 62138.
Train used to test AC or DC lines. Can be based at RM (when testing DC) or ZI
(when testing AC).

Formation: BDTS–MBS–MBS (AC/DC)–DTC
Supply System: 25 kV AC 50 Hz overhead or 750 V DC third rail.
Traction Motors: Four English Electric 546 of 201.5 kW each or four English
Electric 507 of 185 kW each (977979).

Construction: Steel.	**Doors:** Slam.
Gangways: Within unit.	**Bogies:** B4/Mark 4/B5 (SR)
Couplers: Buckeye.	**Maximum Speed:** 75 m.p.h.
Dimensions: 20.29 x 2.82 m.	

Non-standard Livery: Deep green & black.

977977. BDTS. Lot No. 30745 Derby 1965–1967. 37.5 t.
977978. MBS. Lot No. 30746 Derby 1965–1967. 57.0 t.
977979. MBS. Lot No. 30746 Derby 1965–1967. 57.0 t.
977980. DTC. Lot No. 30748 Derby 1965–1967. 34.5 t.
977981. MBS. Lot No. 30760 Derby 1967. 49.0 t.

960 201	**0**	H	*AE*	RM/ZI	977977	(76137)	977978	(62090)
					977981	(62138)	977980	(76187)
Spare	**0**	H	*AE*	RM/ZI	977979	(62078)		

4.5. EMUS AWAITING DISPOSAL

The list below comprises vehicles awaiting disposal which are stored on Network Rail, together with those stored at other locations which, although awaiting disposal, remain Network Rail registered.

Generally, units that are stored but where others in that class are still in service are listed in the main part of this book. This list mainly comprises classes of units of which there are none of that particular class still in revenue earning service. However all slam-door rolling stock now not in use is listed here because of its short future life. Spare cars which are unlikely to run on Network Rail again are also listed here.

IMPORTANT NOTE: EMUs still intact but already at scrapyards are not included in this list.

25 kV AC 50 Hz OVERHEAD UNITS:

Non-standard livery: 960 101 and 960 102 – Light blue & white.

310 046	N	H	PY	76130	62071	70731	76180
310 047	N	H	PY	76131	62072	70732	76181
310 049	N	H	KT	76133	62074	70734	76183
310 050	N	H	KT	76134	62075	70735	76184
310 051	N	H	KT	76135	62076	70736	76185
310 052	N	H	PY	76136	62077	70737	76186
310 057	N	H	PY	76141	62082	70742	76191
310 058	N	H	PY	76142	62083	70743	76192
310 059	N	H	KT	76143	62084	70744	76205
310 060	N	H	PY	76144	62085	70745	76194
310 064	N	H	PY	76148	62089	70749	76198
310 067	N	H	PY	76151	62092	70752	76201
310 068	N	H	PY	76152	62093	70753	76202
310 069	N	H	PY	76153	62094	70754	76203
310 070	N	H	PY	76154	62095	70755	76204
310 101	RR	H	PY	76157	62098		76207
310 102	RR	H	PY	76139	62080		76189
310 107	RR	H	PY	76146	62087		76196
310 108	RR	H	PY	76132	62073		76182
310 110	RR	H	PY	76138	62079		76188
310 111	RR	H	PY	76147	62088		76197
312 730	N	A	PY	76997	62660	71280	78048
312 782	N	A	PY	76976	62511	71195	78027
312 792	N	A	PY	76986	62521	71205	78037

960 101	0	A	PY	977962 (75642) 977963 (61937) 977964 (75981)
960 102	0	A	PY	977965 (75965) 977966 (61928) 977967 (75972)

Spare Cars:

Cl. 307	**BG**	MD	KT	75023				
Cl. 308	**N**	A	PY	70612	70631	70640		
Cl. 309	**RN**	A	PY	71758				
Cl. 310	**RR**	H	PY	62086	76140	76156	76190	76193
	N	H	PY	62091	70751	76145	76200	76206

750 V DC THIRD RAIL UNITS:

Non-standard liveries: 932 620 – One side of each vehicle painted in GEC-Alstom white & orange and the other side in Porterbrook livery. Vehicle 61948 has been used for paint trials, has carried different liveries.

1303	**ST**	H	PY	76581	62287	70967	76611
1315	**ST**	H	PY	76608	62314	70994	76638
1318	**ST**	H	PY	76590	62296	70976	76620
1319	**ST**	H	PY	76591	62297	70977	76621
1320	**ST**	H	PY	76593	62299	70979	76623
1401	**CX**	P	AF	76568	62284		76578
1512	**ST**	P	BM	61321		70268	61320
1704	**CX**	A	BI	76092	62033	70711	76038
1705	**CX**	SN	SU	76076	62017	70695	76022
1711	**CX**	A	PY	76114	62055	71766	76060
1753	**CX**	A	PY	76102	62043	70721	76048
1804	**CX**	A	PY	76778	62416	70711	76849
1832	**CX**	A	PY	76719	62357	71037	76790
1850	**CX**	NR	TH	76629		71036	76789
1855	**CX**	A	PY	76720	62358	71038	76791
1857	**GA**	A	PY	76610	62316	70996	76640
1874	**CX**	A	SU	76755	62393	71073	76826
1889	**ST**	H	PY	76774	62412	71092	76845
1903	**CX**	A	PY	76081	62022	70700	76027
1904	**CX**	A	PY	76107	62048	70726	76053
3423	**CX**	A	PY	76452	62222	70912	76451
3473	**CX**	A	PY	76502	62245	70937	76339
3582	**CX**	A	PY	76891	62472	71130	76275
3588	**CX**	A	PY	76923	62467	71146	76924
4308	**N**	H	PY	61275	75395		
6213	**BG**	NR	PY	65327	77512		
6308	**N**	NR	PY	14564	16108		
6309	**N**	NR	PY	14562	16106		
932 620	**O**	AM	ZG	61948	70653	70660	61949
930 010	**RK**	MA	DY	975600	(10988)	975601	(10843)
930 101	**N**	NR	AF	977207	(61658)	977609	(65414)

Spare Cars:

Non-standard livery: 76112 – Silver (prototype Class 424 "Networker Classic" conversion).

Cl. 411	**N**	H	ZI	61390	70293			
	ST	AM	ZG	69343				
Cl. 416	**IC**	AM	ZG	977296	(65319)			
Cl. 421	**CX**	A	PY	76030	76031	76049	76062	76066
				76073	76084	76085	76103	76116
				76120	76127			
	GA	A	PY	76051	76069	76072	76117	76126
				76129				
	U	A	PY	76061	76067	76115	76121	
	N	AM	ZG	62395				
Cl. 424	**0**	BT	ZD	76112				
Cl. 438	**N**	X	ZG	977764	(70866)			
Cl. 455	**SS**	AM	ZG	71731				
Cl. 930	**RO**	NR	AF	975598 (10989)			975605 (10940)	

5. NON-PASSENGER-CARRYING COACHING STOCK

The notes shown for locomotive-hauled passenger stock generally apply also to non-passenger-carrying coaching stock (often abbreviated to NPCCS).

TOPS TYPE CODES

TOPS type codes for NPCCS are made up as follows:

(1) Two letters denoting the type of the vehicle:

AX	Nightstar generator van
AY	Eurostar barrier vehicle
NA	Propelling control vehicle.
NB	High security brake van (100 m.p.h.).
ND	Gangwayed brake van (90 m.p.h.).
NE	Gangwayed brake van (100 m.p.h.).
NG	Motorail loading wagon.
NH	Gangwayed brake van (110 m.p.h.).
NI	High security brake van (110 m.p.h.).
NJ	General utility van (90 m.p.h.).
NK	High security general utility van (100 m.p.h.).
NL	Newspaper van.
NN	Courier vehicle.
NO	General utility van (100 m.p.h. e.t.h. wired).
NP	General utility van for post office use or Motorail van (110 m.p.h.).
NQ	High security brake van (110 m.p.h.).
NR	BAA container van (100 m.p.h.).
NV	Motorail van (side loading).
NX	Motorail van (100 m.p.h.).
NY	Exhibition van.
NZ	Driving brake van (also known as driving van trailer).
YR	Ferry van (special Southern Region version of NJ with two pairs of side doors instead of three).

(2) A third letter denoting the brake type:

A	Air braked
V	Vacuum braked
X	Dual braked

OPERATING CODES

The normal operating codes are given in parentheses after the TOPS type codes. These are as follows:

BG	Gangwayed brake van.
DLV	Driving brake van (also known as driving van trailer – DVT).
GUV	General utility van.
PCV	Propelling control van.

AK51 (RK)   KITCHEN CAR

Mark 1. Converted 1989 from RBR. Fluorescent lighting. Commonwealth bogies.
ETH 2X.

Lot No. 30628 Pressed Steel 1960–61. 39 t.

Note: Kitchen cars have traditionally been numbered in the NPCCS series, but
have passenger coach diagram numbers!

80041	(1690)	x	**M**	E	*E*	OM

NN   COURIER VEHICLE

Mark 1. Converted 1986–7 from BSKs. One compartment and toilet retained for
courier use. One set of roller shutter doors inserted on each side. ETH 2.

80204/11/23. Lot No. 30699 Wolverton 1962. Commonwealth bogies. 37 t.
80207. Lot No. 30721 Wolverton 1963. Commonwealth bogies. 37 t.
80220. Lot No. 30573 Gloucester 1960. B4 bogies. 33 t.

Notes:

Roller shutter doors removed and aperture plated over on 80207.
80223 has been converted to a bar car with the former stowage area becoming
an open saloon with a bar.

80204	(35297)	x	**M**	WC	*LS*	CS
80207	(35466)	x	**PC**	VS	*VS*	SL
80211	(35296)		**NR**	NR		DY
80220	(35276)	x	**M**	NE	*LS*	NY
80223	(35331)	x	**G**	MH	*MH*	RL

Name: 80207 is branded 'BAGGAGE CAR No.11'.

ND (BG) GANGWAYED BRAKE VAN (90 m.p.h.)

Mark 1. Short frames (57'). Load 10t. All vehicles were built with BR Mark 1
bogies. ETH 1. Vehicles numbered 81xxx had 3000 added to the original numbers
to avoid confusion with Class 81 locomotives. The full lot number list is listed
here for reference purposes with renumbered vehicles. No unmodified vehicles
remain in service.

80621. Lot No. 30046 York 1954. 31.5 t.
80826. Lot No. 30144 Cravens 1955. 31.5 t.
80855–80959. Lot No. 30162 Pressed Steel 1956–57. 32 t.
80980–81001. Lot No. 30173 York 1956. 31.5 t.
81025–81026. Lot No. 30224 Cravens 1956. 31.5 t.

81077–81175. Lot No. 30228 Metro-Cammell 1957–58. 31.5 t.
81205–81265. Lot No. 30163 Pressed Steel 1957. 31.5 t.
81266–81309. Lot No. 30323 Pressed Steel 1957. 32 t.
81325–81497. Lot No. 30400 Pressed Steel 1957–58. 32 t.
81498–81568. Lot No. 30484 Pressed Steel 1958. 32 t.
81606. Lot No. 30716 Gloucester 1962. 31 t.
Non-standard Livery: 81025 is British racing green with gold lining.

The following vehicle is an ND rebogied with Commonwealth bogies and adapted for use as exhibition van 1998 at Lancastrian Carriage & Wagon Co. Ltd. 33 t.

81025 (81025, 84025)   **0**   RA *RA*   CP

Name: 81025 VALIANT

NZ (DLV)　　DRIVING BRAKE VAN (110 m.p.h.)

Mark 3B. Air conditioned. T4 bogies. dg. ETH 5X.

Lot No. 31042 Derby 1988. 45.18 t.

Non-standard Livery: 82146 is EWS silver.

82101	V	P	VW	MA	82127	V	P	VW	MA
82102	V	P		MA	82128	V	P	E	OM
82103	V	P	VW	MA	82129	V	P		ZB
82104	V	P		PC	82130	V	P		LT
82105	V	P		MA	82131	V	P	E	OM
82106	V	P	SR	PC	82132	V	P	SR	PC
82107	V	P	VW	MA	82133	V	P	1A	NC
82108	V	P		LT	82134	V	P		LT
82109	V	P	SR	PC	82135	V	P		LT
82110	V	P	1A	NC	82136	V	P		LT
82111	V	P		PC	82137	V	P		LT
82112	V	P	SR	PC	82138	V	P		LT
82113	V	P		LT	82139	V	P		LT
82114	V	P		PC	82140	V	P		MA
82115	V	P		LT	82141	V	P		LT
82116	V	P		LT	82142	V	P		LT
82117	V	P		LT	82143	V	P	VW	MA
82118	V	P	VW	MA	82144	V	P		LT
82119	1	P	1A	NC	82145	V	P	E	OM
82120	V	P	SR	PC	82146	0	E	E	TO
82121	V	P		PC	82147	V	P		LT
82122	V	P	1A	NC	82148	V	P		LT
82123	V	P		LT	82149	V	P		LT
82124	V	P		PC	82150	V	P	VW	MA
82125	V	P		PC	82151	V	P	E	OM
82126	V	P	VW	MA	82152	V	P	1A	NC

Name:

82101　101 Squadron

NZ (DLV)   DRIVING BRAKE VAN (140 m.p.h.)

Mark 4. Air conditioned. Swiss-built (SIG) bogies. dg. ETH 6X.

Lot No. 31043 Metro-Cammell 1988. 45.18 t.

82200	**GN**	H	*GN*	BN	82216	**GN**	H	*GN*	BN
82201	**GN**	H	*GN*	BN	82217	**GN**	H	*GN*	BN
82202	**GN**	H	*GN*	BN	82218	**GN**	H	*GN*	BN
82203	**GN**	H	*GN*	BN	82219	**GN**	H	*GN*	BN
82204	**GN**	H	*GN*	BN	82220	**GN**	H	*GN*	BN
82205	**GN**	H	*GN*	BN	82222	**GN**	H	*GN*	BN
82206	**GN**	H	*GN*	BN	82223	**GN**	H	*GN*	BN
82207	**GN**	H	*GN*	BN	82224	**GN**	H	*GN*	BN
82208	**GN**	H	*GN*	BN	82225	**GN**	H	*GN*	BN
82209	**GN**	H	*GN*	BN	82226	**GN**	H	*GN*	BN
82210	**GN**	H	*GN*	BN	82227	**GN**	H	*GN*	BN
82211	**GN**	H	*GN*	BN	82228	**GN**	H	*GN*	BN
82212	**GN**	H	*GN*	BN	82229	**GN**	H	*GN*	BN
82213	**GN**	H	*GN*	BN	82230	**GN**	H	*GN*	BN
82214	**GN**	H	*GN*	BN	82231	**GN**	H	*GN*	BN
82215	**GN**	H	*GN*	BN					

Name: 82219   Duke of Edinburgh

NJ (GUV)   GENERAL UTILITY VAN

Mark 1. Short frames. Load 14 t. Screw couplings. These vehicles had 7000 added to the original numbers to avoid confusion with Class 86 locomotives. The full lot number list is listed here for reference purposes with renumbered vehicles. No unmodified vehicles remain in service. All vehicles were built with BR Mark 2 bogies. ETH 0 or 0X*.

86081–86499. Lot No. 30417 Pressed Steel 1958–59. 30 t.
86508–86518. Lot No. 30343 York 1957. 30 t.
86521–86648. Lot No. 30403 York/Glasgow 1958–60. 30 t.
86656–86820. Lot No. 30565 Pressed Steel 1959. 30 t.
86849–86956. Lot No. 30616 Pressed Steel 1959–60. 30 t.

NE/NH (BG)
GANGWAYED BRAKE VAN (100/110 m.p.h.)

NE are ND but rebogied with B4 bogies suitable for 100 m.p.h. NH are identical but are allowed to run at 110 m.p.h. with special maintenance of the bogies. For lot numbers refer to original number series. Deduct 1.5t from weights. 92901–92939 were renumbered from 920xx series by adding 900 to number to avoid conflict with Class 92 locos. All NHA are *pg. ETH 1 (1X*).

b In use as Pendolino barrier vehicle.

92100	(81391)		to	RV	CP
92111	(81432)		NHAb	LW	*FL*	CP

92114	(81443)	NHA	**NR**	NR		DY
92125	(81470)	to		DR		KM
92146	(81498)	NHA		NR		DY
92159	(81534)	NHA		H		KT
92174	(81567)	NHA		H		PY
92175	(81568)	pg		H		CP
92194	(81606)	to		H		PY
92901	(80855, 92001)	NHA		H		PY
92904	(80867, 92004)	*pg	**G**	VS		SL
92908	(80895, 92008)	NHA	**M**	WC	*WC*	CS
92929	(81077, 92029)	NHAb		LW	*FL*	CP
92931	(81102, 92031)	NHA		H		PY
92935	(81150, 92035)	*pg		H		PY
92936	(81158, 92036)	NHA		H	*RV*	CP
92938	(81173, 92038)	NHA		H		PY
92939	(81175, 92039)	NHA		NR		DY

NL   NEWSPAPER VAN

Mark 1. Short frames (57'). Converted from NJ (GUV). Fluorescent lighting, toilets and gangways fitted. Load 14 t. Now used for materials storage. B5 Bogies. ETH 3X.

Lot No. 30922 Wolverton 1977–78. 31 t.

94003	(86281, 93999)	x	**RX**	FG	*GW*	OO
94006	(86202, 85506)		**RX**	FG	*GW*	OO

NKA   HIGH SECURITY GENERAL UTILITY VAN

Mark 1. These vehicles are GUVs further modified with new floors, three roller shutter doors per side and the end doors removed. For lot Nos. see original number series. Commonwealth bogies. Add 2 t to weight. ETH0X.

Non-Standard Livery: 94121 is grey.

94100	(86668, 95100)	**RX**	E	*E*	ML
94101	(86142, 95101)	**RX**	E		MO
94102	(86762, 95102)	**RX**	E		OM
94103	(86956, 95103)	**RX**	E		SD
94104	(86942, 95104)	**RX**	E		OM
94106	(86353, 95106)	**RX**	E	*E*	ML
94107	(86576, 95107)	**RX**	E		OM
94108	(86600, 95108)	**RX**	E		CD
94110	(86393, 95110)	**RX**	E		ER
94111	(86578, 95111)	**RX**	E		ML
94112	(86673, 95112)	**RX**	E		OM
94113	(86235, 95113)	**RX**	E		OM
94114	(86081, 95114)	**RX**	E		WE
94116	(86426, 95116)	**RX**	E		TY
94117	(86534, 95117)	**RX**	E		MO
94118	(86675, 95118)	**RX**	E		EN
94119	(86167, 95119)	**RX**	E		TY
94121	(86518, 95121)	**0**	E		TO

94123	(86376, 95123)	**RX**	E		ML
94126	(86692, 95126)	**RX**	E		ER
94132	(86607, 95132)	**RX**	E	*E*	ML
94133	(86604, 95133)	**RX**	E		ML
94137	(86610, 95137)	**RX**	E		MO
94138	(86212, 95138)	**RX**	E		YN
94140	(86571, 95140)	**RX**	E		TY
94146	(86648, 95146)	**RX**	E		OM
94147	(86091, 95147)	**RX**	E		MO
94148	(86416, 95148)	**RX**	E		ER
94150	(86560, 95150)	**RX**	E		ML
94153	(86798, 95153)	**RX**	E		WE
94155	(86820, 95155)	**RX**	E		ML
94157	(86523, 95157)	**RX**	E		CY
94160	(86581, 95160)	**RX**	E	*E*	ML
94164	(86104, 95164)	**RX**	E		ML
94166	(86112, 95166)	**RX**	E	*E*	ML
94168	(86914, 95168)	**RX**	E		TY
94170	(86395, 95170)	**RX**	E	*E*	ML
94172	(86429, 95172)	**RX**	E		MO
94174	(86852, 95174)	**RX**	E		WE
94175	(86521, 95175)	**RX**	E		MO
94176	(86210, 95176)	**RX**	E	*E*	ML
94177	(86411, 95177)	**RX**	E		SM
94180	(86362, 95141)	**RX**	E		ML
94182	(86710, 95182)	**RX**	E		MO
94190	(86624, 95350)	**RX**	E		BK
94191	(86596, 95351)	**RX**	E		MO
94192	(86727, 95352)	**RX**	E	*E*	ML
94193	(86514, 95353)	**RX**	E		WE
94195	(86375, 95355)	**RX**	E		MO
94196	(86478, 95356)	**RX**	E	*E*	ML
94197	(86508, 95357)	**RX**	E		MO
94198	(86195, 95358)	**RX**	E		ML
94199	(86854, 95359)	**RX**	E		MO
94200	(86207, 95360)	**RX**	E		MO
94202	(86563, 95362)	**RX**	E	*E*	ML
94203	(86345, 95363)	**RX**	E		TY
94204	(86715, 95364)	**RX**	E		ER
94205	(86857, 95365)	**RX**	E		MO
94207	(86529, 95367)	**RX**	E		OM
94208	(86656, 95368)	**RX**	E		SM
94209	(86390, 95369)	**RX**	E		SD
94211	(86713, 95371)	**RX**	E		YN
94212	(86728, 95372)	**RX**	E		MO
94213	(86258, 95373)	**RX**	E		ML
94214	(86367, 95374)	**RX**	E		TY
94215	(86862, 94077)	**RX**	E		MO
94216	(86711, 93711)	**RX**	E		YN
94217	(86131, 93131)	**RX**	E		ML
94218	(86541, 93541)	**RX**	E		MO

94221	(86905, 93905)	**RX** E	*E*	ML
94222	(86474, 93474)	**RX** E		ML
94223	(86660, 93660)	**RX** E		TY
94224	(86273, 93273)	**RX** E		CY
94225	(86849, 93849)	**RX** E		MO
94226	(86525, 93525)	**RX** E		MO
94227	(86585, 93585)	**RX** E		MO
94228	(86511, 93511)	**RX** E		MO
94229	(86720, 93720)	**RX** E		OM

NAA   PROPELLING CONTROL VEHICLE

Mark 1. Class 307 driving trailers converted for use in propelling mail trains out of termini. Fitted with roller shutter doors. Equipment fitted for communication between cab of PCV and locomotive. B5 bogies. ETH 2X.

Lot No. 30206 Eastleigh 1954–56. Converted at Hunslet-Barclay, Kilmarnock 1994–96.

94302	(75124)	**RX** E	TY	94323	(75110)	**RX** E	ML
94303	(75131)	**RX** E	TY	94324	(75103)	**RX** E	MG
94304	(75107)	**RX** E	ML	94325	(75113)	**RX** E	EN
94305	(75104)	**RX** E	EN	94326	(75123)	**RX** E	TY
94306	(75112)	**RX** E	MO	94327	(75116)	**RX** E	EN
94307	(75127)	**RX** E	SD	94331	(75022)	**RX** E	SD
94308	(75125)	**RX** E	ML	94332	(75011)	**RX** E	TY
94309	(75130)	**RX** E	EN	94333	(75016)	**RX** E	TY
94310	(75119)	**RX** E	WE	94334	(75017)	**RX** E	CY
94311	(75105)	**RX** E	WE	94335	(75032)	**RX** E	TY
94312	(75126)	**RX** E	MG	94336	(75031)	**RX** E	TY
94313	(75129)	**RX** E	WE	94337	(75029)	**RX** E	WE
94314	(75109)	**RX** E	MG	94338	(75008)	**RX** E	WE
94315	(75132)	**RX** E	Rugby	94339	(75024)	**RX** E	TD
94316	(75108)	**RX** E	SM	94340	(75012)	**RX** E	CY
94317	(75117)	**RX** E	OM	94341	(75007)	**RX** E	EN
94318	(75115)	**RX** E	SD	94342	(75005)	**RX** E	EN
94319	(75128)	**RX** E	EN	94343	(75027)	**RX** E	ML
94320	(75120)	**RX** E	Norwich	94344	(75014)	**RX** E	SM
94321	(75122)	**RX** E	EN	94345	(75004)	**RX** E	EN
94322	(75111)	**RX** E	ML				

NBA   HIGH SECURITY BRAKE VAN (100 m.p.h.)

Mark 1. These vehicles are NEs further modified with sealed gangways, new floors, built-in tail lights and roller shutter doors. For lot Nos. see original number series. B4 bogies. 31.4 t. ETH 1X.

94400	(81224, 92954)	**RX** E		SD
94401	(81277, 92224)	**RX** E	*E*	ML
94402	(81479, 92629)	**RX** E		ML
94403	(81486, 92135)	**RX** E		MG
94405	(80890, 92233)	**RX** E		EN

94406	(81226, 92956)	**RX**	E	*E*	ML
94407	(81223, 92553)	**RX**	E		MG
94408	(81264, 92981)	**RX**	E	*E*	TY
94410	(81205, 92941)	**RX**	E		WE
94411	(81378, 92997)	**RX**	E		SD
94412	(81210, 92945)	**RX**	E		ML
94413	(80909, 92236)	**RX**	E		MO
94414	(81377, 92996)	**RX**	E		EN
94415	(81309, 92992)	**RX**	E		YN
94416	(80929, 92746)	**RX**	E		TY
94418	(81248, 92244)	**RX**	E		EN
94420	(81325, 92263)	**RX**	E		ML
94422	(81516, 92651)	**RX**	E		OM
94423	(80923, 92914)	**RX**	E	*E*	ML
94424	(81400, 92103)	**RX**	E		ML
94427	(80894, 92754)	**RX**	E		WE
94428	(81550, 92166)	**RX**	E		ML
94429	(80870, 92232)	**RX**	E		MO
94431	(81401, 92604)	**RX**	E		MO
94432	(81383, 92999)	**RX**	E		TY
94433	(81495, 92643)	**RX**	E		AC
94434	(81268, 92584)	**RX**	E		TY
94435	(81485, 92134)	**RX**	E		WE
94436	(81237, 92565)	**RX**	E		EN
94437	(81403, 92208)	**RX**	E		EN
94438	(81425, 92251)	**RX**	E		YN
94439	(81480, 92130)	**RX**	E		ER
94440	(81497, 92645)	**RX**	E		TY
94441	(81492, 92140)	**RX**	E		ML
94442	(80932, 92723)	**RX**	E		ER
94443	(81473, 92127)	**RX**	E		ML
94444	(81484, 92133)	**RX**	E		ML
94445	(81444, 92615)	**RX**	E		WE
94446	(80857, 92242)	**RX**	E		ER
94447	(81515, 92266)	**RX**	E		EN
94448	(81541, 92664)	**RX**	E		TY
94449	(81536, 92747)	**RX**	E		SD
94450	(80927, 92915)	**RX**	E		WE
94451	(80955, 92257)	**RX**	E		WE
94452	(81394, 92602)	**RX**	E		YN
94453	(81170, 92239)	**RX**	E		MO
94454	(81465, 92124)	**RX**	E		WE
94455	(81239, 92264)	**RX**	E		SD
94458	(81255, 92974)	**RX**	E		SD
94459	(81490, 92138)	**RX**	E		ML
94460	(81266, 92983)	**RX**	E		ML
94461	(81487, 92136)	**RX**	E		TY
94462	(81289, 92270)	**RX**	E		CY
94463	(81375, 92995)	**RX**	E		TY
94464	(81240, 92262)	**RX**	E		TY
94465	(81481, 92131)	**RX**	E		TY

94466	(81236, 92964)	**RX**	E	WE
94467	(81245, 92969)	**RX**	E	EN
94468	(81259, 92978)	**RX**	E	ML
94469	(81260, 92979)	**RX**	E	TY
94470	(81442, 92113)	**RX**	E	OM
94471	(81518, 92152)	**RX**	E	ER
94472	(81256, 92975)	**RX**	E	ML
94473	(81262, 92272)	**RX**	E	TY
94474	(81452, 92618)	**RX**	E	ML
94475	(81208, 92943)	**RX**	E	TY
94476	(81209, 92944)	**RX**	E	CY
94477	(81494, 92642)	**RX**	E	TY
94478	(81488, 92637)	**RX**	E	TY
94479	(81482, 92132)	**RX**	E	OM
94480	(81411, 92608)	**RX**	E	ML
94481	(81493, 92641)	**RX**	E	SD
94482	(81491, 92639)	**RX**	E	ML
94483	(81500, 92647)	**RX**	E	SD
94484	(81426, 92110)	**RX**	E	EN
94485	(81496, 92644)	**RX**	E	SD
94486	(81254, 92973)	**RX**	E	ML
94487	(81413, 92609)	**RX**	E	ML
94488	(81405, 92105)	**RX**	E	CY
94490	(81409, 92606)	**RX**	E	MO
94492	(80888, 92721)	**RX**	E	WE
94493	(80944, 92919)	**RX**	E	YN
94494	(81451, 92617)	**RX**	E	EN
94495	(80871, 92755)	**RX**	E	TY
94496	(81514, 92650)	**RX**	E	EN
94497	(80877, 92717)	**RX**	E	ML
94498	(81225, 92555)	**RX**	E	MO
94499	(81258, 92577)	**RX**	E	CY

NBA/NIA/NQA
HIGH SECURITY BRAKE VAN (100/110 m.p.h.)

Mark 1. These vehicles are NEs further modified with sealed gangways, new floors, built-in tail lights and roller shutter doors. For lot Nos. see original number series. B4 bogies. 31.4 t. ETH 1X.

These vehicles are identical to the 94400–94499 series. Certain vehicles are being given a special maintenance regime whereby tyres are reprofiled more frequently than normal and are then allowed to run at 110 m.p.h. Vehicles from the 94400 series upgraded to 110 m.p.h. are being renumbered in this series. Vehicles are NBA (100 m.p.h.) unless marked NIA or NQA (110 m.p.h.). NQA are vehicles which were modified for haulage by Class 90/2 locomotives which were fitted with composition brake blocks.

94500	(81457, 92121)	NIA	**RX**	E	OM
94501	(80891, 92725)		**RX**	E	OM
94502	(80924, 92720)	NQA	**RX**	E	ML

94503	(80873, 92709)	NIA	**RX**	E		SD
94504	(80935, 92748)	NQA	**RX**	E		MO
94505	(81235, 92750)	NIA	**RX**	E		YN
94506	(80958, 92922)	NIA	**RX**	E		MO
94507	(80876, 92505)	NIA	**RX**	E		YN
94508	(80887, 92722)	NQA	**RX**	E		ML
94509	(80897, 92509)	NQA	**RX**	E		OM
94510	(80945, 92265)		**RX**	E		WE
94511	(81504, 92714)	NIA	**RX**	E		OM
94512	(81265, 92582)		**RX**	E		TY
94513	(81257, 92576)		**RX**	E		YN
94514	(81459, 92122)	NIA	**RX**	E		TY
94515	(80916, 92513)	NQA	**RX**	E	E	ML
94516	(81267, 92211)	NQA	**RX**	E		TY
94517	(81489, 92243)	NIA	**RX**	E		CY
94518	(81346, 92258)		**RX**	E		ML
94519	(80930, 92916)	NQA	**RX**	E		OM
94520	(80940, 92917)	NQA	**RX**	E		TY
94521	(80900, 92510)	NIA	**RX**	E		CY
94522	(80880, 92907)	NIA	**RX**	E		TY
94523	(81509, 92649)	NIA	**RX**	E		EN
94524	(81454, 94457)	NQA	**RX**	E		SD
94525	(80902, 92229)	NIA	**RX**	E		TY
94526	(80941, 92518)	NIA	**RX**	E		TY
94527	(80921, 92728)	NQA	**RX**	E		TY
94528	(81404, 92267)		**RX**	E	E	ML
94529	(80959, 92252)	NQA	**RX**	E		CY
94530	(81511, 94409)	NIA	**RX**	E		TY
94531	(80879, 94456)	NQA	**RX**	E		TY
94532	(81423, 94489)	NQA	**RX**	E		OM
94534	(80908, 94430)	NIA	**RX**	E		TY
94535	(80858, 94419)	NIA	**RX**	E		EN
94536	(80936, 94491)	NIA	**RX**	E	E	ML
94537	(81230, 94421)	NIA	**RX**	E		MG
94538	(81283, 94426)	NQA	**RX**	E	E	ML

NBA HIGH SECURITY BRAKE VAN (100 m.p.h.)

Mark 1. Details as for 94400–99 but fitted with Commonwealth bogies. 34.4 t. ETH 1X.

94539	(81501, 92302)	**RX**	E		MO
94540	(81431, 92860)	**RX**	E		TJ
94541	(80980, 92316)	**RX**	E		ML
94542	(80995, 92330)	**RX**	E		MO
94543	(81026, 92389)	**RX**	E	E	ML
94544	(81083, 92345)	**RX**	E		MO
94545	(81001, 92329)	**RX**	E		MO
94546	(81339, 92804)	**RX**	E		MO
94547	(80861, 92392)	**RX**	E	E	ML
94548	(81154, 92344)	**RX**	E		TY

NRA   BAA CONTAINER VAN (100 m.p.h.)

Mark 1. Modified for carriage of British Airports Authority containers with roller
shutter doors and roller floors and gangways removed. Now used for general
parcels traffic. For lot Nos. see original number series. Commonwealth bogies.
Add 2 t to weight. ETH3.

95400	(80621, 95203)	**E**	E		MO
95410	(80826, 95213)	**E**	E		ML

NOA   HIGH SECURITY GENERAL UTILITY VAN

Mark 1. These vehicles are GUVs further modified with new floors, two roller
shutter doors per side, middle doors sealed and end doors removed. For lot Nos.
see original number series. Commonwealth bogies. Add 2 t to weight. ETH 0X.

95715	(86174, 95115)	**R**	E		TY
95727	(86323, 95127)	**R**	E		WE
95734	(86462, 95134)	**R**	E		EN
95739	(86172, 95139)	**R**	E		WE
95743	(86485, 95143)	**R**	E		EN
95749	(86265, 95149)	**R**	E		TY
95754	(86897, 95154)	**R**	E		TY
95758	(86499, 95158)	**R**	E		TY
95759	(86084, 95159)	**R**	E		EN
95761	(86205, 95161)	**R**	E		WE
95762	(86122, 95162)	**R**	E		WE
95763	(86407, 95163)	**R**	E		TY

NP/NX/NV (GUV)   MOTORAIL VAN (100 m.p.h.)

Mark 1. For details and lot numbers see original number series. ETH 0 (0X*).

Notes: 96100 was authorised for 110 m.p.h. and is classified NP.
96101 has a new prototype body built 1998 by Marcroft Engineering with side
loading and one end sealed and is classified NV.

b In use as Pendolino barrier vehicle.

96100	(86734, 93734)	*B5		H		TM
96101	(86741, 93741)	*B5	**HB**	H		PY
96110	(86738, 93738)	*C		H		PY
96132	(86754, 93754)	*C		H		LT
96135	(86755, 93755)	C		H		KT
96139	(86751, 93751)	C		H	*VW*	MA
96164	(86880, 93880)	*C		H		LT
96165	(86784, 93784)	*C		WC		CS
96170	(86159, 93159)	x*C		WC		CS
96175	(86628, 93628)	x*C		WC		CS
96178	(86782, 93782)	*C		WC		CS
96181	(86875, 93875)	*C		WC		ZH
96182	(86944, 93944)	*C b	**K**	LW	*FL*	CP
96191	(86665, 93665)	x*C		WC		CS

NP (GUV)   MOTORAIL VAN (110 m.p.h.)

Mark 1. Vehicles modified with concertina end doors. For details and lot numbers
see original number series. B5 Bogies. ETH 0X.

96210	(86355, 96159)	NR	DY
96212	(86443, 96161)	NR	DY
96218	(86286, 96151)	NR	DY

AX5G   NIGHTSTAR GENERATOR VAN

Mark 3A. Generator vans converted from sleeping cars for use on 'Nightstar'
services. Designed to operate between two Class 37/6 locomotives. Gangways
removed. Two Cummins diesel generator groups providing a 1500 V train supply.
Hydraulic parking brake. 61-way ENS interface jumpers. BT10 bogies.

Lot No. 30960 Derby 1981–83. 46.01 t.

96371	(10545, 6371)	**EP**	EU	NP
96372	(10564, 6372)	**EP**	EU	NP
96373	(10568, 6373)	**EP**	EU	NP
96374	(10585, 6374)	**EP**	EU	NP
96375	(10587, 6375)	**EP**	EU	NP

AY5 (BV)   EUROSTAR BARRIER VEHICLE

Mark 1. Converted from GUVs. Bodies removed. B4 bogies.

96380–96382. Lot No. 30417 Pressed Steel 1958–59. 40 t.
96383. Lot No. 30565 Pressed Steel 1959. 40 t.
96384. Lot No. 30616 Pressed Steel 1959–60. 40 t.

96380	(86386, 6380)	**B**	EU	*EU*	NP
96381	(86187, 6381)	**B**	EU	*EU*	NP
96382	(86295, 6382)	**B**	EU	*EU*	NP
96383	(86664, 6383)	**B**	EU	*EU*	NP
96384	(86955, 6384)	**B**	EU	*EU*	NP

NVA   MOTORAIL VAN (100 m.p.h.)

Mark 1. Built 1998–9 by Marcroft Engineering using underframe and running
gear from Motorail GUVs. Side loading with one end sealed. The vehicles run in
pairs and access is available to the adjacent vehicle. For details and lot numbers
see original number series. B5 bogies. ETH 0X.

96602	(86097, 96150)	**GL**	H	*GW*	PZ
96603	(86334, 96155)	**GL**	H	*GW*	PZ
96604	(86337, 96156)	**GL**	H	*GW*	PZ
96605	(86344, 96157)	**GL**	H	*GW*	PZ
96606	(86324, 96213)	**GL**	H	*GW*	PZ
96607	(86351, 96215)	**GL**	H	*GW*	PZ
96608	(86385, 96216)	**GL**	H	*GW*	PZ
96609	(86327, 96217)	**GL**	H	*GW*	PZ

NY   ULTRASONIC TEST COACH

Converted Railway Age, Crewe 1996 from FO to Exhibition Van. Further converted at Alstom, Wolverton Works 2002 to Ultrasonic Test Coach. B4 bogies.

Lot No. 30843 Derby 1972–73.

99666   (3250)   **RK**   NR   *SO*   ZA

YR   FERRY VAN

This vehicle was built to a wagon lot although the design closely resembles that of NJ except it only has two sets of doors per side. Short Frames (57'). Load 14 t. Commonwealth bogies.

Built Eastleigh 1958. Wagon Lot. No. 2849. 30 t.

Non-Standard Livery: 889202 is Pullman Car umber with gold lining and lettering.

889202   **0**   VS   *VS*   CP

Name: 889202 is branded 'BAGGAGE CAR No.8'.

NPCCS AWAITING DISPOSAL

80319	ER	80371	MG	80429	EN
80320	EN	80372	TJ	80430	EN
80321	EN	80373	EN	80431	EN
80322	SD	80374	WE	80432	TO
80323	EN	80375	EN	80433	EN
80324	WE	80376	WE	80434	TO
80325	WE	80377	EN	80435	EN
80326	EN	80378	EN	80436	ER
80327	EN	80379	EN	80437	EN
80331	EN	80380	EN	80438	EN
80332	WE	80381	WE	80439	MG
80333	TJ	80382	EN	80456	EN
80334	WE	80383	WE	80457	EN
80337	EN	80384	TJ	80458	EN
80339	EN	80385	EN	80865	Hornsey Sand Terminal
80340	TJ	80386	SD	84364	Doncaster West Yard
80341	ER	80387	YN	84387	CY
80342	ER	80390	YN	84519	CY
80343	WE	80392	ER	92193	Preston Carriage Sidings
80344	EN	80393	WE	92198	ZB
80345	EN	80394	EN	92303	OM
80346	EN	80395	EN	92314	CY
80347	EN	80400	MG	92350	FP
80348	WE	80401	TO	92350	OM
80349	EN	80402	EN	92400	CY
80350	EN	80403	WE	92410	CY
80351	EN	80404	WE	92412	CY
80352	EN	80405	WE	92413	CY
80353	ER	80406	TJ	92530	OM
80354	EN	80411	ER	92872	CY
80355	ER	80412	ER	93180	Derby South Dock Siding
80356	EN	80413	WE	93446	CY
80357	SD	80414	EN	93723	Bletchley T&RSMD
80358	EN	80415	ER	93930	CY
80359	EN	80416	TJ	94027	FP
80360	EN	80417	EN	95128	CY
80361	EN	80419	EN	95129	CY
80362	ER	80420	ER	95228	NC
80363	EN	80421	WE	95300	ML
80364	SD	80422	SD	95301	ML
80365	EN	80423	EN	96177	CP
80366	WE	80424	SD	96452	BR
80367	EN	80425	TJ	96453	BR
80368	EN	80426	EN	99645	FP
80369	SD	80427	EN	99646	FP
80370	YN	80428	EN		

6. SERVICE STOCK

Vehicles in this section are numbered in the former BR departmental number series. They are used for internal purposes within the railway industry, i.e. they do not generate revenue from outside the industry.

EMU TRANSLATOR VEHICLES

These vehicles are used to move EMU vehicles around the National Rail system in the same way as other vehicles included in this book. Similar vehicles numbered in the BR capital stock series are included elsewhere in this book. Converted from Mark 1 TSO, RSOs, RUOs, BSKs and GUVs (NP/NL).

975864. Lot No. 30054 Eastleigh 1951–54. Commonwealth bogies.
975867. Lot No. 30014 York 1950–51. Commonwealth bogies.
975875. Lot No. 30143 Charles Roberts 1954–55. Commonwealth bogies.
975974–975978. Lot No. 30647 Wolverton 1959–61. Commonwealth bogies.
977087. Lot No. 30229 Metro–Cammell 1955–57. Commonwealth bogies.
977942/948. Lot No. 30417 Pressed Steel 1958–59. B5 bogies.
977943/949. Lot No. 30565 Pressed Steel 1959. B5 bogies.

Non-standard livery: 975974 and 975978 are in plain grey.

975864	(3849)	**HB**	H	*SR*	GW
975867	(1006)	**HB**	H	*SR*	GW
975875	(34643)	**HB**	H	*WN*	HE
975974	(1030)	**0**	A	*ME*	BD
975976	(1033)	**N**	A		KT
975977	(1023)	**N**	A		KT
975978	(1025)	**0**	A	*ME*	BD
977087	(34971)	**HB**	H	*WN*	HE
977942	(86467, 80251)	**E**	E	*E*	TO
977943	(86718, 80252)	**E**	E	*E*	TO
977948	(86733, 94028)	**E**	E	*E*	TO
977949	(86377, 94025)	**E**	E	*E*	TO

CLASS 390 PENDOLINO BARRIER VEHICLES

These vehicles are used to move Class 390 EMUs around the National Rail system in the same way as other vehicles included in this book. Converted from Mark 1 GUVs (NL).

977944–977946. Lot No. 30417 Pressed Steel 1958–59. B5 bogies.
977947. Lot No. 30565 Pressed Steel 1959. B5 bogies.

977944	(86151, 94010)	**E**	E		TO
977945	(86437, 94011)	**E**	E		TO
977946	(86106, 94024)	**E**	E		TO
977947	(86730, 94032)	**E**	E		TO

LABORATORY, TESTING & INSTRUCTION COACHES

These coaches are used for research, development, instruction, testing and inspection on the National Rail system. Many are fitted with sophisticated technical equipment.

Structure Gauging Driving Trailer Coach. Converted from BR Mark 1 BSK. Lot No. 30699 Wolverton 1961–63. B4 bogies.

975081 (35313)   **Y**   NR   *SO*   ZA

Overhead Line Equipment Test Coach. Can either be locomotive hauled or included between DMU vehicles 977391/2. Converted from BR Mark 1 BSK Lot No. 30142 Gloucester 1954–5. B4 bogies.

975091 (34615)   **Y**   NR   *SO*   ZA

Structure Gauging Train Dormitory and Generator Coach. Converted from BR Mark 1 BCK Lot No. 30732 Derby 1962–4. B4 bogies.

975280 (21263)   **Y**   NR   *SO*   ZA

Test Coach. Converted from BR Mark 2 FK Lot No. 30734 Derby 1962–64. B4 bogies.

975290 (13396)   **SO**   SO   *SO*   ZA

Test Coach. Converted from BR Mark 1 BSK Lot No. 30699 Wolverton 1961–63. Commonwealth bogies.

975397 (35386)   **SO**   SO   *SO*   ZA

Cinema Coach. Converted from BR Mark 1 TSO Lot No. 30243 York 1955–57. BR Mark 1 bogies.

975403 (4598)   **FG**   FG   *GW*   PM

Test Coach. Converted from BR Mark 1 BSK Lot No. 30223 Charles Roberts 1955–56. BT5 bogies.

975422 (34875)   **SO**   SO   *SO*   ZA

New Measurement Train Conference Coach. Converted from prototype HST TF Lot No. 30848 Derby 1972. BT10 bogies.

975814 (11000,41000)   **Y**   NR   *SO*   EC

New Measurement Train Lecture Coach. Converted from prototype HST TRUB Lot No. 30849 Derby 1972–3. BT10 bogies.

975984 (10000, 40000)   **Y**   NR   *SO*   EC

Track Recording Train Dormitory Coach. Converted from BR Mark 2 BSO. Lot No 30757 Derby 1965–66. B4 bogies.

977337 (9395)   **SO**   NR   *SO*   ZA

Track Recording Train Brake & Stores Coach. Converted from Mark 2 BSO. Lot No. 30757 Derby 1965–66. B4 bogies.

977338 (9387)   **SO**   SO   *SO*   ZA

Test Train Staff and Dormitory Coach. Converted from BR Mark 3 SLEP. Lot No. 30960 Derby 1979–83. BT5 bogies.

| 977855 (10576) | **SO** | NR | | ZA |

Radio Equipment Survey Coaches. Converted from BR Mark 2E TSO. Lot No. 30844 Derby 1972–73. B4 bogies.

| 977868 (5846) | **RK** | NR | *SO* | ZA |
| 977869 (5858) | **RK** | NR | *SO* | ZA |

Test Train Staff Coach. Converted from Royal Household couchette Lot No. 30889, which in turn had been converted from BR Mark 2B BFK Lot No. 30790 Derby 1969. B5 bogies.

| 977969 (14112, 2906) | **Y** | NR | *SO* | ZA |

New Measurement Train Laboratory Coach. Converted from BR Mark 2E TSO. Lot No. 30844 Derby 1972–73. B4 bogies.

| 977974 (5854) | **Y** | AE | *SO* | ZA |

Hot Box Detection Coach. Converted from BR Mark 2F FO converted to Class 488/2 EMU TFOH. Lot No. 30859 Derby 1973–74. B4 bogies.

| 977983 (3407, 72503) | **RK** | NR | *SO* | ZA |

New Measurement Train Staff Coach. Converted from HST TRFK. Lot No. 30884 Derby 1976–77. BT10 bogies.

| 977984 (40501) | **Y** | P | *SO* | EC |

Structure Gauging Train Coach. Converted from BR Mark 2F TSO converted to Class 488/3 EMU TSO. Lot No. 30860 Derby 1973–74. B4 bogies.

| 977985 (6019, 72715) | **Y** | NR | *SO* | ZA |

Structure Gauging Train Coach. Converted from BR Mark 2D FO subsequently declassified to SO and then converted to exhibition van. Lot No. 30821 Derby 1971.

| 977986 (3189, 99664) | **Y** | NR | *SO* | ZA |

New Measurement Train Laboratory Coach. Converted from HST TGS. Lot No. 30949 Derby 1982. BT10 bogies.

| 977994 (44087) | **Y** | P | *SO* | EC |

Inspection Coach. Converted from BR Inspection Saloon. BR Wagon Lot No. 3095. Swindon 1957. B4 bogies.

| 999506 AMANDA | **M** | NR | *SO* | ZA |

Track Recording Coach. Converted from BR Inspection Saloon. BR Wagon Lot No. 3379. Swindon 1960. B4 bogies.

| 999508 | **SO** | SO | *SO* | ZA |

New Measurement Train Track Recording Coach. Purpose built Mark 2. B4 bogies.

| 999550 | **Y** | NR | *SO* | EC |

TEST TRAIN BRAKE FORCE RUNNERS

These vehicles are included in test trains to provide brake force and are not used for any other purposes. Other vehicles included in this book may also be similarly used on a temporary basis if required. Converted from BR Mark 1 BSK and BR Mark 2 TSO, BFKs.

977331. Lot No. 30721 Swindon 1961–63. B4 bogies.
977468/470/801/2. Lot No. 30751 Derby 1964–7. B4 bogies.
977789. Lot No. 30837 Derby 1971–72. B4 bogies.
977790/1/6. Lot No. 30844 Derby 1972–73. B4 bogies.
977793. Lot No. 30795 Derby 1969–70. B4 bogies.
977794. Lot No. 30823 Derby 1969–72. B4 bogies.
977905. Lot No. 30573 GRCW 1959–60. B4 bogies.

Non-Standard Liveries: 977788–94 are Adtranz White with yellow stripe. 977331 and 977796 are olive with yellow stripe.

977331	(35444)	**O**	H		BR
977468	(5169)	**SO**	SO	*SO*	ZA
977470	(5134)	**SO**	SO	*SO*	ZA
977789	(5765)	**O**	FM		LU
977790	(5830)	**O**	FM		LU
977791	(5855)	**O**	FM		LU
977793	(5596)	**O**	FM		LU
977794	(14139, 17139)	**O**	FM		LU
977796	(5898)	**O**	H		ZH
977801	(5153)	**SO**	SO	*SO*	ZA
977802	(5176)	**SO**	SO	*SO*	ZA
977905	(35292, 80215)	**SO**	SO		EH

BREAKDOWN TRAIN COACHES

These coaches are formed in trains used for the recovery of derailed railway vehicles and were converted from BR Mark 1 BCK, BG, BSK and SK. The current use of each vehicle is given. 975611–613 were previously converted to trailer luggage vans in 1968. BR Mark 1 bogies.

975080. Lot No. 30155 Wolverton 1955–56.
975087. Lot No. 30032 Wolverton 1951–52.
975463/573. Lot No. 30156 Wolverton 1954–55.
975465/477/494. Lot No. 30233 GRCW 1955–57.
975471. Lot No. 30095 Wolverton 1953–55.
975481/482/484/574. Lot No. 30141 GRCW 1954–55.
975498. Lot No. 30074 Wolverton 1953–54.
975611–613. Lot No. 30162 Pressed Steel 1954–57.
975639, 977088/235. Lot No. 30229 Metro-Cammell 1955–57.
977095/107. Lot No. 30425 Metro-Cammell 1956–58.

r refurbished

975080	(25079)	r	Y	NR	E	TO	Tool Van
975087	(34289)	r	NR	NR	E	LU	Generator Van
975463	(34721)	r	Y	NR	E	TE	Staff Coach
975465	(35109)	r	Y	NR	E	TO	Staff Coach
975471	(34543)	r	NR	NR	E	LU	Staff & Tool Coach
975477	(35108)	r	NR	NR	E	LU	Staff Coach
975481	(34606)	r	Y	NR	E	TO	Generator Van
975482	(34602)	r	Y	NR	E	TE	Generator Van
975484	(34591)		Y	DR		CS	Generator Van
975494	(35082)	r	Y	NR	E	MG	Generator Van
975498	(34367)	r	Y	NR	E	TE	Tool Van
975573	(34729)	r	Y	NR	E	MG	Staff Coach
975574	(34599)	r	Y	NR	E	OC	Staff Coach
975611	(80915, 68201)	r	Y	NR	E	OC	Generator Van
975612	(80922, 68203)	r	Y	NR	E	MG	Tool Van
975613	(80918, 68202)	r	Y	NR	E	OC	Tool Van
975639	(35016)		Y	DR		CS	Tool Van
977088	(34990)		Y	NR	E	CE	Generator Van
977095	(21210)		Y	DR		CS	Staff Coach
977101	(21202)		Y	NR	E	CE	Staff Coach
977235	(34989, 083172)		Y	NR	E	CE	Tool Van

Note: 975087/471/477 are currently in use on the Southern Power upgrade Project.

INFRASTRUCTURE MAINTENANCE COACHES

Overhead Line Maintenance Coaches

These coaches are formed in trains used for the maintenance, repair and renewal of overhead lines and were converted from BR Mark 1 BSK, CK and SK. The current use of each vehicle is given.
Non-standard livery: 975697/698/713/723/733/743 are light grey with red stripe, 975699/700/714/724/734/744 are light grey with blue stripe.

975697/698, 975700. Lot No. 30025 Wolverton 1950–52. BR Mark 1 bogies.
975699. Lot No. 30233 GRCW 1955–57. BR Mark 1 bogies.
975713/744. Lot No. 30350 Wolverton 1956–57.BR Mark 1 bogies.
975714. Lot No. 30374. York 1958. Commonwealth bogies.
975723/743. Lot No. 30349 Wolverton 1956–57. BR Mark 1 bogies.
975724. Lot No. 30471 Metro-Cammell 1957–59. Commonwealth bogies.
975733. Lot No. 30351 Wolverton 1956–57. BR Mark 1 bogies.
975734. Lot No. 30426 Wolverton 1956–58. BR Mark 1 Bogies.

r refurbished

975697	(34147)	r	0	CA	CA	RU	Pantograph coach
975698	(34148)	r	0	CA	CA	RU	Pantograph coach
975699	(35105)	r	0	CA	CA	Preston	Pantograph coach
975700	(34138)	r	0	CA	CA	Preston	Pantograph coach
975713	(25420)	r	0	CA	CA	RU	Stores van
975714	(25466)	r	0	CA	CA	Preston	Stores van

975723	(25388)	r	**0**	CA	*CA*	RU	Stores & generator van
975724	(16079)	r	**0**	CA	*CA*	Preston	Stores & generator van
975733	(16001)	r	**0**	CA	*CA*	RU	Stores & roof access coach
975734	(25695)	r	**0**	CA	*CA*	Preston	Stores & roof access coach
975743	(25358)	r	**0**	CA	*CA*	RU	Staff & office coach
975744	(25440)	r	**0**	CA	*CA*	Preston	Staff & office coach

Snowblower Train Coaches

These coaches work with Snowblower ADB 968501. They were converted from BR Mark 1 BSK. The current use of each vehicle is given. Commonwealth bogies.

975464. Lot No. 30386 Charles Roberts 1956–58.
975486. Lot No. 30025 Wolverton 1950–52.

975464	(35171)	**Y**	NR	*E*	ZK	Staff & dormitory coach
975486	(34100)	**Y**	NR	*E*	ZK	Tool van

Snowblower Train Tool Vans

These vans work with Snowblower ADB 968500.

200715. Wagon Lot No. 3855 Ashford 1976. 4-wheeled.
787395. Wagon Lot No. 3567 Eastleigh 1966. 4-wheeled.

200715	**Y**	NR	*E*	IS
787395	**Y**	NR	*E*	IS

Severn Tunnel Emergency Train Coaches

These coaches are formed in a train used in the event of incidents in the Severn Tunnel. They were converted from BR Mark 1 BSK & BG. The current use of each vehicle is given. 975615 was previously converted to a trailer luggage van in 1968.

975497. Lot No. 30427 Wolverton 1956–59. BR Mark 1 bogies.
975615. Lot No. 30162 Pressed Steel 1954–57. BR Mark 1 bogies.
977526. Lot No. 30229 Metro-Cammell 1955–57. Commonwealth bogies.

975497	(35218)	**Y**	NR *E*	SJ	Tool & generator van
975615	(80951, 68206)	**Y**	NR *E*	SJ	Tool van
977526	(35010)	**BG**	NR *E*	SJ	Emergency casualty coach

Spray Coaches

These coaches are used to spray various concoctions onto the rails or trackbed. In addition to spraying equipment they contain storage tanks. They were converted from BR Mark 1 RMB & GUV.

99019. Lot No. 30702 Wolverton 1961–62. Commonwealth bogies.
99025/26. Lot No. 30565 Pressed Steel 1959. B5 bogies.
99027. Lot No. 30417 Pressed Steel 1958–59. B5 bogies.

99019	(1870)	**NR**	NR	*E*	ZA
99025	(86744, 96103)	**RK**	NR		KT
99026	(86745, 96211)	**RK**	NR		KT
99027	(86331, 96214)	**RK**	NR		KT

Miscellaneous Infrastructure Coaches

These coaches are used for various infrastructure projects on National Rail. They were converted from BR Mark 1 BSK & BG, BR Mark 2 BSO, BFK and BR Mark 3 SLEP. The current use of each vehicle is given.

977163/165/166. Lot No. 30721 Wolverton 1961–63. Commonwealth bogies.
977167. Lot No. 30699 Wolverton 1961–63. Commonwealth bogies.
977168. Lot No. 30573 GRCW 1959–60. B4 bogies.
977169. Lot No. 30232 GRCW 1955–56. B4 bogies.
977591. Lot No. 30756 Derby 1965–66. B4 bogies.
977787. Lot No. 30820 Derby 1969–71. B4 bogies.
977989. Lot No. 30960 Derby 1981–83. BT 10 bogies.
977990. Lot No. 30228 Metro-Cammell 1957-58. B4 bogies.
977991. Lot No. 30323 Pressed steel 1957. B4 bogies.

Non-standard liveries:

977163/165–168 are all over white.
977591 is red and yellow.

977163	(35487)	**O**	BB	*BB*	AP	Staff & generator coach
977165	(35408)	**O**	BB	*BB*	AP	Staff & generator coach
977166	(35419)	**O**	BB	*BB*	AP	Staff & generator coach
977167	(35400)	**O**	BB	*BB*	AP	Staff & generator coach
977168	(35289)	**O**	BB	*BB*	AP	Staff & generator coach
977169	(35027)	**E**	E		OM	Staff & tool coach
977591	(14033, 17033)	**O**	E	*E*	Newport	Staff & tool coach
977787	(9453)	**CE**	NR		TH	Staff, tool & generator coach
977989	(10536)	**M**	J	*J*	Washwood Heath	Staff & Dormitory Coach
977990	(81165, 92937)	**NR**	NR	*E*	LU	Tool Van
977991	(81308, 92991)	**NR**	NR	*E*	LU	Tool Van

INTERNAL USER VEHICLES

These vehicles are confined to yards and depots or do not normally move at all.
Details are given of the internal user number, type and former identity, current
use and location. Many of these listed no longer see regular use.

024611	BR CCT 94237	Stores van	MA
024709	BR fish van 87122	Stores van	Wembley heavy repair shop
024710	BR fish van 87146	Stores van	Wembley heavy repair shop
024711	BR fish van 87227	Stores van	Wembley heavy repair shop
024877	BR CCT 94698	Stores van	Wavertree Yard,Edge Hill
024909	BR BSOT 9106	Staff accommodation	Preston Station
024919	BR GUV 93697	Stores van	Wembley Yard
024953	BR GUV 93682	Stores van	DY
025000	BR BSO 9423	Staff accommodation	Preston Station
025026	BR TSO 5259	Staff accommodation	Wavertree Yard,Edge Hill
025027	LMS CCT 37210	Stores van	RTC Business Park, Derby
041379	LMS CCT 35527	Stores van	Leeman Road EY, York
041898	BR BG 84608	Stores van	Leeman Road EY, York
041947	BR GUV 93425	Stores van	IL
041963	LMS milk tank 44047	Storage tank	DR
042154	BR GUV 93975	Stores van	Ipswich Upper Yard
061034	BR CCT 94798	Stores van	Marsh Junction, Bristol
061061	BR CCT 94135	Stores van	Oxford station
061171	BR GUV 93480	Stores van	RG
061223	BR GUV 93714	Stores van	Oxford station
083264	BR TSO 4047	Staff accommodation	Ashford station down sidings
083439	BR CCT 94752	Stores van	WD
083602	BR CCT 94494	Stores van	Three Bridges station
083633	BR GUV 93724	Stores van	BI
083644	BR Ferry Van 889201	Stores van	EH
083650	BR GUV 93100	Stores van	Ashford station down sidings
083664	BR Ferry Van 889203	Stores van	EH
095020	LNER BG 70170	Stores van	Inverness Yard
095030	BR GUV 96140	Stores van	EC

Note: CCT = Covered Carriage Truck (a 4-wheeled van similar to a GUV)

SERVICE STOCK AWAITING DISPOSAL

This list contains the last known locations of service vehicles awaiting disposal. The definition of which vehicles are "awaiting disposal" is somewhat vague, but generally speaking these are vehicles of types not now in normal service or vehicles which have been damaged by fire, vandalism or collision.

230	Horsham Yard		975717	Oxford Hinksey Yard*
99014	Horsham Yard		975721	Doncaster West Yard
99015	Horsham Yard		975727	Oxford Hinksey Yard*
320645	Leeman Road EY, York		975737	Oxford Hinksey Yard*
975000	ZA		975747	Oxford Hinksey Yard*
975051	CY		975966	Three Bridges WRD
975379	Leeman Road EY, York		975991	CY
975454	TO		975995	Wolverhampton Low Level Stn
975456	Horsham Yard		977077	Ripple Lane Yard
975491	TH		977084	CY
975535	Carnforth Bottom End Sidings		977085	CY
975554	Doncaster West Yard		977111	Ripple Lane Yard
975555	Doncaster West Yard		977112	Ripple Lane Yard
975557	Carstairs		977182	Eastleigh Down CS
975558	Carstairs		977183	Eastleigh Down CS
975559	Carstairs		977193	CY
975638	Horsham Yard		977359	ZN
975658	York South Sidings		977390	CY
975680	Carstairs		977399	NL
975681	Portobello		977449	CY
975682	Portobello		977450	CY
975683	Carstairs		977510	FP
975684	Carstairs		977595	CY
975685	Portobello		977618	Bletchley T&RSMD
975686	Portobello		977695	Eastleigh Down CS
975687	Portobello		977788	ZF
975688	Portobello		977792	ZF
975706	Oxford Hinksey Yard*		977795	ZN

* In use as environmental sound protection barrier.

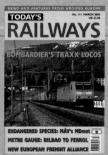

7. CODES

7.1. LIVERY CODES

Livery codes are used to denote the various liveries carried. It is impossible to list every livery variation which currently exists. In particular items ignored for this publication include:

- Minor colour variations.
- Omission of logos.
- All numbering, lettering and brandings.

Descriptions quoted are thus a general guide only. Logos as appropriate for each livery are normally deemed to be carried.

The colour of the lower half of the bodyside is stated first. Minor variations to these liveries are ignored.

Code Description

1	"One" (metallic grey with a broad black bodyside stripe. Pink, yellow, grey, pale green and light blue stripes at the unit/vehicle ends).
1S	One Stansted Express (metallic grey with a broad black bodyside stripe. Orange stripes at unit ends).
ACT	ACTS (Netherlands) (Deep blue with a broad yellow stripe).
AL	Advertising livery (see class heading for details).
AN	Anglia Railways Class 170s (white & turquoise with blue vignette).
AR	Anglia Railways (turquoise blue with a white stripe).
AV	Arriva Trains (turquoise blue with white doors with a cream "swish").
B	BR blue.
BG	BR blue & grey lined out in white.
BI	"Visit Bristol" promotional livery (deep blue with various images).
BL	BR Revised blue with yellow cabs, grey roof, large numbers & logo.
BR	BR blue with a red solebar stripe.
C2	c2c Rail (blue with metallic grey doors & pink c2c branding).
CB	Old Connex South Eastern (NSE blue with a yellow lower bodyside).
CD	Cotswold Rail (silver with blue & red logo).
CE	BR Civil Engineers (yellow & grey with black cab doors & window surrounds).
CH	BR Western Region/GWR (chocolate & cream lined out in gold).
CO	Centro (grey/green with light blue, white & yellow stripes).
CM	Revised old Midland Mainline (Midland Mainline teal green with white Central logos).
CN	Revised Connex South Eastern/South Eastern Trains (white with yellow doors, black window surrounds & grey lower band).
CR	Chiltern Railways (blue & white with a thin red stripe).
CS	ScotRail Caledonian Sleepers (two-tone purple with a silver stripe).
CT	Central Trains (two-tone green with yellow doors. Blue flash and red strpe at vehicle ends).
CU	Corus (silver with red logos).
CX	Connex (white with yellow lower body & blue solebar).
DC	Scenic lines of Devon & Cornwall promotional livery (black with gold cantrail stripe).

DG	BR Departmental (plain dark grey with black cab doors & window surrounds).
DR	Direct Rail Services (dark blue with light blue or dark grey roof).
DS	Revised Direct Rail Services (dark blue, light blue & green).
E	English Welsh & Scottish Railway (maroon bodyside & roof with a broad gold bodyside band).
EB	Eurotunnel (two-tone grey with a broad blue stripe).
EN	Enron Teesside Operations (Trafalgar blue with red solebar stripe).
EP	European Passenger Services (two-tone grey with dark blue roof).
ES	Eurailscout GB (Light orange with a blue and purple logo).
EU	Eurostar (white with dark blue & yellow stripes).
F	BR Trainload Freight (two-tone grey with black cab doors & window surrounds. Various logos).
FB	Revised Fragonset (freight locos) (Black with large bodyside FRAGONSET lettering).
FE	Railfreight Distribution International (two tone-grey with black cab doors & dark blue roof).
FER	Fertis (light grey with a dark grey roof and solebar). Locos for VFLI freight contract in France.
FF	Freightliner grey (two-tone grey with black cab doors & window surrounds. Freightliner logo).
FG	First Group corporate Inter-City livery (indigo blue with a white roof & gold, pink & white stripes).
FL	Freightliner (dark green with yellow cabs).
FO	BR Railfreight (grey bodysides, yellow cabs & large BR double arrow).
FP	Old First Great Western (green & ivory with thin green & broad gold stripes).
FR	Fragonset Railways (black with silver roof & a red bodyside band lined out in white).
FS	First Group corporate regional/suburban livery (indigo blue with pink & white stripes).
FX	Felixstowe Dock Company.
FY	Foster Yeoman (blue/silver. Cast numberplates).
G¹	BR Green (plain green, with white stripe on main line locomotives).
G²	BR Southern Region/SR or BR DMU green.
GA	Southern "Heritage" EMUs (white & dark green with light green semi-circular patches at cab ends. Light green stripe along length of unit).
GB	GB Railfreight (blue with orange cantrail & solebar stripes, orange cabs).
GC	British racing green & cream lined out in gold.
GE	First Great Eastern (grey, green, blue & white).
GG	BR green (two-tone green).
GIF	GIF (Spain) light blue with dark blue band.
GL	First Great Western locos/Motorail vans (green with a gold stripe).
GN	Great North Eastern Railway (dark blue with a red stripe).
GP	Ginsters Cornish Pasties promotional livery (Black & red with various images and cartoons etc.)
GS	Royal Scotsman/Great Scottish & Western Railway (maroon).
GV	Gatwick Express EMU (red, white & indigo blue with mauve & blue doors).
GW	Great Western Railway (green, lined out in black & orange. Cast numberplates).
GX	Gatwick Express InterCity (dark grey/white/burgundy/white).
GY	Eurotunnel (grey & yellow).

PLATFORM 5 MAIL ORDER

Don't miss your copies of the PLATFORM 5 BRITISH RAILWAYS POCKET BOOKS or BRITISH RAILWAYS LOCOMOTIVES & COACHING STOCK.

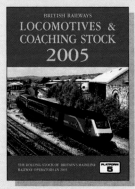

Our annual guides to the rolling stock operating on Britain's mainline railways are published every year in December and March/April respectively. You can make sure you never miss your copy by joining our free mailing list.

Customers on our mailing list receive advance notice of these books a few weeks before they are published, plus a full catalogue of new titles from other transport publishers. To subscribe to this free service, simply register your name and address with our Mail Order Department and we'll send details of the 2006 editions to you shortly before they are published. We do not pass customer details on to any other organisations and we do not conduct any telesales activity.

Please be aware that by subscribing to our mailing lists you are NOT obliged to order any books at any time.

Note: Customers ordering books from the Platform 5 Mail Order Department are automatically added to our mailing list unless specifically requested otherwise. Any customers already on our mailing list who would rather not receive information from us, please contact our Mail Order Department. We will be happy to remove your details from our mailing list.

Details of new publications from Platform 5 and a range of other publishers can also be found in the latest issues of **entrain** and **Today's Railways** magazines.

HA Hanson Quarry Products (dark blue & silver).
HB HSBC Rail (Oxford blue & white).
HC Heathrow Connect (grey with a broad deep blue bodyside band and orange doors).
HE Heathrow Express (silver grey & indigo blue with black window surrounds).
HP Hull Trains "Pioneer" Class (dark green and silver with an orange stripe).
HN Harry Needle Railroad Company (orange/grey, lined out in black).
HW Heart of Wales Line promotional livery (orange with yellow doors).
HT Hull Trains (white with a broad green band on the lower bodyside).
IC BR InterCity (dark grey/white/red/white).
IL Island Line (light blue, with illustrations featuring dinosaurs etc).
IM BR InterCity Mainline (dark grey/white/red/light grey & yellow lower cabsides except shunters).
IR Ian Riley Engineering (grey with green band).
K Black.
LA Lafarge (white, orange & blue).
LH BR Loadhaul (black with orange cabsides).
LN LNER Tourist (green & cream).
LW LNWR black with grey & red lining.
M BR maroon (Maroon lined out in straw & black).
MA Maintrain (blue).
ME Refurbished Merseyrail Electrics (metallic silver with yellow doors).
ML BR Mainline Freight (Aircraft blue with silver stripe).
MM Old Midland Mainline (Teal green with grey lower body sides & three tangerine stripes).
MN New Midland Mainline (Thin tangerine stripe on the lower bodyside, ocean blue, grey & white).
MR Mendip Rail (Green, red & silver).
MT Old Merseytravel (yellow/white with grey & black stripes).
MY Revised Merseytravel (yellow/white with grey stripe).
N BR Network South East (white & blue with red lower bodyside stripe, grey solebar & cab ends).
NR Network Rail (blue with a red stripe).
NS Northern Spirit (turquoise blue with lime green "N").
NT BR Network SouthEast (white & blue with red lower bodyside & cantrail stripes).
NW North Western Trains (blue with gold cantrail stripe & star).
O Non standard livery (see class heading for details).
P Porterbrook Leasing Company (purple & grey).
PC Pullman Car Company (umber & cream with gold lettering) lined out in gold.
PS Provincial Services (dark blue/grey with light blue & white stripes).
R Plain red.
RE Provincial Services/Regional Railways Express (light grey/buff/dark grey with white, dark blue & light blue stripes).
RG BR Parcels (dark grey & red).
RK New Railtrack (green & blue).
RL RMS Locotech (light grey).
RM Royal Mail (red with yellow stripes above solebar).
RN North West Regional Railways (dark blue/grey with green & white stripes).
RO Old Railtrack (orange with white & grey stripes).
RP Royal Train (claret, lined out in red & black).

RR	Regional Railways (dark blue/grey with light blue & white stripes, three narrow dark blue stripes at vehicle ends).
RT	RT Rail (black, lined out in red).
RV	Riviera Trains (Oxford blue & cream, lined out in gold {blue only for locos}).
RX	Rail Express Systems (dark grey & red with or without blue markings).
RZ	Royal Train revised (plain claret, no lining).
S	Old Strathclyde PTE (orange & black lined out in white).
SB	Serco Railtest blue (deep blue with white Serco brandings).
SC	New Strathclyde PTE (carmine & cream lined out in black & gold).
SD	South West Trains outer suburban livery {Class 450} (deep blue with red doors & orange & red cab sides).
SCO	Seco-Rail (orange with a broad yellow bodyside band). For use in France.
SL	Silverlink (indigo blue with white stripe, green lower body & yellow doors).
SP	New Strathclyde PTE {Class 334 style} (carmine & cream, with a turquoise stripe).
SN	Southern (white & dark green with light green semi-circles at one end of each vehicle. Light grey band at solebar level).
SO	Serco Railtest (red & grey).
SR	ScotRail (white, terracotta, purple & aquamarine).
SS	South West Trains inner suburban (Class 455) (red with blue and orange flashes at unit ends).
ST	Stagecoach (white & blue with orange & red stripes).
SW	South West Trains {long-distance stock} (white & dark blue with black window surrounds, red doors & red panel with orange stripe at unit ends).
SX	Stansted Express (two-tone metallic blue with grey doors).
TSO	TSO (all over yellow with a blue solebar). For use in France.
TP	First Trans-Pennine Express (Plum with a yellow "N" and First Group indigo blue lower bodyside band).
TR	Thameslink Rail (dark blue with a broad orange stripe & two narrower white bodyside stripes plus white cantrail stripe).
TT	Thames Trains (blue with lime green doors).
U	Plain white or grey undercoat.
V	Virgin Trains (red with black doors extending into bodysides, three white lower bodysides stripes).
VL	Valley Lines (dark green & red with white & light green stripes. Light green doors).
VP	Virgin Trains shunters (black with a large black & white chequered flag on the bodyside).
VN	Venice Simplon Orient Express "Northern Belle" (crimson lake & cream).
VT	New Virgin Trains (silver, with black window surrounds, white cantrail stripe & red roof. Red swept down at unit ends. Black and white striped doors on units).
VW	Visit Wales promotional livery (green & red with various images).
WA	Wabtec Rail (black).
WB	Wales & Borders Alphaline (metallic silver with blue doors).
WC	West Coast Railway Company (all over maroon with a black bodyside stripe).
WD	West Coast Main Line Desiro (grey with broad blue bodyside band).
WE	Wessex Trains Alphaline promotional livery (metallic silver with various images, pink doors).

WN Old West Anglia Great Northern (white with blue, grey & orange stripes).
WP New West Anglia Great Northern (deep purple with white doors).
WR Waterman Railways (maroon with cream stripes).
WT Wessex Trains Alphaline (metallic silver with maroon or pink doors).
WX Heart of Wessex Line promotional livery (cerise pink with various images.)
WY Old West Yorkshire PTE (red/cream with thin yellow stripe).
WZ Wessex Trains claret promotional livery with various images.
Y   Plain yellow.
YN West Yorkshire PTE (red with light grey "N").
YP New West Yorkshire PTE (red with grey semi-circles).

PLATFORM 5 MAIL ORDER

EISENBAHNATLAS DEUTSCHLAND 2005/2006
Schweers & Wall

The definitive colour atlas of Germany's railways in 1:300000 scale, completely revised and updated. Shows all lines with identification of double track, single track, narrow gauge, freight only, not in use, former line now removed, rack lines and lines under construction. Colours are used to show lines of different electrification voltages and German timetable numbers are shown beside passenger lines. Also shows all stations, halts, junctions, yards, freight facilities, preservation centres, museum lines, tramways and funiculars, plus many general geographical features including rivers and motorways. Includes enlargements of major centres, index maps and a full index to stations and other significant places. Key is in German, English, French and Dutch. 192 pages. Large format hardback. **£27.95.** entrain/*Today's Railways* subscriber price **£24.95.**

EISENBAHNATLAS SCHWEIZ
Schweers & Wall

The definitive atlas of Switzerland's railways in 1:150000 scale. Shows the same extensive detail as in Eisenbahnatlas Deutschland above, with additional identification of the operator of each line. Also includes diagrammatic tramway maps and a full list of railway companies with contact details. Key is in German, English, French and Italian. 96 pages. Large format hardback. **£21.95.** entrain/*Today's Railways* subscriber price **£18.95.**

SIGNALLING ATLAS & SIGNAL BOX DIRECTORY
Signalling Record Society

Detailed listing of all signal boxes in Great Britain and Ireland. Covers Network Rail, London Underground, other systems, NIR, IE, heritage railways and other preserved or disused boxes. For every box gives details of name, Quail map reference, type, date, frame equipment, number of levers, locking and other notation. Also includes 18 colour maps showing box locations and methods of working. Comprehensive. 96 pages. **£9.95.**

Please add postage: 10% UK, 20% Europe, 30% Rest of World.

Telephone, fax or send your order to the Platform 5 Mail Order Department. See page 384 of this book for details.

7.2. OWNER CODES

Locomotives and rolling stock are owned by various companies and are allotted codes as follows:

Code	Owner
11	Class 33/1 Preservation Company
24	6024 Preservation Society
40	The Class 40 Preservation Society
50	The Fifty Fund
62	The Princess Royal Locomotive Trust
71	71A Locomotive Group
A	Angel Trains
AE	AEA Technology Rail
AM	Alstom
B1	Thompson B1 Locomotive Society
BB	Balfour Beatty Rail Plant
BC	Bridgend County Borough Council
BK	The Scottish Railway Preservation Society
BT	Bombardier Transportation
CA	Carillion Rail Plant
CD	Cotswold Rail Engineering
CM	Cambrian Trains
CR	Chiltern Railways
DG	Duke of Gloucester Steam Locomotive Trust
DP	The Deltic Preservation Society
DR	Direct Rail Services
DT	The Diesel Traction Group
E	English Welsh & Scottish Railway
EN	Enron Teesside Operations
ES	Eurailscout GB
ET	Eurotunnel
EU	Eurostar (UK)
FG	First Group
FL	Freightliner
FM	FM Rail (Fragonset Merlin Railways)
FS	Flying Scotsman Railways
FX	The Felixstowe Dock & Railway Company
FY	Foster Yeoman
GB	GB Railfreight (owned by First Group)
GD	Garsdale Railtours
GS	The Great Scottish & Western Railway Company
GW	The Great Western Society
H	HSBC Rail (UK)
HA	The Hanson Group
HD	Hastings Diesels
HE	British Airports Authority
HJ	Howard Johnston Engineering
HN	Harry Needle Railroad Company
HS	Harry Schneider

HX	Halifax Asset Finance
IR	Ian Riley Engineering
J	Fastline
JK	Dr. John Kennedy
LW	London & North Western Railway Company
MA	Maintrain
MD	Ministry of Defence
MH	Mid-Hants Railway
MN	Merchant Navy Locomotive Preservation Society
MW	Martin Walker (Beaver Sports)
NE	North Eastern Locomotive Preservation Group
NM	National Railway Museum
NR	Network Rail
P	Porterbrook Leasing Company
PO	Other owner
RA	Railfilms
RD	Rhondda Cynon Taff District Council
RI	Rail Assets Investments
RL	RMS Locotec
RM	Royal Mail
RP	Rampart Carriage & Wagon Services
RT	RT Rail Tours
RV	Riviera Trains
SA	Sea Containers Rail Services
SB	SNCB/NMBS (Société Nationale des Chemins de fer Belges/ Nationale Maatschappij der Belgische Spoorwegen)
SF	SNCF (Société Nationale des Chemins de fer Français)
SH	Scottish Highland Railway Company
SM	Siemens Transportation
SN	Southern
SO	Serco Railtest
SV	Severn Valley Railway
SW	South West Trains
VS	Venice-Simplon Orient Express
VT	Vintage Trains
VW	Virgin West Coast
WA	Wabtec Rail
WC	West Coast Railway Company
WF	Western Falcon Rail (Alan and Tracy Lear)
WH	Waterman Heritage Trust
WN	West Anglia Great Northern Railway
WT	Wessex Trains
X	Sold for scrap/further use and awaiting collection or owner unknown

7.3. LOCOMOTIVE POOL CODES

Locomotives are split into operational groups ("pools") for diagramming and maintenance purposes. The official codes used to denote these pools are shown in this publication.

Code	Pool
ARZG	Alstom Class 08 (Eastleigh).
ARZH	Alstom Class 08 (Glasgow Springburn).
ARZN	Alstom Class 08 (Wolverton).
ATLO	Alstom Class 08.
ATSP	Alstom Class 47.
ATTB	Alstom Class 57.
ATXX	Alstom locos for long-term repair.
CDJD	Serco Railtest Class 08.
CREL	Cotswold Rail operational locomotives – contract hire.
CROL	Cotswold Rail stored locomotives.
CRRH	Cotswold Rail operational locomotives – spot-hire contracts.
CRUR	Cotswold Rail stored locomotives – undergoing restoration.
DFFT	Freightliner Class 47 with "Dock Mode" for the Felixstowe branch.
DFGC	Freightliner Class 86/5.
DFGM	Freightliner Class 66/5, Intermodal traffic.
DFHC	Freightliner Class 66/9.
DFHH	Freightliner Heavy Haul Classes 66/5 and 66/6.
DFLC	Freightliner Class 90.
DFLH	Freightliner Heavy Haul Class 47.
DFLM	Freightliner Class 47 with multiple working equipment.
DFLS	Freightliner Class 08.
DFNC	Freightliner Class 86/6.
DFRT	Freightliner Class 66/5 & 66/6. Network Rail contracts and general traffic.
DFTZ	Freightliner Class 57.
DHLT	Freightliner locomotives awaiting maintenance/repair/disposal.
FGXP	First Group Class 43 (stored).
GBAC	GB Railfreight Class 87.
GBCM	GB Railfreight Class 66. Railfreight contracts.
GBED	GB Railfreight Class 73.
GBRT	GB Railfreight Class 66. Network Rail contracts.
GBZZ	GB Railfreight. Stored pool.
GPSN	Eurostar (UK) Class 73.
GPSS	Eurostar (UK) Class 08.
GPSV	Eurostar (UK) Class 37.
HBSH	Wabtec hire shunting locomotives.
HGSS	Maintrain Class 08 (Tyseley/Soho)
HISE	Maintrain Class 08 (Derby).
HISL	Maintrain Class 08 (Neville Hill).
HJSE	First Great Western Class 08 (Landore).
HJSL	First Great Western Class 08 (Laira).
HJXX	First Great Western Class 08 (Old Oak HST & St. Philips Marsh).
HNRL	Harry Needle Railroad Company hire locomotives.
HNRS	Harry Needle Railroad Company stored locomotives.

HQXX	West Anglia Great Northern Railway Class 03.
HWSU	Southern Class 09.
HYSB	South West Trains standby locomotives.
IANA	One Anglia Classes 47, 86 & 90.
IECA	Great North Eastern Railway Class 91.
IECB	Great North Eastern Railway Class 89.
IECP	Great North Eastern Railway Class 43.
IMLP	Midland Mainline Class 43.
IVGA	Gatwick Express Class 73.
IWCA	Virgin West Coast Class 87.
IWLA	First Great Western Class 57.
IWRP	First Great Western Class 43.
KCSI	Bombardier Class 08 (Ilford).
KDSD	Bombardier Class 08 (Doncaster).
MBDL	Non TOC-owned diesel locomotives.
MOLO	RT Rail Tours locos.
MOLS	RT Rail Tours stored locos.
QACL	Network Rail Class 86.
QADD	Network Rail Class 31.
QAED	Network Rail Class 73.
QCAR	Network Rail New Measurement Train Class 43.
RFSH	Wabtec hire fleet.
RTLO	Riviera Trains operational fleet.
RTLS	Riviera Trains stored locos.
SAXL	HSBC Rail (UK) off-lease locomotives.
SBXL	Porterbrook Leasing Company off-lease locomotives.
SCXL	Angel Trains off-lease locomotives.
SDED	FM Rail Class 73.
SDFL	FM Rail locomotives (freight traffic).
SDFR	FM Rail locomotives (general).
SDPP	FM Rail operational locomotives (push-pull capability).
SDMS	FM Rail museum locomotives.
SDXL	FM Rail stored locomotives.
WAAK	EWS Class 67.
WABK	EWS Class 67 RETB fitted.
WBAN	EWS Class 66.
WBBM	EWS Class 66 RETB fitted.
WBLN	EWS Class 66 dedicated locos for Lickey Incline banking duties. Fitted with additional lights and drawgear.
WCAN	EWS Class 60 standard fuel tanks.
WCBN	EWS Class 60 extended-range fuel tanks.
WDAG	EWS Class 59/2.
WEFE	EWS Class 90.
WKAD	EWS Class 37 general.
WKBM	EWS Class 37 Scotland.
WKCK	EWS Class 37 hired to Arriva Trains Wales.
WKSN	EWS Class 37 Special operations.
WMOC	EWS heritage locomotives.
WNSO	EWS main line locomotives – sold awaiting collection.
WNSS	EWS main line locomotives – stored serviceable.
WNTA	EWS locomotives – stored Sandite locos.

WNTR EWS locomotives – tactical reserve.
WNTS EWS locomotives – tactical stored serviceable.
WNWX EWS main line locomotives – for major repairs.
WNXX EWS locomotives – stored unserviceable.
WNYX EWS locomotives – authorised for component recovery.
WNZX EWS locomotives – awaiting disposal.
WREM EWS Shunting locomotives (Eastern and East Midlands – contract hire).
WRGW EWS Shunting locomotives (Great Western and South Wales – contract hire).
WRLS EWS Shunting locomotives (South London – contract hire).
WRSC EWS Shunting locomotives (Scotland and Carlisle area – contract hire).
WRWM EWS Shunting locomotives (West Midlands and North West – contract hire).
WRWR EWS Shunting locomotives (Western Region – contract hire).
WSAW EWS Shunting locomotives (South Wales, on hire to Celsa (formerly Allied Steel & Wire).
WSEM EWS Shunting locomotives (Eastern and East Midlands).
WSGW EWS Shunting locomotives (Great Western and South Wales).
WSLN EWS Shunting locomotives (North London).
WSLS EWS Shunting locomotives (South London).
WSNE EWS Shunting locomotives (North East).
WSSC EWS Shunting locomotives (Scotland and Carlisle area).
WSWM EWS Shunting locomotives (West Midlands and North West).
WSWR EWS Shunting locomotives (Western Region).
WSXX EWS Shunting locomotives – stored.
WSYX EWS Shunting locomotives – authorised for component recovery.
WTAE EWS Class 92.
WZFF EWS Class 58 – hire locos France.
WZFH EWS Class 58 – hire locos The Netherlands.
WZFS EWS Class 58 – hire locos Spain.
WZGF EWS Class 56 – hire locos France.
WZKF EWS Class 37 – possible hire locos France.
WZKS EWS Class 37 – hire locos Spain.
WZTS EWS Shunting locomotives – tactical stored serviceable.
XHAC Direct Rail Services Class 87.
XHCK Direct Rail Services operational locomotives (Classes 37 & 66).
XHMW Direct Rail Services locomotives undergoing long-term repairs.
XHSD Direct Rail Services operational locomotives (Classes 20, 33, 37 & 47).
XHSS Direct Rail Services stored locomotives.
XYPA Mendip Rail Class 59/1.
XYPO Mendip Rail Class 59/0.

7.4. OPERATOR CODES

Operator codes are used to denote the organisation that facilitates the use of
that vehicle, and may not be the actual Train Operating Company which runs
the train. Where no operator code is shown, vehicles are currently not in use.

Code	Operator
62	The Princess Royal Locomotive Trust
1A	One Anglia
1E	One Great Eastern
1S	One Stansted Express
1W	One West Anglia
AE	AEA Technology Rail
AW	Arriva Trains Wales
BB	Balfour Beatty Rail Plant
BK	The Scottish Railway Preservation Society
C2	c2c Rail
CA	Carillion Rail Plant
CD	Cotswold Rail Engineering
CR	Chiltern Railways
CT	Central Trains
DR	Direct Rail Services
E	English Welsh & Scottish Railway
EU	Eurostar (UK)
FL	Freightliner
FK	First Great Western Link
FM	FM Rail (Fragonset Merlin Railways)
GB	GB Railfreight (owned by First Group)
GN	Great North Eastern Raiway
GS	The Great Scottish & Western Railway Company
GW	First Great Western
GX	Gatwick Express
HC	Heathrow Connect (joint Heathrow Express/FGW Link operation)
HD	Hastings Diesels
HE	Heathrow Express
HT	Hull Trains
IL	Island Line
J	Fastline
LS	Locomotive support coach
ME	Merseyrail Electrics
MH	Mid-Hants Railway
MM	Midland Mainline
NO	Northern
RA	Railfilms
RP	Royal Train
RV	Riviera Trains
SE	South Eastern Trains
SF	SNCF (French Railways)
SH	Scottish Highland Railway Company
SL	Silverlink

SN	Southern
SO	Serco Railtest
SR	First ScotRail
SW	South West Trains
TP	First Trans-Pennine Express
TR	Thameslink Rail
VS	Venice-Simplon Orient Express
VT	Vintage Trains
VW	Virgin West Coast
VX	Virgin Cross-Country
WC	West Coast Railway Company
WN	(West Anglia) Great Northern
WT	Wessex Trains
WX	Wessex Trains (TOC)

7.5. ALLOCATION & LOCATION CODES

Allocation codes are used in this publication to denote the normal maintenance base ("depots") of each operational locomotive, multiple unit or coach. However, maintenance may be carried out at other locations and may also be carried out by mobile maintenance teams.

Location codes are used to denote common storage locations whilst the full place name is used for other locations. The designation (S) denotes stored. However, when a locomotive pool code denotes that a loco is stored anyway then the (S) is not shown.

Code	Depot	Operator
AC	Aberdeen Clayhills	*Storage location only*
AF	Ashford Chart Leacon (Kent)	Bombardier Transportation
AL	Aylesbury	Chiltern Railways
AN	Allerton (Liverpool)	EWS
AP*	Ashford Rail Plant	Balfour Beatty Rail Plant
AS	Allely's, Studley (Warwickshire)	*Storage location only*
AY	Ayr	EWS
BA	Basford Hall Yard (Crewe)	*Storage location only*
BD	Birkenhead North	Merseyrail Electrics
BF*	Battlefield Line (Shackerstone)	Battlefield Line
BG*	Billingham, Teeside	Enron Teesside Operations
BH	Barrow Hill (Chesterfield)	Barrow Hill Engine Shed Society
BI	Brighton Lovers Walk	Southern
BK	Bristol Barton Hill	EWS
BM	Bournemouth	South West Trains
BN	Bounds Green (London)	GNER
BR*	MoD DSDC Bicester	Ministry of Defence
BQ	Bury (Greater Manchester)	East Lancashire Railway
BS	Bescot (Walsall)	EWS
BT	Bo'ness (West Lothian)	Bo'ness & Kinneil Railway
BY	Bletchley	Silverlink
BZ	St. Blazey (Par)	EWS
CD	Crewe Diesel	EWS
CE	Crewe International Electric	EWS
CF	Cardiff Canton	Arriva Trains Wales/Pullman Rail
CH	Chester	Arriva Trains Wales/Alstom
CJ	Clapham Yard (London)	South West Trains
CK	Corkerhill (Glasgow)	First ScotRail
CL	Carlisle Upperby	*Storage location only*
CO	Cranmore (Somerset)	East Somerset Railway
CP	Crewe Carriage	London & North Western Railway Co.
CQ	Crewe (The Railway Age)	London & North Western Railway Co.
CS	Carnforth	West Coast Railway Company
CT*	MoD Caerwent AFD (Chepstow)	Ministry of Defence
CU	Carlisle Currock	*Storage location only*
CY*	Crewe South Yard	*Storage location only*
CZ	Central Rivers (Burton)	Bombardier Transportation
DC*	Didcot yard	EWS

DF	Derby FM Rail	FM Rail
DI	Didcot Railway Centre	Great Western Society
DM*	Dee Marsh yard (Shotton steelworks)	Corus
DR	Doncaster	EWS
DV*	Daventry Freight Terminal (DIRFT)	Tibbett & Britten
DY	Derby Etches Park	Maintrain
EA*	Earles Sidings (Hope)	Lafarge
EC	Edinburgh Craigentinny	GNER
EH	Eastleigh	EWS
EM	East Ham (London)	c2c
EN	Euston Downside (London)	*Storage location only*
ER	Exeter Riverside Yard	*Storage location only*
ES*	On hire to GIF, Spain	GIF
EU	Coquelles Eurotunnel (France)	Eurotunnel
EX	Exeter	Wessex Trains
FB	Ferrybridge	EWS
FD	Freightliner diesels (general code)	Freightliner
FE	Freightliner electrics (general code)	Freightliner
FF	Forest (Brussels)	SNCB/NMBS
FN*	On hire to Fertis/TSO/Seco, France	Fertis/TSO/Seco-Rail
FP	Ferme Park sidings	*Storage location only*
FR	Fratton (Portsmouth)	South West Trains
FX*	Felixstowe	Felixstowe Dock & Railway Company
GI	Gillingham (Kent)	South Eastern Trains
GW	Shields Road (Glasgow)	First ScotRail
HA	Haymarket (Edinburgh)	First ScotRail
HE	Hornsey (London)	WAGN/One West Anglia
HG	Hither Green (London)	EWS
HM	Healey Mills (Wakefield)	EWS
HT	Heaton (Newcastle)	Northern
IM	Immingham	EWS
IL	Ilford (London)	One Great Eastern
IP*	Ipswich stabling point	Freightliner
IR*	Immingham Railfreight Terminal	*Storage location only*
IS	Inverness	First ScotRail
KM	Carlisle Kingmoor	Direct Rail Services
KR	Kidderminster	Severn Valley Railway
KT	MoD Kineton (Warwickshire)	Ministry of Defence
KY	Knottingley	EWS
LA	Laira (Plymouth)	First Great Western
LB	Loughborough	Brush Traction
LC	Lancastrian C&W Company, Heysham	Lancastrian C&W Company
LD	Leeds Midland Road	LNWR/Freightliner
LE	Landore (Swansea)	First Great Western
LG	Longsight (Manchester)	Northern
LH*	LH Group, Barton-under-Needwood	LH Group Services
LL	Edge Hill (Liverpool)	West Coast Traincare
LR	Leicester	EWS
LT	MoD Longtown (Cumbria)	Ministry of Defence
LU	MoD Ludgershall	Ministry of Defence
LY	Le Landy (Paris)	SNCF

RAILWAY TIMETABLES ON CD-ROM

The **ELECTRONIC TIMETABLE CD-ROM** contains full railway timetable information* for most European countries, including Great Britain, France, Germany, Belgium, Netherlands, Luxembourg, Italy, Switzerland, Austria etc.

Simply specify the following:
- Date of travel
- Destination station
- Departure station
- Preferred time of travel (arrival or departure)

The journey planner facility will calculate your rail travel options.
- Specify a particular route or routes for your journey.
- Print a full itinerary for each journey option.
- Print full arrival/departure listings for any station.
- Print a diagrammatic map of your route for each journey option.
- Simple reverse facility for calculating your return journey.

* In some countries where a timetable change occurs during the period of validity, information is included only up to the date of timetable change. Regular updates can be downloaded over the internet, by choosing 'file', 'update' and following the instructions given. You MUST have the CD-ROM in your CD-ROM drive to successfully download updates.

RAILWAY TIMETABLES ON CD-ROM

The system is not restricted to international travel and also works for entirely domestic journeys within any country selected.

Also includes a useful German hotel guide. Capable of running in English, French, German or Italian languages. Minimum system requirements: Windows 98 or later, 486/33 MHz, 8MB RAM.

PRICE: £9.95 (post free to UK and Europe, please add £1.00 postage to rest of World).
ENTRAIN TODAY'S RAILWAYS SUBSCRIBER PRICE: £7.95

Note: The electronic timetable is released twice a year in June and December. Our mail order department will be able to take advance orders from the beginning of May and November for each forthcoming timetable. To register on our CD-ROM timetable mailing list, please contact our Mail Order Department.

HOW TO ORDER:

Telephone your order and credit card details to our 24 hour sales hotline:
0114-255-8000 (UK), +44-114-255-8000 (from overseas), or fax: +44(0)114-255-2471.

Or send your credit/debit card details, sterling cheque, or British postal order payable to 'Platform 5 Publishing Limited' to:
Mail Order Department (LCS), Platform 5 Publishing Ltd., 3 Wyvern House, Sark Road, SHEFFIELD, S2 4HG, ENGLAND.

MA	Manchester Longsight	West Coast Traincare
MD	Merehead	Mendip Rail
MG	Margam (Port Talbot)	EWS
MH	Millerhill Yard	EWS
ML	Motherwell (Glasgow)	EWS
MM	Fire Service College, Moreton-in-Marsh	Cotswold Rail
MO*	Mossend Yard	EWS
MQ*	Meldon Quarry (Okehampton)	Dartmoor Railways
MW	MoD Marchwood (Southampton)	Ministry of Defence
MY*	Whitemoor Yard (March)	GBRf
NC	Norwich Crown Point	One Anglia
NH	Newton Heath (Manchester)	Northern
NL	Neville Hill (Leeds)	Northern/Maintrain
NP	North Pole International (London)	Eurostar (UK)
NT	Northam (Southampton)	Siemens/South West Trains
NW	Brunner Mond Works, Northwich (Cheshire)	Brunner Mond
NY	Grosmont (North Yorkshire)	North Yorkshire Moors Railway
OC	Old Oak Common locomotive (London)	EWS
OH	Old Oak Common EMUs (London)	Heathrow Express
OO	Old Oak Common HST (London)	First Great Western
OM	Old Oak Common carriage(London)	EWS
OY	Oxley (Wolverhampton)	West Coast Traincare
PB	Peterborough yards	EWS/GBRf
PC	Polmadie (Glasgow)	West Coast Traincare
PM	St. Philips Marsh (Bristol)	First Great Western
PY	MoD DERA Pig's Bay (Shoeburyness)	Ministry of Defence
PZ	Penzance	First Great Western
QU*	Quidhampton (Salisbury)	Imerys
RD	Nottingham Heritage Centre, Ruddington	Great Central Railway (North)
RG	Reading	First Great Western Link
RL	Ropley (Hampshire)	Mid-Hants Railway
RM	Ramsgate	South Eastern Trains
RU*	Rugby Rail Plant	Carillion Rail Plant
RY	Ryde (Isle of Wight)	Island Line
SA	Salisbury	South West Trains
SD	Stoke Gifford Yard (Bristol Parkway)	*Storage location only*
SE	St. Leonards (Hastings)	St. Leonards Railway Engineering
SG	Slade Green (London)	South Eastern Trains
SI	Soho (Birmingham)	Maintrain
SJ	Severn Tunnel Junction	EWS
SK	Swanwick Junction (Derbyshire)	Midland Railway-Butterley
SL	Stewarts Lane (London)	Gatwick Express/VSOE
SM	Swansea Maliphant Sidings	*Storage location only*
SO	Southall (Greater London)	Flying Scotsman Railways
SP	Springs Branch CRDC (Wigan)	EWS
SU	Selhurst (Croydon)	Southern
SY	Saltley (Birmingham)	EWS
SZ	Southampton Maritime	Freightliner
TB	Tilburg (Netherlands)	NedTrain
TD	Temple Mills (Stratford, London)	EWS
TE	Thornaby (Middlesbrough)	EWS

TH	Pershore Airfield, Throckmorton, Worcs	*Storage location only*
TJ	Tavistock Junction Yard	*Storage location only*
TM	Tyseley Locomotive Works	Birmingham Railway Mueseum
TO	Toton (Nottinghamshire)	EWS
TS	Tyseley (Birmingham)	Maintrain
TT*	Toton Training School Compound (Notts)	*Storage location only*
TY	Tyne Yard (Newcastle)	EWS
WA	Warrington	EWS
WB	Wembley (London)	EWS
WD	Wimbledon (London)	South West Trains
WE	Willesden Brent sidings	*Storage location only*
WI	Wilton, Teesside	SembCorp Utilities
WN	Willesden (London)	West Coast Traincare
WS	West Somerset Railway (Minehead)	West Somerset Railway
WY	Westbury Yard	EWS
XW	Crofton	Bombardier Transportation
YJ	Yeovil Junction Railway Centre	Somerset & Dorset Loco Company
YK	National Railway Museum (York)	Science Mueseum
YN	York Yard North, North Sidings	*Storage location only*
ZA	RTC Business Park (Derby)	Serco/AEA Technology
ZB	Doncaster Works	Wabtec
ZC	Crewe Works	Bombardier Transportation
ZD	Derby Litchurch Lane Works	Bombardier Transportation
ZF	Doncaster Works (closed)	Bombardier Transportation
ZG	Eastleigh Works	Alstom
ZH	Springburn Works, Glasgow	Alstom
ZI	Ilford Works	Bombardier Transportation
ZK	Kilmarnock Works	Hunslet-Barclay
ZN	Wolverton Works	Alstom
ZP	Horbury Works (Wakefield)	Bombardier Transportation

*= unofficial code.

7.6. ABBREVIATIONS

The following general abbreviations are used in this book:

AC	Alternating Current (i.e. Overhead supply).
AFD	Air Force Department
BR	British Railways.
BSI	Bergische Stahl Industrie.
CRDC	Component Recovery & Disposal Centre
C&W	Carriage & Wagon
DC	Direct Current (i.e. Third Rail).
DEMU	Diesel Electric Multiple Unit.
DERA	Defence Evaluation & Research Agency
Dia.	Diagram number.
DMU	Diesel Multiple Unit (general term).
DSDC	Defence Storage & Distribution CentreEMU Electric Multiple Unit.
GNER	Great North Eastern Railway
GWR	Great Western Railway.
H-B	Hunslet-Barclay.
h.p.	horse power.
HNRC	Harry Needle Railroad Company
Hz	Hertz.
kN	kilonewtons.
km/h	kilometres per hour.
kW	kilowatts.
lbf	pounds force.
LT	London Transport.
LUL	London Underground Limited.
m.	metres.
mm.	millimetres.
m.p.h.	miles per hour.
RCH	Railway Clearing House.
r.p.m.	revolutions per minute.
RR	Rolls Royce.
RSL	Rolling Stock Library.
SR	BR Southern Region.
t.	tonnes.
T	Toilets.
TD	Toilets suitable for disabled passengers.
TDM	Time Division Multiplex.
V	volts.
w	wheelchair spaces.

7.7 BUILDERS

These are shown in class headings. The workshops of British Railways and the pre-nationalisation and pre-grouping companies were first transferred to a wholly-owned subsidiary called 'British Rail Engineering Ltd.', abbreviated to BREL. These workshops were later privatised, BREL then becoming 'BREL Ltd.'. Some of the works were then taken over by ABB, which was later merged with Daimler-Benz Transportation to become 'Adtranz'. This company has now been taken over by Bombardier Transportation, which had taken over Procor at Horbury previously. Bombardier also builds vehicles for the British market in Brugge, Belgium.

Other workshops were the subject of separate sales, Springburn, Glasgow and Wolverton becoming 'Railcare' and Eastleigh becoming 'Wessex Traincare'. These are now owned by Alstom (previously GEC-Alsthom), as is the former Metro-Cammell Works in Birmingham.

Note: Part of Doncaster works was sold to RFS Engineering, which became insolvent and was bought out and renamed RFS Industries. This has now been taken over by Wabtec.

The builder details in the class headings show the owner at the time of vehicle construction followed by the works as follows:

Ashford	Ashford Works (Note that this is not the same as the current Bombardier Ashford depot which is at Chart Leacon)
Birmingham	The former Metro-Cammel works at Saltley, Birmingham.
Cowlairs	Cowlairs Works, Glasgow
Derby	Derby Carriage Works (also known as Litchurch Lane)
Doncaster	Doncaster Works.
Eastleigh	Eastleigh Works
Swindon	Swindon Works.
Wolverton	Wolverton Works.
York	York Carriage Works.

Other builders are:

Alexander	Walter Alexander, Falkirk.
Barclay	Andrew Barclay, Caledonia Works, Kilmarnock (now Hunslet-Barclay).
BRCW	Birmingham Railway Carriage & Wagon, Smethwick.
CAF	Construcciones y Auxiliar de Ferrocarriles, Zaragosa, Spain.
Cravens	Cravens, Sheffield.
Gloucester	Gloucester Railway Carriage & Wagon, Gloucester.
Hunslet-Barclay	Hunslet-Barclay, Caledonia Works, Kilmarnock.
Hunslet TPL	Hunslet Transportation Projects, Leeds.
Lancing	SR, Lancing Works.
Leyland Bus	Leyland Bus, Workington.
Metro-Cammell	Metropolitan-Cammell, Saltley, Birmingham
Pressed Steel	Pressed Steel, Linwood.
Charles Roberts	Charles Roberts, Horbury Junction, Wakefield.
SGP	Simmering-Graz-Pauker, Austria (now owned by Siemens).
Siemens	Siemens Transportation Systems (various works in Germany and Austria).
SRP	Specialist Rail Products Ltd (A subsidiary of RFS).

ENGINEERING INNOVATION AND INVESTMENT

in off balance sheet train leasing